THE JEW IN THE
MEDIEVAL COMMUNITY

'il n'ont pais ne ieu propre aucun en toute Chretianté, ou ils puissent demourer, frequanter ne y habiter, se ce n'est de la propre et pure licence et volenté du Seigneur ou Seigneurs soubz qui il se vouldroient asseoir pour demourer soubz eulz comme leurs subgiez, et qui à ce les vouldroient recueillir et recevoir.'—*Charter of John of France*, 1361.

THE JEW IN THE
MEDIEVAL COMMUNITY

A study of his political and economic situation

By
JAMES PARKES

Second Edition

with a new Introduction

Foreword by

MORTON C. FIERMAN

HERMON PRESS
NEW YORK

THE JEW IN THE MEDIEVAL COMMUNITY
Second edition
Copyright © 1976 James Parkes
Published by
SEPHER-HERMON PRESS, INC.
New York, N.Y.
LCCC No. 74-78328
ISBN 0-87203-059-8 (cloth)
ISBN 0-87203-060-1 (paper)

FOREWORD

In December of 1976, Rev. Dr. James Parkes will be eighty years old. He is to be congratulated on reaching this age and for having made such a magnificent contribution to the world of religion during his lifetime as well.

Dr. Parkes wrote the seminal work in the area of Jewish-Christian relations, *The Conflict of the Church and the Synagogue,* followed by *The Jew in the Medieval Community,* a work of equal eminence, which is now being published in a new edition. To have written these two works alone would have been a sufficient contribution to humanity, but, since 1938, Dr. Parkes wrote much more. Hopefully, some time this year the University of Southampton will publish a bibliography of his works. This project will consist of approximately 72 printed pages, reflecting indeed a library of writing, but better still, an excellent collection of creative work in various areas of concern under both his name, James Parkes, and under his pseudonym, John Hadham. For all these munificent gifts, we are grateful to the Rev. Dr. James Parkes; and yet, he made other contributions. He did not remain in the ivory tower. He ventured out of it.

It is interesting to note that even as a young man he participated in unusual activities. For example, he joined the army in 1916 but unfortunately was gassed. Upon his recuperation he became a Brigade Gas officer engaged in the protection against gas. After the war while an undergraduate he organized the League of Nations Union at Oxford University. He joined the Student Christian Movement in 1923 after which he worked for the International Student service until 1935. In 1933 he aided emigres from Nazi Germany. His research into antisemitism led to his involvement with the fate of German Jewry, and in 1935, his seven-year residence in

Geneva ended with the discovery that the Nazis had ordered his liquidation! Since then he has endeavored in countless ways to assist the contemporary world to come to grips with problems in Jewish-Christian relationships, antisemitism, Israel-Arab relations, and theological problems of various kinds. He has traveled the world to talk to people about his ideas; hoping thereby to influence them to understand, to comprehend each other, and hopefully to live at peace one with the other.

This distinguished Christian gentleman has been the President of the Jewish Historical Society of England (1949-51). No mean honor this. He was singled out for his ability as a distinguished historian of the Jewish people.

Dr. Parkes at eighty has the spiritual and mental vigor of a man much his junior. When my wife and I saw him and his beloved wife in June, 1975, at their home in Iwerne Minster in Dorset, not far from Salisbury, his mind was as alert as it was when I first met him in 1944 in England. He is a stalwart. He is one of the great men of our time, blessed not only with insight and much ability, but a fine sense of humor. His wit is like a fine dry sherry. All who know him, enjoy it.

Our best wishes to Dr. Parkes as he enters his eightieth year. May he live to 120, bright of mind, excellent in health, continuing to give of his capabilities to mankind. Congratulations also on this new edition of *The Jew in the Medieval Community*.

MORTON C. FIERMAN
California State University, Fullerton
Fullerton, California
March 1976

INTRODUCTION TO THE SECOND EDITION

The volume to whose second edition this forms the Introduction traces the origin of both the political and the economic distortion of European Jewish life. Their citizenship disappeared with the disappearance of the Roman empire; and Jews reappeared in medieval Christendom as the completely private property of secular or ecclesiastical princes, private property which could be treated exactly as the owners liked. Jews could live only where they had a formal, written permission to do so, and the prince could lay down what conditions he liked, and revoke the charter and expel his Jews at a moment's notice. Jews had nowhere to appeal to against an unjust prince. Even today Jews instinctively pay immense attention to legal rights, for Nazi Germany reminded them that emancipation itself rested on precise laws. Hence their insistence that Israel, resting on the Balfour Declaration and the United Nations decision, offers them one land where they can live as other people—'as of right and not on sufferance.'

The study of the medieval charters forms the first part of *The Jew in the Medieval Community*. Since it was written the period has been covered in the appropriate volumes of *The Social and Religious History of the Jews* by Salo W. Baron, but a reader is warned that, at the moment of writing, the index extends only to volume 12. Apart from studies of individual charters and communities, the most important field of exploration is probably the medieval Responsa. Charters inevitably prescribed various matters affecting the non-Jewish neighbour, and these might well be the subject of Responsa. There would have been lawsuits between Jews and Christians, now one side providing the defendant, now the other. Which law was to prevail? All kinds of relations with the non-Jew could provide issues on which a small community might ask advice.

The second field with which *The Jew in the Medieval Community* dealt was that of the money-lender, or rather the emergence in the medieval community of a money economy, and the special place occupied in that economy by the Jew, the private property of the prince. Here also there is bound to be material in the appropriate volumes of Baron, but I do not know of any later special study of money-lending. But the story, written chronologically, clearly refutes any idea of *instinctive* Jewish financial ability. Early money-lenders made absurd mistakes; success came from experience, not instinct.

Two volumes indicate the field where details of a community or a period should throw light on the artificial life led by the whole Jewish people. One is *Tradition and Crisis: Jewish Society at the End of the Middle Ages*, by Jacob Katz, published in 1961, and the other is *Harmony and Discord: An Analysis of the Decline of Jewish Self-Government in 15th century Central Europe*, by Eric Zimmer, published in 1970.

For works published before 1971 anywhere in the field, the *Widener Library Shelflist, vol 39, Judaica*, published in 1971 by Harvard University provides a chronologically arranged list which is worth consulting.

The outbreak of war in 1939 prevented the continuation of the history of antisemitism as I had planned it. But since the Jewish people of today,, as well as their Christian or other neighbours, are inevitably influenced by the history they have passed through, it is, perhaps, worth recording my intentions in the succeeding volumes. The research for the second medieval volume was almost completed when the war destroyed my income, and in the post-war world I have never had the tranquillity to return to a life of orderly research. The second medieval volume would have dealt with the Church and the People. So far as the theologians were concerned, the main addition to the patristic period was the knowledge of the actual contemporary beliefs and practices of the Jews in their midst. While this produces the expected antisemitic outpourings, there is a surprising strain of friendly interest running right through the period. The early medieval dialogues, such as that of Rabbi Samuel of Morocco, are astonishingly and deeply spiritual. Gilbert Crispin, Abbot of Westminster in the time of William the Conqueror, writes to the archbishop of

Canterbury of a Jew with whom he has frequent discussions, and he speaks of him with real respect and affection. This strain runs through up to the end of the medieval period and underlies the Biblical scholarship of Luther.

There is, unhappily, a very contrary picture, occupying the main area of the canvas, a picture of false accusations spread by the ignorant and credulous local clergy, and revived in our own day by both Catholic and Protestant antisemites. Ritual murder, the poisoning of wells, the world plot against Christians and Christendom, these are still potent forces of evil, affecting not only Europeans, but, through Russian or Nazi influences, the Arab world, from Saudi Arabia to North Africa.

Coupled with the accusations of the local clergy was the growth of a folk-lore, owing a good deal to the sudden spate of stories created during the iconoclastic controversy which I wrote of in chapter 8 of *The Conflict*. Some of the stories of the miraculous conversions of Jews by images become standard in medieval folklore; and one carries the basic theme of Shakespeare's *Merchant of Venice* back to an iconodule of the 8th century. Besides the local folklore there is an important influence for evil in the prevalence of popular drama, of which the Oberammergau Passion play is a surviving example. They usually link Jews with the devil, again a belief which will be found among peasantry today.

While thus the third volume would have followed relatively familiar paths, the fourth volume would have dealt with subjects till now largely ignored. There are the Christian Hebraists from the 16th up to the middle of the 18th century (admirably described in Meuschen's *Novum Testamentum ex Talmude Illustratum* of 1736). There is a new literature aimed at the conversion of the Jew to Protestant or Catholic Christianity. There are the Deists, and there is the beginning of post-biblical Jewish history. And all the time the traditional anti-Jewish material is ground out, and the antisemites have new grist to their mill.

Thus the sympathetic studies of rabbinic Judaism or

Chasidism are balanced by the violent hostility of Eisenmenger and Wagenseil. But, in addition to the charges of their patristic and medieval predecessors, they now know the Jewish satirical life of Jesus of Nazareth (the *Sepher Toldoth Jeshu*) as well as the Jewish defence against the Christian antisemite. In the same way the brilliant and objective work of Basnage in his *Histoire des Juifs pour servir a continuation de l'Histoire de Josephe* was immediately followed by the Jesuits with a forged edition resurrecting all the charges which Basnage had dismissed. It is worth mentioning that the Parkes Library at Southampton University has a copy of the extremely rare work *'L'Histoire des Juifs reclamee et retablie par son veritable Auteur, Mr. Basnage, contre l'edition anonyme et tronquee qui s'en est faite a Paris chez Roulland, 1710.* A copy of this (almost as rare) forgery exists at the HUC, Cincinnati.

The economic aspect of the period is equally fascinating. The paradoxical characteristic of the Jewish people that their *destiny* has been shaped by their constant encounter with other peoples but their *qualities* have remained identifiably Jewish, is illustrated during the period of this volume by the creation of the modern German economy through the wealthy and powerful 'court Jews,' and of what was to become Rumania by the impoverished and often itinerant Jewish trader.

In other words this volume would have provided the background which explains the nineteenth century paradox— that it is the century in which emancipation became obviously inevitable, and, for totally different reasons, modern political and racial antisemitism became inevitable also—the theme of volume 5, on which a great deal of research has been done by other scholars during the decades since I made my original plans which the war prevented me from carrying out.

It is evidence of the thought of the period involved that it was quite late that I noticed an omission which would have been impossible today—the Jewish destiny under Islam, which provides the excellent second volume of Poliakov's *History of Antisemitism.* But the challenge of Rosemary Ruether exposes yet another gap—the Byzantine story in which Andrew Sharf has pioneered in his *Byzantine Jewry from Justinian to the 4th Crusade*, and of which Christians in the Middle East are the contemporary heirs.

Today, in 1975, in the post-Holocaust era, it would have been right to sum up the picture of two thousand years of relations between Jew and non-Jew with some assessment of the changes in the right direction as well as the persistence of the evils of the past. There is evidence both from the scholar and the general public that change is in the air, theological as well political and social. It would be pleasant, as well as profitable, that the men and women who have made the change possible should be recorded as fully and as carefully as those whom history will record as creators and transmittors of antisemitism.

JAMES PARKES
October 1975

TABLE OF CONTENTS

reasons for the failure of the Church—the
failure of substitutes—the conflict with the
Roman view of usury—the conflict and the
Jewish usurer.

PREFACE

The story of antisemitism is long and complicated. If it requires for its understanding neither the supernatural maledictions beloved of the theologians of a past age, nor the racial mysticism of the present, yet it needs the slow and patient following of its thread through the successive periods in which Jewish history is inextricably interwoven with that of the nations among whom the Jewish people have lived, worked and suffered. In the previous volume, *The Conflict of the Church and the Synagogue*, the story was taken from its beginnings in the coming of Christianity, and the separation of the new faith from its parent Judaism, down to the disappearance of the last threads of Roman custom in the empire of Charlemagne.

In this volume the story is taken a stage further, but along the same road. The future lines of Jewish history were determined when the youthful Church took advantage of her first access to the throne of the legislator to penalise and to degrade the members of the older faith. In the pagan empire the Jews had enjoyed the minimum special privileges which enabled them to remain loyal to their monotheism. Apart from this, they were indistinguishable from other Roman citizens. From the fourth century onwards they were gradually thrust into a position of inferiority by the restrictions of their rights, first in the religious, but later also in the political, civil and economic fields. This conception of the inferior status of the Jews the medieval legislator inherited from the Christian Roman Empire.

The picture which is disclosed in these pages only represents one-half of the consequences of this inheritance. It deals with the political and economic status of the Jews of medieval Europe. The reason for allotting two volumes to this period lies in the impossibility of making neat and tidy generalisations, or tracing logical sequences of development in a period where everything was arbitrary. For, whereas in the Roman world it was one law, one economic system, one theological attitude which determined the whole of the

XVII

history of Jewish-Christian relations, in the medieval period there is only one certain rule, and that is that there are no certain rules by which any aspect of the status or of the conditions of the medieval Jewries may be safely decided on the basis of the situation elsewhere. To write a comprehensive story of the period from the tenth to the fifteenth century would require a volume the size of an encyclopaedia, and even then it would be unsafe to make conjecture to fill gaps in the surviving evidence. Was the estate of a Jew confiscated at his death? Certainly it was; there is ample evidence to prove it. Did his heir have normal rights of inheritance? Of course he did; there are innumerable examples of such successions. And it is possible that evidence of these two contradictory solutions of the problem of testamentary rights would be found in examples from the same Jewish community, during the same period. For everything in medieval Jewish history is arbitrary, and that is the only stable rule.

It is for this reason that the book is made up so largely of examples, and that these are chosen in apparently so haphazard a way. For sometimes it seemed best to illustrate similar conditions from countries and centuries as widely separated as possible; and at others the clearest picture emerged from the exposure of varieties within a narrow compass. To give all the examples, or even the most familiar, was clearly impossible, for this is not a continuous history of the Jews; even to have taken the smaller subject of Jewish-Christian relations, and to have dealt with it comprehensively, country by country, and century by century, would have produced a work of incredible length and still more incredible monotony.

As the period has been treated by subjects, and neither by countries nor by periods, examples have been chosen far more frequently from the northern and western countries than from the southern and eastern. In the south conditions were usually better than in the north, and it is true that more space given to Italy, Sicily and Provence would have lightened sometimes the gloom of the colours, and diversified the monotony of the decline; but the lightening would have been but a falsification, for the essential fact is that it was the decline of the northern Jewries in England, France and Germany, which determined the future. The Jewries of

Italy and Poland fell more slowly into degradation, but they fell. The northern and western countries dragged them down; they did not avail to lighten or to alter the tragedy.

It had originally been intended to deal with the whole of the Middle Ages within a single volume. This has been abandoned, and in this volume it is only the political and economic situation of the Jews which is described; their relations with the Church and the population will be reserved for the next. Such a division obviously presents inconveniences in a subject in which every factor is interwoven with every other; but its most unfortunate consequence is that it results in a somewhat unfair picture being presented of the Church, since here the Church appears as a single whole, in almost continuous opposition both to the political and to the economic situation of the Jews. The subsequent volume, dealing with the attitude of the Church in detail, will, I hope, correct the impression.

Finally, I would add for the benefit of those who possess the first volume of the series, *The Conflict of the Church and the Synagogue*, that they will find on page 406 a list of alterations and corrections of passages in that volume. For many of these I am indebted to friendly scholars and reviewers, and I trust that I shall receive the same for the present volume, the results of which will be similarly listed in the third. No man can expect to survey so wide a field without many mistakes, for it would be enough for one lifetime to master in every known detail the subject dealt with in any single chapter. Yet, in spite of the immense need for more and better study of the details of medieval Jewish life, there is also a place for a work which attempts to indicate the general balance of the picture and to cull from the mass of available material that which assists the student of present problems to understand the cause of a contemporary phenomenon.

JAMES PARKES

BARLEY
January 1938

ABBREVIATIONS

Agobard A, B, C, D, E	See bibliography of Chapter II.
Aronius	Aronius, J., *Regesten zur Geschichte der Juden im Fränkischen und Deutschen Reiche bis zum Jahre 1273.* Berlin, 1902.
Baer, *Aragon*	Baer, F., *Die Juden im christlichen Spanien. Pt. I. Urkunden und Regesten.* Vol. I. Aragonien und Navarra. Berlin, 1929.
Baer, *Castile*	—— Vol. II. Kastilien/Inquisitionsakten. Berlin, 1936.
Bondy	Bondy, G., and Dworský, F., *Zur Geschichte der Juden in Böhmen, Mähren und Schlesien.* Vol. I. Prague, 1906.
Bouquet	*Rerum Gallicarum et Francicarum scriptores* (Recueil des Historiens de Gaule et de la France). Ed. M. Bouquet and others. Twenty-four volumes. Paris, 1738-1904.
c.	In Mansi and PL indicates column as the books are not divided into pages.
CJ	*Codex Justinianus.* Ed. Krueger, 9th Edition. Berlin, 1915.
Col. doc.	*Collection de documents inédits sur l'histoire de France.* Paris, 1835 ff., in progress.
CT	*Codex Theodosianus.* Ed. Mommsen and Meyer. Berlin, 1905.
Diss.	Dissertation (thesis for a Doctorate).
Ep.	Epistola.
Gall. Jud.	Gross, H., *Gallia Judaica.* Paris, 1897.
JQR	*Jewish Quarterly Review.* London, 1888-1908.
JQR, n.s.	—— New Series. Philadelphia, 1910 ff., in progress.
Laurière	*Ordonnances des Rois de France de la IIIe race.* Ed. E. J. de Laurière. Twenty-one volumes. Paris, 1723-1849.
Mansi	Mansi, J. D., *Sacrorum conciliorum collectio.* Thirty-one volumes. Florence and Venice, 1759-98.
MGH	*Monumenta Germaniae Historica.* Ed. G. H. Pertz, T. Mommsen, and others. Hannover, 1826 ff., in progress.
Conc.	Legum Sect. III. *Concilia.* Two volumes in 4. 1893-1924. Quarto.
Const.	Legum Sect. IV. *Constitutiones,* etc. 1893 ff. Quarto.
Dipl.	*Diplomata Regum et Imperatorum Germaniae,* 1879 ff.
Formulae	Legum Sect. V. *Formulae Merovingici et Karolini aevi.* 1886. Quarto.

LL	*Leges.* I-V. 1835-89. Fol.
SS	*Scriptores.* Thirty volumes in 31. 1826-96.
MGWJ	*Monatsschrift für die Geschichte und Wissenschaft des Judenthums.* Dresden and (later) Breslau, 1851 ff., in progress.
Neubauer & Stern N. and S. NS, A, B, C	For all these see bibliography of Chapter III.
Nov. Theod.	See CT.
PL	*Patrologiae cursus completus.* Series latina. Ed. J. P. Migne. 221 volumes. Paris, 1844-55.
Régné, *Catalogue*	Régné, J., *Catalogue des Actes de Jaime Ier, Pedro III, et Alfonso III, rois d'Aragon, concernant les Juifs* (1213-91). REJ, LX-LXX, 1910-20, and *Catalogue d'Actes pour servir à l'histoire des Juifs de la Couronne d'Aragon sous le règne de Jaime II* (1291-1327). REJ, LXXIII-LXXVIII, 1921-24.
Régné, *Narbonne*	See bibliography of Chapter II.
REJ	*Revue des Études Juives.* Paris, 1880 ff., in progress.
Scherer	Scherer, J. E., *Die Rechtsverhältnisse der Juden in den deutsch-österreichischen Ländern.* Leipzig, 1901.
Teulet	Teulet, J. B. A. T., *Layettes du Trésor des Chartes.* Three volumes. Paris, 1863-75.
The Conflict	Parkes, J., *The Conflict of the Church and the Synagogue.* London, 1934.
Wiener, *Regesten* Wiener	M. Wiener, *Regesten zur Geschichte der Juden in Deutschland während des Mittelalters.* Hannover, 1862.
ZGJD	*Zeitschrift für die Geschichte der Juden in Deutschland.* Ed. L. Geiger. Five volumes Braunschweig, 1887-1892.

PART I

THE BACKGROUND

CHAPTER ONE

THE ROMAN CHRISTIAN INHERITANCE

The reign of Charlemagne marks the end of an epoch in the history of Jewish-Christian relationships. By the eighth century their legal status as Roman citizens under the Theodosian Code had ceased to give them any protection. It is still referred to in parts of Europe up to the beginning of the fourteenth century, but even then it offers only a shadow of a past security. Their new status, as specially protected exceptions to the Common Law, makes its first hesitating appearance in the beginning of the ninth century. By the tenth century has already begun the practice of giving Jews away, like any other chattel. In the same period, though our sources are few and scattered, the commercial significance of the Jewish population of Western Europe begins to attract attention; and at the end of the tenth century we come across the first traces of moneylending as a natural activity of a Jewish merchant class.

In the relations of everyday life also, changes began to be noticeable. The hostility of the clergy, when it was aroused, was able to develop with less and less restraint as secular authority waned with the collapse of the empire of Charlemagne. In various centres the season of Easter was accompanied by licensed ' Jew-baiting ' at particular religious ceremonies. New complaints occurred, and old attacks took on new forms.

To understand these new manifestations it is, of course, necessary to study contemporary conditions in the general society of western Europe. But it is even more essential to have some picture of the attitude to the Jews and to Judaism which the early makers of medieval Europe inherited from the preceding centuries. It is frequently assumed that ' anti-semitism ' is ' as old as the hills ', and manifests itself instantly and continuously wherever there is a Jewish community. Events of remote history, whether in the Egypt of the period of the Exodus, in the Rome of Caesar, or in the Alexandria of the Ptolemies, are torn out of their

context, and their contemporary explanation ignored, in order
to provide arguments for this assertion. But the enmities of
these periods, such as they were, can be paralleled in the
history of every people and, in so far as they are capable of
a normal explanation, do not explain an ' abnormal ' movement such as antisemitism. The memories of peoples last
long; a certain suspicion of the unlike is normal to human
societies; but neither of these truisms explain the phenomenon with which we are here concerned. There are, in fact,
only two possible explanations: that advanced by the racist,
which sees in Jewish blood and in the unalterable physical
characteristics of the ' Jewish race ' something against which
other ' races ' automatically react; and that of the historian,
which seeks special historical circumstances to account for
a special historical development, and yet circumstances
whose emergence and influence do not necessitate the
introduction of the mythical or the supernatural for their
explanation.

The answer to the ' racist ' is simple and final. To speak of
' race ' in any biological sense when speaking of the Jews is
pure nonsense. There is no such thing as ' a Jewish race '.
And if race be used as a substitute for ' civilisation ', ' religious community ' or ' people ', the answer is equally clear.
There is ample evidence throughout the history of the
relations of the Jews with their neighbours, that where the
situation has been normal the relations have been equally so.

The true explanation of antisemitism is to be found in the
history of the early centuries of Christianity, the daughter
religion of Judaism, in the theology evolved by the Church,
in the interpretation of the Old Testament which became
current among her theologians and preachers, and in the
legislation which was inspired by these interpretations. This
is not to assert that the Jews, unlike other human groups,
never made themselves unpopular through their own fault,
that they were never disliked by their neighbours for reasons
similar to those which have animated dislikes of other
peoples. Evidence of normal conflict is certainly to be found
throughout their history. The dislike of the Egyptians for
the Jews of Alexandria was a normal dislike. The jealousy
of the Greek cities in the time of Pompey was a normal
jealousy. The riots against the Jews in the eastern provinces

of the Byzantine empire during the Persian wars were normal riots. And yet in all these cases, where Jewish conduct was responsible for the dislike which the rest of the population felt for the Jews, it can also be said that such conduct was normal by the standard of human failings. Other peoples have applied uncomplimentary epithets to, and told offensive stories about, their neighbours, epithets and stories which have been bitterly resented. Other groups have secured for themselves privileged positions which have placed on the rest of the inhabitants extra burdens. And there are other examples in history of the revolts of oppressed peoples and the indignation of their oppressors. Incidents of such a character are no more and no less frequent in Jewish history than in the history of others. They only appear to be exceptional when seen from the standpoint of later developments.

The common feature of all such incidents, whether in Jewish or in other history, is that the responsibility is mutual, and the immediate causes explain the immediate effects. That which makes of 'antisemitism' an abnormality in history is that there are not adequate immediate causes to explain the results. A single example will be enough to illustrate this statement. Since 1933 the Jews of Germany have undergone a persecution which has no parallel even in their history. But, when every allowance has been made for the maximum indignation which the activities or misdemeanours of certain individuals within German Jewry might legitimately have aroused, it is impossible to discover in contemporary Jewish history any crimes which have merited so terrible a punishment.

The same disparity between cause and effect appears in the history of every Jewish persecution since the massacres of 1096 which disgraced the First Crusade. This is the abnormality whose ultimate explanation lies in the history of the Christian Church to which reference has already been made.

Christianity began as a Jewish sect. Its earliest members were either Synagogue-frequenting Jews or Synagogue-frequenting Gentiles. Apart from their peculiar belief that they knew the Name of the Messiah, nothing distinguished them from their fellow members of the Synagogue. Their ethics were Jewish—Pharisaic—ethics. Their Messiah was a Jew. Their leaders were all Jews. The Temple was still the centre of their worship. The brethren in the Holy City itself enjoyed a particular esteem. But within a century of its birth all this changed, and Christianity appeared as an entirely separate religion, and was recognised as such by the Roman authorities.

The stages of the separation overlap, and are inevitably obscure in many details, but their main lines can still be traced. For a brief while after the Crucifixion the only active opposition came from the hierarchy at Jerusalem. They naturally found it intolerable that, through having surrendered Jesus of Nazareth to Pilate, they should be accused of having betrayed their Messiah to a Roman death; and they forbade the Apostles to speak in His name.

The second stage of the separation is more pregnant with future consequence: Gentiles in considerable numbers were attracted by the power of the new preaching, and many accepted the new Messiah. From the time of the missionary journeys of Paul, many of these Gentiles were pure pagans, not people who had already been drawn to the worship of the Synagogue, and who were therefore acquainted with the Ceremonial Law. Were the new converts to be asked to observe it? The Christian leaders at first did not treat the question as fundamental. It seemed to them natural that the Gentiles should be asked to conform to the ways of the Jews. The increasing success of Paul necessitated a more serious study of the question. A strong party, with direct contact with the mission field, felt that the leaders in Jerusalem did not appreciate the realities of the problem. A deputation was sent to Jerusalem, a council was held, and a decision of the greatest importance for the future Church was taken. That decision was that the Gentiles should be asked to obey the Moral Law which was binding on everyone (the Noachic Commandments), but not the full Mosaic or Ceremonial Law[1]. It is important to realise that this decision was taken

---

[1] My reasons for deciding in this sense the vexed question of the nature of the decisions given in Acts xv, 29 cannot be related in full. The present text appears to suggest a novel series of dietary regulations. Such a solution is difficult to accept. The decision must have been one which would have seemed proper and natural to a group of Jews who believed themselves to be living in the Messianic Age. It must, therefore, have been something in their existing traditions which seemed appropriate

by a Council of orthodox Jews, and without in the least infringing their orthodoxy. Just as there were many interpretations within Judaism of the character of the coming Messiah, so there were many views as to the position of the Law in the Messianic Age. Any of these views could be held by a Jew without its affecting his loyalty to Judaism.

The decision taken may be called a ' liberal decision '. Its orthodoxy is vouched for by the fact that it was the proposal of that Leader who through all his life enjoyed the highest esteem of those Jews who did not accept his Messianic views—James. But there was a party within the new Church, especially in Asia Minor, which could not accept this liberal decision. Its members wished to insist on the strictest conformity to the whole of the Ceremonial Law. They are the people known as ' the Judaisers ', and they are not to be confused with the ' Judeo-Christians ', or with members of the ' Jewish ' as opposed to the ' Gentile ' Church.

Through the action of this party observance of the Law became the basis of a violent controversy within the Church; but the decisions of Jerusalem also inevitably led to controversy between the nascent Church and the Synagogue in the Diaspora. In the congregations of Palestine the question did not arise until later, but in the Greek cities of the Pauline Mission, and in similar places, it came quickly to the front. The new liberty towards the Ceremonial Law was offered to Gentiles on the basis of the Arrival of the Messianic Age. Those Jews who also believed that the Messianic Age had come mostly accepted the decision of the Council; but if a Jew did not accept that hypothesis, or, in other words, did not accept Jesus of Nazareth as Messiah, then all argument for admitting Gentiles into the fellowship of Israel, without any other ceremony than that of Baptism in the Name of Jesus, fell to the ground.

to this new development. Jewish traditions offer two possibilities: regulations for Jews exposed to mortal danger in the Gentile world (Talmud, *Sanhedrin*, 74a) or the commandments binding on the Sons of Noah, that is, all humanity (*ibid.*, 56a). Personally, I accept the latter, as I cannot see that the former applies at this stage of the development of the Church.

I have used the word ' Law ' instead of ' Torah ' throughout, as it is more familiar to ordinary readers. But it must be remembered that in its proper meaning the ideas of ' revelation ' and ' instruction ' are both contained in what we call Jewish ' Law '.

The policy of Paul much embittered the situation. Those whom Paul brought within the fold were persons, often of the lowest class, who had no idea, not merely of ceremonial matters of procedure, but of what we, in common with the Jews of the time, would consider common decency. They included people with ' manners none and morals beastly '. They believed that they had obtained a new form of ' Salvation ', and this did not automatically imply to them any reformation of their lives. On the contrary, the certainty of being saved gave rather an excuse for indulgence. The cases with which Paul deals in his letters, the repeated lists of ' the works of the flesh ' which are to be rejected, enable us to sympathise with what must have been the feelings of those who did not accept the coming of the Messianic Age which he preached. Their cry that this man was overthrowing the Law was not the niggling pedantry of narrowminded ' legalists ', but extremely similar to the violent protests of established Church circles against the similar activity of the Salvation Army in its early days.

In fact, Paul himself was the first person to admit the justice of their complaints, and to reply to the protests of Jews and Jewish Christians by disclaiming any intention of overthrowing the Law as a moral rule of life. The later chapters of his epistles are the finest source which we possess for an understanding of the popular teaching of the Pharisees in the first century.

There were thus three parties to the dispute in the Diaspora, Paul and his followers, the Judaisers, and the Jews; and the position of each may be roughly summed up as follows:

Paul argued, the Messiah has come; my task is to preach Him to the Gentiles. Those who accept Him enter the New Israel by baptism, the new ceremonial which replaces circumcision for the Gentiles. Within the new Israel distinctions between Jew and Gentile have ceased to exist; and although the Ceremonial Law is still valid for Jews, it is impossible for Gentiles[1].

---

[1] It is this point which lends the bitterness to his attacks on ' the Law ' in his epistles. The Hellenistic world was only too ready to accept ceremonies as effecting moral changes, and the teaching of a new and complicated way of life, in addition to new morals, would have been more than his converts would have understood. They would certainly have given false values to ceremonial acts.

The Judaisers argued, the Messiah has come, but entry into His Kingdom is by the old terms of loyalty in full to the Covenant given to Moses. Christ fulfils that covenant; He does not supersede it in any detail. Gentiles must be admitted to the Messianic Kingdom, but for admission they must become as Jews.

The Jewish opponents of Paul argued, the Messiah has not come, therefore action taken upon the assumption that He has is false. In the present circumstances there is no authority for the admission of Gentiles to the Synagogue on new and more liberal conditions than formerly.

Thus the Judaisers attacked Paul for the non-observance of the Ceremonial Law by his Gentile converts, the Jews for non-observance of the Law in general. Hence the reply of Paul to the first was an absolute refusal to compromise; his reply to the second was that they had completely misunderstood him.

This is the first phase of the controversy over the Law, a real issue between two parties within the Church, and a false issue, based on misunderstanding, between ' Christian ' and Jew. In the second phase of the controversy the situation changed completely. The conflict within the Church was at an end. All Christians, whether of Jewish or pagan origin, were expected to abandon the Law. But between Christian and Jew the issue became a real one. The attack was led by Gentile Christians; the defence was in the hands of the official Jewish authorities in Palestine. The question at issue was no longer whether the Law was still binding on Gentiles who had accepted the Messiah, but whether it was ever binding on any one in the way in which the Jews had understood it. ' The Law ' was opposed to ' The Gospel ' as a different and erroneous way of life. While some Christians recognised that it was divinely appointed and operative up to the time of the coming of the Messiah, some would not even accept this limited approval. They condemned it root and branch, and would not recognise that it had ever consisted in other than ceremonial observances. In such conditions it is not unnatural that the fury, which in the days of Paul had been local, became a general hatred of the new sect, and an uncompromising rejection of fellowship with them.

But if the Christians made themselves impossible to the

Jews, the hostility was not less marked in the opposite direction. The Jews gradually ruled out of possibility the idea that the crucified Jesus of Nazareth, as interpreted by the Gentile theologians, could be the Messiah. As time went on, they evolved in support of their contention contemptuous and often—from a Christian point of view—blasphemous stories of His life.

Considering that the Church, after the separation, turned her back on the way of life described in the Old Testament as ' life under the Law ', it might at first be thought that the Old Testament would gradually have dropped out of use in Christian circles, and that, bit by bit, the old animosities would have disappeared, as they have in most countries to-day between Catholic and Protestant. The reason why this did not happen is twofold. Firstly, the New Testament so constantly refers to the authority of the Old that a violent reinterpretation of their own position would have been needed for such a revolution to have been accepted by the theologians. Secondly, the Church required the Old Testament to establish her position in the Roman Empire. The ancient world prized antiquity highly, and it was the first task of a new religion in the Roman Empire to acquire a respectable pedigree. Such a pedigree could only be adduced for Christianity by rooting it in the Old Testament. The Apologists constantly justified Christian claims by the antiquity of the Christian religion, since Abraham and Moses were far earlier than Homer, Plato or Socrates. Such a method of argument was based upon a particular interpretation of the Scriptures. Proofs of the Messianic authority of Jesus were read into every page of it; Moses and the prophets were said themselves to have considered their revelation only partial and preparatory, and all the heroes of Jewish history were gradually transformed into pre-Incarnation Christians.

Such a reading of the one treasure left to the Jews after the destruction of Jerusalem and their exile from the Holy Land was enough in itself to keep alight the flames of Jewish bitterness and hatred. But the Church did not even rest content with this interpretation. The Old Testament is full of both praise and blame, promise and threat. She claimed the praise and promise for herself; but she did not accept that the failures of the Old Testament were her failures, and that the blame and the threat were addressed to her. By what seemed to her an inevitable exegetical necessity, she allotted the blame and the denunciation to the Jew. It is here that we can put our finger on the real birthplace of antisemitism. Like all great social tragedies it was not deliberately intended by human wickedness. Just as the nineteenth-century industrialist never intended the slums which were, in fact, the inevitable outcome of his economic policy, so the early fathers never intended the pogroms and massacres, the humiliating legislation, the insults and misrepresentations, which succeeding centuries have reared upon the foundations which they laid. None of the other factors, psychological, economic or cultural, which lie dormant in all human relationships for good or evil, could of themselves have brought this monstrous spawn to birth, much though they may have contributed to its subsequent growth. Its ' onlie begetter ' was the Christian theologian, with the ceaseless abuse of the Jews which exegetical necessity imposed upon him—abuse delivered, so far as we can see, with little or no hatred of his Jewish contemporaries. For the same centuries which in the pages of the preachers and commentators contain the most ghastly picture of Jewish depravity, reveal also continuous good relationships, both social and religious, between Jews and Christians, both laymen and clerics.

It is, in fact, the greatest proof of the normality of ordinary social relationships that it was a thousand years before this preaching had its natural effect in the massacres which accompanied the First Crusade—massacres which without this preparation remain completely inexplicable. This is not to say that it is impossible to find in the history of the previous centuries those shadows which coming events cast before them, but that those shadows in their turn are only explicable when successive incidents are traced to the same source, the picture of Jewish depravity in patristic literature.

In the fourth century the Peace of the Church, coupled with the new political influence of the clergy, introduced a new phase. The protagonist was henceforth the imperial or ecclesiastical legislator, and no longer the theologian and the biblical commentator. But the work of the latter was well and truly done by the end of the fourth century. It was not possible to say more against the Law than Jerome, when he wrote that God had sent it deliberately to deceive the Jews and to lead them to their destruction[1]. Eusebius of Caesarea, in two lengthy treatises[2], had claimed each Jewish patriarch, prophet and hero exclusively for Christian history. It was but logical for an anonymous contemporary to seek to express this hostility in legal terms, and to claim that the Jews were to be treated as apostates from Christianity, as men who had known the truth and deliberately rejected it[3]; and a flood of apocryphal Acts and Gospels existed to prove the assertion.

The mantle fell from the preacher to the legislator; but, that we might be assured that the continuity was unbroken, the laws themselves were clothed in language of clerical vituperation, and varied in intensity directly with the piety and orthodoxy of the Sovereign in question. Even the bitterest edicts of the Middle Ages lacked the abuse showered upon the Jews by the pious Emperors of the fourth and fifth centuries. Jerome had curtly called a Jewish house of prayer a ' synagogue of Satan ': the very first law of Constantine which dealt with such an edifice referred to it by a term which was never used of a religious building, and which in Roman slang meant a brothel[4]. Few of the laws passed against the Jews before the fall of the Western Empire were the result of any political or constitutional necessity. The laws of the pagan second century had dealt with the menace of a rebel nation: those of the Christian fourth and fifth were designed to crush a hated religious sect. Even if a legitimate Christian interest was involved in the repeated legislation for the protection or removal of Christian slaves in the possession of Jews[5], nothing but hatred and petty spite forbade the adequate repair, the rebuilding or the adornment of Jewish synagogues[6]; or ordered the exclusion of Jews from the privileges or honours which accompanied such ranks as

---

[1] Jer., *Ep.* cxxi, when he applied Ezek. xx, 25 to the actual prescriptions of Torah. PL, XXII, c. 1032.

[2] In the *Preparatio Evangelica* and the *Demonstratio Evangelica*.

[3] ps-Ambrose, *Commentary on Romans*, ix, 27; PL, XVII, c. 139.

[4] CT, 16, 8, 1, the word is *conciliabulum*.

[5] For a list of these see *The Conflict of the Church and the Synagogue*, p. 391.

[6] *Ibid.*

they were allowed to hold[1], and the degradation, with terms of abuse and opprobrium, of the Jewish Patriarch, on whom had been conferred by previous emperors the titles of *His Excellency* and *His Eminence*, and in whose favour special laws had been passed only a few years earlier[2].

The hostile laws of the later Empire did not perish with its fall, as did those designed to assure the minimum of civic rights to the Jewish population. The basic statement of Theodosius the Great: ' it is quite clear that no law forbids the existence of a Jewish sect[3] ' was forgotten: the trivial pin-pricks against the adornment of synagogues were sometimes still enforced in the eighteenth century.

Humiliating and exasperating as were such regulations, they were less pregnant with future evil than the series of measures by which the political and economic equality of the Jews was steadily undermined. For the repetitions of these laws in the canons of the Church transmitted them directly to the legislators, secular and clerical, of the Middle Ages. The process began with Constantine himself. In the pagan Empire Jews had enjoyed immunity from all offices which involved the offering of sacrifice, an immunity which had pressed hardly on the small numbers in the provincial cities who possessed the necessary wealth for the undertaking of civic duties. When pagan sacrifices were themselves abolished, all justification for these immunities vanished, and, since the offices in question were exceedingly burden-some, it was not unreasonable that the Jews should share in them[4]. Constantius followed by confiscating the property of a citizen who was converted from Christianity to Judaism[5]. Gratian deprived the convert of testamentary rights, and applied the same penalty to the Jew who received him; and he set the precedent for the hateful practices of the Inquisi-tion, by allowing the accusation of apostasy to be made up to five years after the death of the accused person[6]. Theodo-sius the Great assimilated marriage with a Jew or Jewess to

[1] Nov. Theod. 3.
[2] CT, 16, 8, 11 and 22.
[3] *Ibid.*, 16, 8, 9.
[4] *Ibid.*, 16, 8, 3.
[5] *Ibid.*, 16, 8, 7.
[6] *Ibid.*, 16, 7, 3.

adultery[1], and further allowed the Jews themselves to marry
only according to the Christian Table of Affinity[2]. A new
departure was made by Honorius, who excluded Jews from
military and political functions[3]. Theodosius II closed the
list in an obscure edict in which it appears that he compelled
them to observe the Christian calendar of Fasts and Feasts.[4]

Many of these laws were embodied in canons by the
contemporaries of the imperial legislators, and so passed
naturally into the tradition of western Europe by the channel
of the great collections of canons which were a feature of the
pre-Carolingian epoch. Others were repeated in the shortened editions of the Theodosian Code which were prepared
for the various successor states.

With the exception of one country, little change was made
for many centuries in the civic position of the Jews as defined
in the Roman Codes. The exception was Visigothic Spain.
Nothing better illustrates the fact that religion, and not
political necessity, determined the whole of this type of
legislation, than the Spanish sequence of edicts against the
Jews. In the days when the Visigoths were Arians, no laws
of any significance were passed. But the transition of the
monarchs, and subsequently of the people, from Arianism
to Catholicism, did not by some economic alchemy transform
the Jewish section of the population from good citizens into
bad ones. The only significant change was that the Catholic
clergy, until then merely members of the Roman minority,
now had the ear of the prince; and to confirm the fact that
it was wholly a clerical impulse which inspired a legislation
so fanatical that, in little more than a century, it entirely
ruined the Jewish population of Spain, those kings who were
not elected by the favour of the clerical party, either passed
no laws against the Jews at all, or reversed and ignored those
of their more pious predecessors. One king, Chintilla,
legislated on this matter entirely by ecclesiastical canons, and
his successors, Recceswinth and Erwig, made use of laws
and canons to confirm each other, in the successive councils
of Toledo.

[1] CT, 3, 7, 2.
[2] CJ, 1, 9, 7.
[3] CT, 16, 8, 16 and 24. The law was frequently repeated.
[4] *Ibid.*, 15, 5, 5.

Fortunately for the medieval Jew, the destruction of the Visigothic kingdom by the Moors largely destroyed the memory of the Toledan legislation. The canons of these councils were but rarely quoted in collections, and it would be difficult to find evidence for medieval action based on the sole precedent of Visigothic legislation.

In the rest of Christendom the clergy seemed to be temporarily satisfied with the position as defined in the Roman Code, and devoted their time to a slow struggle to secure its enforcement among secular princes who saw no reason to deprive themselves of the services of trusted and intelligent servants for the simple reason that they were Jews. But, while satisfied with the civic restrictions imposed on the Jewish population, they were active in another direction. The Roman legislators had devoted considerable attention to the protection of slaves from Jewish influence. The rest of the population might be presumed to be sufficiently educated to protect itself. The peasant and urban population of Merovingian and Carolingian Europe was in as dangerous a position—from the clerical point of view—as had been the slaves of Rome. They might well be tempted to yield to the arguments of intelligent Jews against Christianity and in favour of their own religion. This, coupled with the fact that normal relations between the Jews of western Europe and their Christian neighbours were good, caused them to repeat, at practically every council, canons against close intercourse, social or religious, between Jew and Christian.

In the place of new legislation a different phenomenon appeared, the arbitrary action of secular and ecclesiastical princes. This action was almost always couched in the terms of the simplest alternative—baptism or expulsion. Only in two cases is it reported that a serious effort was made to convert the Jews by argument before the alternative came into operation, and in neither case did the effort meet with success. Ferreol of Uzès was able to claim no single convert, and Avitus of Clermont, who had tried sermons in place of the banquets advocated by Ferreol, secured but one[1]. The result was that a number of forced baptisms took place, and that those who refused baptism suffered summary expulsion. It is even possible that, at the order of Dagobert,

[1] For a list of various incidents of this kind see *The Conflict*, pp. 333 ff.

a general expulsion from all France took place at the beginning of the seventh century.

Such action was a direct infringement of the rights of the Jewish population as guaranteed by the general permission granted to them to live according to Roman Law. For the Jews were still 'cives Romani', a privilege which they shared with the Catholic subjects of Arian kings, and retained in shadowy form after the conversions of the different sovereigns to Catholicism. But it is evident that it would have been useless for them to have adduced these traditional rights as an argument against the arbitrary will of the prince. Bribery and flattery, were they in the position to offer either, would have been far more likely to achieve their goal. In view of the curious status which, in the full development of the Middle Ages, took the place of their Roman citizenship, and which originated primarily in the Germanic attitude towards the resident stranger, it is important to note that in this earlier period no suggestion is made that Germanic custom authorised these arbitrary acts. Even in Visigothic Spain, where the influence of such customs pervaded the whole re-edition of the Roman Codes more fully than elsewhere, those sections which deal with Jewish affairs are grounded entirely in Roman and Catholic practice. Only in the introduction of certain strange penalties and personal mutilations is the influence of an alternative tradition discernible.

While such illegalities were not infrequent among the ordinary princes of the time, including episcopal rulers, the Papacy and the greatest of the secular rulers set their faces sternly against them. In a number of cases submitted to his judgment Theodoric the Ostrogoth kept firmly to the paths traced by the Theodosian Code; and Gregory the Great, in twenty letters dealing with Jewish affairs, strongly opposed forced baptisms, or any other infringement of the legal rights still enjoyed by the Jews under his sway[1]. But both were equally firm in suppressing any attempt of the Jews to obtain privileges which were not theirs by law, and which seemed to menace either the security of their Christian subjects or the dignity of the Christian Church.

In a period with so little scholarship it is not unnatural

[1] *The Conflict*, pp. 206-221.

that the theological picture of the Jew should sink somewhat into the background. It was still there, but it rarely appeared, and when it did so, nothing was added to the established colouring. Disputations, written or oral, can rarely have taken place, though in Visigothic Spain, where from every point of view conditions were unlike those elsewhere in western Europe, it was necessary to prevent unlettered Christians from arguing with Jews, lest the latter should succeed in sowing doubts in the minds of the former as to the truths of Christianity.

In the economic field it was a period in which Jews shared the normal insecurities of the times, but little more; and there is ample evidence that daily relations were normal. One may even say that they improved rather than declined in the period from the breakdown of Rome up to the Carolingian epoch—Visigothic Spain being an exception. At least, when we begin to have fuller information of the Jews in the ninth century, they are occupying a much more favourable position than they were three or four hundred years earlier.

In their actual circumstances there was, indeed, little reason why their position should be unfavourable. In the period from the fifth to the eighth century they gradually took the place previously occupied by the Syrians as ' international' traders; and they continued, and perhaps developed, the trade in slaves. But these two occupations only employed a relatively small proportion of the Jewish population, and the rest were indistinguishable from other town dwellers. They were to be found in most of the Roman towns of southern France, and spread as far as the Rhineland; they frequented the fairs of northern Europe, penetrating even through the Slav fringes to north and east, and into the British Isles towards the end of the period under review. But the groups in which they lived were mostly small, and it is probable that few towns could count more than a dozen Jewish families. In many places, even as late as the eleventh century, single families were to be found living completely alone among the Christian population.

Such conditions favoured friendly relations, for there was not yet anything strange in the normal life of the Jew to attract attention. The cities were only slowly becoming

C

homogeneous, especially in the south where the Jewish population was more numerous. Christianity was only slowly penetrating into the masses of the people and into the consciousness of their rulers themselves. The Jews were a factor making for prosperity. There was plenty of room for their activities without their arousing the jealousy of rivals. Nothing suggests that such outbreaks as there were possessed an economic basis. And in general, it must be reckoned that the times were lawless, and the Jews could not expect to escape wholly from the consequences of a violence from which every other section of the population also suffered. It was the evil inheritance of past ages rather than contemporary conditions which decided the turn for the worse which took place in the succeeding centuries, and which indeed made that turn inevitable.

CHAPTER TWO

THE THRESHOLD OF THE MIDDLE AGES

BIBLIOGRAPHICAL INTRODUCTION

One of the main difficulties in building a bridge from the Roman to the medieval world is the extreme paucity of solid material wherewith to construct the approaches from either side. The ' bridge ' itself may be considered to be the Carolingian era of the ninth century, and it stands out as a relatively solid and, if one may employ the term, well documented structure. But it rests on almost nothing on either side! The Jews emerge into the searchlight of the correspondence of Agobard after a century and a half of almost complete obscurity. We do not even know whether they were continuously resident in France, the main country of their western settlement, or not. And again, when we have crossed the bridge, we find its other pier also rests on nothing, for we are without any but the most scanty material for the period from 850 to 1000.

The main interest is, therefore, the Carolingian era, and in particular the long reign of Louis the Pious, son of Charlemagne. For this period we have his own Diplomata, the earliest examples of special charters issued to the Jews; a number of ecclesiastical regulations; and, above all, the correspondence of Agobard, Archbishop of Lyons from 816 to 840. Agobard is said to have been a Spaniard by birth, and he belongs to the brilliant circle of reforming bishops gathered by Charlemagne, and to a lesser extent by his son. He was an ecclesiastical administrator rather than a theologian, and his writings are mostly short tracts or letters on subjects of immediate interest. They cover a wide field, and though they are conspicuous for fiery ardour, rather than academic calm, they are singularly free from either superstition or blind passion. There is nothing in them to equal the beastliness of the sermons of Chrysostom at Antioch on the subject of the Jews, or the crass ignorance of some of the eastern documents.

The question as to whether Agobard was justified in his conflict with the Jews, or is to be considered simply as an ' antisemite ', will probably remain permanently in debate. Material representing both points of view is given in the list of books. Apart, however, from his standpoint, his information as to the details of Jewish-Christian relations is of inestimable value. The writings of his successors, Amulo and Remigius of Lyons and Rathere of Verona, are also of considerable use as supplements to his own.

Apart from this group from Lyons and their Veronese imitator, few writers of the period deserve special mention. The books of Fulbert of Chartres and Peter Damian on the Jews possess no special interest. They are briefly referred to in a supplementary note in the *Adversus Judaeos* of Lukyn Williams. The one author who merits attention is Rabbi Samuel of Morocco, but only to draw attention to the sweetness and sympathy of his work in a period when those two qualities were rare indeed. A fuller discussion of Rabbi Samuel will come more appropriately in the succeeding volume, on the relations of the Jew to the medieval Church. The reasons for including him at all are given in footnote 4 on page 31.

Modern works are also scarce. In the earlier sections of the chapter I have been compelled perforce to refer largely to the predecessor to this volume, *The Conflict of the Church and the Synagogue*, in order to explain the survivals from the Roman world. Aronius contains most of the relevant scraps from chroniclers, together with summaries of the diplomata of Louis and the arguments of Agobard. But for serious study it is necessary to go to the texts presented in Bouquet and PL respectively. There is a valuable work by Bruno Hahn on the economic aspects of the period; and for France there are the two studies of Levi and Regné which contain much material. The introductory sections in the different chapters of Scherer are very valuable. The early chapters of Stobbe and Caro are also useful. Bedarride is very unreliable, though there is useful material in his notes, once they are disentangled from the confusion into which the printer has plunged them.

NOTE.—Since writing this I have received the work of Katz which is undoubtedly the most comprehensive study of the first half of the period treated in this chapter.

LIST OF BOOKS

A. Texts

AGOBARD

A. *Consultatio et Supplicatio . . . ad Proceres Palatii de baptismo Judaicorum mancipiorum. Reverendissimis . . . Adalardo, Walae, et Helisarcho* (before 826). Migne, PL, CVI, c. 99-106.

B. *Epistola ad Proceres Palatii contra Praeceptum impium de baptismo Judaicorum mancipiorum* (826). *Ibid.*, CIV, c. 173-178.

C. *De Insolentia Judaeorum* (826-827). *Ibid.*, CIV, c. 69-76.

D. *Epistola Agobardi, Bernardi, et Eaof de Judaicis superstitionibus* (same date). *Ibid.*, CIV, c. 77-100.

E. *Epistola . . . ad Nibridium Episcopum Narbonensem de cavendo convictu et societate Judaica. Ibid.*, CIV, c. 107-114.

Referred to in the text as Agobard A, B, C, D, E.

AMULO

Epistola, seu Liber contra Judaeos, ad Carolum Regem (843-877). *Ibid.*, CXVI, c. 141-184.

REMIGIUS

Epistola ad imperatorem de baptizatis Hebraeis (852-875). *Ibid.*, CXIX, c. 422 ff.

RATHERIUS

Qualitatis Conjectura. Ibid., CXXXVI, c. 535.

BOUQUET

Rerum Gallicarum et Francicarum scriptores. (Recueil des historiens de Gaule et de la France.) Ed. M. Bouquet and others. Vol. VI.

B. WORKS ON AGOBARD

CHEVALLARD, ABBÉ P.   *Saint Agobard, Archévêque de Lyon.*
Lyon, 1869.

LUKYN WILLIAMS, A.   *Adversus Judaeos*, xxxix, pp. 348-
357. Cambridge, 1935.

REINACH, T.   *Agobard et les Juifs* (Conférence).
REJ, L, Actes, pp. lxxxi ff.

C. GENERAL.

ARONIUS, J.   *Regesten zur Geschichte der Juden im
Fränkischen und Deutschen Reiche
bis zum Jahre 1273.* Berlin, 1902.

BEDARRIDE, I.   *Les Juifs en France, en Italie et en
Espagne.* Paris, 1859.

CARO, G.   *Sozial- und Wirtschaftsgeschichte der
Juden im Mittelalter und der Neuzeit.*
Vol. I. Leipzig, 1908.

HAHN, B.   *Die wirtschaftliche Tätigkeit der
Juden im Fränkischen und Deutschen
Reich bis zum 2. Kreuzzug.* Diss.
Freiburg i.B., 1911.

KATZ, S.   *The Jews in the Visigothic and Frankish Kingdoms of Spain and Gaul.*
Cambridge (Mass.), 1937.

LÉVI, I.   *Les Juifs de France du milieu du IXe
siècle aux Croisades.* REJ, LII.

REGNÉ, J.   *Etude sur la condition des Juifs de
Narbonne du Ve au XIVe siècle.*
REJ, LV, pp. 1-36, 221-243; LVIII,
pp. 75-105, 200-225; LIX, pp. 59-
89; LXI, pp. 228-254; LXII, pp. 1-
27, 248-266; LXIII, pp. 75-99.

SCHERER, J. E.   *Die Rechtsverhältnisse der Juden in
den deutsch-österreichischen Ländern.*
Leipzig, 1901.

STOBBE, O.   *Die Juden in Deutschland während
des Mittelalters, in politischer, socialer und rechtlicher Beziehung.*
Braunschweig, 1866; Berlin, 1923.

I. THE NATURE OF THE PERIOD

There are few periods of Jewish history in which generalisations are so apt to replace facts as that which lies between the end of the Roman Empire and the First Crusade. Both Jewish and Gentile writers fall into the easy temptation to read back from the following period an interpretation of events which they would not otherwise bear. To do so is not only unscientific; it has a particular danger in the present subject. It obscures the study of the actual historical origin of the present Jewish situation—largely a creation of the Middle Ages—and it falsifies conceptions of the relations between the Jews and their neighbours; and these two errors in combination lend ready support to theories of unalterable Jewish characteristics on the one hand, and unvarying Gentile hostility on the other. Nor are these generalisations justified by a complete absence of precise information as to Jewish life during the age under review. Naturally, sources are fewer than for the following period, and much must be left to conjecture. But it is possible to arrive at a fairly safe basis for this reconstruction. The main lines of the picture, the essential shapes within which that reconstruction must take place, are clearly indicated to us by the sources themselves.

For the Jews, more perhaps than for any other group in western Europe, the reign of Charlemagne stands as the end of the Roman period rather than as the first suggestion of the medieval empire and of medieval history. The many principalities out of which his dominions had been built up either knew no Jewish inhabitants or treated them as Roman citizens, citizens indeed of second rank whose rights might with almost complete impunity be infringed by princely or clerical violence, but still citizens. Charlemagne himself made no general regulations to govern their status. Had he done so, there might have been more unity in the treatment which they received from subsequent authorities. As it was, when his empire broke up, their position was left completely undefined.

This lack of definition in no way marked them out from the rest of their contemporaries. The chaos and disorder which followed the disappearance of a strong central authority left everything else also vague. For two hundred years there was, within both Church and State, a struggle for new definitions of relationships until finally the recognisable hierarchies of the Middle Ages took shape, with Pope and Emperor, national kings, semi-independent vassal princes, towns and peasants, linked together by a complicated system of feudal and other bonds.

From the standpoint of the Jewish population the most significant tendency of the period was the multiplication of separate sovereignties. The decisive influence, in domestic affairs at least, fell to the owners of the great fiefs, whether hereditary—dukes, counts, and barons, or ecclesiastical—archbishops, bishops and abbots. It was these who were the actual rulers of the territories which they held from their sovereigns. In England their claim never, so far as we know, included the right to possess their own Jews, and in consequence the Jews, up to the time of their expulsion in 1290, remained the possession of the crown itself. But in France the barons owned their own Jews as of right, and until the fourteenth century the kings did not even challenge this possession. The same was more or less true within the empire. It is this subdivision in the ownership of Jews which led both to their calamities and to their survival, their calamities, in that each man was anxious to exploit, and jealously guarded the right to exploit, his own property; and their salvation, in that there was never any possibility of all the princes of Christendom agreeing simultaneously to their expulsion, so that their flight had rarely to be farther than to the domain of the next prince, sometimes merely a matter of a few miles.

While the subdivision of authority was the most potent influence on the political situation of the Jews, the greatest influence in their social development came from movements within the Church. While the Carolingian Renaissance produced a remarkable flowering of intellectual and spiritual life, much of this ground was lost in the next two centuries. The Christian religion as an influence moulding daily thought and practice lost almost all effective power in large stretches of the continent. But the revived discipline of the monasteries of the tenth century, and the reform of the secular clergy which followed it, ensured for the Church an effective influence in the moulding of the social forms which were developing simultaneously. This inevitably meant a check to the close relations between Jews and Christians which existed during the period between Charlemagne and the eleventh century. And, in fact, when the feudal society of the country-side and the communal organisation of the towns had completed their control of every aspect of medieval life, it was found to be practically a closed system in which the erstwhile Roman citizen and equal member, the Jew, had no place.

In the economic field the period offers the nearest approach to a Jewish monopoly in certain departments of trade which is to be found anywhere in European history. After the disappearance of the Syrians, and before the appearance of the northern commercial centres of France, Flanders and Germany, the international trade of western Europe was almost exclusively in the hands of a few north Italian cities, and of small Jewish colonies settled along the Rhone, the Loire, the Seine and the Rhine. Even in local trade these groups seem to have had a considerable share. While the Jews were thus never, even then, the only traders, it is possible that the slave trade through north-eastern Europe to the Slav countries and the land trade to the East were for practical purposes Jewish monopolies.

II. THE TRANSMISSION OF THE ROMAN STATUS

As has been already said, the Jews of northern Europe did not lose their status as Roman citizens by any particular official cancellation of their rights. It sank rather into that oblivion in which was lost so much of the Roman inheritance. Even the Jews themselves seem to have forgotten its existence. To this general statement there is one exception. In the south of France, the Roman tradition lingered longer than elsewhere. Even to-day in the towns and villages of Provence Gothic, the stone symbol of medieval society, wears always an alien air, and in the true architecture of Provence it is often impossible to say, from a consideration of the actual detail, whether a building is late Roman, medieval or

Renaissance, so imperceptibly did the styles glide into each other. In such an atmosphere it was natural that the old system of ownership of land should have survived longer than elsewhere, and that among the citizens who freely owned land, and enjoyed all the lordships connected with ownership, should occasionally have been Jews. Even in 1276 a group of clerics, giving an arbitral decision in a dispute at Narbonne, issued their decision ' on the basis that the Jews are subjected to the laws, and should live according to the Code of Rome '[1].

But while elsewhere the Roman citizenship vanished, leaving no trace, there is a long interregnum between this vanishing and any new regulation; and the latter, when it came, differed from place to place, and often from year to year. Such an interregnum was natural in an evolving society, and too much stress must not be laid on the absence of precision. In common with others, the Jews enjoyed such permission to live as the powerful chose to allow them. Records of violence and injustice to them are paralleled by similar acts towards different sections of Christian society.

It was only through the influence of the clergy that any details of the Theodosian and canonical conception of the Jew survived at all. It was in their libraries that copies of old laws and canons were kept. Charlemagne, when he wished to know the Catholic laws governing society, wrote to the Pope, Hadrian I, for an abstract of conciliar law[2]. In the same way Agobard, Archbishop of Lyons, wishing to recall Louis the Pious and his empress Judith from their undue familiarity with Jews, collected for him the enactments of Church Councils, especially those of the Frankish Church itself, as a guide to his action[3]; and his successor, Amulo, addressed almost the same collection to Charles the Bald a couple of decades later[4]. Similarly, when Frederick (Archbishop of Mainz in the tenth century, but more prince than bishop) wished to know the right way in which to treat

---

[1] ' attento quod Judaei subsunt legibus et jure romano vivere debent. . . .' G. Saige, Les Juifs de Languedoc, p. 203.

[2] Cap. Aquisgran., xlv; MGH, LL, I, p. 61.

[3] Agobard, D, i; c. 77 ff.

[4] Amulo, Epistola, seu Liber contra Judaeos ad Carolum Regem, i; PL, CXVI, c. 141.

his Jews, he wrote to a priest to collect for him the laws of the Church on the subject[1].

The most serious effort of the Church to secure the attention of the secular authorities for the observance of these laws was made at the Council of Meaux in 845. This Council was called by the leading Churchmen of northern and central France, the famous Hincmar of Rheims being one of the principal figures. It presented to the king, Charles the Bald, an abstract of laws of Constantine, Theodosius II, and Childebert, letters of Gregory the Great, and canons of Epaone, Agde, Mâcon, Orleans, Laodicea, Clermont and Toledo[2]. The decisions of the Council were, however, quashed by Charles, and not put into effect.

While occasionally there are references to such matters as the construction of synagogues[3], or the sale to Christians of meat unfit for Jews[4], the main interest of the clergy was focussed upon three points: the possession of, or trade in, Christian slaves; the occupation of positions of authority over Christians; and the presence of Jews among Christians during the solemnities of Holy Week. All these were points on which there was copious existing legislation, both from princes and from councils[5]. It was neither a desire to inflict humiliations on the Jews, nor mere legalism, which induced the clerics of the Carolingian era to concentrate upon these questions. Their choice of these issues, out of all that they might have raised, was due to a purely practical consideration —their alarm at the close and friendly relations between Jews and Christians which seem to have existed in many walks of society within the Frankish dominions.

That the laws themselves were merely secondary to this ultimate object we can most easily realise from two writings of Agobard, addressed to Louis the Pious, during the period in which his court was dominated by the Empress Judith. Of these letters, one was written by himself, and the other jointly composed by himself and two of his colleagues[6].

[1] Aronius, No. 128.
[2] Mansi, XIV, c. 836 ff.
[3] Agobard, C, v; c. 74.
[4] *Ibid.*, iii; c. 73.
[5] For laws on these subjects see *The Conflict*, App. I, ii, p. 389.
[6] C and D; c. 69 ff. and 77 ff.

In these two documents none of the laws of the Roman Codes are quoted at all. It is canons of councils, opinions of the saints of the Church, and anecdotes from their lives which are collected to convey to the Emperor the warning which the Archbishop wished to give.

So great was the authority of the Roman tradition, however, that when a precise issue was in question, none of the Carolingians asked for more than that which the Roman Code required. At times they even asked less. Agobard, who violently disapproved of the Jewish possession of Christian slaves, was yet willing to pay for them at a price which an early Gallic Council had fixed[1]. He could have found authority in the Theodosian Code for evading any payment whatsoever[2]. But on the main issue they asked for the confirmation of the established position: a Christian was not to be sold into servitude to a Jew or pagan[3], and a Jew was not to circumcise a pagan or Christian slave[4]. On the question of a time limit within which a slave trader might retain Christian slaves whom he had bought, they probably followed the ruling of Gregory[5]; but they tried to limit the field of the trader by forbidding the sale of slaves outside the frontiers of the kingdom[6]. The English clergy in this matter followed the same line as their Frankish colleagues[7].

The second desire of the clergy was to see a strict enforcement of the laws excluding the Jews from any position of authority over Christians[8]. This also possessed Roman

[1] D, vi; c. 84.

[2] CT, 16, 9, 4.

[3] Cf. *Capitularia Caroli Magni et Ludovici Pii*, VI, ccccxxiii; Mansi, XV, *appendix*, c. 672. Based on canon ix of the twelfth council of Toledo (681).

[4] *Ibid.*, VII, cclxxxvi; Mansi, XV, *appendix*, c. 727. Based on CT, 16, 9, 4.

[5] Gregory allowed a trader forty ⊔ays to dispose of a Christian slave, unless illness prolonged the period. Gregory, *Ep.*, IX, civ; MGH, Epistolae, II, p. 111.

[6] Agobard, C, iii; c. 72.

[7] Cf. the eighth-century canons of Egbert of York, cl and cli; Mansi, XII, c. 429, and Conc. Aenham. of 1009, vi; *ibid.*, XIX, c. 307.

[8] Cf. Pavia (850), xx, Mansi, XIV, c. 937, and Rome (1078), *ibid.*, XX, c. 508; also the *Capitularia Caroli Magni et Ludovici Pii*, VI, cxxii; *ibid.*, XV, *appendix*, c. 630, and the letter of Gregory VII to Alphonso of Castile, *ibid.*, XX, c. 341.

sanction, and was reasonable from their standpoint. Since there were many other classes in the community unlikely ever to be able to enjoy office, it would have seemed to them no excessive discipline to demand of the Jews. Finally, they desired to see a proper respect observed by the Jews for the dignity and the solemnities of the Church—abstention from work on Sundays, absence from the streets during Holy Week, and liberty of conscience for their Christian servants. Authority for such an attitude was again to be found in past enactments, secular and ecclesiastical.

Nearly all our evidence for the life of this period inevitably comes from the activities of the Frankish Church. But as the influence of Christendom was extended into northern and eastern Europe, the same attitude was adopted in new provinces. A Hungarian council at Szabolcs of the end of the eleventh century, for example, decreed the exclusion of the Jews from the streets during Holy Week, prohibited intermarriage between Jews and Christians, and any work being done on Sundays[1]. Another at Gran, twenty years later, forbade any kind of service being given to Jews by Christians[2].

III. THE TRANSMISSION OF ROMAN THEOLOGY

As they were exact in their demand that the laws and canons of the previous period should be enforced, so also were the Carolingian clergy faithful in representing no more and no less than the earlier theological position. Again, they did not desire to transgress the limits laid down. It is interesting to see both Agobard and Amulo insisting that Christians are not to attack the lives, comfort and wealth of the Jews, but only to abstain from their society and observe punctiliously what the Church enjoins[3].

As to what the Church enjoined they were quite clear. The basis of the Christian Faith was the Shema Israel, the great declaration of the unity of God in Deuteronomy[4],

[1] Szabolcs (1092), x and xxvi; Mansi, XX, c. 763 and 773.
[2] Gran (1114), lxi, *ibid.*, XXI, c. 112.
[3] Agobard, C, iv, c. 74, and Amulo, *Contra Judaeos*, lix; PL, CXVI, c. 184.
[4] *Capitulare I, an.* 789, lxi; MGH, Legum Sectio II, Capit. I, p. 58. Repeated in *Capitularia Caroli Magni et Ludovici Pii*, I, lviii; Mansi, XV, *appendix*, c. 480.

but the Christians understood it, and the Jews did not. For
the Old Testament contained partly ' mysteries ' and partly
' moral precepts '. The Jews did not understand that the
former were carnal, and had been abolished at the coming
of the Messiah. They included such ' mysteries ' as the
permission to the priesthood to marry. The ' precepts ',
however, retained an eternal validity[1]. Of these precepts
the Church was the guardian against both heretics and Jews.
But the latter were to be distinguished from the former in
that the heretics were wrong on some points, whereas the
Jews were wrong on all[2]. Hence, it is not personal spite but
a mere restatement of the accepted position when Agobard
says: ' all who are under the Law are under a curse, and are
clothed with the curse as with a garment. It (the curse)
has entered, like water, inside them, and like oil into their
bones. They are, moreover, cursed in the city, and cursed in
the field; cursed in coming in, and cursed in going out;
cursed in the fruits of the womb, the land and the flock;
cursed are their cellars, their barns, their medicines, their
food, and the crumbs that drop from it, and none of them
can escape from this appalling, this ghastly, curse of the
Law, except by Him who was made a Curse for us '[3].

Nothing of this is new. And, in fact, it was difficult to see
what could be added to what the earlier centuries had
devised. There could only be a varying of intensity. Origin-
ality of basis was no longer possible. From Agobard in the
beginning of the period covered by this chapter, to Bruno of
Würzburg[4] at the end, the same note and the same violence
are to be found in many writers. But just as they are the
normal successors of Ambrose and Chrysostom, so also there
were successors to the slightly more gentle preachers of the
past. One such was Remigius of Auxerre. In a sermon on
the Crucifixion, he warned his hearers that they must think
not merely of the Jews alone, but rather of all sinners, as
responsible for the Cross; and he went on to warn them
also that they must not even condemn the Jews for their part

---

[1] Council of Rome (1074), xii; Mansi, XX, c. 415.
[2] Agobard, D, ix; c. 86. Repeated by Amulo, *op. cit.*, iv; *ibid.*, CXVI,
c. 143.
[3] Agobard, E; c. 113.
[4] See especially his commentary on Ps. xxi, in PL, CXLII, c. 109 ff.

in it, since God has given them until the Second Coming to repent of their action[1]. Commonplace as these words may sound to-day, they are almost unique in the period of their utterance.

Only in the eleventh century does a new argument emerge in three writings. The passage of the millennium emphasised the length of the Jewish exile. No prophecy of which the Jews might make use predicted anything so terrible as a thousand years of punishment for their sins. Fulbert, Bishop of Chartres[2], writing at the beginning of the century, Peter Damian[3] and Rabbi Samuel of Morocco[4] writing towards the end, make telling use of this argument. Fulbert reveals that its significance was not lost upon the Jews themselves; for he refers to their claim that ' the sceptre ' had not in fact ' departed from Judah ', in that every Jewish householder was a king in his own household. Of much greater interest is the *Letter of Rabbi Samuel*.

This letter, addressed to a fellow scholar of Morocco, is unique in the whole field of Jewish Christian polemics. In all its pages is no single word of abuse, no sneer at the misfortunes of the Jews, no word of contempt, no gibe, no threat. As do Fulbert and Peter Damian, the Rabbi begins with the tragedy of the thousand years of exile and suffering.

[1] *Fifth Homily on S. Matthew;* PL, CXXXI, c. 892.

[2] *Tractatus contra Judaeos;* PL, CXLI, c. 305.

[3] *Antilogus contra Judaeos* and *Dialogus inter Judaeum et Christianum;* PL, CXLV, c. 41, and c. 57.

[4] In spite of the arguments of Steinschneider and others I am convinced of the authenticity of this document. It claims to be written in the middle of the eleventh century by a Rabbi who had been converted to Christianity, presumably under Moslem rule. The argument of Steinschneider and of those who reject its authenticity, is that it was actually written by the fourteenth-century Dominican of Spain, who claimed to have discovered it and to have translated it from the Arabic. This hypothesis, however, entirely ignores two facts. Nothing in the document itself suggests the theology of the fourteenth century, and, still more important, nothing in the tone of it suggests the method of medieval, and Dominican, controversy. If there really was a Dominican of the sweetness and saintliness of the author of this document, writing in the fourteenth century, it is incredible that there are no traces of his influence elsewhere. For a fuller discussion of the authorship, and for references to the various authorities who have discussed it, see Lukyn Williams, *Adversus Judaeos*, pp. 228 ff. Dr Lukyn Williams himself, whose authority in this field is unique, inclines to the acceptance of the document as genuine. The letter is printed in innumerable editions. It will also be found in PL, CXLIX, c. 333-368.

He paints with deep pathos the despair which follows the realisation that no prophecy of Scripture deals with so long an exile, or promises a restoration therefrom.   Now, for their former sins, the Jews were sent into exile for a deter-mined period with a promise of return. What crime, other than that which the Christians allege, the killing of the Messiah himself, can explain an exile so long and hopeless? From this he passes gradually to the evidence that Jesus was in fact the Messiah, and to his own acceptance of Him. Each chapter of the letter opens in a tone of gentle melan-choly with an address to ' the Master ' to whom the letter is written, and ends with a note of encouragement: ' but, whatever may happen, we are all children of God '.

Among the polemics of the period should, perhaps, be included the *Defence of the Catholic Faith against the Jews* of Isidore of Seville; for, though it was written in the seventh century, it was translated into German at the monastery of Murbach near Strasbourg, in the eighth or ninth century, and is one of the earliest documents in the German vernacular.

Not unnaturally, formal theology and written disputations were not all that was transmitted by the Carolingians. The popular conception of the Jew in legend and hagiology also found a place in their writings. The Jew as the subject of a miracle leading to his conversion, already familiar in the Iconoclastic controversy[1], provided useful material for the discussions in the tenth and eleventh centuries as to the nature of the Eucharist. Gezo of Tortona relates a story which provides an interesting bridge between the Iconodules and the clergy of the Middle Ages who created the legend of the Profanation of the Host. A Jew wishes to insult Christ in the wafer. He goes with Christians to Mass, and com-municates. Receiving the wafer on his tongue, he is about to transfer it to his pocket, when he is seized with fearful pains, and is unable to shut his mouth. The sacred wafer hangs miraculously between his lips, touching nothing, until the priest comes and removes it. The Jew and many with him are converted[2].

---

[1] See *The Conflict*, viii. The Iconoclasts desired to abolish images; the ' Iconodules ' were the party defending their use. They proved the efficiency of images by a pleasant series of stories in which images converted Jews.

[2] *De Corpore et Sanguine Christi*, xxxix; PL, CXXXVII, c. 390.

Yet another sinister transition appears in a legend of the Jews of Rome. The Iconodules had many versions of the story of the mockery of a crucifix, but none were attended with results as terrible as those which befell the Eternal City itself in 1020. For, as a result of the evil actions of some Jews (subsequently confessed in horror at the consequences by one of the evil-doers themselves), a whirlwind and earthquake descended on the city and almost destroyed the entire population. Nor did it seem a curious manifestation of Divine Power to the chronicler of the event, that the anger of Heaven continued indiscriminately to destroy the innocent and unconscious Romans, until the Pope discovered the guilty parties by means of the confession already mentioned, and immediately executed them by the mundane process of decapitation[1]. The Byzantines were both more logical and more conscious of a reason in Divine Righteousness. In their stories the punishment fell upon the guilty parties, and was usually but a prelude to a glorious conversion.

IV. THE TRANSMISSION OF POPULAR TRADITION

The idea of Jewish hostility to Christianity expressed itself in other familiar ways also. Just as the Jews had been accused of the very improbable intention of betraying Arian Visigothic Arles to the Catholic Clovis[2], so they were accused of betraying Bordeaux to the Normans in 848. While it is impossible to deny that they may have done so, the action seems extremely improbable, for the Normans were raiders who ravaged the country in search of loot, and one would have thought that merchants, above all others, would have been anxious to defend the town from them. The incident is only reported once, in a chronicle written by Prudentius of Troyes, and Troyes is somewhat distant from Bordeaux[3]. Other chroniclers of the period make no mention of it.

[1] Adhemar, *Historia*, iii, s.a. 1020; MGH, SS, IV, p. 139. Cf. Mansi, XIX, c. 323.

[2] *The Conflict*, p. 321.

[3] Prudentius, *Annales*, s.a. 848; MGH, SS, I, p. 443. It is worth noting that there is no definite record of Jews in Bordeaux before the eleventh century, though this is not conclusive evidence against an earlier settlement.

D

The same authority is responsible for another story of a
Jewish betrayal in this century. Four years after the betrayal
of Bordeaux, Prudentius tells us that the Jews betrayed
Barcelona to the Moors[1]. On this occasion a *prima facie* case
can be made out for the probability of the story; for the
Jews were much better treated by the Moors than by the
Christian rulers in Spain. But, unfortunately for Prudentius,
there is only one record of an attack on Barcelona during the
period in question—an attack which did not take place in
852—and that attack in any case was unsuccessful. Equally
unfortunate for its author is the accusation that the Jews
betrayed the town of Toulouse to the Moors, and that in
consequence one of the community was condemned annually
to receive a buffet on the cheek[2]. The buffet was certainly
administered, but Toulouse happens to be a city which the
Moors failed ever to take[3]. A somewhat similar story occurs
again in the beginning of the eleventh century. This time
it is the destruction of the Church of the Holy Sepulchre
which was attributed to the treachery of the Jews, or of
Jews and Moors of Spain. But while a persecution of Christians certainly took place during the reign of Hakim, the
Fatimite Caliph, the Jews suffered equally with them, so
that the story possesses little or no probability[4].

More serious for the life of the Jews than the struggle of
the clergy to maintain intact the Roman discipline and
theology, discussed in the last section, was the repetition and
intensification of acts of lawlessness such as had taken place
even before the complete downfall of Roman law and order.

Three expulsions are recorded during the two centuries
which followed the death of Charlemagne. In 855 the Jews
were expelled by the Emperor Louis II from Italy[5]. No
reason whatever is given for this action, and we know too

---

[1] Prudentius, *Annales*, s.a. 852; p. 447.

[2] See below, pp. 43 ff.

[3] See I. Levi, *Les Juifs de France du milieu du IXe siècle aux Croisades*;
REJ, LII, p. 162.

[4] See Glaber Rodulfus, *Hist.*, III, vii, s.a. 1010; Bouquet, X, p. 34.
Cf. Adhemar, *Hist.*, III, xlvii, s.a. 1010; MGH, SS, IV, p. 137, and
Hugo, *Chron.*, xxvii, s.a. 1028; *ibid.*, VIII, p. 399. Elmacinus (*Hist.
Sarac.*, III, vi, quoted in Bouquet, X, p. 152, note g) recognises that
Jews and Christians were equally suppressed by Hakim.

[5] Conventus Ticinensis III, Statut. iv; MGH, LL, I, p. 437.

little of conditions at the time to be able to supply one. The
same is true of the expulsion thirty years later from Sens.
Here there is the added mystery that, whether for the same
reason or for totally unconnected causes, the nuns were
expelled at the same time[1]. In 1012 Henry II expelled the
Jews from Mainz[2]. On this occasion a possible explanation
can be given. Just about this time an important personality,
Wecelinus, Chaplain of a certain Duke Conrad, was converted to Judaism; and such an act may well have aroused
sufficient indignation to have led to the expulsion of the
community adjudged responsible[3].

There are four incidents of varying gravity reported in
which the baptism of Jews figures as the central interest.
They are all told in sufficient detail to merit attention.

The first case is extraordinarily interesting, and it is
difficult to be at all sure that it may be legitimately classed
as ' compulsory '. The successor of Agobard and Amulo
in the See of Lyons was Remigius, and he was no less concerned with the Jewish question than his predecessors. In a
long letter to the emperor he recorded his experience. The
order in which he related events has some importance. By
divine grace, he told the emperor, his labours had been
blessed with a number of conversions, both men and women,
old and young, youths and children, together with many of
their servants. As the number of the converted multiplied,
they began to invite other Jews to follow them, especially the
boys and young people, since the old were immovable.
A large number of the young began to feel a yearning for an
experience similar to that enjoyed by the converted; and he
then adds: ' *especially, I think, because every Sabbath the
word of God is preached in the synagogue by our brothers and
priests* '. The unconverted Jews then began to send their
children to Arles down the Rhone. The converted were very
troubled by this, and reported it to the bishop. He ordered
the children who were left to be brought before him, without
any harm being done to them, so that if any wished freely

---

[1] ' Ansegisus (the Archbishop) Judaeos certa de causa et moniales ab
urbe Senonica expulit ', Odoramnus, s.a. 883; Bouquet, VIII, p. 237.

[2] *Annales Quedlinburg.*, s.a. 1012, MGH, SS, III, p. 81.

[3] Alpertus, *De diversitate temporum*, I, vii; MGH, SS, IV, p. 704.
Cf. H. Tykocinski, in *Philippson Festschrift*, p. 1.

to enter the Church they might do so. Six small children (pueruli) asked for baptism, and, seeing this, forty-seven more followed them. Finding that the rest would not be moved, he returned them unharmed to their parents. But he requested the emperor to see that a similar opportunity was given by the Bishop of Arles to the children who had been sent there[1].

This is clearly not a story of violent baptism. The question is whether there is evidence of undue pressure. Jewish scholars have, not unnaturally, seen such evidence in the letter[2], but it is probable that they are mistaken. Comparing the letter with that written some centuries earlier by Severus of Majorca, in which actions of violence are presented under a camouflage of miracle[3], and with the frankness with which forced baptisms are presented as such throughout the Middle Ages, such a difference of tone is revealed that it is reasonable to grant to Remigius a *prima facie* acceptance of the events which he recounts as a genuine example of a mass conversion. For, unquestionably, such have happened in the history of all religions. Supposing him to have been a man of different type from his predecessors, it may well be that, because of the very friendliness between Jews and Christians of which they complained, he succeeded where their methods failed. The critical sentence in his account is the one given in italics. According to Remigius the sequence was: a number of conversions as a result of his mission; then, largely owing to the enthusiasm of the converts, actual preaching in the synagogue. It is only if the preaching in the synagogue was, in fact, parallel to the compulsory sermons of later days; and if it had been the cause of the first ' conversions ', that the story assumes an appearance of a pressure indistinguishable from compulsion. For reasons given later in the chapter, it seems more probable that the story should be accepted at its face value as an instance of genuine conversions from Judaism to Christianity.

[1] Remigius, *Ep. de baptizatis Hebraeis*; PL, CXIX, p. 422. The ascription of the letter to Remigius is uncertain, but the name of the writer is of secondary importance.

[2] E.g. Gross, in MGWJ, XXVII, p. 136. ' (Remigius) ahmte ihnen (Agobard and Amulo) in seinem Fanatismus gegen die Juden nach und bildet mit ihnen zusammen das judenfeindliche Trifolium von Lyon.'

[3] See *The Conflict*, pp. 203 ff.

The next case of which we possess information is almost equally interesting. We have already seen that the Archbishop Frederick of Mainz was sufficiently concerned with the position of Jewish residents within his jurisdiction to request a priest to provide him with an abstract of the regulations of canon law affecting the Jews[1]. Some years before this he wrote to the Pope Leo VII for his advice on the same subject. The reply of the Pope was that ' he should have the religion of the Holy Trinity and the Mystery of the Incarnation preached to them with the utmost wisdom and prudence ' . . . but, if they refused to believe it, then the Pope gave the Archbishop authority to expel them from his territories, ' since we ought not to dwell with the enemies of God '. But on no account was he to baptize them against their will[2]. How matters turned out we do not know.

The third example is more tragic. At the beginning of the eleventh century Robert the Pious was king of France. The epithet ' pious ' only implies that he was possessed of some learning, and reverenced the Church. In fact, he was a man of astute character playing an extremely difficult game at a time when the fortunes of the French monarchy were at their very lowest ebb. This is the king who is said to have ordered the Jews of France to choose between baptism and death.

Four separate documents appear to deal with the event; and though scholars, considering them individually, have cast doubts upon their accuracy, their mutual confirmation assures us that something occurred. A Hebrew manuscript of the beginning of the eleventh century says that Robert, in agreement with the barons, offered the Jews baptism or death, and that many were killed or committed suicide[3]. A Norman chronicler of the middle of the eleventh century, William Godell, has the curt statement under the year 1010: ' in this year many Jews were baptized under duress '[4]. Under the same date a Burgundian monk, Rudolf Glaber, has a highly pictorial account of the massacres which took place everywhere in indignation at the action of the Jews of

[1] See above, pp. 26 ff.
[2] Leo VII, Ep. xiv; PL, CXXXII, c. 1084 ff.
[3] REJ, LII, p. 165; Gall. Jud., p. 71.
[4] Bouquet, X, p. 262.

Orleans in procuring the destruction of the Church of the Holy Sepulchre in Jerusalem[1].

Under the same year, in another chronicle, we have a substantial account of the repercussion in Limoges of the happenings in Jerusalem. The chronicler was Adhemar, and he was in the city at the time. According to his report, Hilduin, Bishop of Limoges, announced to the Jews that they must either accept Christianity or leave the city; he gave them a month for reflection, and during this month theologians were ordered to argue with them. The result was three or four conversions; and the rest left the city with their wives and children. One manuscript adds that many committed suicide fearing that they would be violently baptized[2].

To these four documents a further piece of evidence may be added. There lived at this time a famous Jewish scholar, Rabbi Gershom of Metz. In the ' Responsa ' which he addressed to many communities which wrote to him for advice, there are a number of references to apostates[3]. His own son was baptized, apparently by force, and died a Christian. The fact that Rabbi Gershom observed full mourning for him, as though he had died a Jew, suggests that there was something unusual in the ' conversion '; and his general gentleness in dealing with those who returned to Judaism is most easily explained by the fact that he was not dealing with those who had left Judaism in the first place of their own free will. If there had been a wave of indignation against the Jews, during which many had been baptized by force, and if clerical and popular indifference had then allowed the ' converts ' to return to the religion in which they really believed, this would account for the attitude of Rabbi Gershom. Later on it is very unlikely that many ' converts ' would have succeeded in returning openly to Judaism, but they did so, both in 1096, and after some forced baptisms, of which we know no details, in central Germany, about 1085[4]. There is, therefore, no reason for not believing that the same happened in 1010.

[1] Bouquet, X, p. 34.
[2] Adhemar, *Hist.*, III, xlvii; MGH, SS, IV, p. 136. For the arguments against the veracity of these accounts see Aronius, No. 142.
[3] Cf. *Gallia Judaica*, p. 303.
[4] Letter of Antipope Clement III reproaching the Bishop of Bamberg for allowing such returns; Mansi, XX, c. 600.

That 1010 was a year of floods, pestilence and famine, and that an eclipse took place about the same time, lends colour to the possibility that what we know to have happened in Limoges was scheduled to happen elsewhere also. The cases dealt with by Rabbi Gershom prove that in the north-east of France there was disorder about this period, and we have no reason for linking his statements to any events other than those reported of this year. Whether the expulsion in Mainz two years later should also be linked to this series, and not to the conversion of Wecelin, is more open to doubt. But that 1010 was a tragic year for the Jews in many places seems to be well established. Though we may doubt whether the Jews had any share in the destruction of the Church of the Holy Sepulchre, it may well be that the people of that time were convinced of their guilt. It is certain that violent indignation was felt at the destruction of the church. The eclipse, the floods and the famine may have seemed to be divine punishments for this tragic event. If this were so, then to massacre or baptize the wicked Jews who had planned it would have been an act of necessary piety.

Finally, there is a case from Trier which suggests a ' Golem ' story of Rabbi Loew of Prague[1]. Everard the Bishop decreed in 1066 that the Jews should accept baptism or expulsion on the following Easter day. The Jews—or ' certain of that unspeakable people '—proceeded to make a waxen image, a ' mommet' in fact, of the Bishop. Through it was threaded a wick. They bribed a Christian priest to baptize the mommet—a curious blending of black and white magic. When Easter Sunday arrived, the Jews lit the wick, and the Bishop donned his robes and proceeded to the font. But at this very moment the wick reached the middle of the figure, and the Bishop was seized with great pains and expired in the vestry[2]. While modern scholars may doubt the efficacy of waxen images, there seems no reason to doubt either that the Bishop did plan such an act, or that he was prevented from carrying it out only by a coincidence which was not unnaturally ascribed to magic.

[1] A Golem is a clay image miraculously endowed with life by special prayers, and created to preserve the Jews at a time of great danger. Cf. Chajim Bloch, Le Golem, légendes du ghetto de Prague, Strasbourg, 1928.

[2] Gesta Treverorum, s.a. 1066; MGH, SS, VIII, p. 182.

V. THE BEGINNING OF NEW REGULATIONS

While so far there has been recorded the continuation of laws, ideas and traditions which the Carolingians had inherited from an earlier age, it was inevitable that, as time progressed, novel problems should arise and require new solutions. The most important innovation was the granting of special letters of protection to individuals or to communities. We possess several of these granted about the year 825 by Louis the Pious[1]. Their purpose was to protect the Jews from arbitrary acts of violence, to allow them to carry on their trade undisturbed, to secure them from molestation in their observances, and to confirm their enjoyment of special courts on all matters affecting Jewish Law. There was no attempt at any comprehensive regulation of their status, though the phrase that ' as long as they remain loyal subjects, the Emperor takes them under his patronage and protection ', forecasts unconsciously their future position as imperial or other private property.

The few ' Diplomata ' of Louis are the only prescriptions of Jewish conditions of settlement that we possess over a period of more than two centuries. Doubtless some others existed and have been lost, but there cannot have been many. For either they would have left some trace in the literature which remains to us from those centuries, or, more likely, they would be referred to in later documents of similar character. Jews, in times of stress or persecution, would have quoted them as evidence in their favour, would have referred to the antiquity of their privileges, and have based their claims to fresh confirmation of their rights on existing ancient documents. The real conclusion to be drawn from the scarcity of Jewish charters is that few were issued, because few were needed; and that few were needed because there was nothing sufficiently abnormal in the Jewish situation to demand continual regulation. They lived the lives of ordinary townsfolk, shared in the privileges and responsibilities of their fellows, and were distinguished from them only by their religion.

[1] The discussion of the actual clauses of these Diplomata will be found in Ch. V, pp. 158 ff. The question of Christian slaves is considered below, pp. 45 ff.

A natural development from the conferring of a letter of protection on Jews resident directly under the imperial authority, was the transference of this authority to others. Louis of Provence in 920, in confirming the Archbishop of Arles in the possession of his city, confirmed him also in the possession of its Jews[1]. Similarly, Otto the Great in 965 placed the Jews and other merchants of Magdeburg directly under the authority of the Archbishop[2], and his successor Otto II acted in exactly the same way towards the Jews of Merseburg near Halle[3].

As a practical consequence of the special Letters of Protection granted by Louis the Pious, a special officer, the ' Master of the Jews ', was appointed by him to see that the privileges were observed[4]. We have no record of the office being a permanent one at this time, though such an official is frequently found in later medieval regulations.

While these innovations to some extent marked the Jews out as a separate group within society, another reminded them that they had still to take their share in the duties imposed on the rest of the population. During the whole period the Church was gradually establishing her claim that all land ought to pay tithe to some religious object. The first stage was naturally to claim this tithe from those who, being themselves Christians, would recognise the obligation—at any rate, in principle. The next stage was to demand it on all land situated within a Christian parish. A difficulty arose, however, when land, which had been in the possession of Christians, and on which tithe had been paid, passed into the hands of a Jew. A complaint on this score was made to Charles the Simple by the clergy of Narbonne in 899; and the king ruled that of the land occupied by Jews in the parishes in question, all that had once paid tithe was to continue to pay it[5]. The Jews continued to resist payment,

[1] Dipl. xviii; Bouquet, IX, p. 686.
[2] Dipl. ccc; MGH, *Dipl.*, I, p. 416.
[3] Thietmar, *Chron.*, III, i; MGH, SS, III, p. 758.
[4] There are several references to him in the letters of Agobard, e.g. A and B; c. 105 and 178. He clearly took his duties seriously, cf. C and E ii; c. 70.
[5] Dipl. xiii; Bouquet, IX, p. 480. Cf. also Dips. 54 and 88. On the question of the authority by which Charles intervened in a dispute in Narbonne, see Israel Levi and J. Regné in REJ, LII, p. 164, and LV, pp. 223 ff.

and in 1068 a Council meeting at Gerona confirmed that, throughout the provinces of southern France and northern Spain, Jews were to pay tithes on any land which had been bought from Christians[1]. A second council, meeting ten years later at the same place, extended the principle to all land owned by Jews. It was to pay tithes to the parish in which it was situated[2]. This solution was not confined to this area. It gradually found its way into practice elsewhere, until it came to be the accepted rule[3]. A further limitation on Jewish land-ownership dates, in theory at least, from the time of Louis the Pious, or from later in the ninth century. This was the law forbidding Christians and either Jews or heretics to be tenants of each other[4]. That there were not more regulations during this period is probably due, as has already been said, to the fact that the abnormality of the Jews in a Christian society was not yet sufficiently marked to attract the attention of reforming princes and bishops whose hands were already sufficiently full with more urgent matters.

VI. NEW FORMS OF POPULAR VIOLENCE

Signs are not wanting at this time of other and less pleasant harbingers of the Middle Ages. It was a feature of the earlier period that it needed a special occasion, and usually special inflammation, to produce a hatred of the Jew in the man in the street. But already at the beginning of the tenth century a council at Mainz had to remind the faithful that to kill a Jew was no light offence, but homicide, ' since war is not even made on enemies abroad unless they have broken the peace '[5].

The most curious acts of violence took place in three French towns, Chalons-sur-Saône, Béziers and Toulouse. In Chalons, on Palm Sunday, ' the Jews are stoned by the

---

[1] Canon xiv; Mansi, XIX, c. 1072.

[2] Canon x; *ibid.*, XX, c. 519.

[3] Cf., e.g., App. to Council of Clermont, 1095; *ibid.*, XX, c. 911.

[4] *Ad Cap. Caroli M. et Ludovici P. Add.*, III, xc; Mansi, XVI App. c. 586.

[5] Aronius, No. 121.

clergy and people, because they stoned Jesus '[1]. In Béziers
the custom received a still more definite ecclesiastical sanction. A sermon was preached in the cathedral by the bishop,
in which he reminded the people that ' they could observe
around them the grandchildren of those who condemned
Jesus, people who denied the existence of Mary the Mother
of God '. He went on to tell them that for that one week,
' when their hearts were agonised by the thoughts of the
insults offered to their Saviour, they had his blessing, and
the Governor's licence, to revenge themselves upon the
Jews—but only with stones '. No other weapon might be
used. As a result of the sermon the Jewish houses were
bombarded daily with stones throughout the week. One
imagines that if this really happened every year, the houses
were largely empty at that season. There were many Jewish
communities in the neighbourhood to which the inhabitants
might move. The chronicler who relates the story, however,
accepting the Jews to be of sterner stuff, states that very many
of them were wounded yearly[2]. The custom was not abolished until the twelfth century, but a hundred years later
the tradition was still living among the populace[3].

Even more serious was the licensed violence of Toulouse.
There, in alleged memory of a betrayal of the town to the
Moors—a story whose authenticity is contradicted by the
fact that the Moors never took the town—every year a Jew
had to stand up in the square before S. Stephen's Church
and receive a blow in the face. The custom certainly goes

---

[1] *Ordinary of S. Vincent of Chalons.* Courtepée, the historian of
Burgundy, says that even in his day (the end of the eighteenth century)
children, on the return of the Palm Sunday procession, which always
followed the Rue des Juifs, used to knock on the doors with stones, in
memory of this custom (*Histoire de la Bourgogne*, III, p. 219). Reminders
of the events of Passion Week in various forms are found all through the
Middle Ages; e.g., the dice which Jews entering the Archbishopric of
Mainz had to pay the Archbishop in memory of the dice with which the
soldiers cast lots for Our Lord's clothes (J. Menczel, *Beiträge zur
Geschichte der Juden in Mainz*, p. 25).

[2] Gaufredus Vosiensis, *Chron.*, s.a. 1152; Bouquet, XII, p. 436.

[3] The *Constitutio de Judaeis*, continually repeated by Popes during the
twelfth century, explicitly forbids such violence. It was originally issued
by Calixtus II in about 1120. A council of Béziers in 1246 specially
warns the bishops and clergy to protect the Jews from the attacks
of the Christians during Holy Week; see canon xli; Mansi, XXIII,
c. 702.

back to the ninth century, and was not abolished until the twelfth. In one case at least it is recorded that the Jew was killed on the spot by the blow[1].

VII. THE ECONOMIC POSITION OF THE JEWS

When we turn from these different Christian activities to examine the position of the Jews, it may at first appear astonishing that there was not a greater agitation of the clergy against them. For, whether we examine their position from the economic, social or religious standpoint, the prominence of what must have been extremely small and scattered Jewish communities in western Europe is remarkable.

It is absurd to talk, as do many authors, of any Jewish monopoly of all trade; but it was almost impossible for law-givers and writers of the ninth and tenth centuries to think of ' merchants ' without at the same time thinking of ' Jews '. The phrase ' Jews and other merchants ' is almost as common as the phrase ' merchants including Jews '[2]. On the other hand, commercial legislation which *exclusively* refers to Jews is non-existent, except in cases where the principle to be enforced was religious and not commercial.

In the second half of the period under review, the commercial cities of north-western Europe were already coming into existence, and merchants of northern Europe were beginning to acquire importance. In the first half, commerce was largely dealt with through the many ' markets ' established by princes and bishops. Here most of the local trade was carried on; and to these markets came merchants from many parts. Christian and Jewish traders from Byzantium, Venice, and the cities of southern France and southern

---

[1] Adhemar, *Hist.*, III, lii, s.a. 1020; MGH, SS, IV, p. 139. The story is also told at length and with many embroideries in the *Vita S. Theodardi, Aep. Narbon.* (Bouquet, IX, p. 115).

[2] Examples of Jews and Christians being mentioned together are: *Capit. Caroli Magni et Ludovici Pii*, I, cxvii, Mansi, XV, *app.* V, c. 490; *Capit. of Lothar I*, of 832, xix, MGH, LL, I, p. 363; *Capit. Regum Francorum*, of 864, XXXIV, xxiii; Mansi, XVII, *app.*, c. 125 f.; *Conventus Carisiac.* of 877, xxxi, MGH, LL, I, p. 540; *Leges Baiuwar.*, Add. X Leg. Port., c.a. 906, MGH, LL, II, 2, p. 481; *Bull of Investiture of Otho*, of 963, MGH, LL, II, 2, p. 168 (*n.*); *Council of Leon*, xxv, Mansi, XIX, c. 340.

Italy were to be found in these northern markets all through the period. The sea trade with the Orient was at this time largely in the hands of those who did not have to use the pirate-infested waters of the western Mediterranean. But there was also a land trade by caravans across southern Russia, as well as a land route to the Baltic countries, both used by merchants of the south-west. In the sea-borne trade Jews probably took a considerable share[1]; the caravan trade came as near to being a Jewish monopoly as existed at the time. Certainly the slave trade which formed an important element in this land trade fell increasingly into their hands, until its gradual disappearance from the eleventh century onwards.

The particular spheres of Jewish commercial activity were thus three: a share in all the normal trade of western Europe, a very important part in the land-borne trade with the East, and a predominant share of the trade in slaves.

Of these three it was the last which raised most problems, especially in the minds of the clergy. The legal position of Jewish slave dealers has been already discussed. But it may also be suggested that actual conditions were likely to be very different from what the strict interpreters of Roman and canon law desired. It would appear that Jews had little difficulty in obtaining slaves in the eastern provinces of the Empire and in Poland, in spite of the protection which the acceptance of Christianity in those regions should have given the inhabitants. References to this traffic in Christian slaves are not infrequent. The Emperor Henry II received continual complaints that the Margrave Guizelin of Meissen sold his Christian serfs to Jews, but he was unable to prevent it[2]. It is recorded of the mother of Boleslav III of Poland that she was of such piety that she left money to redeem all Christian captives who had fallen into the hands of Jewish slave-dealers[3]; and the Duke Wladislav of Bohemia also purchased all Christians whom he found in the possession of

---

[1] Ibn Khordadbeh, French translation in *Journal Asiatique*, VI, v. See B. Hahn, *Die Wirtschaftliche Tätigkeit der Juden im fränkischen und deutschen Reich*, pp. 35 ff., and Monachus Sangall., *Gesta Karoli*, II; MGH, SS, II, p. 757.

[2] Thietmar, *Chron.*, s.a. 1009; MGH, SS, III, p. 821.

[3] *Chron. Polon.*, II, i, s.a. 1085; MGH, SS, IX, p. 445.

Jews[1]. A century earlier his inability to find sufficient funds for the same work, owing to the large number of slaves involved, helped to break the heart of Saint Adalbert, Bishop of Prague[2]. It may be that the failure of Adalbert, and the success of Wladislav, indicated the gradual decline in the quantities of slaves involved. The evidence is thus enough to show that the Church possessed a genuine grievance against the section of the Jewish population involved in the slave trade. But the misdeeds of slave traders did not cease at the purchase of Christians in eastern Europe. Agobard quotes cases—and there is no reason to refuse his evidence— of the theft of children in France for sale to the Moors of Spain[3]; and a chronicler of the middle of the tenth century brings an even more unpleasant story of the castration of boys in eastern France for their sale as eunuchs to the Moorish harems, a trade which was, apparently, extremely profitable[4].

It must also be remembered that at this period the Church, herself becoming the largest landowner of western Europe, had set her face against the possession of slaves on her own estates. She owned immense numbers of serfs, but about the possession of slaves she was beginning to have scruples of conscience. At the time of the original legislation of Roman emperors and Church councils, all that had concerned her was the possession of Christians by Jews, but the noble defence of the liberty of the human soul in the letters of Agobard goes far beyond what the Roman authorities had had in mind.

On this question, Agobard was both morally and legally in the right in his conflict with Louis the Pious. Louis had, in defiance of Canon Law and Biblical precept, authorised Jewish slave owners to refuse permission for the baptism of those among their slaves who wished to become Christians. By some misunderstanding, or in simple ' bluff ', he quoted

---

[1] Cosmas, *Chron. Bohem.*, III, lvii, s.a. 1124; MGH, SS, IX, p. 129.

[2] *Vita S. Adalberti Pragensis*, iv; MGH, SS, IV, pp. 586 ff., and *De S. Adalb.*, iv; *ibid.*, XV, p. 1179.

[3] C. Postscriptum; c. 76.

[4] Liudprand, *Antapod.*, VI, vi; MGH, SS, III, p. 338.

' canon law ' as his authority for doing so[1]. Agobard went to see the emperor, but, overcome with confusion, he failed to make his case, and returned, deeply mortified, to Lyons. From his own city he wrote to the Court and explained his position. ' Every human being ', he wrote, ' is the child of God; and the Lord God, Who has created him in the womb, Who has brought him forth into the light of this life, Who preserves for him the life He gave him, and Who guards his health, has more rights in every man, even in the slave, than he who pays twenty or thirty shillings for him, and enjoys the work of his body. Nor can any man doubt that each single slave, owing his earthly lord the work done by his bodily limbs, owes His Creator alone the devotion of his soul '[2]. It was not that he demanded, as he might legally have done, that the slave who desired baptism should be surrendered by his Jewish master without compensation. He was prepared to pay for each slave whom he received into the Church. It was an extremely foolish action of the Jews of Lyons to have made use of their favour at Court to secure for themselves the privilege against which Agobard protested, for they could secure no advantage from so violent an insult to the Church. The question as to whether Christianity ought to be a missionary religion or not may be one for metaphysicians to argue. We cannot blame Agobard as a Prince of the Church for accepting the implications of its fundamental doctrines. The utmost liberality which a Churchman could have been expected to practise in the matter was shown by Rüdiger, Bishop of Speyer in 1084, when he permitted the Jews of Speyer to retain the services of servants who had been baptized, on condition that they allowed them to carry out their religious observances[3].

---

[1] Such an authorisation actually occurs in one of the surviving Diplomata, that granted to Rabbi Domatus (Bouquet, VI, p. 649). The only canon which the Emperor might have thought to be in favour of his view is Gangres, iii: ' si quis servum praetextu divini cultus doceat dominum contemnere proprium, ut discedat ab eius obsequio, nec ei cum benevolentia et omni honore deserviat, anathema sit.' But this really deals with a totally different aspect of the question, contempt for a pagan master on the part of a Christian slave.

[2] A, c. 103.

[3] Aronius, No. 168.

If the conduct of Jewish slave traders and owners was open to reprobation, there was little other complaint to make about Jewish commercial activities or their economic situation. For Agobard wins less of our sympathies when he finds an insult to the Christian Faith in the sale to Christians of meat condemned for Jewish use or the dregs of Jewish wine[1]. At worst, it was not the Jewish seller but the Christian buyer who merited censure.

The same is true of the accusation that Jews purchased Church plate. The disposal of Church property, whether to Jewish or to Christian merchants, had troubled the Christian conscience since the days of Charlemagne[2]. But it is probable that in most cases blame for such transactions was unmerited. Money was hard to get, currency short, and the merchant, whether Jew or Christian, who obliged with a loan in times of need, cannot be blamed either for lending, or charging interest for his loan—though it is interesting to note that there are no protests at this period as to the rate of interest. Nor can the borrower be blamed either, for he might well have needed the money for an important purpose. The crime was, in fact, formal and ecclésiastical, rather than moral or religious[3].

The main interest in the references to Church plate lies in the fact that they reveal the natural and gradual origins of money-lending. There has been no society which has not required facilities for borrowing money at one time or other. At the same time the paucity of references to borrowing from merchants confirms the fact that at this stage of European development the bulk of the lending was in the hands of the clergy themselves, especially the monastic clergy. For we may contrast the few scattered references to merchant lenders already quoted with the numerous denunciations of clerical usury in local councils[4].

---

[1] C, iii; c. 73.

[2] *Capit. Caroli Magni et Ludovici Pii*, I, cxvii; Mansi, XV, *app.*, c. 490.

[3] References to this subject are not infrequent; cf. *Cap. Caroli Magni et Ludovici Pii*, I, cxvii, Mansi, XV, *app.*, c. 490; Clothaire I, *Cap. of* 832, xxiii, MGH, LL, I, p. 364; Flodoard, *Hist. Remensis Eccl.*, III, xiii; MGH, SS, XIII, p. 493; *Chron. Mon. Casinensis*, s.a. 1022, *ibid.*, VII, p. 656.

[4] From the ninth century alone there still survive, e.g., Halitgar of Cambrai, V, ix and x (PL, CIV, c. 688); Rudolf of Bourges, xxxv (Mansi, XIV, c. 959).

From the south of France and Spain we get the beginnings of more formal transactions in the tenth century. About A.D. 900 Arsinde, Countess of Narbonne, borrowed 1,000 solidi from some Jews of that town[1]. From Catalonia a hundred years later we have two records of the same kind, but it is an interesting coincidence that in one Amatus and his wife borrow from the Jew Joseph, and in the other the Jew Bonisach and his wife borrow from the Christians Raymund William and Raymund Desplegad[2].

VIII. SOCIAL POSITION AND SOCIAL RELATIONSHIPS

Apart from their possession and treatment of Christian slaves, it was not the economic life of the Jews which created difficulties in the minds of churchmen like Agobard. It was Jewish social and religious conduct which appeared to them to endanger the faith of their Christian brethren. For the Jewish population was not easily distinguished from the rest. The serf and peasant at one end of the social scale, and the nobility at the other, would know the Jew as a passing merchant among other passing merchants. The townsman knew the Jewish resident as a fellow-townsman. It was these last who knew the Jews best, for the Jews were town-dwellers. This does not, of course, mean that they neither owned land nor cultivated it; it means only that they did not either possess villages and manors or own or work on great landed estates. But the towns were surrounded by fields, and many fields lay within the more spacious boundaries of the earlier Roman cities. These the Jews owned and worked in the same way as their Christian neighbours[3]. Neither does the

---

[1] J. Régné, *Etude sur la Condition des Juifs de Narbonne*; REJ, LVIII, p. 77.

[2] J. Miret y Sans and M. Schwab, *Documents sur les Juifs Catalans aux XIe, XIIe et XIIIe siècles*, Nos. i and x; REJ, LXVIII, pp. 54 and 70. The Charter of Leon of 1091 makes provision for lending in both directions; Baer, *Castile*, No. 14.

[3] References to Jews owning land are frequent. See, e.g., the Diploma of Louis the Pious for some Jews of Septimania (Bouquet, VI, p. 624), the privileges conferred by Henry IV on the Jews of Speyer (Aronius, No. 170) and Worms (*ibid.*, No. 171), and also the discussion on the payment of tithe by Jews, pp. 41 ff.

F.

lack of Jews among the great nobility of Church and State necessarily mean that they never occupied positions of the highest importance in the service of the sovereign. Charlemagne employed a Jew as ambassador[1], and the habit of using great Jewish merchants as ambassadors lasted all through the Middle Ages, especially when embassies to non-Christian countries were required. And, in various countries, but especially in Aragon and Castile, Jews held high financial office under Christian sovereigns. Such Jews would have met clergy and nobility on an equal footing, even though they lacked their high-sounding titles.

But it was among the townsmen of all classes that the ordinary Jew was most at home. He was to be found numbered among the artisans, the shopkeepers, the clerks, the lawyers, and the doctors. Naturally, we rarely hear of these ordinary folk. There was nothing in their lives to distinguish them. We do hear of two doctors, but only because their patients died! If a king had a Jewish physician, and did not actually perish on the battlefield, cloven in two by the battle-axe of the enemy, there is nothing surprising in his unfortunate doctor being accused of poisoning him. This happened to the doctors of Carloman[2] and Hugh Capet[3], though in the former case the historian who recorded the event is honest enough to add *as it is said* to his account.

Together with the towns, it is in a certain number of princely courts that the closest fellowship between Jews and Christians existed. Agobard knew that the power and influence of the Jews in Lyons was bound up with the favour they received at the court of Louis and Judith. A century later another bishop, Rathere of Verona, who had a curious and varied career in many different centres, repeats many of the remarks of Agobard. His words suggest that in the cities of northern Italy the same friendship existed as in France[4].

---

[1] Einhard, *Annals*, s.a. 801; MGH, SS, I, p. 190.

[2] Regino, *Chronicon*, s.a. 877; MGH, SS, I, p. 589.

[3] Richer, *Hist.*, III add., s.a. 996; MGH, SS, III, p. 657.

[4] *Qualitatis Conjectura;* PL, CXXXVI, c. 535 ff. His remarks follow so closely the lines of those of Agobard, that it would be arguable that he was copying them rather than basing his views on his own experience. But there is no reason for believing that the situation in Verona in the beginning of the tenth century was substantially different from that of Lyons in the ninth.

Of the princely courts there are three in which the amity which reigned between Jews and Christians shocked the orthodox. Rainard II of Sens, who lived at the beginning of the eleventh century, was said to be so fond of them that he was called ' the king of the Jews '[1]. William Rufus was equally amiable towards them[2], though this may well have been more out of dislike for the clergy than for any positive reason. But the most famous of these courts, and the one of which we have the fullest information, was that of Louis the Pious.

It was particularly during the period in which the emperor was under the influence of his second wife, Judith, that the Jews obtained a remarkable ascendancy. Our chief information on the subject comes from the letter of Agobard *on the Insolence of the Jews*, to which reference has already been made. The description is, therefore, written from a definite ecclesiastical point of view, and is full of horror at conditions which raise in us no moral indignation, as well as of righteous wrath at actual assaults upon Christian theory and practice. When Agobard protests that the Jews are allowed to build new synagogues, that courtiers buy wine from Jewish merchants, that women at the court receive presents of oriental robes from Jews, it is difficult to share his indignation. When he denounces the blasphemy of Christians who had been heard telling the Jews that they wished that Christianity possessed a law-giver like Moses, that they preferred Jewish scholars to Christian preachers, our sympathies may even be on the side of the Jews. Such facts are but evidence of the strange light of humanity which spread over the Carolingian age, a light of which Agobard himself, in his struggle against superstition and legal barbarity, was no mean reflection. It is, on the other hand, possible to realise that such things did seem terrible to one brought up in the traditions of canon law and patristic literature, for there is no tolerance of Judaism in either of these. Nor was Agobard in error in believing that such fellowship would not stop at artificial limits; but that if Christians said that there were things in Judaism which seemed preferable to their own

[1] D'Arbois de Jubainville, *Hist. des comtes de Champagne*, I, p. 229.

[2] William of Malmesbury, *Gesta Regum*, IV, cccxvii, ed. Stubbs (Rolls Series), II, p. 371.

practices, so Jews would proceed to pungent criticism of the weaknesses of ninth-century Christianity. He was right also in believing that the ease with which formal prohibitions as to the sale of wine and meat were set aside, would but embolden the Jews to ignore more important precepts of the Church. For this had happened in the matter of slaves; and, flushed with this victory, the Jews of Lyons had proceeded to indulge in malicious revenge upon the Church's disapproval and oppression, by securing the removal of the market from the Sabbath to Sunday[1], whereby their observances were secured, but the repose of the Christian Sunday destroyed.

Though to Agobard these latter consequences were convincing evidence that the whole fellowship with Jews which existed in the court and elsewhere was a sign of degeneracy, and even of the near approach of Antichrist, it is difficult for the modern mind to accord him that sympathy which is certainly his due. The Carolingian age was a birth premature by nearly half a millennium. Men were not ready for the freedom of thought which for a brief epoch had dawned among them. The long and more formal discipline of the medieval Church still had its work to do in shaping European life. The Carolingian renaissance was followed by a dreadful epoch of chaos. The friendship which had reigned between Jews and Christians had nothing to do with the creation of that chaos. But the chaos was a proof that the times were not yet ripe for the liberty of which that friendship was a symbol. In the actual and tragic course of history it was not because some Jews and some Christians abused their liberty that the friendship was to be drowned in blood, but because for good or ill it was the Church alone which possessed the power and the steadfastness to create a new spirit out of the chaos. And by the principles of the Church that friendship was a forbidden thing. It was the

---

[1] It has usually been taken by scholars that the change is to Sunday, for, though Agobard does not expressly say so, this appears a legitimate deduction from his words. But I make the statement with a certain reserve. Agobard's argument is that the Saturday market brought the country folk to the city, so that they stayed over for the Sunday Mass. But if the market were moved to a day in the middle of the week, the result would be the same; for the countryman would not make two journeys to the city.

Church's stern attitude of a meagre justice untempered by mercy which was destined to reign; not the gentle words of Louis the Pious in setting right an injustice done to three Jews in a French village, when he wrote that ' although apostolic teaching ordains that we should do good to our brethren in the faith, it does not forbid us to benefit the unfaithful with our kindly service. It exhorts us rather to seek humbly our inspiration in the Divine mercy, and to make no distinction between the faithful and the unfaithful '[1].

IX. THE RELIGIOUS INFLUENCE OF THE JEWS

That Agobard was right in believing that close social friendship between Jews and Christians, in the particular circumstances with which he was concerned, led to abuses, we have already seen: that they involved also a religious danger, we have ample evidence to show. There has hardly been a period in the history of Jewish-Christian relationships from the time of the separation up to the nineteenth century when there was such free exchange of ideas between Jews and Christians.

The extreme freedom with which Jews spoke about the Christian Faith, and the Person of its Founder, is revealed by the extensive knowledge which Agobard and Amulo possessed of the contents of the *Sepher Toldoth Jeshu*, the Jewish life of Jesus[2]. This was a work which originated in the centuries following the separation of the Church from the Synagogue, as an alternative explanation of the life of Christ to that presented in the Gospel narratives. But the bitterness produced by the legislation of the Church of the Roman Empire had broadened the caricature and embittered the satire of its contents[3]. Naturally, the centre of the work was a justification of the condemnation of Christ and alternative explanations of the miracles and the Resurrection. While the theologians of the Middle Ages were well aware of the

---

[1] Bouquet, VI, p. 624.

[2] For the earlier versions see *The Conflict*, pp. 109 and 114.

[3] Agobard, D, c. 87 f.; Amulo, *Contra Judaeos*, xxv, xxxix and xl, PL, CXVI, adds further information. Both will be found discussed in Lukyn Williams, *Adversus Judaeos*, pp. 352 and 362.

existence of this book, it was kept carefully concealed by the Jews, and only discovered on rare occasions by searches carried out under the Inquisition, for its discovery meant death to its possessor. The Carolingian Jew seems to have spoken of it openly[1]. In addition to caricaturing the life of Christ, the Jews treated with contempt the stories of the founding of the Church and the miraculous delivery of Peter from prison[2]. The apostles they called ' apostates ', and the Gospels ' a revelation of iniquity '[3]; the Sacraments they dismissed as idolatry[4].

It has already been said that they were not less frank in criticising their Christian contemporaries; as, for example, when they replied to the claim of the Church to possess miraculous powers by the simple statement that God was everywhere, and could work miracles where He would[5]. Such frankness, coupled with their vaunting of their own religion and themselves as descendants of the Patriarchs and Prophets[6], render it not surprising that Agobard and his followers used an equal freedom in describing Judaism and Jewish practices. What is more curious is to find Jews telling converts that there is no harm in their believing in Jesus, provided that they do not believe in him as God[7]. A situation where such a subtle point of view was possible reveals an extraordinary interpenetration between Jews and Christians.

Christians in the service of Jews, whether free or slave, were particularly susceptible to their influence, and unlikely to be sufficiently well educated to reply to their arguments. The result was that they feasted in Lent, worked on Sunday, and rested on the Sabbath[8]. Country priests bought from the Jews wine for the Eucharist which Agobard believed to

---

[1] Rabanus Maurus, *Expositio in Leviticum*, VII, xiii; PL, CVIII, c. 563.
[2] Acts xii, 3 ff.
[3] A Hebrew pun on the word Evangelion.
[4] Gezo of Tortona, *De Corpore et Sanguine Christi*, xxxix; PL, CXXXVII, c. 390.
[5] Arnold of S. Emmeranus, *De Miraculis S. Emmerani*, I, xv; PL, CXLI, c. 1014.
[6] Agobard, E; c. 111.
[7] Amulo, *Contra Judaeos*, xlii; PL, CXVI, c. 171.
[8] Agobard, E ; c. 111.

be filthily polluted by them[1]; and country people lent a willing ear to Jewish tax collectors who bribed them by the promise of reduced taxes if they would accept conversion to Judaism[2]. It was largely for warning his flock against the insidious results of contacts with Jews, as revealed in these practices[3], that Agobard incurred their bitter enmity in Lyons, an enmity which their friendship with the court enabled them to make effective in a real persecution of the archbishop[4].

But it was not only simple people or worldly courtiers who were impressed by Jewish practices; nor is it merely a tribute to wealth or secular power which caused the Carolingian artists to represent the Synagogue as a figure of equal dignity with the Church[5]. Church councils themselves at times bore witness to Jewish merits. The Council of Paris of 829 refers with wonder to the faithful observance of the Sabbath by the Jews, ' in spite of the absence of any earthly power to compel them '[6]; and a council at Dortmund in 1005, though reflecting the usual Christian disapproval of the licence which Jews possessed to marry within the degrees forbidden to Christians, admitted that actual practice among Christians had sanctioned marriages of which even the Jews would have disapproved[7].

While all this is evidence of considerable mutual knowledge, there is little evidence of contact between scholars. Mentions of ' disputations ' are rare, and of Christian scholars who knew Hebrew, rarer. Rabanus Maurus speaks of a Hebrew teacher who had explained to him the Hebrew interpretation of the Scriptures—which he is careful to add that he did not accept[8]. But the clergy with whom the Jews came into contact were the secular clergy, and learning, such as it was, was mostly confined to monasteries situated in

---

[1] Agobard, C, iv; c. 73; Amulo, *Contra Judaeos*, xli; PL, CXVI, c. 170.

[2] Amulo, *ibid.*, xlii; c. 170.

[3] Agobard, C, i and ii; c. 69 f.

[4] *Ibid.*, ii; c. 70.

[5] P. Hildenfinger, REJ, XLVII, p. 187.

[6] Cap. i, 50; MGH, Conc., II, p. 643.

[7] Conc. Tremon., *Adnotatio P. Pagi*; Mansi, XIX, c. 281.

[8] *Praef. in Comm. Lib. IV. Regum*, PL, CIX, c. 10. The contact may not have been personal; cf. Rieger in MGWJ, LXVIII, pp. 66 ff.

remote places. It was only in a few centres, such as Rome, that Christian and Jewish scholars were likely to meet, and, in fact, Alcuin does tell us of a disputation which he attended during the period of his Roman studies[1].

That there were few disputations is, perhaps, not unnatural, but it is surprising to find how few conversions to Judaism seem actually to have taken place, in view of the continual alarm of the Church at the influence of the Jews. It is probable that a number of obscure people in the service of the Jews were accepted into the Synagogue, but only two converts of note are known to us, Bodo, the Chaplain of Louis the Pious[2] in the ninth century, and Wecelin a couple of centuries later[3]. During the first Crusade, however, there is mention of proselytes among the victims of the massacres in the Rhineland[4], so that it would appear that there were more conversions than are actually recorded.

In the opposite direction there were certainly a considerable number. The converts of Lyons in the days of Remigius have already been mentioned. While this is the only known mass conversion, a number of distinguished individuals in each of the centuries under consideration are said to have been of Jewish origin[5]. From the type of men concerned, it would seem that the conversions had been sincere. There is only one doubtful reference to that hateful type of convert, common in the later Middle Ages, who proved his sincerity to his new faith by continuous denunciations of the faith which he had quitted[6]; and there is also but a single reference to the converted charlatan, who planned to make a good thing out of his conversion. This amiable adventurer went beyond the conventional humbug who promised to make

---

[1] *Ep.*, ci; PL, C, c. 314.

[2] Prudentius Trec., *Ann.*, s.a. 839; MGH, SS, I, p. 433.

[3] See above, pp. 35 and 39.

[4] E.g., *Chronicle of Salomo b. Simeon*, Neubauer and Stern, p. 126.

[5] Cf. Adhemar, *Hist.*, III, s.a. 1003, MGH, SS, IV, p. 135; Cosmas, *Chron. Boëm.*, s.a. 1067, MGH, SS, IX, p. 80; Benzo, *Ad Henr. IV Imp. Libri*, s.a. 1062, MGH, XI, p. 616; Ad. Neubauer and E. A. Renan, *Histoire Littéraire de la France*, VII, p. 262; and H. Vogelstein and P. Rieger, *Geschichte der Juden in Rom*, I, p. 214.

[6] A persecution at Limoges in 994 is said to have been due to the accusations of a converted Jew (*Gallia Judaica*, p. 308).

gold out of copper; for he also undertook to make philosophers out of fools[1].

Of more interest are a number of extremely emotional cases which rationalists might dismiss as the typical miracles of fable, but which accord well enough with the experience of emotional revivals in modern times. They are connected with experiences of the Eucharist. In one case a Jew saw a lamb in the hands of the priest[2]; in another he saw an actual body broken by him, and blood sprinkled over all the worshippers[3]. While it would be rash to deny that these cases might have been invented, they are not in themselves impossible.

X. COMING STORMS

The period which has been thus briefly passed under review is one of curious fascination, and of a mystery made more obscure by the paucity of documents. The whole Carolingian interlude and its survivals stand as an unexpected interruption of what is otherwise a logical sequence from Theodosius II, to the establishment of the badge and the ghetto, to the accusations of ritual murder, the poisoning of wells, and the profanation of the Host. The sequence is, in fact, unbroken, for Agobard, Amulo and Rathere bridge the gulf as the inheritors of the Roman tradition and the precursors of the medieval Jew-baiters. But for a brief moment the Church was not the Government, but the Opposition, and to crown the whole, the emperor under whom much of the interlude took place was called ' the Pious '[4]. For a few years Judaism and Christianity stood together as standards of life in a world of barbarism, and men saw the attractiveness of each. But tradition was too strong, and the conflict between them could only be really healed by means not available to that age—an objective re-examination of its basis, and an independence of judgment towards patristic values which it is idle to demand of the actors of the time.

---

[1] Adam., *Hammaburg. Eccl. Pontif. Gesta*, III, xxxvii, Scholia lxxviii; MGH, SS, VII, p. 349.

[2] Agnellus Abbas, *Liber Pontificalis, Vita Damiani*, v; PL, CVI, c. 697.

[3] Gezo of Tortona, *De Corpore et Sanguine*, xlii; PL, CXXXVII, p. 393.

[4] Latin *Ludovicus Pius*; the French, more logically, call him *Louis le Debonnaire*.

From the standpoint of historical continuity, it is the steady effort to reintroduce the laws and canons of Rome, the introduction of new regulations against the Jews, the stoning of Chalons and Béziers, the buffeting of Toulouse, and not the friendship and free criticism of the Court of Louis which are the significant episodes of the period. By the beginning of the eleventh century the last flicker of the Carolingian freedom expired; and before the middle a new series of outrages heralded the massacres of the first Crusade.

In 1063 a Crusade was launched against the Saracens of Spain. Knights assembled for it throughout the south of France, a district in which there were many and rich Jewish communities. Thence they passed into the Spanish Marches, where also the Jews were numerous. In both these districts there were outbreaks against the Jewish population, and the Jews were massacred in the name of the Crusade, and with the approval, tacit or open, of the Archbishop of Narbonne. But he stood alone in his approval. The Viscount of Narbonne did all that he could to protect the Jews, and, to their honour, the Spanish clergy did the same. The incident is known to us from the letters which the Pope, Alexander II, addressed to the various actors. To the Archbishop he wrote expressing his strong condemnation[1]; to the Viscount and the Spanish clergy his warm approval[2]. The Crusaders themselves he rebuked for their stupidity, in that ' they foolishly wished to kill those whom the Divine Mercy had predestined to Salvation '. This episode is indeed a curtain-raiser for the main act of 1096. All the actors are there; the fanaticism, half-religious, half-greedy, of the soldier, the divided Church, the prince anxious to protect valuable subjects, and the Pope aloof and dignified, the repository of the Catholic tradition—for had not Paul said that at the last all Israel should be gathered in?

[1] Mansi, XIX, 980.
[2] *Ibid.*

CHAPTER THREE

THE FIRST CRUSADE

BIBLIOGRAPHICAL INTRODUCTION

For our purpose, the First Crusade is far more important than its successors. Though the Crusades were always nervous periods for the Jewish population, it is only in 1096 that the popular effervescence vitally affected their whole future development in western Europe. The most important sources for the events of this year are three Hebrew reports of the persecutions in the Rhineland, edited by Neubauer and Stern. The relation of these reports to each other does not directly concern us, though it is a matter of considerable controversy. For our purpose it is sufficient that they all contain contemporary materials and that, by good fortune, each of them gives in full detail happenings related only summarily by the others. In this way we have excellent information about the events in Speyer, Worms, Mainz and Cologne. For the events in Trier we have fuller information in a Christian chronicle, the *Gesta* of the Archbishops of Trier, of which the part interesting us was written in the first half of the twelfth century.

From various other Christian chroniclers we can obtain a number of general references to the Jews, those of Ekkehard being the most interesting. They are referred to in the appropriate places.

Of modern works, the most important are the Introduction to the texts in Neubauer and Stern and the articles discussing this introduction by Porgès and Sonne in the *Revue des Etudes Juives*, and by Elbogen in the *Philippson Festschrift*. A useful summary of the different points of view is to be found in the book of Schiffmann. This will also be found useful for ordering and relating the sometimes confused and unchronologically arranged information of the Hebrew Chronicles.

LIST OF BOOKS

NEUBAUER, A., AND STERN, M.
Hebräische Berichte über die Juden-verfolgungen während der Kreuzzüge. Herausgegeben von A. Neubauer und M. Stern. Ins Deutsche übersetzt von S. Baer. (*Quellen zur Geschichte der Juden in Deutschland,* II). Berlin, 1892.
Contains, in Hebrew and German texts, reports of the following chroniclers on the First Crusade:
(1) Salomo bar Simeon.
(2) Elieser bar Nathan.
(3) An anonymous chronicler from Mainz.
In the text referred to as NS, A; NS, B; NS, C.

GESTA TREVERORUM
Ed. G. Waitz. MGH, SS, VIII, pp. 111-200.

ELBOGEN, I.
Zu den hebräischen Berichten über die Judenverfolgungen im Jahre 1096. Festschrift zum 70. Geburtstage Martin Philippsons, Leipzig, 1916, p. 6.

PORGÈS, N.
Les Relations hébraïques des persécutions des Juifs pendant la première croisade. REJ, XXV, p. 181; XXVI, p. 183; XXVII, p. 317.

SCHIFFMANN, SARAH
Heinrich IV und die Bischöfe in ihrem Verhalten zu den deutschen Juden zur Zeit des ersten Kreuzzuges. Diss. Berlin, 1931.

SONNE, I.
Nouvel examen des trois relations hébraïques sur les persécutions de 1096. REJ, LXXXV, p. 113.

STEINHERZ, S.
Kreuzfahrer und Juden in Prag (1096). Jahrbuch der Gesellschaft für Geschichte der Juden in der čecho-slovakischen Republik, I, p. 1.

I. THE CRUSADING MOVEMENT

The Crusades must be considered as part of the interminable
conflict between Christendom and Islam. As such, they were
both religious and political in their nature. For the conflict
with Islam was not merely a competition for the religious
domination of various peoples, but, even more, a struggle
for the political domination of the countries around the
Mediterranean.

From the appearance of Mahomet in the seventh century,
up to the tenth, the fortunes of war had gone with the
Islamic invaders of what had once been Christendom. The
Byzantine Empire, which stood in the forefront of the attack,
lost control of the greater part of its Asiatic possessions, and
had, at times, to fear even for the security of Constantinople.
The Visigothic Kingdom of Spain disappeared almost
entirely in the beginning of the eighth century, and the
Arabs crossed the Pyrenees, and even menaced western
Christendom as far north as the Loire until their total defeat
at Tours in 732. They gained Sicily in the ninth century and
held it until the Norman conquest in the middle of the
eleventh. Their ships threatened all the ports of the Mediterranean, and they penetrated so far up the river valleys that
Saracen invaders appeared on the shores of the lake of
Geneva. Naturally, this triumphant movement roused the
continual opposition of Christian powers; and the Papacy, as
representative of the rival religion, was ever interested in
military attempts to repel the invader who was also an
infidel.

Another potent cause for the First Crusade was the
indignation of the Christians over the treatment of pilgrims.
The visit to the Holy Places had been the supreme attraction
among all pilgrimages since the early days of the Church.
From the time of Charlemagne up to the end of the tenth
century the pilgrims had been treated with favour, for the
Caliphs recognised that their country benefited economically
from such visits. But the third of the Fatimite Caliphs,
Hakim, was a man of cruel and fanatical temperament, and
under his rule at the end of the tenth century the pilgrims
began to suffer a violent persecution. Nevertheless they

continued to come, but now they came armed. Hakim retorted in 1008 by destroying the Church of the Holy Sepulchre, the holiest of all the Christian sites in Palestine. This aroused tremendous indignation in Europe. In 1071 yet another change for the worse took place. The Seljuks conquered Jerusalem, and treated pilgrims even worse than Hakim. Moreover, they pressed their conquests almost as far as the Sea of Marmora, and menaced Constantinople itself. Thus the religious and political motives coalesced towards the end of the eleventh century; for Constantinople was the essential bulwark of Christendom against heathendom and Islam.

The wars between Christendom and Islam did not, however, all partake of the nature of Crusades; and not all Crusades are of interest for a study of Jewish-Christian relationships. But in such a conflict the stimulation of religious fanaticism was a useful aid to recruitment, and religious fanaticism and excesses against Jews usually went side by side. Certainly this was the case in the earliest of these movements, the call to the deliverance of the Christians in Spain, which resulted in the Jewish massacres of 1063.

II. THE FIRST CRUSADE IN 1096

While previous Popes had attempted unsuccessfully to rally all Christendom in a concerted effort to assist the Byzantine emperor, and to reconquer the Holy Land, it was not until 1095 that the project became capable of realisation. In November of that year Urban II, at a general council at Clermont, gave a moving picture of the dangerous situation of the Christian power in the east, the sufferings of pilgrims to the Holy places, and the general menace of Islam. He called on all the princes of Christendom to forsake their mutual quarrels and wars, and to unite in a march through Constantinople to Jerusalem. The appeal, made with great eloquence, met with amazing success. As a sign of his concern for the victory of the armies, the Pope appointed Adhemar, Bishop of Puy, as his personal representative and leader of the movement. He himself travelled extensively in France preaching the Crusade; and in his wake followed an immense horde of popular preachers, who stirred up the enthusiasm of the populace. Among them Peter of Achery in the diocese of Amiens, called ' Peter the Hermit ', gained a rather dubious notoriety.

Adhemar of Puy proclaimed August 1096 as the date of assembly of the Crusading force, and the great barons and princes who took part began to move at about this time. But before the leaders were ready, popular assemblages took place. In northern France, in Lorraine and in Flanders, where the preaching of Peter and his fellow-enthusiasts had been exceedingly effective, groups of ' pauperes '—poor men—began to assemble in the early spring of 1096. Equipped neither with military training, nor with adequate financial or other resources, they set out to cross Europe towards Constantinople. While some of the nobles who took part in the movement certainly hoped to carve out for themselves kingdoms in the territories which the Crusaders expected to win from the Saracens, these ill-trained bands, though doubtless they had nothing economically to lose, were moved by pure religious fanaticism—and that of a most unbridled kind. For it was these bands who were responsible for all the massacres of the Jews; and in many places they treated the local Christian populations along the line of their march little better. Many of them perished at the hands of the Hungarians and Bulgarians whose territories they ravaged; and those who ultimately reached Constantinople did so only to fall before the trained soldiers of Islam, in a futile attack on a Saracen fortress near Nicea in Asia Minor.

It is possible, even probable, that many of their misdeeds were due to lack of provision for the route, and to an exalted, and in the event incorrect, expectation that God would provide for His soldiers. But even before their departure, and before the fatigues and dangers of the long march had had time to embitter them, they proclaimed their hostility to the Jews.

We do not know whether the preaching of Peter himself was directly responsible for raising the Jewish issue. Events in Spain had proved how naturally the thought of massacring the Jews came to a Crusading army; and Peter was not himself present at any of the terrible massacres in the Rhineland[1]. But the first group which attacked the Jews was one which assembled in Normandy, and fell upon the Jews of Rouen[2]; and this was either the group of Peter, or the followers of a French knight of Poissy, Walter Sansavoir, who remained in contact with him as far as Cologne. Peter himself arrived at Trier in the beginning of April, preached for a week in Cologne and its neighbourhood (April 12-19), and then turned south-east towards the Danube. On his way he was joined by a German band, and continued his route eastwards. Meanwhile, a number of other bands had collected in Germany. A priest, Volkmar, collected an army in Saxony, and marched through Bohemia, massacring the Jews of Prague[3]. Another priest, Gottschalk, descended from the Rhineland to the Danube and massacred the communities of Ratisbon, and possibly other Danubian cities[4]. Yet another band was led by a Rhineland count, Emicho or Emmerich, and was responsible for the worst of the massacres in the Rhineland itself[5]. His forces attacked the Jews of Speyer, Worms and Mainz. A band from Flanders, coming up the Rhine to join him, attacked those of Cologne. A final band, associated improbably by the Hebrew chroniclers with Godfrey of Bouillon himself, came from Lorraine, and plundered the communities of Lorraine and especially Metz[6].

How many thousand Jews perished in these slaughters we have no means of estimating, but it is important to recognise that such bloodshed formed no part of the original plan of the Crusade, and that we have no record of ill-treatment of the Jews anywhere in Europe by the great nobles of the official armies of Adhemar of Puy. All the accounts deal with armies of ' pauperes ', who assembled and set out

[1] See H. Hagenmayer, *Peter der Eremite*, pp. 139 and 374.

[2] Guiberti, *De Vita sua*, II, v; Bouquet, XII, p. 240.

[3] Ekkehard, *Chron. Univ. Sax.*, s.a. 1096; MGH, SS, VI, p. 208.

[4] *Ibid.*

[5] *Ibid.*; MGH, SS, VI, p. 215.

[6] NS, A, reports the hostility of Godfrey, but Godfrey did not start until August, and these massacres took place earlier. Cf. NS, p. 87.

independently, but under the predominating influence of the preaching of Peter the Hermit. Since his was the influence which inspired the bands, and since there is no record of a single word from him condemning the massacres, he certainly cannot be acquitted of some responsibility for the events which followed his appeals.

III. THE CALL TO MASSACRE

Frutolf, Prior of Michelsberg, near Bamberg[1], in relating the movements of all the three priests concerned, Peter, Volkmar and Gottschalk, expresses his dislike of them. Of Peter himself he says that ' many afterwards came to consider him a hypocrite '; and he calls Gottschalk ' no true servant of God, but a traitor '[2]. He ascribes anti-Jewish excesses directly to both of them: ' in the cities through which they passed, they either massacred, or forced to accept baptism, the beastly remnants of Jewry whom they found, considering them to be the enemies of the Church in her midst '. And he adds that ' most of them after their baptism returned like dogs to their vomit '[3]. His hostile and contemptuous references to Jews indicate that his disapproval of these priests was in no way connected with their anti-Jewish behaviour, and it is significant of the general feeling that no Christian chronicler views the situation otherwise.

It is in Rouen, which lay within the district roused by Peter and possibly also by Gottschalk, that the words, soon to become familiar throughout Germany, were first heard: ' We have set out to march on a long road against the enemies of God in the east, and behold, before our eyes are the Jews, His worst foes. To ignore them is preposterous '[4]. The Hebrew reports of the events in the Rhineland relate the same story[5], and add that the Crusaders said ' Jesus

[1] Frutolf was the author of the first half of the *Universal Chronicle* which bears the name of Ekkehard of Aura, author of the second part. Frutolf was a supporter of Henry IV and an opponent of the Pope. This may colour his condemnation of the priests who led the crusading bands.

[2] *Op. cit.*, s.a. 1096.

[3] *Ibid.*

[4] Guiberti, *De Vita sua*, II, v; Bouquet, XII, p. 240. ' Preposterous ' in the literal sense of putting the cart before the horse.

[5] NS, A, pp. 80, 82 and 89.

F

Himself said: " the day will come when my disciples will avenge my blood." We are those disciples and will fulfil the duty. For God hates the Jews for their evil doing, and has made the Christians His portion.' Another form is given by another chronicler who relates the advent of the first German bands to the Crusade. They are said to have issued a declaration that ' whoever killed a Jew had all his sins forgiven him '; and one of them, a certain Count Dithmar, announced that he would not start until he had murdered at least one Jew[1]. Even Godfrey of Bouillon is credited with the same sentiments, and is related to have sworn that he would not leave a single Jew alive in his path, until, cautioned by the Emperor, and assisted perhaps by a large bribe from the Jews of Cologne, he changed his mind and promised them his protection[2]. And, in fact, we hear of no ill-treatment of Jews on his march along the Rhine and Danube.

All these accounts suggest that the massacres owed their origin entirely to religious fanaticism, and this is supported by the fact that in no case was a Jew who accepted baptism injured. But we shall probably not be wrong if we see in this bloodshed one of the expressions of medieval piety which looked for an earthly as well as a heavenly reward. For the Lord, who clearly desired the extermination of the Jews, had also allowed them to become very wealthy—and these were bands of poor men. It is not illegitimate to assume that this happy combination of circumstances might well appear to them the Divine method by which the needs of their journey might be met. For it is not without interest that Peter himself carried with him into the Rhineland a letter, which by some means he had obtained from the communities of northern France, in which it was suggested that the Jewish communities of the towns through which he passed should provide his followers with the necessities of their journey[3]. In return for this, they assured their brethren that Peter would give them his protection. In the event we hear no single word of his attempting to do so. This suggests that the letter was obtained by threats, and that the protection was never intended to be given.

[1] NS, C, p. 170.
[2] NS, A, pp. 87 ff.
[3] NS, A, p. 131.

The only evidence which might invalidate the idea that plunder as well as piety moved ' the poor men ' would be that serious attempts at conversion preceded the menace of the sword. It is true that in certain accounts of the declaration it is put in the form ' either the Jew shall accept Christianity, or he will be killed '[1], but there is no sign of serious attempts at preaching to the Jews on the part of the priests who led these Crusaders. The Archbishop of Trier suggested —successfully—to the Jewish community of that town that they should be baptized and so save themselves, but this was because the Crusaders already menaced them with death[2]. While the Crusaders in many cases forcibly baptized large numbers of Jews, these baptisms either followed the sack of the Jewish quarter, or the acceptance of large Jewish bribes. In such circumstances it must be assumed that the desire for plunder and a religious blood-lust were the real sources of their actions, not a sincere desire for the conversion of the Jews.

IV. THE MASSACRES

It was in the Duchy of Normandy that the Crusaders first put their declaration into practice. In Rouen they collected the Jews into a church, either by force or by a trick, and there menaced them with either death or baptism. Those who did not accept the latter were immediately killed[3]. From Rouen the trouble spread to other towns of northern France, and possibly to other parts of the country as well[4].

Of the early history of the band which collected in Flanders we know nothing, and we hear of no Jewish massacres there. But those who started from Lorraine ravaged the Jewries of that region, though we know no details except of their activities in Metz, where twenty-two Jews are reported to have been killed, and the rest of the community forcibly baptized[5].

---

[1] E.g., NS, C, p. 169.

[2] *Gesta Ep. Trev.*, Cont. Prima, xvii; MGH, SS, VIII, p. 190.

[3] Guiberti, *De Vita sua*, II, v; Bouquet, XII, p. 240.

[4] Richard of Poitiers, *Chron.*, s.a. 1096; Bouquet, XII, p. 411. Gaufredus Voss., *Chron.*, s.a. 1096; *ibid.*, p. 428.

[5] NS, A, pp. 132 and 137.

On April 10 Peter the Hermit arrived in Trier with his letter from the French Jewish communities. For some weeks he was occupied with preaching in the Rhineland, collecting, perhaps, those German contingents which appeared in the month of May. During this period nothing is heard of the Jews, but in the beginning of May the first act of the Rhineland drama took place at Speyer. The events are related in full detail, based on the account of an eye-witness, in the ' Darmstadt Chronicle '[1]. The diocese at this time was administered by John I, successor of Rüdiger the giver of the Charter to the Jewish community in 1084. The secular authority over the city was wholly in his hands, and the Jews were his property. Both he and his predecessor were anxious to strengthen and increase the city, and both were men of powerful personality, capable of exercising their authority. John is also said by the ' Darmstadt Chronicle ' to have been a man of outstanding piety. The Jews, therefore, were in good hands, and could reckon that all that was humanly possible would be done to protect them. On a Sabbath evening in the beginning of May the Crusaders, who may have been camping near the city for some days already, plotted with some of the citizens to fall upon the Jews during the synagogue service. The plan came to the ears of the latter, and they advanced the hour of service sufficiently for the building to be empty when the Crusaders and citizens arrived. Enraged by this trick, they fell upon those whom they met in the street, and killed eleven of them. News of this quickly came to the ears of the Bishop, who assembled his troops, descended on the rioters, seized certain culprits, and, carrying off the Jews, lodged them in his castle[2]. The guilty citizens were punished by having their hands cut off—which is ascribed by a Christian chronicler quite unnecessarily to Jewish bribery—and the Jews remained safely in the castle until the immediate danger was over. They were then lodged in a fortified place outside the town, where they were safe even from Emicho, the butcher of the Jewry of Mainz.

---

[1] NS, C, pp. 171 ff. The anonymous Chronicle of Mainz is known as the ' Darmstadt Chronicle ' as it exists in a unique MS. in the library of that town.

[2] Bernold, *Chron.*, MGH, SS, V, p. 465.

The next community to be attacked was that of Worms. This also is most fully related by the ' Darmstadt Chronicle '[1]. On May 5 someone, either Crusader or citizen, dug up a corpse which had been buried for a month, and paraded it through the town, crying out that the Jews had killed a Christian, boiled him, and thrown the resulting concoction into various wells in order to poison the water supply. This naturally enraged the mob, who prepared to fall on the Jews.

The situation in Worms was very different from that in Speyer. The authority of the Bishop was by no means universally recognised in the town, and the main power was in the hands of the burghers. This explains the behaviour of the Jews. Some preferred to trust the one authority, some the other. As it happened, in neither case did it save them, though we have no real evidence that the Christians concerned lacked the will as well as the power to do so. Since the discovery of the corpse is said to have taken place on May 5[2], and the first massacre was not until May 18[3], it may be suggested that the interval was taken up with municipal and episcopal efforts to protect the Jews. The result in any case was that some of the Jews took refuge in different houses, their own or those of citizens who promised them protection, and others took refuge in the castle of the Bishop. Their treasures were similarly divided between individual houses and the castle. On the 18th a mob of Crusaders and townsfolk fell upon the Jewish quarter. The synagogue was sacked, and the Scrolls of the Law were desecrated and destroyed. The Jews whom they discovered hiding in their houses were killed, and their houses plundered. Children were either killed or taken away to be brought up as Christians. The survivors thereupon decided to accept the formality of baptism in order both to bury their dead and to rescue their children.

The attack upon the Jews in the castle, whom the Bishop was as powerless to protect as had been the citizens, came next. They had been witnesses of the sack of the Jewish quarter, and had approved the decision of the survivors to accept baptism. The same alternative was now put before

[1] NS, C, pp. 172 ff.; cf. also NS, A, p. 84.
[2] NS, C, p. 172.
[3] NS, B, p. 155.

them themselves, for the Bishop informed them that, unless they would be baptized, he could not hope to protect them[1]. The Jews asked for a short delay, in order to make up their minds, but when, at its termination, the Crusaders entered the building, it was to find that the whole of the community was dead. For, realising that there was no hope of rescue, they had decided to kill each other. On these two days eight hundred are said to have died at the hands of their fellows or of the mob.

From the few survivors the full horror of this heroic but ghastly holocaust, in which mothers killed their children, husbands their wives, sons their fathers, and fathers their sons, is known to us in detail, for it is all related in the different Hebrew chronicles. Some of the incidents formed the subject of elegies sung in the synagogues of Germany for many centuries[2]. But, in truth, the stories of Worms and the other cities of the Rhineland in 1096 stand out as a page, not in the history of the Jews alone, but in the history of all humanity, as an example, rarely equalled and never excelled, of the power of the human spirit over the weakness of the flesh.

Of the many stories of the fates of individuals who survived the different assaults, two may be given. A youth called Isaac was found to be still alive, and offered his life if he would accept baptism. He refused. A cord was tied round his neck and he was dragged through the city to a church. There, as he was still living, he was again offered baptism. Again he refused. Thereupon the Crusaders killed him[3]. Another feigned acceptance, and asked to be taken to the Bishop. In his presence he suddenly drew a knife, stabbed the Bishop's nephew, and was not slain until he had killed two others also[4]. Of these two incidents, the former was constantly repeated in many hideous ways: the latter is almost the only occasion on which a Jewish victim attempted to revenge himself on his persecutors.

---

[1] Bernold, *Chron.*, s.a. 1096; MGH, SS, V, p. 465.

[2] I. Elbogen, *Der Jüdische Gottesdienst*, pp. 335 ff.

[3] NS, C, p. 175.

[4] NS, B, p. 156.

In attempting to assess responsibility we shall probably be right, as against the Hebrew chroniclers, in ascribing no deliberate intention to betray the Jews either to the burghers or the Bishop. The promise of the latter to protect them appears to have been given in all sincerity. This is confirmed by the fortnight which elapsed between the alleged discovery of the corpse and the first outbreak. Nor is there any reason to doubt the Bishop's subsequent statement that he could not save the Jews unless they would accept baptism. It was a painful but exact description of his powerlessness. Neither bishop nor burgher had the requisite authority to withstand the Crusaders, when the latter were aided by a mob of their own citizens. On the other hand, we need not, with the Chronicler Bernold, ascribe the heroic decision of the Jews to ' the devil and their own hard hearts ! '[1]

After the massacre of Worms it was the turn of Mainz, the leading city and the leading Jewish community of the Rhineland. A letter had come to them in the early spring from the Jewries of northern France, relating their own tragedy, warning their fellow-Jews of what they might expect, and asking them to establish a special fast to avert further bloodshed. It is interesting that the Mainz community replied that, while they would fast, they ' needed to have no fears for themselves, since they had never observed a suspicion of danger, and had heard nothing of a sword hanging over their own heads '[2]. Nevertheless, after information reached them of the massacres of Worms, they took counsel with the Archbishop as to their protection and offered a large ransom for their safety. The Archbishop recommended them to deposit their treasures, and to take up residence, in his castle. With a few exceptions they did so. Some, however, took refuge in the castle of the Count, and a few in the houses of Christian friends.

To understand the sequel, it is again necessary to review the distribution of power in the city at that time. The authority of Ruthard, Archbishop of Mainz, was very limited. Further, he could not count on the loyalty of his own forces, which were nominally considerable[3]. The

[1] Bernold, *Chron.*, s.a. 1096; MGH, SS, V, p. 465.

[2] NS, C, pp. 169 ff.

[3] *Analista Sax.*, s.a. 1096; MGH, SS, VI, p. 729.

reason given by a Chronicler, that ' perhaps Christians would not fight against Christians for the sake of the Jews,' may well be true, especially if the soldiers had been subjected to the appeals of Peter the Hermit or similar preachers. The forces at the disposal of the Count and City Fathers seem to have been so slight that they are not heard of after their first failure to prevent the Crusaders from entering the city. The action of the different authorities was, consequently, only capable of delaying events for a few days.

The downfall of this, the greatest community of the Rhineland, began, incongruously, with a piece of farce. It was not a Christian corpse, as at Worms, but a pet goose whose conduct excited the crowd! The mistress of the goose had decided to go on the Crusade, and—what seemed a miracle to the beholders—the goose had decided to accompany her. In some curious fashion this was taken as a Divine endorsement of the whole purpose of the Crusade, including the determination either to massacre or to baptize the Jews![1]

The Crusaders at this time were assembled outside the city, and a mob formed with the purpose of entering the town and falling on the Jews. But the burghers resisted, and a struggle ensued, in which one of the Crusaders was killed[2]. The Jewish community were by this time dispersed in their various places of refuge, some in the episcopal palace, some in the Count's castle, some in the cathedral, some with Christian friends, and some still hidden in their own houses. They ventured out only for the Sabbath service in the synagogue. After the struggle already related, opinion in the city began to turn against the Jews, as responsible for the bloodshed. The danger greatly increased when, on May 25, Emicho of Leiningen arrived outside the walls with a large force. The Archbishop was about to leave the city for a pastoral visitation; but the Jews, by means of a present, persuaded him to stay in the hope that his presence might protect them. Both he and the Count promised their protection, but asked the Jews to pay the expenses involved. For this purpose the Jews provided them with 400 pounds of silver, and at the same time sent a useless bribe to Emicho[3].

[1] NS, A, p. 90.
[2] *Ibid.*, p. 91.
[3] *Ibid.*, pp. 92-3.

The Archbishop's share in demanding this payment was to cause him trouble when the Emperor returned to Germany[1].

On May 27 someone from within opened the gates of the city to Emicho, and a mob of Crusaders and townsfolk rushed to the episcopal palace. The Jews, led by their Rabbi, Kalonymus, put up a resistance. But they were too weak with fasting for it to be effective, and the Crusaders won the outer court. The Archbishop and his troops fled, leaving the Jews to their fate[2].

On entering the court, the Crusaders found some of the elders sitting passively waiting for their martyrdom. These they killed and pressed on into the building[3]. The bulk of the Jews had barricaded themselves into the great hall, and thus gained a short respite. But, realising that it could be only for a few hours, they decided to kill themselves. Fearing most that their children would be taken from them and baptized, they killed these first, while mothers threw money from the windows to distract and occupy the Crusaders[4]. When, a few hours later, the latter broke in, all were dead or dying. Pressing on, they found that other Jews had shut themselves into different rooms of the Palace. But the Crusaders made short work of breaking down the doors and of massacring all they found within.

In the evening, when they began to throw the bodies from the windows, they found a number to be living and calling feebly for water. The dying were told that they would be given water only if they would accept baptism. Almost all still had the strength to refuse. They were martyred[5]. By the following day only a handful of Jews were still alive of the hundreds who had taken refuge in the building[6].

Meanwhile, Rabbi Kalonymus and fifty-three of the elders had hidden in the sacristy of the Cathedral. There they succeeded in escaping notice[7], while the Crusaders passed on to the castle of the Count, where the tragedy of the Archbishop's palace was repeated. The forces of the Count

---

[1] See below, p. 81.
[2] NS, A, p. 95.
[3] *Ibid.*, pp. 96 and 100.
[4] *Ibid.*, C, p. 181.
[5] *Ibid.*, A, p. 109.
[6] *Ibid.*, p. 104.
[7] *Ibid.*, p. 111.

and the Jews were together too weak to withstand them. The doors were broken in, and all who had not killed themselves were massacred. Among the bodies were found some rolls of the Law. They were torn to pieces and desecrated[1]. The Crusaders then proceeded to the middle of the city, seeking houses where Jews had taken refuge. A priest had given shelter to one family, that of a tax collector, David son of Nathanael. The mob demanded his surrender, and the priest came to him, counselling him to accept baptism, as he could not possibly protect him. Nathanael asked that the Crusaders might be brought into the courtyard of the house, where he could address them. When they entered Nathanael came forward, but instead of the request for mercy in return for baptism which his host expected, he hurled insults at them as apostates and false believers. The enraged mob fell on him and his family and slaughtered them[2]. Other victims followed; and the Crusaders then seized two old men and violently baptized them. These two, Isaac and Uri, had remained in their own houses. Two days after their baptism, overcome with shame, they met with their families in the house of Isaac. They then set fire to the house, and to the synagogue which stood near-by. They and their families perished in the flames, which spread until a considerable quarter of the city was destroyed[3]. Women who had been taken alive were dragged to a church, and on refusing baptism, murdered[4]. The city presented the appearance of a shambles. Round the palaces of the Archbishop and the Count lay the naked bodies of hundreds of victims. Others lay in the streets of the town, where they had been struck down. In pity the burghers took the money which they had been given to protect the unhappy community, and used it for the burial of the bodies[5].

Meanwhile, the Archbishop himself, seeing his palace in the hands of the mob, had fled from the city and taken refuge across the Rhine at Rüdesheim. There he heard that Kalonymus and the fifty-three elders with him were still alive,

---

[1] *Ibid.*, p. 102.

[2] *Ibid.*, p. 104.

[3] *Ibid.*, p. 105.

[4] *Ibid.*, p. 108.

[5] *Ibid.*, p. 110,

hidden in the sacristy of the Cathedral. He secretly sent
three hundred soldiers to rescue them, and to bring them
over to Rüdesheim. The escape, however, became known,
and the mob followed across the river. The unhappy prelate
had again to avow his impotence, and to confess to the
refugees that he could only protect them if they would allow
themselves to be baptized. Rabbi Kalonymus asked for a
night for reflection, and, leaving his presence, first slew his
son and then, according to some accounts, himself. Others
say that when he returned to the Archbishop in the morning
and avowed his deed, the Archbishop turned away from him
in horror, and that Kalonymus sprang forward and tried to
kill him, meeting death at the hands of his attendants. The
Archbishop then drove the rest of the Jews out of his castle.
There, trying to hide themselves in the woods surrounding
the village, they were miserably cut down by the Crusaders
and villagers[1].

Such is the story of the tragedy of Mainz as told by the
few who survived, either by baptism, or by fleeing to Speyer.
Little by little the community grew again from the ruins,
and a new synagogue was consecrated in 1104. But it is not
surprising to find that instead of the two separate quarters
which had existed before 1096, one was enough for the new
settlers[2]. In all, one thousand and fourteen are said to have
perished in the massacre[3].

While the bands of Emicho were thus occupied at Mainz,
a new horde, coming perhaps from Flanders, appeared at
Cologne. Ever since they had received news of the catas-
trophes which had befallen their brethren in the more
southerly communities, the Jews of Cologne had been
waiting in great anxiety, and in strict fasting, to see what
their own fate would be. The civic power of the Archbishop
in Cologne was even less than that of his colleague in Mainz.
In consequence, on the first appearance of the hated cross
on an armed band approaching the city, the Jews fled to the
houses of Christian acquaintances. There they remained
for nearly a week, while the Crusaders sacked the synagogue
and plundered their homes. Where they discovered a Jew,

[1] *Ibid.*, pp. 111 ff.

[2] *Ibid.*, p. 143.

[3] *Annales Wirziburg.*, s.a. 1096; MGH, SS, II, p. 246.

they put him to death if he refused baptism. After a week, the Bishop rescued and hid the survivors in seven villages belonging to the diocese. There they hoped to escape the notice of the Crusaders or the mob. All went well for three weeks, but then the hiding-places of the Jews were discovered, and their security was changed into a trap. On June 24 the Feast of Saint John drew a large crowd of peasants to the village of Neuss. The assembled crowd murdered all the refugees whom they could find. Here, and in other villages, the assassins are simply called ' the enemies ', but it is to be presumed that it is the usual medley of Crusaders and inhabitants, such as had been responsible elsewhere for the massacres. One detail will reveal the full horror of these days. A certain Isaac was tortured until he was unconscious, and then, while unconscious, baptized. Three days later he recovered consciousness and was told that he was a Christian. He struggled back to Cologne, rested an hour in his home, and then went down to the Rhine and threw himself in. His dead body floated down the river, and was found lying by that of his son on the shore at Neuss.

The same day, or the next, the refugees at Wevelinghofen were discovered and tortured to accept baptism. They refused, and either killed themselves or were murdered. In the two villages of the name of Altenahr, over three hundred met the same fate a day later. At the same time, on a Sabbath eve, the Crusaders appeared at Xanten. The Jews were just celebrating their evening meal when they heard of their arrival. The rabbi continued the customary Benedictions, and at the end, ' making themselves their offering to God ', they spoke the final Benediction, and then all killed each other. Next it was the turn of the refugees of Mörs. There the mayor tried for two days to protect them, but it was the same story: protection was only possible if they would accept baptism. The Jews refused, and the mayor handed them over to the Crusaders. Some were killed, the rest forcibly baptized[1]. The same fate befell the Jews of Kerpen and of Geldern; and, with this last attack, the destruction of the community of Cologne was complete.

[1] Thus far the details are from NS, A, pp. 116 ff. What follows is from NS, B, p. 165.

While this was happening to the Jews of Mainz and Cologne, catastrophe menaced also the Jews of Trier, the city where Peter the Hermit had made his first appearance in the region. This is the only case in which a Christian source is more detailed than the Hebrew Chronicles. The ' Gesta ' of the Archbishops of Trier and the report of Salomo b. Simeon supplement each other. Some time during May the forces of the Crusaders appeared beneath the walls of the city. Hearing of their approach, some of the Jews at once killed themselves and their children, to save the latter from the hands of the Crusaders. Some of the women rushed to the bridge and, filling their skirts with stones, threw themselves into the river. The rest took refuge in the castle of the Archbishop which was an impregnable fortress. The Archbishop was at that moment absent, but returned within a few days, and before the Crusaders and the mob had decided what to do. On June 1 there was an important market, bringing large numbers of villagers from the surrounding region into the town. This seemed a favourable moment for the attack. But the Archbishop also took advantage of the presence of the crowds to preach a sermon in his cathedral in defence of the Jews. This so enraged the mob that he was forced to flee, and hid himself in a chamber attached to the building. There he lay concealed for a week, while the Jews barricaded themselves into the castle. Realising that there was no hope of his being able to rescue them, he finally got into touch with them and urged them to be baptized—these events, humiliating to the episcopal dignity, the Gesta omit. On reflection and on the advice of their rabbi, Micheas, the Jews decided to accept, and asked the Archbishop to explain to them the Christian Faith, ' since it is better to accept that than to lie daily in fear for ourselves and our possessions '. All those in the castle were baptized, but all except Micheas reverted to Judaism the following year, when the Emperor gave them permission to do so. The majority of the community was thus spared, and the martyrs of Trier were either those who perished voluntarily in the beginning, or those who were discovered in the town during the siege of the castle[1].

[1] Gesta Treverorum, Cont. prima, xvii, MGH, SS, VIII, pp. 190 ff.; NS, A, pp. 131 ff.

During the following weeks similar events took place in Bohemia and the Danube cities, wherever the bands of 'poor men' passed. In Ratisbon the burghers tried vainly to defend their Jews, but all were herded into the river and baptized by the simple method of signing the water with the cross[1]. In a city which may be Halle or Wessel in Bohemia, the prince and the Jews between them managed to rout the Crusaders with the loss of only six of their own side[2]. In Prague, the Bishop, Cosmas, did his best to prevent their forcible baptism; but the Duke was absent in Poland, and he had no force at his command. Many of the Jews of Bohemia fled either to Poland or to Hungary to escape from the Crusaders' march.

Finally, in the summer, the armies passed across the Hungarian border on their long march to Constantinople, and the remnants of the Jews were left in peace to rebuild the ruins of their lives. These groups of Crusaders perished miserably, either in the Balkans or before the walls of Nicea, and it is not surprising that contemporary chroniclers saw in their wretched fate a punishment for all the ill deeds with which they had dishonoured what should have been, if a mistaken, yet a glorious and romantic movement. The atrocities for which they were responsible have been briefly given. The Hebrew chronicles are full of details from eye-witnesses which are even more harrowing than those which have been related. To give all is, happily, unnecessary, but unless the reader can seize some of the horror of those fatal weeks, it is not possible to understand the subsequent history of the Middle Ages or the bitterness of the hatred of the Jews for Christianity and for those Jews who accepted conversion to it. For, whether there was or was not some economic motive in their actions, the Crusaders murdered in the Name of Christ, killing 'His enemies', mercilessly and with torture, as a deed well pleasing in His sight.

[1] NS, A, p. 137.
[2] *Ibid.*, the place is called שלא or (p. 131) ושׁל.

V. THE ATTITUDE OF THE EMPEROR

While these events were taking place the Emperor, Henry IV, was in northern Italy. So far as we know he first learnt of them from Kalonymus of Mainz[1] who, as soon as he heard of the menaces of Godfrey of Bouillon and, perhaps, the events of northern France, hastily sent him a message appealing for protection. The Emperor consented to do what he could, and sent an imperial order to the responsible authorities, instructing them to take the necessary steps to put the Jews into places of security[2]. To this order may be attributed the successful actions of Bishop John of Speyer, and the unsuccessful attempt of Archbishop Herman of Cologne to distribute the Jews in the different villages of the diocese. This was as much as the Emperor was able to do at the time, for all was over long before he returned to Germany.

On his return he had to deal with two questions: the situation of the hundreds of Jews who had been violently baptized, and the possible punishment of the guilty. To the disapproval of the Pope, and in contradiction to the express rules of Canon Law, he allowed the first to return to Judaism[3]. That the Pope disapproved would only encourage the Emperor to this action, for there was no love lost between them. As a matter of fact, all those who could had already returned to their own way of life. They ate only kosher meat, and never entered the churches except under compulsion[4]. It may appear extraordinary that in spite of the fact that, as the Chronicle of Salomo b. Simeon expresses it, everyone knew that they had accepted baptism out of no inner conviction but out of fear of the Crusaders, yet the Church

---

[1] NS, A, p. 87.

[2] *Ibid.*, C, p. 171.

[3] *Reg. Pont.*, cited in Aronius, No. 204; Ekk., *Chron. Univ.*, s.a. 1097, MGH, SS, VI, p. 208. According to a Hebrew account (NS, C, p. 171) this act of Henry was secured by the intercession of Rabbi Moses b. Jekuthiel, President of the Community of Speyer, in the middle of the outbreak. The permission was, in fact, given by Henry at Ratisbon in 1097, so that the baptized Jews had to wait about a year for their permission to return (Ekkehard).

[4] NS, A, p. 138.

should have insisted on their remaining members of a faith in which they did not believe. The explanation lies in the Catholic conception of baptism. By the performance of that Sacrament, even upon unwilling or unconscious persons, an actual change is considered to be effected in their spiritual situation. Even the Revised Prayer Book of the Church of England of 1928 still retains the words that baptism is ' a death unto sin and a new birth unto righteousness, for *being by nature born in sin and children of wrath we are hereby made the children of Grace* '[1]. This effect is secured *ex opere operato*, independently of the person concerned. If, therefore, a Jew had had the waters of baptism poured on him, the act had been performed, and for him to ' return to his vomit ' was to insult the Sacrament, and to commit an act of blasphemous sacrilege. Moreover, as the act had not only an independent but an eternal validity, it was impossible for him to renounce it and to ' unbaptize himself '. Finally, since he was a baptized person, the clergy had the right to supervise the education of his children, and to ensure that they were brought up in the Christian Faith. These reasons produced the paradoxical result that to spiritually minded clergy of the time the act of the Emperor was an act of appalling impiety, which involved the irretrievable damnation of the unhappy Jews concerned; while it was those who were indifferent to the Faith who saw in the act a truly Christian reparation for a crime of horrible brutality.

A more difficult question was the punishment of the guilty. Even if the Emperor had not fully taken over the possession of the Jews of the empire by 1096[2], yet they were under his general protection. His difficulty lay in the fact that the actual criminals were either the Crusaders, who were no longer within his territory, or the town mobs, who were impossible to identify. The comment of a chronicler reveals the dilemma: ' it certainly seems remarkable that on a single day in many different places, moved by a single violent inspiration, such massacres should have taken place, in spite of the fact that many disapproved of them, and the clergy were hostile to them. But they could evidently not

[1] In ' a catechism ' in *The Prayer Book as proposed in* 1928.

[2] See following chapter, pp. 106 ff.

have been avoided since they occurred in the face of excommunication, which many of the clergy pronounced on those who took part in them, and of menaces of punishment on the part of many of the princes '[1]. In other words, all those whom the Emperor might have been able to identify had done their best to prevent them, and had been swept out of the way by a wave of popular feeling. The only group on whom he was able to fix were certain of the relatives of the Archbishop of Mainz, who had looted Jewish property which the Emperor considered should revert to himself. The Archbishop was not immune from suspicion on the same grounds, but as both he and his relatives took refuge in Thuringia, we do not know whether the Emperor succeeded in recovering anything[2].

One precaution which Henry took for the future was carefully to include the Jews in the ' general peace ' which he caused to be sworn in 1103 by all the rulers of the empire. The habit thus begun was frequently followed, both in imperial declarations, and in treaties between different authorities within the empire[3]. How much protection this afforded the Jews it is difficult to assess. Sometimes no doubt it was effective; but it is to be feared that it was only during the relatively rare periods of quiet that a Jew could count upon its action[4].

VI. EFFECT OF THE FIRST CRUSADE ON THE JEWS

Looking back, it is easy to see that the First Crusade was the decisive turning point in medieval Jewish-Christian relations, but this was not immediately evident to those

---

[1] Hugo, *Chron.*; MGH, SS, VI, p. 209.

[2] Ekkehard, *Chron. Univ.*, s.a. 1098; MGH, SS, VI, p. 209.

[3] *Constitutio Pacis Generalis*; MGH, LL, II, p. 60. For similar formulas of later emperors, see *ibid.*, pp. 267, 368, 375. A similar paragraph is included in the treaty of the Confederation of certain Rhineland cities in 1179, MGH, LL, IV, Const. I, p. 381; and in 1254, *op. cit.*, Const. II, p. 581. At the Cortes of Villafranca in Aragon in 1218 a similar oath included both Moors and Jews; Regné, *Catalogue*, No. 1; REJ, LX, p. 161.

[4] Cf. MGH, LL, IV, Const. V, p. 375, where a judge and jury find that Heyne von Slatheym in seizing a Jew has broken the Land's Peace.

G

living at the time. It is, on the contrary, interesting to see how, in successive Crusades, Jewish communities which had not yet suffered were unable to believe that anything evil would happen to them. Thus, while the Jewries of the Rhineland took immediate refuge in different strongholds on the approach of the forces of the Second Crusade in 1146, those of Würzburg, less than a hundred miles from Mainz, refused to believe that they were in any danger, and suffered severely in consequence[1]. In France it is the same story. The communities of Normandy placed themselves in security, but there were sporadic massacres in other places where before all had been peaceful[2]. In the Third Crusade it was the turn of England. Such a situation is proof, not only that previous relations had not been bad, but that they only changed slowly for the worse. They possessed, however, a new quality of brittleness. Any incident was enough to turn the general population, previously indifferent, into a mob seeking blood.

This new insecurity had a profound effect upon Jewish economic life. The Jew had been accustomed to the life of a travelling merchant, and his voyages had been long and frequent. In spite of the dangers of the road and the burden of frequent tolls—legal or illegal—such trade was profitable, and was probably growing at the time when the Crusades occurred to interrupt Jewish participation in it. Within the next century much of it passed to the rising cities of Italy and Flanders, and the Jews never regained any predominant position. For, apart from the rivalry of the Flemings and Italians, the new situation created by the Crusades caused a change in their occupations. As long as bands of Crusaders were wandering across country, so long the roads were scarcely safe for Jewish merchants— it is significant that in the Second Crusade most of the recorded victims in Germany were caught on the road. An occupation containing fewer risks became desirable, and it was found in the ever-increasing demand for money in a society which was rapidly developing. Whereas previously the Jewish merchants had occasionally ' obliged ' a friend

---

[1] *Chronicle* of Ephraim b. Jacob, NS, p. 192.

[2] *Ibid.*, p. 194.

with a loan, taking some object as security, now commerce began to take the second place, and the lending of money, an occupation which could be carried on at home, the first. Yet other reasons than personal security contributed thereto. Money and precious objects could be hidden or carried away more easily than cumbrous merchandise—or crops, cattle and houses! Lastly, money was the best bulwark of security, in that it was the only form in which the Jews could buy protection, or bribe their enemies. The Hebrew Chronicles of the Crusades speak in a way, curious to us, of this power of bribery, and so far from mourning over the costliness of this continual necessity, regard the wealth of the Jewish communities as a gift of God whereby they are able to preserve their religious loyalty to Him[1].

In the Roman world, the word Jew meant simply a member of the Jewish nation or religion—the ideas were interchangeable: in the Carolingian world, and up to the eleventh century, Jew often meant merchant. It is only after the First Crusade that the word Jew comes to have any connection with money-lender, but within a century the two words almost became synonyms.

VII. EFFECT ON THE AUTHORITIES

If the Crusade had a fundamental and far-reaching effect upon the Jews, it had an equally important effect on the attitude which the different secular authorities adopted towards them. Firstly, it became necessary to take serious steps for their protection, but it is doubtful whether for humanitarian reasons alone this would have received the attention which it merited. It was here that the change in their economic activity was of great value to the Jews, for the princes came to discover a strong financial interest in their security. Lack of money was a chronic ailment of the sovereigns of the twelfth century. With their increasing responsibilities, they were still largely dependent on their own feudal estates for their resources. The Jews, however, were their private property; and it followed naturally that

[1]See *Chronicles* of Ephraim b. Jacob and Elasar b. Judah, in NS, *passim.*

their wealth could be used to replenish the ever-empty royal and baronial treasuries. To rob a Jew was, therefore, to rob a prince. To kill him was to deprive the prince of his property. Even to convert him was a wrong from the royal point of view, for converted, he could no longer produce money for his sovereign from his moneylending.

The period which follows 1096, therefore, is marked by a succession of charters of settlement, containing regulations of economic privileges and responsibilities designed to secure the maximum benefit to the donor from the presence of a Jewish community. Kings, princes and cities disputed the ownership of Jews; they were exchanged, pawned and given away. Minor princes and cities obtained special permission to establish Jewish colonies. It became a special favour to be allowed to keep a Jew, and a gift of one was a valuable present. And all this was done with no other motive than profit. The comfort or security of the Jew only played any rôle with the most enlightened or humanitarian rulers, and protection apart from a return in cash was so rare that Jewish chroniclers note it with amazement when a Christian risks himself in their defence and accepts no bribe therefore. Bishop John of Speyer obtained this glory in the First Crusade, and Bernard of Clairvaux and an unnamed priest in the second[1].

VIII. EFFECT ON THE CHURCH

While the attitude of the secular authorities, as it developed in the twelfth and thirteenth centuries, was fairly straightforward, that of the Church was more complex. In the actual period of the massacres this difference was evident. The royal and civic authorities failed to protect the Jews through lack of power, not lack of will. For they all seemed to have done their best. But among the churchmen, three different attitudes can be observed.

The greatest puzzle of all is the silence of Pope Urban himself, and the fact that there was no appeal to him from the Jewish communities. He did not leave France until the

[1] See NS, C, pp. 171 f., and Report of Ephraim b. Jacob, NS, pp. 188 and 196.

middle of August 1096, and by this time the deadly work of
the Crusaders was complete, and the Rhineland communities
in ruins. It is impossible to believe that he was entirely
ignorant of all that was happening; but, on the other hand,
it is almost equally difficult to believe that he did, in fact,
intervene, but that his intervention was entirely fruitless, and
that all record of it has perished. His only recorded action
was to condemn Henry IV for permitting the baptized Jews
to return to Judaism in 1098. His silence is the more extraordinary in that the massacres in Spain during the Crusade
of 1063 had met with energetic condemnation from Pope
Alexander II.

As against the silence of Urban on this occasion must be
set the activity of his successors during subsequent Crusades.
Of all medieval authorities their general record is the cleanest.
While it is to be expected that they would accept as fundamental the two principles in Jewish-Christian relations, that
every effort must be made to convert the Jews to Christianity
and that no licence must be allowed to Jews to influence, or
exercise authority over, Christians, they constantly raised
their voice against acts of violence or lawlessness.

When they considered that harsh legislation was required
for the maintenance of the two fundamentals, they were not
squeamish to apply it. The Jewish badge, the ghetto, the
conversional sermon, all have their origin in papal legislation.
On the other hand, they protected the Jews, as far as they
could, in the enjoyment of tranquillity, and in the possession
of rights which presented no dangers to their Christian
flocks. While they did not sanction the return to Judaism
of Jews baptized by force, and could, indeed, doctrinally not
do so, they strongly disapproved of this violence, and exercised what power they possessed to ensure the protection
of Jewish communities against such baptisms during the
subsequent Crusades and at other times of popular effervescence. Equally they condemned those accusations against
the Jews and the Jewish religion which medieval superstition
raised with such appalling results. They accepted neither
the accusation of ritual murder, which they rightly held to
be abhorrent to the religious principles of Judaism, nor that
of poisoning the wells of Europe. While they considered
that the Jews should live in subjection and degradation for

the crime of deicide, they saw in this condition no licence for massacre or violence on the part of Christians.

The record of the local clergy, deeply imbued with all the ignorance and superstition of their flocks, is a much less honourable one. It is no accident that the first massacres owed their origin to clerical preaching, and that three of the murderous bands of Crusaders were led by priests. The subsequent accusations, especially that of ritual murder and of the profanation of Hosts, find their origin and their chief support in the local clergy, both secular and monastic. Even that of poisoning wells was readily accepted by them. And while we hear of the greater clergy and outstanding personalities such as Bernard of Clairvaux intervening to protect the Jew from the mob, we hear of very few such actions on the part of lesser men in clerical orders. One priest alone appears as a protector of the Jews in 1147. In the records of the efforts made in the cities to defend the Jews only one chronicler mentions the clergy either in 1096 or in later Crusades. It is not unfair to see in this class the pivot around which the tragedy of medieval Jewry turned.

Less brutal, but equally hostile is the record of the great preaching orders of the Dominicans and Franciscans. While men like Vincent Ferrer and Raymund Martini were fortunately rare, the Orders were primarily responsible for the destruction of Jewish books, for the perpetuation of the theological conception of the Jews as deicides, and for those laws of humiliation by which the medieval Jew was prevented from corrupting his Christian neighbour. And it was to the Orders, especially the Dominicans, that was entrusted the Office of the Inquisition. If the local clergy and monasteries must be held responsible for the deaths of thousands at the hands of the mob, the Orders must equally be held responsible for the degradation of those who survived.

The third group which merits consideration contains the bishops and ecclesiastical rulers. Their attitude was determined alternately by the dual nature of their office. A worldly bishop might concentrate on the economic advantages which a Jewish settlement might bring to his dominions, and grant privileges which his own clergy would view with disapproval. A saintly bishop might equally well adopt an attitude which his secular officers considered to be to the disadvantage of his states. In the events of 1096, the only bishop whose motives are suspect is Ruthard of Mainz. He was considered by the Emperor to have illegally collected the property of the Jewish victims, but it is not suggested that he connived at the massacres in order to get this into his hands. What is interesting is that, while all seem to have done their best, their religious power over the populace was very slight. The Bishop of Trier tried to turn the mob from their purpose by a sermon, but he not only failed to influence them, but was compelled to hide from their rage in his own cathedral. Clergy who threatened with excommunication those who murdered Jews fared no better.

IX. EFFECT ON THE POPULACE

In considering the effect of these events on the populace it is again necessary to distinguish different groups. The lower classes of the city discovered that the Jews had rich houses to loot, and even the most irreligious found that religion was a good cloak under which to loot them. The merchant class, and the middle classes generally, remained for a long while the Jews' best friends, the class most likely to offer them shelter in case of danger, least likely to be swept away into fanatical attacks upon them—and there is here an important tribute to the essential virtue of the ordinary Jew, for this was the class with whom he came into the closest social and business contact.

Finally, there are the civil urban authorities to be considered. With them the protection of the Jew was largely a matter of pride in the good government of their towns. Even in the wave of hysteria which accompanied the Black Death there were some municipalities which attempted to protect the Jewish population from the mob. On the other hand, there were times when they petitioned to be allowed to expel their Jews in order that they might not be constantly exhausted by the effort to protect them. As the commercial importance of the middle classes grew, and the power in the cities fell into their hands, commercial rivalry began to play a larger rôle in the civic attitude to the Jews, and the clerical effort to segregate them lest they corrupted the Christian population came to be seconded by the civic authorities in order to dispose of an inconvenient rival.

While the forces let loose in 1096 came ultimately to determine the situation of the Jews in the whole of Europe, things changed more slowly in Spain, Italy and the south of France than in the north. Civilisation was more highly developed in the south, so that the commercial rivalry of the Jews was less feared on the one hand, and, on the other, the traditions of their Roman citizenship died much more slowly in regions in which it had for centuries been a dominant reality, and in which Jewish communities could look back over a thousand years of relatively friendly relations with their Christian neighbours. In the south of France and in Spain serious trouble did not occur before the fourteenth century, and in Italy it came even later. But in the end it came, and the final act of the medieval tragedy was the expulsion from Spain in 1492, and the last relic of medieval policy was the ghetto of Rome, which was not abolished until 1870.

X. RELATIONSHIPS IN THE MEDIEVAL PERIOD

It will be seen from the foregoing pages how complex is the study of the medieval period. Church and State touched Jewish life at every point, and in their attitudes were moved by widely differing motives. Within each group there were again deep contradictions. As a generalisation it has to be admitted that the major note of the period is tragedy. In no other way can one explain how the flourishing Jewish civilisation at the beginning of the period came to be the narrow and cringing society found at the end. But if humanity has an appalling aptitude for falling short of its ideals, it has an equal gift for rising above its principles, and throughout the period there are traces of individual friendship and mutual respect which do something to lighten the gloom. Nor was the Jewish spirit entirely broken by the appalling ordeal through which it passed. Life within the narrow walls of their houses still offered something of joy and refinement even after four centuries of persecution. Traces of scholarship survived the steady destruction of Jewish books and the martyrdom of Jewish scholars. Even the two great communities which finally broke under the strain, and consented to an apparent renunciation of their religion for the sake of material security, redeemed their momentary weakness in the heroic history of the Marranos for three centuries to come.

PART II

THE POLITICAL STATUS
OF THE JEW

BIBLIOGRAPHICAL INTRODUCTION

Whereas in the period of the Christian Roman Empire almost the sole external determinant of the Jewish position in society was the attitude, hostile or neutral, of the theologians and the influence of the ecclesiastical authorities over the Emperor, a new and vitally important element came into play as soon as the northern societies began to develop. In the Roman world, whatever might happen, Jewry could still rely upon the basic fact of citizenship. Actions, local or temporary, might partially invalidate the exercise of this basic right, but they could not annul it. Even the beginning of the actual limitation of Jewish equality before the law left the elementary rights of the Jewish citizen secure. But with the crumbling of the Roman fabric of law an entirely new position arose. In Germanic society there was no determined place for the Jew, and such a place had to be made for him by special action. The basis of the new position was the complete dependence of the individual Jew, or of the local community, on the will of a master. Nowhere could the Jews exist of right. Everywhere they needed a special regulation of their presence; and this special regulation both affected their own communal organisation, and determined in large measure their relations with the non-Jewish community within which they lived.

A system of ' privileges', which grew to meet new needs, naturally presented many varieties in its development; hence the necessity for studying separately the different ' families ' in which these privileges evolved. The reactions of different elements in Christian society were also various, in accordance with the special interests of the element concerned. In view of the earlier situation it is of particular interest that the Church, which had previously taken the initiative and had been the determining factor in the daily contacts of the Jews with their neighbours, now passed into a policy of reaction, favourable or hostile, to the initiative of others. In this second period it was the princes, not the bishops, who took the lead, and they did so because Jewry had become a significant and specialised factor in society, offering specific advantages to whoever controlled it. Hence the charters passed from being little more than passports, authorising a particular group of subjects to go about their normal business, into being carefully drawn-up instruments by which the maximum advantage could be secured out of the activities of a highly specialised group directly depending on—indeed, directly belonging to—the prince who issued them.

To give a list of the books containing the original sources for this political transformation of the Jews in the Middle Ages is impossible. They are to be found scattered through all the great collections, as well as in innumerable monographs on the local history of the Jews in different lands and countries. Moreover, to set out the full story, it would be necessary to give a bibliography also of the main source-books of general political and legal history, for at every point the status of the Jew is intimately related to the political and legal conceptions of the time. The work of relating Jewish regulations to general conceptions is still in its infancy, and the first necessity for a close study of the situation is the work of Guido Kisch, which contains extremely important bibliographical notes.

The main problem which lies at the base of all others is that of the ' Kammerknechtschaft ' or ' servitudo camerae '. Its origin is extremely vague, and it is very possible that it will always remain a matter of controversy, since documents of the tenth or eleventh century are never likely to become common. The phrase first emerges in a text of an eleventh-century charter to the Jews of Worms, but the text itself is a copy of the fourteenth century. It is therefore disputed whether the phrase is original. For this reason a special bibliography is given of the Speyer-Worms charters of 1084 and 1090, in which every point of view is represented. Behind the actual serfdom to the treasury lies the status of the Jew as a stranger in Germanic custom. Since there is no English study of this aspect of that custom, the standard work of Brunner is included as a guide to the literature on this subject. It is a point which is also dealt with in some detail by Scherer and Kisch. Most of the other books reveal their subject from their title. The exception is Scherer, who has included, by way of preliminary study or comparison with the Austrian charters, details of the legal history of the

Jews in every European country. It is thus the most comprehensive collection of material at present available.

The books so far discussed deal mainly with the status imposed upon the Jews by Christian sovereigns. The Jewish community itself, however, was necessarily influenced, and its customs modified, by its position as a scattered minority within Christendom. While, therefore, it is no part of this study to trespass on the work of Jewish scholars who are far more competent to describe the inner life of the Jews during the period, it is necessary to discuss some aspects of the life of the Jewries, because they are intimately connected with the question of Jewish-Gentile relations. For the Christian reader this field is almost completely unknown, and the literature, in other than Hebrew, is not very extensive. The sources of our knowledge are mainly the Responsa of prominent rabbis, and it would be well for those unfamiliar with the nature of these Responsa to consult the article of Lauterbach. The work of Finkelstein includes a survey of the decisions of the rabbinical synods of France, Germany and Spain; and that of Shohet contains a mass of valuable facts. But its brevity occasionally obscures the variety which existed, and its generalisations are sometimes dangerous. Apart from Jewish sources, primarily the Responsa already mentioned, the two largest collections of material dealing with the inner life of the Jewish communities are to be found in Regné and Baer, notices of which are to be found in the list of abbreviations at the beginning of the book.

LIST OF BOOKS

I. GENERAL

BRUNNER, H.

Deutsche Rechtsgeschichte, I, 2nd edition. Leipzig, 1906.

EGAN, C.

The Status of the Jews in England. London, R. Hastings, 1848.

FISCHER, H.

Die verfassungsrechtliche Stellung der Juden in den deutschen Städten während des 13. Jahrhunderts. Breslau, 1931.

KISCH, GUIDO

Research in Medieval Legal History of the Jews. In *Proceedings of the American Academy for Jewish Research,* vol. VI. New York, 1934-35.

KISCH, GUIDO

The Jewry-Law of the Medieval German Law-Books, Part I. In *Proceedings of the American Academy for Jewish Research,* vol. VII. New York, 1935-36.

RÖSEL, I.

Die Reichssteuern der deutschen Judengemeinden von ihren Anfängen bis zur Mitte des 14. Jahrhunderts. Berlin, 1910.

SCHERER, J. E.

Die Rechtsverhältnisse der Juden in den deutsch-österreichischen Ländern. Leipzig, 1901.

STOBBE, O.

Die Juden in Deutschland während des Mittelalters. Braunschweig, 1866; reprinted Berlin, 1923.

ZIMMELS, H. J.

Beiträge zur Geschichte der Juden in Deutschland im 13. Jahrhundert, insbesondere auf Grund der Gutachten des R. Meir Rothenburg. Vienna, 1926.

II. Books dealing with Charters of Worms and Speyer

Aronius, J.   *Regesten*, etc., Nos. 168, 170, 171. Berlin, 1902.

Brann, M., Jakob-sohn, J., & Rosenthal, E.   Article ' Speyer ' in *Germania Judaica*, pp. 326 ff. Breslau, 1934.

Bresslau, H.   *Diplomatische Erläuterungen zu den Judenprivilegien Heinrichs IV.* ZGJD, I, pp. 152 ff. Braunschweig, 1887.

Carlebach, E.   *Die rechtlichen und sozialen Verhältnisse der jüdischen Gemeinden: Speyer, Worms und Mainz von ihren Anfängen bis zur Mitte des 14. Jahrhunderts.* Leipzig, 1901.

Caro, G.   *Sozial- und Wirtschaftsgeschichte der Juden im Mittelalter und der Neuzeit,* I, pp. 170 ff. Leipzig, 1908.

Epstein, A.   *Jüdische Alterthümer in Speier.* MGWJ, XLI, pp. 25 ff. Berlin, 1897.

Graetz, H.   *Geschichte der Juden,* VI, chapter 4. Leipzig, 1861.

Hoeniger, R.   *Zur Geschichte der Juden Deutschlands im frühen Mittelalter,* I, II. ZGJD, I, pp. 65 ff., 136 ff. Braunschweig, 1887.

Jakobsohn, J.   Article ' Worms ' in *Germania Judaica*, pp. 437 ff. Breslau, 1934.

Schiffmann, S.   *Heinrich IV. und die Bischöfe in ihrem Verhalten zu den deutschen Juden zur Zeit des ersten Kreuzzuges.* Diss. Berlin, 1931.

Stobbe, O.   *Die Judenprivilegien Heinrichs IV. für Speier und für Worms.* ZGJD, I, pp. 205 ff. Braunschweig, 1887.

H

TÄUBLER, E.   *Urkundliche Beiträge zur Geschichte der Juden in Deutschland im Mittelalter*, Nos. 2 and 4. In *Mitteilungen des Gesamtarchivs der Deutschen Juden*, IV, pp. 44 ff., and V, pp. 127 ff. Leipzig, 1914-15.

III. Books dealing with the inner life of the Jewish Communities

ABRAHAMS, ISRAEL   *Jewish Life in the Middle Ages.* London (Macmillan), 1896.

BAER, FRITZ   Article ' Gemeinde ', *II. Mittelalter und neuere Zeit*, in *Encyclopaedia Judaica*, vol. VII. Berlin, 1931.

BERLINER, A.   *Aus dem Leben der deutschen Juden im Mittelalter.* Berlin, 1900.

CARLEBACH, E.   *Die rechtlichen und sozialen Verhältnisse der jüdischen Gemeinden: Speyer, Worms und Mainz von ihren Anfängen bis zur Mitte des 14. Jahrhunderts.* Leipzig, 1901.

CARO, G.   *Sozial- und Wirtschaftsgeschichte der Juden im Mittelalter und der Neuzeit.* Two vols. Leipzig, 1908, 1920.

EPSTEIN, I.   *The ' Responsa ' of Rabbi Solomon ben Adreth of Barcelona (1235-1310) as a source of the history of Spain.* London (Kegan Paul, Trench, Trübner), 1925.

FINKELSTEIN, L.   *Jewish self-government in the Middle Ages.* New York, 1924.

FISCHER, H.   *Die verfassungsrechtliche Stellung der Juden in den deutschen Städten während des dreizehnten Jahrhunderts.* Breslau, 1931.

GÜDEMANN, M.   *Geschichte des Erziehungswesens und der Cultur der abendländischen Juden während des Mittelalters und der neueren Zeit.* Three vols. Vienna, 1880-88.

KOBER, A.   *Studien zur mittelalterlichen Geschichte der Juden in Köln a. Rh., insbesondere ihres Grundbesitzes.* Diss. Breslau, 1903.

KRACAUER, I.   *Die politische Geschichte der Frankfurter Juden bis zum Jahre 1349.* Frankfurt a.M., 1911.

LAUTERBACH, J. Z.   Article ' She'elot u-Teshuboth ' (interpellations and decisions) in *Jewish Encyclopedia,* vol. XI. New York, 1905.

RÖSEL, I.   *Die Reichssteuern der deutschen Judengemeinden von ihren Anfängen bis zur Mitte des 14. Jahrhunderts.* Berlin, 1910.

SHOHET, D. M.   *The Jewish Court in the Middle Ages.* New York, 1931.

ZIMMELS, H. J.   *Beiträge zur Geschichte der Juden in Deutschland im 13. Jahrhundert insbesondere auf Grund der Gutachten des R. Meir Rothenburg.* Vienna, 1926.

ZUCROW, S.   *Adjustment of Law to Life in Rabbinic Literature.* Boston, 1928.

The most frequently used source-books will be found in the list of abbreviations at the beginning of the book.

CHAPTER FOUR

THE JEW AS PRIVATE PROPERTY

I. FOUNDATIONS OF THE MEDIEVAL STATUS

The three pillars on which was raised the structure of medieval Jewish society were Roman Law, Canon Law and Germanic Custom.

By Roman Law the Jews had possessed three essential privileges, on which the life of their communities rested. The lawfulness of the practices of Judaism had been recognised by Julius Caesar. When Christian influence endangered this, it was confirmed by Theodosius in the statement that ' it is established that there are no laws by which the sect of the Jews is forbidden to exist. . . . ' This confirmation found its way neither into the Code of Justinian nor into the ' breviaries ' of the Code of Theodosius which were used in western Europe from the barbarian period onwards. The second privilege was that of citizenship, which had been originally granted to the Jews, together with all subjects of the Empire, by Caracalla. This also found no place in the medieval memory of Roman Law, although one of its implications was never wholly lost. The Jews were only slowly deprived of the right to hold land, a right not usually possessed by a stranger in Germanic Custom. Only the third of their privileges remained, that which granted them a wide measure of judicial autonomy.

On the other hand, the restrictions on the social, religious and professional life of the Jews, which the piety of Christian emperors and the zeal of the Church had imposed during the fourth and fifth centuries, these remained embodied in ecclesiastical collections of laws and passed thence into the practice of the Middle Ages. Special taxation also, though it grew up in the Carolingian era without any thought of Roman precedent, ultimately came to find its sanction in the *aurum coronarium* of Roman days.

The second pillar was Canon Law. Whereas Roman Law was succeeded by a long silence on the part of the national law-givers, the Church continued in an uninterrupted sequence her legislation about the Jews. It turned consistently on the two points with which we are already familiar: the prevention of Jewish influence or authority over Christians, and the relegation of the Jews to the status of social inferiority befitting a deicide people. Instead of the protection which had been guaranteed by Roman Law, and which remained effective in principle, even if practice sometimes transgressed it, the Jew had to be satisfied with an ineffective ban on excessive persecution. Nowhere is the conception of the Jew as an accursed deicide more apparent than in this substitution, and nothing illustrates more vividly his utter rightlessness in medieval society. Only against his murder would the Church, the guardian of the oppressed, lift up her voice. If an order went out for his expulsion, the Church approved, for Christian society was better without his presence; if his property were confiscated, the Church rejoiced, for his wealth had been collected by forbidden means; if his children were baptized by force, the Church regretted it, but doctrine forbade any attempt to restore the child to the home and the religion of his fathers.

The third pillar was Germanic Custom. When the pagan or Arian barbarians succeeded to the western provinces of the Roman empire they regarded the Roman citizens as strangers, and usually allowed them to enjoy their existing laws. But, when the barbarians became Catholic, the distinction between the two societies gradually vanished; the 'Romans' came to think of themselves by the same names as their conquerors, Franks, Burgundians or Visigoths, and only the Jews remained distinct. To retain the whole structure even of the shortened Roman Codes for their special benefit was evidently impracticable, apart from the fact that it would have run counter to the universal tradition of the Church. The Jews therefore remained in the position of 'strangers', with the additions already indicated, that they did not automatically forfeit their traditional autonomy in the regulation of their own community, and that they continued to hold land.

According to Germanic Custom, a stranger was an object without a master. In so far as he was not protected, either by a powerful individual, or by inter-tribal or international arrangement, he did not enjoy the most elementary rights. He could be killed, and his murderer could not be punished; any man who gave him lodging was responsible for his actions; his property was ownerless, and his heir had no right of inheritance.

At a later period royal protection was extended to those who had no other. But the normal procedure was for the stranger to seek the protection of the chief man on the spot. To him he paid a tax. If he failed to seek it and to pay the tax, and if the sovereign had not accorded it, then at the end of a year and a day he became a slave. The stranger lived according to the laws of his protector, and an attack on him was regarded as an attack on the latter. In the case of an important chief, such as a king, a special official was sometimes appointed who saw that he was protected for his master's sake.

We have here many of the elements of the Jewish position, but it is obvious that this custom was evolved to deal with men of a very different category from the settled Jewries of western Europe. The stranger contemplated was more likely to be a pilgrim, or travelling merchant, who would need the protection but for a short period; or, if he sought residence, he was more likely to be a fugitive or refugee. Certainly nothing was contemplated so abnormal as two resident communities living side by side, following similar occupations, pursuing the same daily life, but governed by different laws and customs. With but little modification established custom could be fitted to meet the needs of the first Jewish arrivals amid the Germanic tribes and nations, for they were travelling merchants in search of slaves, skins, amber, and other products of north-eastern Europe or of Russia. They sought no right of residence, and the only privileges which they required were on questions of tax and toll. But they were succeeded by settlers, and it was soon evident that more would be needed than Germanic Custom by itself offered a precedent for supplying.

II. SUBSEQUENT DEVELOPMENT

It was when more regulation was needed that the one remaining relic of Roman privilege appeared the most priceless possession of European Jewry—their communal autonomy. Judaism naturally needs buildings for worship, but its religious principles also compel a community to have in its own control all the mechanism for governing daily life and the relations between members. It is possible that the tolerance with which the Arian barbarians had left the Catholic churches in the possession of the Catholic Romans might have enabled them to overlook the possession of synagogues by Jews. But since Canon Law forbade new synagogues to be built, this would have been a very slender reed for a new Jewish community to count on. Certainly Christian tradition would never have sanctioned anything parallel to the special courts, special butchers, baths, schools and other manifestations of difference, the enjoyment of which was, in fact, never fundamentally questioned, since they were already established, and had the sanction of Roman Law. Without this sanction, and the toleration it encountered, Jewish life would have become impossible in Europe in the measure in which Christian conceptions reared the structure of feudal society. Certain foreign communities, merchants of the Hanse, of the different Italian towns and others, did acquire communal autonomy for their settlements, but this was by mutual arrangement, and the Jews had nothing ' mutually ' to offer. The result could only have been their total departure from the continent in the search for more tolerant surroundings. For it is on the basis of this essential communal autonomy that the Jewish communities faced the increasing rigour with which their lives were circumscribed.

The earliest innovations were connected with the occupation of travelling merchant, and the tax, which the Jew had originally paid merely for the right to exist, came to be considered a duty on his merchandise, so that it is sometimes stated that a Jew entering a place without goods, does so without paying a toll. But though its original explanation was completely forgotten, it never wholly lost its original meaning, and later German lawyers identified it with the *aurum coronarium*, and considered it an additional poll tax, to be paid direct to the emperor, whatever other taxes the Jew within the empire might pay to him or to any other authority. This change of explanation is an interesting example of the complexity of the origins of the Jewish status. For while the taxes on Jews tended to increase, and to find new justifications, other strangers saw special taxes diminish—and, indeed, vanish—before the period was very far developed.

It was primarily to protect them on their commercial journeys that Louis the Pious granted a number of ' passports ' to Jewish families, for it was almost only as merchants that attention was drawn to the Jews. But when attention was drawn to them, then their status as Jews was likely to bring them a slightly heavier burden than that placed on Christian merchants. From the decisions of the Assembly of Quierzy in the ninth century, by which Jews paid tolls of one-tenth, and Christians of one-eleventh[1], down to the charters of Jewish and Lombard money-lenders of the fourteenth century, this rule holds good. The discrimination, which began with slightly higher tolls, ended with the complete exclusion of the Jews from one profession after another as the centuries passed on, until they were forced to accept the openings left to them, and, in particular, the trade of money-lender and dealer in second-hand goods.

The eleventh century revealed that it was not enough to consider the Jew merely as a travelling merchant. The number of cities in which permanent Jewish settlements existed was undoubtedly increasing, and a regulation of their status desirable. This was all the more necessary as the spread of the communal movement towards the end of the century made the whole development of the towns a burning issue. In these new settlements there was no tradition of citizenship behind the Jewish residence. Hence, while the Jews of the ninth century required passports, those of the eleventh required communal statutes. The earliest of these which has survived incorporated a Jewish commune within the growing city of Speyer in 1084.

But these new privileges, extensive as they often were, were granted for the profit of their owners, and not for the sake of justice or generosity to the Jews themselves. It was only by express permission that any of the rightlessness of the Germanic ' stranger ' was waived in their favour. When Henry IV fined the murderers of Jews in 1096, or sought

---

[1] Cap. xxxi; MGH, LL, I, p. 540.

to regain their property which had been stolen, it was for his own treasury that he did it[1]. Similarly, when a Jew died, his property was the possession of his owner. In practice the heir was usually allowed to purchase it back for a sum, but, when the owner decided so to do, he took it. There are many cases of this, the most famous being that of Aaron of Lincoln, whose property was so extensive that a special department of the Exchequer had to be created to administer it. A case which occurred in northern France in 1240 is very instructive, for it showed that apart from a written privilege, the owner's right to the property could not be contested even in the thirteenth century. Three Jews challenged the right of Gimbaud, Baron of S. Veranus, to the property of their parents who had lived on the Baron's territory, apparently without any special position in relation to him. The Baron consented to submit the case to the arbitration of the Archbishop of Sens. The Archbishop decided that the parents had belonged to Gimbaud, together with all their property, and all claims and rights which they possessed at the time of their deaths[2].

The First Crusade introduced yet another problem. For it made it clear that the Jews needed protection not merely as merchants or as residents, but as non-Christians, exposed to the violence of Christian fanaticism, and inadequately protected by the mere fact of possessing a regular position in the social scheme. Hence came the inclusion of the Jews in the General Peace sworn by the different powers within the empire in 1103[3]. In it the Jews are classed with women and clergy as people who cannot protect themselves—but it is to be noted that they are classed with groups which by no means lacked civil rights.

All these separate threads were woven into a single cord in the evolution of the idea of the 'servitudo camerae', the position of 'serfs of the treasury', which was the final

---

[1] While this was the normal procedure there are, as usual, exceptions, especially in the south. As late as 1289 the Parliament of Toulouse ordered damages to be paid to some Jews of the Archbishop of Narbonne who had been illegally tortured by the servants of the Viscount of Narbonne. Regné, *Etude sur la Condition des Juifs de Narbonne*; REJ, LVIII, p. 223.

[2] Teulet, II, p. 431, No. 2873.

[3] See Ch. III, p. 81.

medieval definition of Jewish status. In this evolution the conception of ' stranger ' was in some aspects linked to the conception of ' villein ', for the villein was also a person who was rightless in so far as his personal lord was concerned. But in practice custom gave the villein more security than the Jew, and as the Middle Ages developed the disparity became more marked.

It is in the beginning of the twelfth century that the conception makes its first recognisable appearance. In the *Laws of Saint Edward*, a compilation of that period, it is written that ' the Jews and all their property belong to the king '[1]. Either in 1157 or 1182 the actual phrase, ' servi camerae ', first occurs in a German charter[2]. The conception of belonging to the treasury, however, was independent of the actual phrase[3].

Even in Spain the Germanic custom finally prevailed over the local tradition. For in the Spain of the Reconquest the Jews did not pass from almost complete rightlessness to the relative security of dependence on a prince, but rather in the opposite direction. The Jews lived under both Moorish and Christian sovereigns. In each territory members of the dominant religion naturally had certain privileges. But in almost every respect the religious minorities enjoyed equality. The increase of religious intolerance in the Christian kingdoms from the thirteenth century onwards weighed heavily on both Moor and Jew, but it is not till the fourteenth century that local history came to be so far forgotten that a Spanish king declared in the exact manner of the emperor, that ' the Jews are ours and the peculiar patrimony of the royal treasury '[4]. The phrase occurs in a number of forms in different countries, but it is difficult to imagine a more sweeping declaration of complete possession than that made by Henry III of England that ' no Jew shall remain in

---

[1] *Leges Ecclesiasticae S. Edwardi Regis*, xxi; Mansi, XIX, c. 719. Cf. Maitland and Pollock, *History of English Law*, 2nd ed., 1898, I, p. 468.

[2] Confirmation by Frederick I of Charter to Jews of Worms in 1157, or the Privilege of the same emperor to the Jews of Regensburg in 1182. The doubt is due to the fact that the former charter exists only in a thirteenth-century copy.

[3] See *Mitteilungen des Gesamt-Archivs der Deutschen Juden*, IV, pp. 45 ff., for a discussion of the whole question.

[4] Baer, *Aragon*, No. 317.

England, unless he serve the king, and as soon as any Jew is born, whether male or female, let him serve Us in some way '[1].

Of the development of the attitude of the Church, little needs to be said. The violence of popular superstition must be distinguished from the judgments of Popes and Councils. But the latter remained effective guardians of the principle that the Jews must be kept in a condition of servitude. By the establishment of the Jewish badge at the fourth Lateran Council in 1215, and the slow establishment of the ghetto culminating in its official enactment at Basel in 1434, the Church did far more than the princes to ensure the final degradation of the Jewish communities of medieval Europe.

Finally, the slow and complicated growth of the peculiar status of the Jew was completely forgotten, and the jurist of the thirteenth century seeking an explanation of it found it in Roman history. The Saxon Law Code of 1230 traced the origin of their protection to the promise granted by Vespasian to Josephus who had cured Titus of gout; and the Swabian Code, half a century later, discovered the origin of the imperial right to exact special taxes from the Jews in the confiscation by Vespasian of the Temple Tax, and his conversion of it into a tax into the Privy Purse. Alternatively, a personal ' passport ' granted to two Jews by the Emperor Frederick II in 1234 implies that the cause for the need of such documents was ' the defencelessness of the Jews ' and the origin of the right to give it ' the prerogative of Christian Law '[2]. By a contrary fiction the same emperor, in granting a charter to the citizens of Vienna in 1237, excluded the Jews from office ' because from primitive times the imperial authority has decreed perpetual servitude to the Jews as a perpetual punishment for their crime '[3].

III. THE GRANTORS OF THE CHARTERS

Germanic custom allowed either the king or some local magnate to assume the protection of a ' stranger '. This explains the diverse origin of the charters which we possess.

[1] Tovey, *Anglia Judaica*, p. 147.
[2] Aronius, No. 468.
[3] Scherer, p. 132.

Some are granted by kings, some by cities, some by clerical
and secular princes. In some cases we possess charters for
the same Jewish community issuing from different sources.
Thus Rüdiger, Bishop of Speyer, issued a charter to his Jews
in 1084, and six years later a different charter was granted
to the same community by the Emperor Henry IV. The
Jewish community of Ratisbon fell under the jurisdiction of
three authorities, the Emperor, the Count, and the City.
The Jews of Narbonne were divided into two Jewries, a
viscountal and an archiepiscopal, each possessing different
rights.

The varying conditions of Jewish settlement also led to
differences in their legal bases. In the south of Europe the
Jewish communities had been settled in many centres from
Roman times. Only their religious privileges differentiated
them from other citizens. Often there was no sign of any
special regulations of their position until the end of the
Middle Ages, when they began to share the decline of western
European Jewry. In the north the settlements were frequently artificial. Jews were introduced or reintroduced into
a centre for the sole purpose of usury. Naturally, such
specialised settlements required a different type of charter
from that needed by a community following many different
occupations.

In the earlier stages of medieval history the only possible
conflict about a settlement was between the secular authority,
granting a charter, and the ecclesiastical, demanding the
strict observance of Canon Law. But in the fourteenth and
fifteenth centuries it is common to find a conflict between
the prince and the city, or between the national authority
and the local, for Jewish settlement had sunk into being
a kind of financial speculation which, at best, benefited only
the speculator. There results a double struggle, first to get
hold of the profits, then, of the defeated party, to prevent
the speculation turning to his disadvantage. The causes of
this conflict are evident. After all, the Jews obtained money
to pay heavy taxes by the usury which they charged. In
Bohemia, at the end of the fifteenth century, in order to meet
these payments they were actually allowed to exact double
the usury demanded by a Christian[1]. If the Jews belonged

[1] Bondy, No. 292.

to the overlord, he collected this money, and could still claim
to tax his subjects. If they belonged to a local baron or a
city, and these possessed the right of taxation, they could pay
a large part of the taxes or exactions demanded of them by
their sovereigns by extracting money from the Jews. The
efforts of the central powers were, therefore, to retain the Jews
in their own hands, that of the cities and the barons to extract
from the Jews their share of the burdens of local taxation.
The same conflict also appears in judicial matters, the kings
and princes striving to retain jurisdiction over the Jews for
themselves, and the barons and cities demanding the subjection of the Jews to the local courts. As monetary fines
formed a large proportion of the punishments meted out, the
reason for the conflict is obvious.

When the granting of the charters had become a mere
speculation, it is not surprising that, like other speculations,
they offered little security to their victims. When the town
of Brüx, which had been temporarily pawned to Saxony, did
homage to their new Elector in 1425, the citizens specified
in writing that they were to retain possession of their Jew,
Michael of Melnik[1]. But forty years later they requested and
received permission to expel their Jews, on condition that
they made good the taxes which the Jews had paid[2]; although
it is probable that, like others who took the same step, they
soon regretted it, and either got the Jews back to pay their
own taxes or obtained a remission of them from their prince.
A similar spirit of speculation possessed the citizens of Eger
throughout the fifteenth century. They were in perpetual
conflict with the King of Bohemia as to whether they would
accept Jews or not. In 1430 it was the king, Sigmund, who
ordered the burghers to expel the Jews, and it was the
burghers who protested, and who, four years later, obtained
permission to invite Jews again to settle in the town[3]. But in
1480 it was the burghers who petitioned the king for permission to expel their Jews, and the king who did not wish
to do it. However, in 1497 the burghers finally got their way,
and Vladyslav IV allowed them to expel the Jews, and

---

[1] Bondy, Nos. 216 and 217.

[2] *Ibid.*, No. 263.

[3] *Ibid.*, Nos. 220 and 225.

promised that he would never again give Jews permission
to settle in the town[1].

IV. THE JEWS AS PRIVATE PROPERTY

One of the greatest trials of the Jewish communities was
that the conferment of a charter never involved a final
surrender of the property rights of the giver of the charter.
It was one of the basic causes of Jewish insecurity during the
whole of the period that the most liberal grants, made with
the most solemn assertions that they would remain un-
changed either in perpetuity or at least for a specified number
of years, might at a moment's notice be either entirely
revoked or at least sensibly modified. Both in the practice and
in the theory of medieval law the Jew was fundamentally
rightless[2]. With but the rarest exceptions the utmost liberty
that an individual could obtain was a privileged exemption
from taxation or from the various humiliations to which
the Jewries were subjected, and a community could hardly
achieve even this. Communal taxes might at times be
remitted, but only because the Jews were at the moment
bled white, and a breathing space would allow them to
collect further profit to be later transferred to the royal
treasury.

Cases have already been quoted from the tenth and
eleventh centuries of the gift or transfer of the Jews of a
particular place to the authority of someone other than the
king or emperor[3]. In 1098 Pedro I of Aragon presented
the monastery of Leire with half the custom dues of the Jews
of Ruesta; and in the following year he presented a church in
Huesca with the tithes paid him by the Jews of Montclus[4].
These two latter gifts excluded transference of property in
the Jews, a point on which the earlier German grants are
completely vague. But the motive of both is clearly financial
advantage; and they are the precursors of a number of later

---

[1] Bondy, Nos. 275, 276 and 293.

[2] Cf. F. I. Schechter, *The Rightlessness of Medieval English Jewry*;
JQR, n.s. IV, pp. 121 ff.

[3] See above, p. 41.

[4] Baer, *Aragon*, Nos. 11 and 12.

grants where the recipient obtained not certain rights but exclusive ownership of the Jew concerned.

As the Middle Ages advanced, different practices grew up in different countries. In England the king never surrendered his authority over the Jews of the whole country[1], even though on three occasions he pawned them or gave them away. In France, up to the expulsion of 1306, the Jews might belong either to the king or the barons. The king could only claim as of right the jurisdiction over Jews on the royal demesne. Questions relative to other Jews were a matter for treaty between him and his barons. In Spain as in France Jews might live on either royal or baronial demesnes, and those who lived on the latter were normally free from taxes imposed on their neighbours in the former. But the king had the right to reclaim royal Jews who fled to baronial lands[2], and to compel the debtors of royal Jews to pay their debts, even if the debtors were subjects of the barons[3]. He could also decree that general regulations as to the rate of interest and other matters should apply to all Jews of the kingdom, wherever they might be living[4].

In the empire, the emperor claimed a final right in all the Jews resident within his frontiers, though he might, and frequently did, surrender this right to others. That in this question his position was far weaker than that of other sovereigns is obvious. It is also natural, for his authority was less than that of most national kings and the need for conciliating powerful interests was greater.

While in most cases the transfers of sovereignty present no particular interest, a few will show the variety of the form of transfer. In 1281 Rudolf of Habsburg surrendered authority over the Jews of the city and diocese of Ratisbon to the Bishop, ordered them to be obedient to him, never to oppose themselves to him in any legal matter, and, further, to remain within their houses in Holy Week, and observe all other

---

[1] This does not apply to the French possessions of the English monarchs. Cf. *Patent Rolls*, 1225-32, p. 387, where Henry allows a baron to keep Jews in Poitou ' sicut . . . ceteri Barones Pictavenses habent in terris suis '.

[2] Regné, *Catalogue*, No. 2324; REJ, LXIX, p. 213.

[3] *Ibid.*, No. 103; LX, p. 181.

[4] *Ibid.*, No. 3410; LXXVIII, p. 139.

canonical restrictions on their behaviour[1]. So unusual a secular insistence on what was primarily an ecclesiastical interest may be due to the effort being made by Rudolf to secure duchies for his two sons, an effort in which he was prepared to make considerable concessions to the German princes.

In 1299 his son, Albert of Habsburg, who had just overcome his rival, Adolf of Nassau, set about restoring the Jewish communities in the Rhineland which had been decimated by fanatical bands of peasants as the result of accusations of ritual murder. One of the chief supporters of Adolf had been his uncle, the Archbishop of Mainz, but when the Archbishop finally came over to Albert, the latter, in order to confirm his support, granted him all the loans of the dead Jews who had been victims of the riots and had not left heirs[2]. Three years later, when he needed the support of the Princes of the Rhineland in his conflict with Boniface VIII, he granted to the Archbishop the living Jews of Frankfurt also[3]. At times we find not a whole community, but a single individual, presented to a needy friend, as when in 1197 Odo of Burgundy gave the Jew Eli and his family to a man named Vigier[4].

Such gifts were not always made in perpetuity. It frequently happened that the emperors made their gifts conditional. Albert himself was less generous to the Archbishop of Cologne than to his colleague of Mainz, for he granted the former a number of Jewish communities with the express proviso that he might himself tax them to any extent he liked when it seemed to him opportune to do so[5]. The Emperor Henry VII stated in some of his grants of Jews the price at which he might redeem them[6]. His successor, Lewis

---

[1] MGH, LL, II, p. 426.

[2] *Ibid.*, p. 471.

[3] *Ibid.*, p. 477.

[4] J. Simmonet, *Juifs et Lombards*, in Mémoires de l'Académie de Dijon, IIe Série, XIII, p. 152, n. 1. In Aragon, Jews were frequently given to the great orders; Regné, *Catalogue*, Nos. 11 and 35; REJ, LX, pp. 164, 168; Baer, *Aragon*, Nos. 26, 38, 41, 46a, 67, 74, 76, 79. Cf. No. 78, where a Jewish Community protests against such gifts which reduce its power of paying its taxes. For the various details involved in such a gift, cf. *Close Rolls of Edward I*, 1279-88, p. 245; *ibid.*, 1288-96, p. 99.

[5] MGH, LL, IV, Const. IV, i, p. 21.

[6] E.g., in gift to Diethmar of Catzenellenbogen; MGH, LL, IV, Const. IV, ii, p. 836.

I

the Bavarian, with a truer sense of the usual condition of imperial finances, used to state the sum that the recipients of the Jews might extract from them, or the period for which they might enjoy them. This extracted[1], or the period expired[2], the Jews reverted to the Imperial Treasury.

He who had no Jews to give away could obtain equally useful results by granting to a subordinate the right to acquire Jews on his own. For example, the Dauphin, in 1315, conceded to certain of his barons the right to have and to hold within their jurisdiction 'Lombards, Jews and other usurers '[3]. In 1435 the Emperor Sigmund, King of Bohemia, granted a property at Falkenhayn to Casper and Matthias Schlick, and allowed them to keep Jews on it[4]. In 1353, when Jews were excluded from the royal territory, John of France allowed the Abbot of Saint Denys to have and to hold under his own jurisdiction up to five Jewish families in the town and castle belonging to the abbey[5].

The kings of Bohemia were in the habit of being very precise as to the number of Jews they allowed to barons or to towns. In 1294 Ulrich von Neuhaus asked Wenceslaus permission to settle at Neuhaus eight Jews and their families. He promised that, if the permission were granted, he would allow only the head of each family to practise money-lending; and, in asking leave to replace any who left, he promised not to take them from the King's Jewries. But he wanted his Jews to be allowed to ' do at the pleasure of his will all those things which the King's Jews do at the King's pleasure, and to perform for him all the services which the King's Jews performed for the King '[6]. King John in 1322 allowed the Bishop of Olmütz to keep one Jew in each of his four towns[7]; in 1334 he allowed Peter of Rosenberg to keep four on his estates[8]; and his successor, the Emperor Charles IV, allowed

[1] E.g., MGH, LL, IV, Const. V, p. 297.
[2] Ibid., p. 320.
[3] Valbonais, Histoire de Dauphiné, I, p. 74.
[4] Bondy, No. 227.
[5] Laurière, IV, p. 139, iv.
[6] Bondy, No. 39.
[7] Ibid., No. 52.
[8] Ibid., No. 70.

the town of Budweis to keep three on specially favourable conditions[1].

Such concessions raised a number of problems for the different parties concerned, which can be illustrated from various gifts of James II of Aragon. In 1316 he granted the Infante Alphonso permission to settle Jews in a number of his towns[2]. But he retained the right of the royal Jewries in the towns which these settlers quitted to collect from them their contribution to the royal taxes. This obviously robbed the gift of much of its attraction, and it is to be presumed that the Infante protested, for next year the king told the community of Lerida not to tax the Infante's Jews who came from that town[3]. In 1324 the same king allowed Otto de Moncade, Lord of Aytona, to settle ten royal Jews from Lerida in his castle[4]. But the community of Lerida tried to stop them going[5]. At the same time the king told the baron that if he could get his Jews from baronial territories, he could settle a larger number. An excellent source of supply for those who wished to collect Jews was also provided by expulsion orders in neighbouring states. A number of Spanish noblemen at this period received permission to settle Jews expelled from France[6].

Towns and barons, once granted these privileges, were tenacious of them, and tried to make settlement attractive. The town of Breslau, for example, in conferring a series of charters on a Jewess and her family was careful to make the conditions as favourable as possible. They were to pay no tax other than the tax to the king; they could preserve their own laws; they would be protected from the clerical courts; and they might leave the city when they wanted to[7]. But it is not so certain that all such favourable conditions were actually carried out.

[1] Bondy, No. 140.

[2] Regné, *Catalogue*, No. 3057; REJ, LXXVII, p. 179.

[3] *Ibid.*, No. 3070; p. 181. This problem occurs on many occasions: e.g. when the Emperor Lewis in 1330 gave the Jews of Thuringia to his son-in-law; Lewinsky, *Regesten zur Geschichte der Juden in Sachsen*; MGWJ, XLIX, p. 746. Cf. below, p. 257, n. 2.

[4] Regné, *Catalogue*, No. 3311; REJ, LXXVIII, p. 123.

[5] *Ibid.*, No. 3367; cf. No. 3445; pp. 132 and 145.

[6] *Ibid.*, Nos. 3245 and 3265; pp. 112 and 116.

[7] Bondy, Nos. 117, 119, 122.

Another right of private property is the right to sell, pawn or exchange it, and cases where Jews are sold, pawned and exchanged are not infrequent. An early example comes from Burgundy, where Duke Odo in 1196 granted his Jews in Dijon to the town in exchange for the town of Fenay[1]. Henry III pawned his Jews once to Richard of Cornwall, and assigned them once to his son Edward, who pawned them to their rivals the Cahorsins[2]. In Spain the gift of a Jew seems sometimes to have been designed to benefit primarily the Jew concerned; for Pedro II of Aragon, in giving Rabbi Asser Abenbentraca and his posterity to the Knights of Saint John, did so in recognition of his faithful services, and at the Rabbi's request[3].

The cases so far quoted deal with the surrender of Jews in one form or another to lesser authorities. But cases frequently occur where, in making a gift of territory, or in conceding a privilege, the Jews are explicitly withheld. One of the earliest instances of this occurred in Spain. In 1106 the Viscount of Gerona ceded the fortress of Balaguer to Arnald Berenger de Anglerola, but explicitly withheld ' the merchants, whether Christians, Moors or Jews, together with their houses, stores, and all the income derived therefrom '[4]. From then onwards the practice became common, and examples of it are found in all parts. In 1218 the Archbishop of Rouen, in a letter to Philip Augustus, recognised that the king had reserved to his justice cases between Jews and citizens in Dieppe[5]. The same king, in conferring a charter on the Abbot of Fécamp, excluded—and the Abbot agreed to the exclusion—all jurisdiction over usurers and Jews, which he reserved to himself[6]. Similarly, Philip of Boulogne, receiving the town of Boulogne from Louis VIII, explicitly recognised that this grant did not include the loans of the Jews settled there, which remained in the king's hands[7]. When Henry III of England in 1256 granted to Guy de

[1] J. Simmonet, loc. cit., p. 151.
[2] Tovey, Anglia Judaica, pp. 135, 157 ff.
[3] Baer, Aragon, No. 66.
[4] Ibid., No. 14.
[5] Teulet, I, p. 461, No. 1282.
[6] Ibid., p. 373, No. 977.
[7] Ibid., II, p. 24, No. 1630.

Roquefort the castle of Colchester and the lands belonging to it, he excluded ' the wood of Kingswood and the Jews of the town '[1]. And just as Henry III retained his Jews and a forest, so Theobald of Champagne, in granting a charter to Provins, excludes ' the jurisdiction and protection of his churches, his knights, his fiefs, and his Jews '[2].

An exercise of the rights of ownership which must have been peculiarly galling to the Jew concerned, was the giving away of all or part of his property, without troubling to inform him. The right existed everywhere, but few seem to have practised it with such regularity as Henry III of England and his successor, Edward I. While Henry was pursuing his inglorious ' war ' in Gascony at various dates during his reign, it was quite common for him to write home to the justices of the Jews to inform them that he had cancelled such and such a debt owing to such and such a Jew by one of his favourites of the moment. The Gascon Rolls are full of such documents[3]. Just according to his pleasure he cancelled the whole debt, half the debt, the interest or any other portion he pleased[4]. This was a fantastic interpretation of the law that a Jew's property belonged to his lord, but Henry III was responsible for other equally curious methods of extracting money. Compensation for excommunication was fairly commonly demanded, in both France and Spain, but there is a special ingenuity in the permission which Henry granted to the Jews of London to excommunicate any member of the community who refused to share in the expenses of maintaining the cemetery only on condition that they fined the delinquent an adequate sum, and that this came to the king and to no one else[5].

If it was possible to dispose of the property of a living Jew, it was even easier to dispose of it when he was dead. The complications of the rights of inheritance are discussed

---

[1] *Patent Rolls*, 1247-58, p. 482; cf. F. I. Schechter, *loc. cit.*; JQR, n.s., IV, p. 142.

[2] Teulet, II, p. 185, No. 2075. Cf. p. 218a, No. 2153, where similar charters are given to Châtillon and Dornans.

[3] Col. doc., *Rôles Gascons*, I, Nos. 52, 62, 84, 115, 133, 152, 1252, 1377, 1391, 1433, 1660, etc.

[4] *Ibid.*, No. 1414 cancellation of interest; Nos. 1396, 1875, 2666, 2862, no interest during service with the king.

[5] *Patent Rolls*, 1247-58, p. 72.

later[1], but that no rights could prevent arbitrary actions is shown by the cynical gifts of the Emperor Charles IV in 1349. In February he gave the Archbishop of Trier the goods of the Jews in Alsace and elsewhere ' who have already been killed or may still be killed '. And in June he offered the Margrave of Brandenburg his own choice of the three best Jewish houses in Nuremberg ' when there is next a massacre of the Jews there '[2]. The sinister background of this princely generosity is the Black Death, which led to the massacre of countless Jews by a superstitious populace which believed that they had caused the pest by poisoning the wells.

Yet one more aspect of the private property in Jews is worth chronicling. The loans of the Jews belonged to their lord. If, therefore, they lent money to another lord, or, worse still, to the subjects of another lord, there was a risk that the loan might be lost through some action over which the owner had no authority. In one case a certain Godfrey of Duilley ran into debt to the Jews belonging to Count Theobald of Champagne, and the latter compelled him to surrender all his dues on certain Champagne fairs until the debt was extinguished[3]. His namesake, Theobald of Troyes, made a treaty in 1198 with his uncle, Philip Augustus, by which each promised that his Jews should not make any loans to the subjects of the other[4]. The converse to the risk involved when a Jew lent to the subjects of another also engaged attention. For if a foreign Jew lent money to a subject, not only was the repayment sent out of the territory, an important consideration when currency was short, but no profit in the loan accrued to the lord concerned. Philip VI of France in 1340, one of the periods during which Jews were not allowed to live in France, had a simple method of dealing with those of his subjects who sought financial assistance elsewhere. Not only did he prohibit them from

---

[1] See below, p. 264.

[2] S. Adler, *Geschichte der Juden in Mülhausen*, p. 18. Henry III of England also offered a house in London Jewry to William of Bedford ' quancito opportunitas se optulerit '. Col. doc., *Rôles Gascons*, I, 1124.

[3] Teulet, II, p. 217b, No. 2150.

[4] *Ibid.*, I, p. 197, No. 479.

making any repayment, but, if any were so rash as to do so, he ordered an equivalent sum to be paid to himself by way of a fine[1].

V. PROTECTION OF JEWS FROM THE SOVEREIGNTY OF OTHERS

In the thirteenth century, when the power of the monarchy in France was scarcely greater than that of the barons, the question of the ownership of Jews continually arose. Louis VIII in 1223 concluded a general treaty with his barons, by which each promised that he would not seize the Jews of another[2]. Louis IX extended this arrangement in a general convention at Melun in 1230. He agreed that any baron might seize one of his Jews whom he found in the domain of another baron, however long he might have resided there; and he made this agreement compulsory among all the barons of the kingdom[3]. Like Louis VIII, he confirmed this agreement by a series of treaties concluded with each separate baron[4]. But he went further and had the agreement embodied also in canons of the Church[5].

These treaties led to a number of disputes the settlement of which needed complicated enquiries. The registers of the Parliament of Louis IX are full of decisions in such cases[6]. In one instance two Jews living on the land of a certain abbess were adjudged to belong to the king. The abbess therefore requested the king either to have them baptized or to remove them, as she did not wish to have Jews on her territory. The king removed them[7]. Sometimes this division of sovereignty led to domestic tragedies, as when the King of Aragon wrote

[1] Laurière, II, p. 143.

[2] Ibid., I, p. 47.

[3] Ibid., p. 53.

[4] For a series of these separate treaties see Teulet, II, pp. 153b, No. 1996, and 174b, No. 2049. For the similar individual treaties made by Louis VIII, before the general agreement of 1223, cf. ibid., I, p. 350, No. 922 (1210), and confirmations of the treaty of 1223, ibid., II, pp. 15-18, Nos. 1612, 1615, 1619, 1620. In some cases the barons also made treaties with each other.

[5] E.g., Béziers, 1255, canon xxvii; Mansi, XXIII, c. 883.

[6] See Col. doc., Les Olim, I, index, ' judaeus ' passim.

[7] Ibid., p. 893.

to Alphonse of Poitiers asking for the return of his Jew, Bonus of Mas d'Agenais in the Seneschaussée of Toulouse. Alphonse agreed, provided that Bonus had paid all tallages due from him, and ordered the seneschal to ascertain from the Jewish community whether he had done so, and whether also they could show any reason why the return should not be allowed. But Bonus had married a Jewess belonging to Alphonse, and the seneschal was therefore ordered to ensure that none of the property of his wife was removed when Bonus was given permission to depart[1].

The first blow at these complications was struck by Philip the Fair, whose need of money was continuous. He ordered his royal officials to see that none of the rights possessed by the different barons interfered with the persons or commercial activities of the Jews of the kingdom[2]. Then, when he expelled them in 1306, he made the order of expulsion valid for the whole Jewry, on whomsoever's territory the individual Jew might be living. He was, however, prepared to allow the lord of that territory a share in the loot[3]. On the return of the Jews in 1315 Louis X, while otherwise leaving the barons in possession of their rights, retained an overriding permission to keep any baronial Jew whom he desired to have[4]; and finally in 1361, on their last sojourn in France, John expressly reserved to himself all rights over them, on whomsoever's territory they might happen to settle[5].

In thus securing the complete hold over the Jews of the country, the kings of France were more successful than those of Spain. Both in Aragon and Castile, the burden of royal taxation was such that there was a steady flight into the territories of the barons or of the great orders. As late as 1462 Henry IV of Castile complained of his inability to arrest the movement, and thus repair the ravages in his revenue which it caused[6].

---

[1] Col. doc., *Correspondance d'Alphonse de Poitiers*, No. 1313, of 1269.

[2] Unpublished document in *Catalogue d'Actes relatifs aux Juifs*; U. Robert, REJ, III, p. 222, No. 86.

[3] Cf. G. Saige, *Les Juifs de Languedoc*, pp. 101 ff.

[4] Laurière, I, pp. 595 ff., clause xi.

[5] *Ibid.*, III, pp. 473 ff., clause iv.

[6] Baer, *Castile*, No. 316; cf. Regné, *Catalogue*, Nos. 1649, 1980, 2255; REJ, LXVII, p. 214, LXIX, pp. 157 and 202.

In Germany the conflict flowed even more strongly in a centrifugal direction. The emperor more and more surrendered his authority over the Jews either to the great secular and ecclesiastical princes or to the towns[1]. This was due partly to their continual need of protection and partly to his continual need of money. But even so he retained a minimum of financial privileges, later represented by the 'opferpfennig' and by special payments on such occasions as his coronation. It was the unmanageable size of the empire rather than policy which created this difference. When they had the power, or could afford to, German emperors were just as anxious to retain their Jews as was any other owner. But in practice it was the princes rather than the emperors who were able to assert the authority exercised by the kings of France. Emperors would have found it useless to take the line of Vladyslav of Bohemia who, in 1499, forbade the Jews of Bohemia, under the enormous penalty of 6,000 Bohemian groschen, to place themselves under the protection of any authority other than himself[2].

Within the empire, even though the Jews belonged to, or were pawned to, innumerable different authorities, there was a certain amount of contact and intercommunication between the Jews of one authority and those of another. The Jews of the Archbishopric of Mainz were allowed to settle in imperial cities and *vice versa*, and it was a criminal offence to prevent such movement[3]. The Jews of the imperial city of Ulm possessed rights of taxation over Jews in the neighbouring territories of Ehingen and Schelklingen, until the owner of the latter Jews, the Duke of Austria, protested[4]. But to attempt to quit the territory of the empire altogether exposed the fugitive to the confiscation of his property within the Imperial territory[5].

How deeply engrained the idea of the possession of the Jews became may be finally illustrated from an example

---

[1] Cf. H. Fischer, *Die verfassungsrechtliche Stellung der Juden in den deutschen Städten während des 13. Jahrhunderts*, pp. 7 ff. See also Graetz, *Geschichte*, VIII, p. 3, on the surrender of the 'Judenregal' by Charles IV in the Golden Bull of 1356.

[2] Bondy, No. 300.

[3] MGH, LL, IV, Const. III, p. 267, n. 3.

[4] *Ibid.*, Const. VIII, p. 642.

[5] *Ibid.*, Const. III, p. 369.

connected with their expulsion from Spain in 1492. Some of the refugees went to Florence, and were there robbed. Whereupon Ferdinand wrote to the magistrates of the city and asked for full information on the subject, intervened in favour of the Jews, and demanded that they should be allowed to give their evidence in the presence both of an official of Florence appointed for the subject, and of the emissary of the King of Spain who was the bearer of the letter[1].

VI. PRESERVATION OF JURISDICTION OVER THE JEWS

Closely akin to the jealousy with which the sovereignty over the Jews was guarded, was the care with which the jurisdiction over suits in which they were involved was preserved. This resolved itself into a double conflict—with the Church and with the local authorities. To a certain extent the motive was the same in both cases—a pecuniary one[2]. For not only was medieval justice expensive for the litigants, so that considerable profits could be made out of it by the authority possessing the right to justice, but punishments consisted largely of fines. Apart also from lawsuits almost every Jewish action involved a payment to the licensing authority. Loans had to be registered, and for this a charge was made. To engage in trade a licence had to be obtained. To marry, or to abstain from marriage, might involve a payment. Change of residence, the burial of the dead, the introduction of a new member of the family or a new servant, all these actions might, and usually did, involve payments. It was therefore no light matter to surrender jurisdiction over the Jews.

In England and in Spain, where the central organisation was stronger than elsewhere, the justices of the Jews and royal judges worked steadily for the attainment of a monopoly of all cases affecting their charges, and with certain exceptions achieved it[3]. In France, Philip the Fair, as usual,

[1] Baer, *Castile*, No. 389.

[2] Other aspects of the struggle with the clergy are considered in the following section.

[3] Ch. Gross, *The Exchequer of the Jews of England*, in *Papers read at the Anglo-Jewish Exhibition*, 1887, I, p. 204.

allowed the financial motive to be perfectly plain. He forbade the Jews to be imprisoned without the permission of the royal bailiffs[1], and allowed the ecclesiastical courts to exercise jurisdiction over them—provided they only imposed canonical punishments, and not pecuniary ones[2]. The struggle in France to achieve royal authority over the Jews is parallel to the general struggle to achieve this supremacy. Louis VIII or Louis IX would never have dreamed of denying baronial courts the right to try the Jews belonging to the barony; but, in this as in other matters, on their final appearance from 1361 to 1395, the king managed to get into his own hands exclusive authority throughout the country, so that all the profits of justice flowed into his own coffers. In Germany such centralisation was never possible. The overriding authority of the emperor, which was incapable of protecting them effectively in times of danger, was too weak to supervise their legal needs and claims. But, on the other hand, in component parts of the empire—for example, in Austria and Bohemia—the same system obtained as in the west, and the prerogative of Jewish justice was jealously guarded by the ducal and royal courts.

VII. PROTECTION FROM CLERICAL SUPERSTITION

A large portion of the public history of the Jews in Roman times and in the Middle Ages is composed of the conflict of the secular and ecclesiastical authorities to enforce their particular view of the place of the Jews in Christian society. The formal reaction of the ecclesiastics to the granting of charters of privileges is considered in a later chapter[3]; but this was but a part of the day-to-day conflict between the two authorities. The two objects which the Church set itself—the protection of the Christian from contamination, and the conversion, or at least repression, of the Jews— could only be achieved in the measure in which she could balk the secular powers of their simpler aim, to squeeze as

[1] Laurière, I, p. 317.
[2] Unpublished ordinance in *Catalogue d'Actes relatifs aux Juifs*, No. 65; REJ, III, p. 220.
[3] See below, pp. 210 ff.

much money as possible out of their subjects through the channel of Jewish usury. In the end both failed to achieve more than a fragmentary victory. The Church lost the battle to defend the Christian community from Jewish influence, for Rashi was the inspiration of Nicholas Lyra, and

Si Lyra non lyrasset
Luther non saltasset.

She also failed to convert the Jew. But she succeeded in repressing Judaism, and in humiliating the Synagogue. The secular authorities failed to secure a permanent or steady revenue from their Jewish property, but they succeeded in creating a certain Jewish aptitude for finance which has enabled the Jews to weather a good many storms.

It is just because victory smiled on neither side that the struggle was so bitter. Only on the rare occasions when the royal power was so strong that the Church was helpless against it, or when an ecclesiastical prince—especially the Pope himself—combined secular and ecclesiastical jurisdiction in one benevolent hand, did matters go smoothly for the Jews. For the rest of the time they lived between the devil of royal extortion and the deep sea of ecclesiastical repression.

This latter manifested itself in four ways. There was, in the first place, the menace of religious superstition, for the accusations of ritual murder, poisoning of wells, and profanation of the Host were all believed by the more superstitious of the clergy. Secondly, there was the menace of the enforcement by ecclesiastical pains of strict obedience to the canons. Thirdly, there was the menace of enforced attendance at conversional activities. Fourthly, and lastly, the menace of the Inquisition threatened those who had fallen under its jurisdiction through involuntary baptism, and the still more involuntary acceptance of a Creed from which they could not recede.

Incidents have already been quoted from the Carolingian era of strange ceremonies connected with Good Friday and Easter[1]. The Jew who was killed by a ' ceremonial ' blow at Toulouse died at the hands of the Count's chaplain. The rioting at Béziers was initiated by a sermon in the cathedral from the bishop. The stoning at Chalons was the accompaniment of a religious procession. On this foundation an

[1] See above, pp. 42 ff.

even more sinister structure was reared by later centuries. In Spain, outrages at Passiontide seem to have continued all through the Middle Ages[1]; and with the growth of organised conversional activities and continual sermons on the crime of deicide, a fresh danger was added to Jewish life in that fanatical hatred might be stirred up at any season. For the Dominicans, and others who had authority to preach in the synagogues and to compel the Jews to listen to them, used to arrive in the Jewish quarter accompanied by a mob of Christians, who assaulted and insulted the unwilling auditors[2]. In Valentia the Knights of Saint John seem to have gone farther, for they broke a door through the wall of the Jewish quarter in order to introduce crucifixes and other religious objects into the streets of the Jews, with a view to raising riots[3].

It was from the clergy that nearly all the accusations of ritual murder arose, and they alone profited by them. The ' saint ' and his shrine brought many pilgrims and offerings to the fortunate possessors of the body. This is evident from an incident connected with the first of all these accusations, the alleged murder of William of Norwich in 1144. At the time when the case first roused interest, the Prior of Lewes happened to be staying in Norwich. Before anything had been ' proved ' as to how the boy met his death, the Prior tried to get the body for Lewes Priory, for he realised that it might become an object ' of conspicuous veneration and worship '[4]. It is also tragically significant that with this first accusation is coupled the name of a monk, Theobald of Cambridge, who was a converted Jew[5].

In the accusation of poisoning wells, the clergy also took a prominent part. The records of the earlier forms of the accusation are too vague to allow of any precise reconstruction, but, in the final rehearsal for the terrible events of the years 1348 and 1349, the whole responsibility rests with the clergy, especially with one priest who was a converted Jew.

---

[1] Cf. Regné, *Catalogue*, Nos. 2474 and 2478; REJ, LXXV, pp. 145 ff. A large number of similar cases are quoted throughout this collection.

[2] *Ibid.*, Nos. 746-748; LXIII, pp. 261 ff., etc.

[3] *Ibid.*, No. 1715; LXVIII, p. 200.

[4] A. Jessop and M. R. James, *St. William of Norwich*, p. 49.

[5] *Ibid.*, p. 93.

In a riot in Parthenay in western France in 1321, a letter with a golden seal was said to have been found in the house of a Jew, Bananias. It was in Hebrew, and was immediately suspected by the clergy to contain matters of importance. The converted Jew 'translated' it, and found that it revealed a huge plot of the Jews, the lepers, and the Saracens of Spain, to destroy the whole Christian population of Europe by poisoning the wells[1].

To say that these accusations were of clerical origin is not to imply that they were always disbelieved by the laity, any more than it implies that all the clergy believed them. The country nobility and the ordinary townsman were just as credulous as the country and urban clergy. The opposition to these accusations, when it came, came from the secular princes; and to a large extent its presence must be set down not merely to their self-interest, but to their obedience to the Papacy itself, which had strictly forbidden the most serious of all accusations, that of ritual murder. Papal action, however, only dates from the year 1247[2], whereas royal action can be traced a century earlier. The first time that such a charge was levelled against the Jews, at Norwich in 1144, they were allowed to take refuge from the anger of the mob in the royal castle, and were effectively protected by the sheriff[3]. In 1171, according to Hebrew reports, after the accusation at Blois and the deaths of a large proportion of the community, the Jews of France petitioned Louis VII for protection. The King replied that he had himself examined a similar accusation at Janville[4], and had found it false, and that he would therefore give them a charter forbidding the accusation. Similar action was taken by the Count of Champagne in the same year; and in 1187 the Archbishop of Mainz extracted an oath from the Jewish community that they did not kill a Christian in preparation for Passover, and accepted their declaration[5]. No traces of these documents

[1] Letter of Pope John XX; Mansi, XXV, c. 569.
[2] M. Stern, *Die Päpstlichen Bullen über die Blutbeschuldigung*, Nos. 1 and 2.
[3] Jessop and James, *op. cit.*, pp. 48 and 49.
[4] According to Gross this must be the place referred to, for Joinville, which is the name given by Salomo b. Simeon, would have been within the jurisdiction of the Counts of Champagne (*Gallia Judaica*, p. 254).
[5] Neubauer and Stern, Report of Salomo b. Simeon, pp. 149 and 152; and report of Elasar b. Judah, p. 214.

remain, and no reference is made to them elsewhere than in the Hebrew reports from which they are quoted. As the Jews had a very clear interest in claiming the existence of such denials, the evidence cannot be called first class. On the other hand, the reports are more or less contemporary, and the accusation was only just making its first appearance. The account of the death of William of Norwich makes it quite clear that people were slow to believe in ritual murder; and it must not be forgotten that this period, the end of the twelfth century, is the period in which different princes came to realise most completely the asset which they possessed in their Jewish property.

The next instance of princely protection is also related by the Hebrew chroniclers. Ephraim b. Jacob, a contemporary of the events which he is describing, relates the story of a riot at Speyer following on the discovery of the body of a Christian girl three miles from the city. The Jewish quarter was sacked, some lives were lost, the synagogue was burned. Duke Otto, brother of the Emperor Henry VI, who was Protector of the Jews, proceeded to harry the land of the bishop and citizens. His imperial brother, arriving shortly afterwards, arrested the murderers, fined the town heavily, and compelled them to pay 500 marks' compensation to the Jews as well as reconstruct the Jewish quarter and its synagogue[1].

The action taken by the Emperor Frederick II, in a case which was brought before him, is even more interesting. In 1236 there was an accusation of ritual murder at Hagenau, related in the chronicles of Marbach and of Richard of Sens. According to the latter, the emperor accepted a large bribe to protect the Jews, but according to the former he convened the wisest men of the empire and asked whether the accusation was true, asserting that if it was he would expel all the Jews from the empire. They were unable to find any proof of it, and the emperor, in consequence, dismissed the charge[2].

More dramatic, if less scholarly, was the action of King Rudolf in 1288. There had been an accusation of ritual murder in the Rhineland, the victim being a youth named

[1] Neubauer and Stern, Report of Ephraim b. Jacob, pp. 211 ff.
[2] MGH, SS, XVII, pp. 178 and XXV, p. 324.

Wernher. Forty Jews had been condemned to death, and many others imprisoned. The survivors appealed to Rudolf, promising him (according to the chronicler) a large sum of money. The king took two thousand marks, and then, we are told, compelled the Archbishop of Mainz to preach a sermon in which he stated that the body of Wernher ought to be burnt and its ashes scattered to the winds—and lest any Christian member of the congregation dared to disagree with this opinion, five hundred armed ' Jews ' were present at the sermon, ready to kill him on the spot[1].

The accusation that bribery was at the root of any acquittal is natural in the monastic chroniclers, and it need only be suspected in so far as it implies that but for the bribe the prince concerned would have believed in the murder. The story of Frederick II and the report of the actions of Louis VII contain nothing either incredible or even improbable; and at least the tradition is constant that the owners of the Jews were very ready to protect them against the accusation. After 1247 they could refer to Papal authority for so doing; and the bulls of Innocent IV and of later popes were not infrequently circulated at the request of different Jewish communities by the princes concerned[2]. A number of the charters of the ' Frederician '[3] family explicitly forbade the accusation, except under the safeguard that the Christian who made it found three Jews as well as three Christians to support it; and that the accuser, if his accusation failed, would meet the punishment which he demanded for the Jews[4].

VIII. PROTECTION OF THE JEWS FROM COURTS CHRISTIAN

Ritual murder and similar accusations, however, were not matters of everyday occurrence. Of much greater import

[1] *Chron. Colmar.;* MGH,SS, XVII, p. 255. Whether the 500 armed Jews are to be put down to monkish imagination, or represent a use of the word ' Jew ', not uncommon in earlier centuries, to denote anyone not behaving as a Christian ought to, must be left to the reader. I suspect it refers simply to the presence of imperial troops.

[2] Cf., for example, the charter of Ottokar II, 1254; Bondy, No. 25.

[3] See below, p. 178 and, e.g., Bondy, No. 25.

[4] Scherer, p. 319.

was the protection of the ordinary activities of the Jews from the jurisdiction of the Courts Christian. There were a number of offences which a Jew might commit, in regard to which the Church possessed an undeniable right of judgment. The difficulty came when the penalties imposed consisted of fines and confiscations which affected the value of the Jews to the prince. There was in the beginning of the fourteenth century an energetic Archbishop of Tarragona who, on charges of assisting conversion to Judaism, fined two Jewish communities 20,000 and 35,000 sous respectively, and decreed confiscation and exile against the chief offenders. The result was the complete inability of these communities to pay their taxes to the king, and the flight of a good many members of the communities concerned[1]. Such considerations alone made the princes anxious not to surrender their justice over the Jews to any other court. But when the Courts Christian were the alternatives, still more important considerations came into force. Canon Law and the charters of the princes viewed the status of the Jews from entirely different standpoints. Therefore, once a cleric succeeded in getting a Jewish plaintiff or defendant before an ecclesiastical judge, he had got him into a position very inferior to that which he would have enjoyed in a royal court.

To complicate the matter still further, clerics themselves were, in theory, outside the royal jurisdiction, so that— theoretically—a Jew and a cleric could never institute proceedings against each other, since the one could only be compelled to appear in the court of the prince and was exempt from other jurisdiction, and the other was similarly placed with regard to the court of the bishop. In actual practice the Church never made good the totality of this claim. In England, for example, clerics were constantly to be found both as plaintiffs and defendants in the royal courts. But the claim itself allowed her to protest against cases in which the change of court gave an unfair advantage to the Jew over the cleric.

The Council of London of 1257 gives the most comprehensive list of matters which were judged to belong exclusively to the jurisdiction of Courts Christian: an offence

---

[1] Regné, *Catalogue*, Nos. 2952, 2954, 2966, 2968; REJ, LXXVI pp. 194 ff.

K

against the person of a cleric, or the property of the Church, sacrilege, assault of a cleric, and adultery with a Christian woman[1]. It is unlikely that anywhere but in England, where the justices of the Jews had secured an extraordinary power in the thirteenth century, would jurisdiction in all these cases have been refused to the ecclesiastical judge. But by far the most frequent cases must have been proceedings for the recovery of a loan. On such a matter a Jew would naturally refuse to appear before an ecclesiastical judge. In the first place, such a judge would not recognise his claim to usury; and in the second the prince, who had licensed his usury, authorised him to sue in the royal courts, and there alone, for payment. But a cleric would be equally unwilling to allow the suit to be treated in the court of the prince, since it was extremely unlikely that this court would regard ecclesiastical property with the respect it obtained in the court of the bishop[2]. Since both the giving and receiving of usury was considered a crime of the same nature as sorcery, blasphemy and heresy, subject, even in Christian laymen, to the Courts Christian, the conflict could scarcely be avoided. Only a few of the possible causes of disputes between Jews and clerics were covered by the inclusion, in almost all the charters issued to the Jews, of a clause excluding Church property and plate from the objects on which they might lend money. And this is the only concession which the secular authorities were normally prepared to make. As a result, the Church remained permanently on the *qui vive* to assert what she believed to be her prerogatives.

It is in the second half of the twelfth century that the battle was first joined. This is natural, since the money-lending activities of the Jews only begin to assume import-ance at that time. The princes, conscious of the new source of revenue which they had acquired, refused to distinguish between a clerical and a lay debtor to their Jews. This situation was sufficiently general for Alexander III, who sum-moned the third Lateran Council in 1179, to complain that ' it has come to our ears that the Jews, dwelling in cities through-out Christendom, have reached such a pitch of arrogance that, if they have a lawsuit with a cleric, or even with a bishop,

---

[1] Canon xxxii; Mansi, XXIII, c. 959.
[2] Cf. Canon of S. Quentin below, pp. 358 ff.

they drag him before the secular judge; in defiance of all reason and justice they conduct their case before any chance magistrate on the basis of a simple document, either without witnesses, or with the evidence of some chance Christian or Jew; and they refuse to accept the evidence of weighty and good men against themselves '. The Pope, therefore, ordered that, since not even good Christians can sue a cleric before a secular court, much less shall the enemies of the Cross be allowed to do so under any circumstances whatever. Further, since it is opposed to the Gospel that any question should be decided on the evidence of one man, even when he is thoroughly trustworthy, no case is to be listened to, unless there are two or more serious witnesses to the facts[1].

From then onwards evidence of the conflict is continuous. The charters regularly allowed the Jews the right to judgment in the court of the prince alone; and the episcopate as steadily protested. Thus, at the beginning of the thirteenth century, when the Jews of the County of Nevers had presumably received a charter similar to that granted to those of the royal demesne by Philip Augustus, the Bishop of Auxerre issued a series of prohibitions on the subject. Among other orders, he very legitimately forbade Christians, under pain of excommunication, to answer a summons in a court in which the Jewish litigant was allowed to reject the evidence of unexceptionable Christian witnesses. The reply of the officials of the count was ruthlessly to imprison such recalcitrant Christians until they received a statement from the Jewish creditor that their debts had been satisfactorily liquidated[2].

Almost at the same time, in England, the Regents for Henry III made it quite clear that they were going to continue the policy of protection granted to the Jews by John. In a general circular letter to the Sheriffs or other royal officials of Hereford, Worcester, York, Lincoln, Stamford, Bristol, Northampton, Southampton, and Winchester, they ordered them to protect the Jews, and in particular to override any orders issued by the bishops. Jews were not to be made to plead in Courts Christian,

---

[1] Reproduced under Lateran III, Pars XX, ii; Mansi, XXII, c. 356-7.
[2] Letter of Innocent III to the Count of Nevers, 1208; Baluze, *Ep. Innoc. III*, X, 190.

' since the Bishops have nothing at all to do with our Jews '[1].

Five months later the Archbishop of Canterbury and the Bishop of Lincoln attempted to enforce their authority by forbidding Christians to sell food to the Jews, or to hold any communion whatever with them; but the Crown replied by ordering the imprisonment of any Christian obeying this instruction of the bishops[2]. Neither side was prepared to give in, and thirty years later, when the justices of the Jews had still further consolidated their authority in all legal matters affecting Jewry, the Constitutions of Boniface of Canterbury of about 1250 reverted to the question. Under pain of excommunication they again forbade Christians to sell food or hold any communication with Jews who refused to appear before a Court Christian in any case touching the person or property of a cleric[3].

In France, Germany and Spain history followed the same course. The conflict of the Bishop of Auxerre and the Count of Nevers was itself a repercussion of two solemn agreements made in 1204 and 1206 between the king and his barons. By these agreements the rights of the clergy were limited to action against Christian nurses in the service of Jews—a matter in which princely owners had no interest[4]—and they were forbidden to prevent commercial relations between Jews and Christians. Jews, on the other hand, were forbidden to make loans on movable Church property at all, or on Church lands without the consent of their prince[5]. The extent to which the owner could enforce his position depended on his general authority. As in so many cases, the emperor himself was the least able to stand up for his own interests against the Church, especially when the interests of

---

[1] *Patent Rolls*, 1216-1225, p. 157. For actual cases where a Jew is given redress against such episcopal action cf. F. I. Schechter, *op. cit.*, in JQR, n.s., IV, p. 143.

[2] Tovey, *op. cit.*, p. 83. Two further orders of the same kind, issued in London in 1235 and 1245, are to be found in the *Close Rolls*. vol. 1234-37, p. 329 and 1242-47, p. 378.

[3] Tovey, p. 146. Cf. Council of London 1257, canon xxxii; Mansi, XXIII, c. 959.

[4] Laurière, I, p. 39.

[5] *Ibid.*, p. 44. Cf. the unpublished document of 1275 of Hugo, Provost of the Church of Orange (*Catalogue d'Actes relatifs aux Juifs;* REJ, III, p. 217, No. 48).

princes or cities were also involved. The city of Heilbronn in 1322 compelled Frederick the Handsome to overlook not only the fact that they had robbed his Jews of their property, but also that they had obtained for themselves decisions of ecclesiastical courts against them[1].

On the other hand, a sovereign like James I of Aragon was prepared to enforce his will by the most strenuous measures. A battle, which lasted at least from 1271 to 1275, opened mildly with a suggestion from the clergy of Gerona and Besalu that they would accept any summons for their debts to Jews, but in the clerical courts. This was met with the curt rejoinder that, except where the property of the Church was in question, they should appear before the royal court[2]. In 1274 the clergy and laity of Montpellier obtained letters of committal summoning Jews before the Courts Christian—in which the fees were higher than in the royal courts. The king sentenced all those who had obtained such letters to confiscation of their goods, and the return to the defendants of the fees they had paid. If the plaintiffs were laymen, they were also to be imprisoned[3]. In the following year the clergy of yet another part of his dominions, Roussillon and Cerdagne, made an attempt to assert their authority, and went so far as to threaten Jews who would not submit to them with complete excommunication from any relations with the Christian population, and even expulsion from their residences. But James was not the king to tolerate this. Avoiding the word ' excommunication ', he simply ordered a similar punishment to be applied to any cleric who summoned a Jew before the ecclesiastical judge—no layman was to give evidence for him, to buy from him, sell or hire anything to him, let him lodgings, cultivate his property, or furnish him any service whatever, until he withdrew his summons. Needless to say, at the same time he ordered the Jew to accept a summons in the royal court, and to ignore any order of excommunication or banishment[4].

An equally interesting skirmish took place in Castile in the beginning of the fourteenth century, showing that all the

[1] MGH, LL, IV, Const. V, p. 527.
[2] Regné, *Catalogue*, No. 486; REJ, LXII, p. 40.
[3] *Ibid.*, No. 596; p. 57.
[4] *Ibid.*, Nos. 625 and 630; pp. 62 and 63.

elements of the battle were still present[1]. Certain clerics and laymen obtained letters from Pope Clement V entitling them to take action to suppress usury in the Archbishopric of Toledo. The Jews of Toledo, and others affected, complained to Ferdinand IV. The king sent a commissioner to extract from the representative of the Chapter of Toledo a solemn promise that they would take no further action in the matter and would revoke any excommunications which they had already issued. He reminded them that the action of the Pope infringed the royal sovereignty, ' for they should know that the Jews and all their possessions are mine, and that if they are injured, their loss prevents them from paying my taxes '. To make his meaning quite clear, the king informed the Chapter that, if he failed to get his accustomed revenue from the Jews, he would take the double from the property of the Church of Toledo.

John XXII, the successor of Clement V, acted in a similar way in Germany, and with equal lack of success. He ordered the emperor, Lewis IV, to suppress the usury of the Jews, and when the emperor refused, this refusal was made one of the grounds of his subsequent futile excommunication by the Pope[2].

It must not, however, be imagined that the two parties opposed each other merely out of spite. The Church remained intransigent on the subject of usury, and the princes on their financial rights; but where these did not come into play, each side might be disposed to make concessions to the other. Only four years after the Fourth Lateran Council had imposed the badge upon all Jews, Honorius, the successor of Innocent III, received a request from the King of Castile, supported by the Archbishop of Toledo, asking for exemption from this canon. If it were enforced, said the King, the Jews would leave his kingdom and emigrate to the neighbouring Moorish kingdoms, and he would lose a large part of his revenue thereby. To this request the Pope agreed, and the Jews of Castile were exempted from wearing the badge[3]. All through the Middle

---

[1] Baer, *Castile*, No. 121. Cf. the situation in the time of John II and Pope Eugenius IV; *ibid.*, Nos. 295, 296.

[2] Letter of C. Spinula, 1323, in MGH, LL, IV, Const. V, p. 615.

[3] Baer, *Castile*, No. 46.

Ages exceptions in the matter of the badge were common, and against such the Church, in spite of her insistence on the general rule, only rarely protested.

In the same way the secular powers rarely interfered with legislation passed by the councils which was directed at the protection of Christianity from either danger or contempt. In fact, they continually embodied such rules in the charters and privileges which they granted to the Jews. Exclusion from the streets at Easter, limitations as to the killing and sale of meat, these and similar matters find their way into the laws of the princes from the canons of the councils. And, in return, the Church used her influence to prevent actual violence against the persons of the Jews, and—so long as usury was not in question—unjust treatment of them. ' Faith must be kept with the Jews ', says the Council of Bourges in 1236, ' and no one may use violence towards them; for the Church protects the Jews, since, as it is written, she desires not the death of a sinner '[1].

A good example of how the two attitudes might come into play in a single situation can be found in an incident in Castile in the beginning of the fifteenth century. The King was a boy, and the Queen-Mother Catherine was under the influence of Vincent Ferrer, a Dominican who hated the Jews with a fanatical hatred. At his instance she issued in 1412 a long order concerning Jewish-Christian relations, which is almost entirely based on canonical regulations, with one significant omission. Nowhere in its twenty-four clauses is money-lending prohibited[2]. In 1442 Eugenius IV issued a bull concerning the Jews of Castile which was based almost textually on those clauses of the Law of 1412 which dealt with the prohibition of intercourse between Jews and Christians. But he added to it copies of a number of canons against usury[3]. Whereupon King John II issued an order, not explicitly referring to usury, but insisting that no state or church laws forbade ' trade ' between Jews and Christians; and ordered those who had been using the papal bull as authority for refusing all intercourse between Jews

[1] Quoted in L. Lazard, *Les Juifs de Touraine*; REJ, XVII, p. 215, n. 2.
[2] Baer, *Castile*, No. 275; full text in E. H. Lindo, *The History of the Jews of Spain and Portugal*, p. 196.
[3] Baer, *Castile*, No. 295.

and Christians to cease from doing so. Moreover—another financial issue—the fines which the Pope had imposed, and which would presumably have been paid into the ecclesiastical courts, were to be suspended until the King had asked the Pope for an explanation[1].

In this conflict one group of rulers stood in a curious position. The Prince Bishops, with their temporal and spiritual lordships, found it difficult to choose between their two responsibilities. In his anxiety to secure more Jews to restore the prosperity of his town, Dietrich von Erbach, Archbishop of Mainz from 1434 to 1459, was prepared to guarantee them immunity from clerical jurisdiction[2]. At exactly the same period Frederick, Archbishop of Magdeburg, inserted an appeal to himself in spiritual questions in a charter granted to a Jew of Halle[3].

IX. PROTECTION FROM THE INQUISITION

In the twelfth century the struggle of the Church against the spread of heresy in the southern provinces of France led to the evolution of a system of enquiry and action which came to be known as the ' Inquisition '. It would be wrong to say that the Inquisition was ' founded ' at any particular date, or with any precise method or sphere of work. It grew by trial and error out of the actual circumstances of the struggle. It was originally practised by Cistercians, who had been charged by Innocent III with the action against heresy in the south of France, and was developed by Saint Dominic who came from Spain to assist them. It was not concerned with Jews as such, and on various occasions, when too zealous Inquisitors exceeded their instructions, effective orders were issued to restrain them. As late as 1422 and 1429, when the Inquisition was more powerful than it had been in the thirteenth century, Martin V by a bull forbade the Inquisitors to exercise any authority over the Jews, who were under the jurisdiction of the Ordinaries (the bishops)

[1] Baer, *Castile*, No. 296; Lindo, *op. cit.*, p. 221.
[2] J. Menczel, *Beiträge zur Geschichte der Juden in Mainz*, No. 14, p. 93.
[3] S. Neufeld, *Die Halleschen Juden*, p. 95.

in ecclesiastical matters, and of their various owners in civil suits[1].

On the other hand, the Inquisition was concerned with blasphemy, witchcraft and usury, and this at times enabled it to claim jurisdiction over the Jews. In fact, a letter of Charles I of Provence in 1276, granted to the Jews to protect them against the financial extortions of the Inquisitors, admits that there are three causes—presumably those mentioned above—for which they may bring Jews under their authority[2]. But he is careful to add that if fines are in question for these crimes, they are to be imposed and collected by his own courts, which had already lost considerable sums from the actions of the Inquisitors. Witchcraft and blasphemy had naturally come into the scope of their work from the beginning. Usury was formally added in 1257 by Pope Alexander IV[3]. The owners of Jews were not, however, willing that Inquisitors should do more than indicate that such and such a Jew was suspect. They repeatedly pointed out that they had their own courts for dealing with such questions—and for collecting the fines.

As in most of the conflicts between the secular and ecclesiastical powers, the fortunes of battle swayed now to one side, now to the other. The Inquisitors themselves were probably at first uncertain of the extent of their powers, and walked warily with regard both to the king's and to the bishop's jurisdiction. In 1269 Inquisitors were appointed in Poitou. They proceeded to consult the ruler of the county, Alphonse of Poitiers, as to whether they should deal with questions of Jewish usury. Alphonse replied that he had appointed his own commissioners to deal with the matter, and the Inquisitors seem to have been satisfied[4]. When James II of Aragon learned that the Dominicans, to whom he had entrusted the suppression of heresy, were proceeding to an Inquisition in Gerona and the neighbourhood, he told them in advance that he considered Jews not to be in the

---

[1] Text in M. Stern, *Die Stellung der Päpste zu den Juden*, p. 33, No. 21. Cf. *ibid.*, No. 31.

[2] Papon, *Histoire gén. de la Provence*, III, Preuves, xv.

[3] L. I. Newman, *Jewish Influence on Christian Reform Movements*, p. 198, n. 15.

[4] Col. doc., *Correspondance d'Alphonse de Poitiers*, Nos. 1014 and 1028.

category of ' heretics ', and therefore outside their jurisdiction. The Inquisitors appear to have circumvented the royal intention by proceeding against them as usurers. But the King wrote to his bailiffs and other officials to protect the Jews from their activity[1].

This gentle approach they soon dropped. Through either excessive enthusiasm or plain greed the Inquisitors were continually exceeding their powers. The most outrageous of these excesses took place at Troyes in 1288. There a trumped-up ritual murder charge was made against the richest Jew of the city, and the mob, after it had sacked his house, delivered him, his family and eight others over to the Order of Preachers. On the very next day, without any reference to any other jurisdiction, the Inquisitors condemned the accused and, on their refusing to abjure their faith, proceeded to hand them over to execution. Thirteen were burnt at the stake[2]. This took place in March, and when in May of the same year Philip at the Parliament of Paris forbade the Orders to judge a Jew without the consent of the secular authorities, he clearly had the excesses of Troyes in mind[3].

It was not only the royal courts which the Inquisitors ignored. In 1295 the Inquisitors of Languedoc, without consulting the Bishop of Nîmes to whose jurisdiction most of the Jews of Nîmes belonged, arrested the richest Jews of the city and accused them of blasphemy. But their power was less than their zeal. The bishop appealed to the king, and the Jews were released[4]. In 1350 they acted in a similar manner at Marseilles. Here the Jews were the property of the town, which immediately took up the matter with the vicar of the King of Provence, since the action of the Inquisitors was contrary to their privileges and liberties. Whether the town was successful in its appeal we do not know[5].

[1] Baer, *Aragon*, No. 133, and Regné, *Catalogue*, No. 2647; REJ, LXXV, p. 173.

[2] A. Neubauer and E. Renan, *Les Rabbins Français du commencement du XIVe siècle*; Hist. Littéraire de la France, XXVII, pp. 475 ff.; and A. Darmesteter, *L'Autodafé de Troyes*; REJ, II, pp. 199 ff.

[3] Laurière, I, p. 317.

[4] *Gallia Judaica*, p. 396; cf. Saige, *Les Juifs de Languedoc*, p. 35.

[5] A. Crémieux, *Les Juifs de Marseille au Moyen Age*, Pièces justificatives, xix; REJ, XLVII, p. 78.

In some cases the conflict lasted over a period of years before victory fell to one side or the other. One such conflict raged in the Aragonese provinces of Roussillon and Cerdagne at the beginning of the fifteenth century. It ended with the victory of the Crown, but the victory was so long delayed that there seem to have been no Jews left to enjoy it. It began with extremely high-handed actions on the part of the Inquisitors, who by menaces and threats compelled a number of Jews to accept baptism, and then arraigned them as heretics. It is true that they had jurisdiction over apostates to Judaism[1], but in this case they seem first to have fitted the Jews for the rôle they were subsequently to play. In 1416 Alphonso V of Aragon complained of this interference in matters outside their province, but they merely replied that they had much greater powers than the King seemed to think[2]. Rebuffed by this reply, the King wrote to Alaman, Cardinal Legate of the Province of Aragon, and begged him to exercise his authority in the matter. Alaman thereupon wrote to the Inquisitors, accused them of the practices referred to, and ordered them to desist, leaving the Jews in peace[3]. The Inquisitors, however, found their practice so profitable that they continued unabashed with their arraignment of the Jews. Meanwhile, the King had left the kingdom, and the Queen-Mother, acting as Regent and feeling the loss to the royal revenue, ordered them firmly to leave the Jews alone. Like all other orders, this failed, and the following year the Jews themselves appealed to the Pope. Martin V replied by a bull strictly forbidding the practice of the Inquisitors[4]. What effect this had we do not know, but at any rate the Jewries of Roussillon from this date onwards rapidly declined. By the middle of the century the Jewish quarters were ruined and abandoned, and the Jews had departed elsewhere.

In Provence the actions of the Inquisitors seem to have been dictated simply by cupidity, for, in the letter of Charles I of 1276 already referred to, it is mainly of the enormous

---

[1] Bull of May 1277, confirmed by Martin III in 1281 (*Catalogue d'Actes*, REJ, III, p. 217, Nos. 50 and 53).

[2] P. Vidal, *Les Juifs de Roussillon et de Cerdagne*; REJ, XVI, p. 14, n. 2.

[3] *Ibid.*, p. 16, n. 4.

[4] *Ibid.*, p. 16, n. 3.

fines which the Inquisitors extracted that the Jews complain. One of the methods by which they obtained them bears a strong resemblance to a not uncommon royal practice. As it was a profitable action suddenly to order all the Jews to get their deeds re-sealed, so the Inquisitors seem to have invented a new and much larger badge than was common, and then compelled all the Jews to wear it.

Sometimes the latitude allowed to the Inquisitors simply depended on political considerations and the relation of the secular power to the Papacy at the moment. Philip the Fair, whose cupidity in regard to his Jews equalled that of his English predecessors John and Henry III, on two occasions, in 1293 and 1302, expressly forbade the Inquisitors to concern themselves even with those matters which came under their jurisdiction, if they affected Jews, and ordered his officials to refuse any co-operation with them in matters of usury, fortune telling, ' and other matters which only concern the king '[1]. And in addition to this general ordinance he issued a special confirmation of it to the seneschals of the south, where the Inquisition was most active. In the earliest of these orders he discloses the motive quite clearly: that such action might impede the payment of tallages to the king. But during a period between the issue of these two orders, an exactly opposite policy prevailed. For in 1299 he not only allowed the Inquisitors the widest authority, but even instructed royal officials to hand over to them any Jew who induced a Christian into heresy, handled the sacred Host, blasphemed the sacraments, circumcised Christians, sheltered heretics, built new synagogues, sang too loudly in them, possessed the Talmud, or deluded Christians[2]. The cause of this temporary change lies in his relations with Pope Boniface VIII. In 1293 he was engaged in a violent quarrel with him, culminating in the issue of the bull *Clericis laicos* in 1296. Then in 1297 a peace was made between them which lasted until 1301; as soon as it came to an end Philip returned to his old policy towards the Inquisitors.

---

[1] Saige, *op. cit.*, pp. 231 ff., of 1293, and Laurière, I, p. 346, and S. Luce, *Catalogue des Documents du Trésor des Chartes*, xv; REJ, II, p. 31, both of 1302.

[2] Saige, *op. cit.*, p. 235.

In all this conflict of interests only one sovereign seems to have discovered a method of satisfying both sides. This was James II of Aragon, who had a subtle manner of dealing with this problem. In a number of cases of various kinds, in which the interference of the Inquisitors could not be entirely condemned, he allowed them to impose enormous punishments and penalties, and then remitted their sentences for a substantial fee—which was, of course, paid into his treasury[1].

Not unnaturally, the extensive powers of the Inquisition seriously alarmed the Jews, and there are cases where they approached not only their usual protectors, but the Inquisitors themselves, to obtain a guarantee of protection. Thus the Jews of Pamiers in 1297 requested the Inquisitor, Arnald John, to examine their charters, and to undertake to allow them to live peaceably according to them, which the Inquisitor then promised to do[2].

With the later history of the Inquisition in Spain we are not here concerned, for, so far from protecting the Jews from its activities, the Crown, which had set it up, was its firmest supporter, and Jews, converted or supposed to have been converted, were its primary victims.

X. PROTECTION FROM COMPULSORY BAPTISM

The conflict between the secular and clerical power over baptised Jews began long before the Inquisition came into being. In fact, it provided the subject on which the interests of the two powers were most obviously at variance. The reason is very simple: a converted Jew could no longer bring revenue to the royal treasury by the practice of usury. For even if the princes drew certain profit from the presence of Christian usurers, it was quite certain that a converted Jew would be too strictly watched by the clergy to be able to continue his previous activity. The conversion of a Jew therefore meant a dead loss to the Treasury. How serious the financial loss might be has already been shown in the

---

[1] Regné, *Catalogue*, Nos. 3256, 3389, 3419; REJ, LXXVIII, pp. 114, 135 and 140.

[2] Saige, *op. cit.*, p. 238, No. xliv.

account of the destruction of the Jewish community of Roussillon. But this instance was not unique. In 1415 the Jews of Teruel had been so reduced by the conversion of their richer brethren that the king had to offer special privileges to encourage new Jewish settlement in the town to enable the community to carry on at all[1].

As a very large percentage of the conversions which took place during the whole period were the result either of direct violence, or at least of strong pressure, the authority which wished to intervene could almost always do so at the request of the Jews—either those who had themselves been forcibly baptized, or, if the latter were infants, their parents or relations. Financial considerations could, therefore, usually be concealed behind a desire to do justice to those who looked to them alone for protection.

The earliest recorded example of royal action allowing apostasy is afforded by William Rufus, whose attitude to the clergy, and indeed to Christianity, was such that, apart from any possible profit, the opportunity to annoy the clergy probably afforded him the greatest pleasure. The Jews of Rouen had lost a number of their community by baptism (we do not know whether the occasion of these baptisms was the First Crusade), and petitioned the king, offering him a considerable sum as bribe, to order them to return. This he did, with success except in a single case[2]. The much more serious example which came before the emperor Henry IV a few years later, has already been discussed[3]. In the history of the succeeding centuries similar cases occasionally occur, but they are rare[4]. For the clergy were usually sufficiently powerful to exact a heavy penance for such an action. Hugues Aubriot, Prevôt of Paris in 1380, was bold enough to allow the Jews to recover the children who had been taken and baptized in the riots of that year. But the ecclesiastical

---

[1] Baer, *Aragon*, No. 512. Many similar incidents can be found in Baer in the period following 1391.

[2] Tovey, *Anglia Judaica*, p. 6.

[3] See pp. 79 ff. above, where also the doctrinal reasons for the attitude of the clergy are discussed.

[4] E.g., the action of Henry of Rodez in 1290, when the seneschal of Rodez tried to make him surrender two Jews and a Jewess who had been converted and then returned to Judaism (*Catalogue d'Actes*, No. 72; REJ, III, p. 220).

authorities compelled him to do penance and to order the restoration to the Church of the children concerned[1]. Louis VII in 1144 was even persuaded to compel by secular action Jewish converts to remain faithful to Catholicism under pain of banishment, death or mutilation[2]; and Louis IX in 1260 made a similar concession in expressly passing converted Jews over to the ordinary jurisdiction of the towns in which they lived[3].

But if the princes were unable to recover those who had been converted, they could at least try to protect Jews from conversion. The larger part of such protection lay in the effective prevention of mob action. But some sovereigns at least were bold enough to forbid the activities of Dominicans, converted Jews and others, although they came armed with power, from the Pope or elsewhere, to compel the Jews to listen to their sermons, or even to admit them as preachers in their synagogues. In the charter granted to the Jews on their return to France in 1361 it was expressly stated that they were not to be compelled to listen to conversional sermons[4]. The chief offenders were Jews who had been themselves converted, and they were particularly active in the southern provinces. As they seem to have persisted in preaching, Denys Quinon, the Procurator of the Jews, petitioned Charles V in 1368 for a confirmation of the order, which the king granted. The complaint which Denys forwarded to the king is delightfully naïve. The Jews protested ' that they had not the habit of going to Church, and obtained no religious satisfaction from their attendance, besides being in considerable danger of bodily harm, or at least of abuse and derision from the rest of the congregation, when they saw them there '[5].

But the greatest weapon against conversion was the fact that a Jew on baptism forfeited all his property. Brutal as this was, it was logical. Before his baptism his property had belonged to the king, and was merely used by the Jew for the king's greater profit. But after his baptism it would have

[1] Col. doc., *Chron. de S. Denys*, I, pp. 102 and 106.
[2] *Ep. ad universos fideles*; Bouquet, XVI, p. 8.
[3] Laurière, XI, p. 333.
[4] *Ibid.*, III, pp. 473 ff., clause xxiii.
[5] *Ibid.*, V, p. 167.

belonged to himself, in the same way as the property of any other Christian. The Church herself at first did not resist this surrender, for she regarded his possessions as the product of the mortal sin of usury, but she would have preferred that his wealth should be returned to those from whom it had been taken[1]. But she soon discovered that the result was that Jewish converts lived in complete misery, and had to beg their way from day to day. There is evidence from every century that this really was the case. In 1137 a young Jew, son of a wealthy money-lender of Ratisbon, desiring to be converted, began to steal money from his father, ' in order to avoid the miserable poverty in which he had frequently seen Jewish converts living '[2]. In 1233 a council at Tours urged on the bishops the need of charity, lest ' poverty should compel converted Jews to return to their vomit '[3]. In 1302 another council, this time in Spain, recognised that the loss of their property and consequent poverty were strong arguments against their conversion[4]. Yet a century later Philip, Duke of Brabant, is found giving a pass to an entire family of converted Jews to beg anywhere in his dominions, and urging people to be generous to them[5].

An old book of specimen letters for use in the Imperial Chancery gives two examples of such letters of protection, one from Charles IV in general terms, and the other issued by Wenceslaus in 1397 specifying in great detail the charitable privileges which the converts were to enjoy. In every town the burgomaster was to appoint two citizens to accompany them from house to house, and to introduce them in the name of the emperor, and to protect them from ill-use; and they were to enjoy freedom from all tolls throughout the length and breadth of the Empire. The inclusion of these letters in such a collection shows that their employment was

---

[1] Cf. the letter of Thomas Aquinas to the Duchess of Brabant. *Opuscula, Editio Romana*, xxi, No. 1.

[2] *Annales Egmundani*, s.a. 1137; MGH, SS, XVI, p. 454.

[3] Quoted by L. Lazard, *Les Juifs de Touraine*, REJ, XVII, p. 215, n. 5.

[4] Pennafiel, x; Mansi, XXV, c. 104.

[5] Ouverleaux, *Notes et Documents sur les Juifs de Belgique*, REJ, IX, p. 284.

not uncommon[1]. Most of the exceptions to this rule are to be found in Aragon, where also conversions were very frequent. At times, it is true, a mass of conversions caused heavy financial loss, but there seems to have been no tradition of confiscating the property of the convert. In one statute he is even allowed explicitly to retain his loans[2].

Some of the members of the Council of Constance in 1416 were actually prepared to compromise on the issue of usury itself. For they recognised that they were playing into the royal hands by demanding the total surrender of the converts' property; and they believed that many Jews would accept conversion if the princes showed leniency in this matter. Some, therefore, suggested that while proven usurious wealth must be returned, in cases of doubt the converts should be given the benefit. Others proposed that, even where the convert had unquestionably lived by usury, he should not have to surrender more than the half of his property[3]. These, however, were opinions, and there is no evidence that they convinced either the Council or the princes.

On the whole, therefore, the princes seem to have been able to maintain their right to the property of a converted Jew, but the Church was not entirely without success in this field. The Decretals of Gregory IX proclaimed the general principle that a convert should be better off after than before his conversion, and sometimes the Church succeeded in convincing a prince that the idea merited consideration. About 1280 Edward I was persuaded to waive his claim to their estates—though in the grant he is careful to record the fact that a valid claim existed, had he wished to revive it—on condition that those who had property surrendered half of it for the maintenance of those who had not[4]. In 1392 Charles VI of France generously allowed converted Jews

---

[1] A. Warschauer, *Mitteilungen aus einem mittelalterlichen Formelbuche*; ZGJD, IV, pp. 278 ff.

[2] James II of Aragon confirming a law of James I, Regné, *Catalogue*, No. 2723; REJ, LXXVI, p. 66. Cf. also No. 2427, LXXIII, p. 205, and No. 2934, LXXVI, p. 191. Henry III of England in one case at least allowed a convert to recover the capital, whilst he himself took the interest (*Close Rolls*, 1253-54, p. 24).

[3] Mansi, XXVIII, c. 286 and 347.

[4] Tovey, *Anglia Judaica*, p. 216.

L

to retain all their possessions; but three years later he reduced it to one-third[1]. It is worth remarking that in each case the act of generosity only preceded by a very few years the final expulsion of the Jews; and it may be conjectured that, since they were certainly ruined in both countries when they left them, increasing want had led to the increase of conversions, and the sums which the sovereigns generously surrendered were sums which it was not worth their while to retain.

However, in spite of the rarity of such successes, the Church continued its attempt to secure rights for converts, either by pensions—even Philip the Fair, when he was on good terms with the Pope, was prepared to allow them four-pence a day[2]—or by the retention of their property, or, lastly, by the establishment of a home for their upkeep.

XI. PROTECTION FROM LOCAL OFFICIALS AND FROM THE MOB

Profitable as it was, the possession of Jews was no sinecure, especially if the territories of the possessor were wide and his authority uncertain. The early French treaties between the king and his barons stand out from a background of each trying to steal the other's Jews, or rather their property. Local officials also might be moved by religious hostility, jealousy, or cupidity to arrest the golden flow in its passage from the coffers of the Jew to those of the sovereign. Such a situation is so obvious that it is needless to quote examples, but the innumerable documents dealing with it have two features of interest.

In the first place, it is nearly always the royal purse and not the Jews which are the primary concern of the sovereign when there has been a disturbance. The fines which Henry

[1] Laurière, VII, p. 557. That the Church watched to see that this was carried out would appear from instructions issued in the Province of Rheims to bishops visiting country parishes. They were to see that Jews, if they wished to be converted, were not entirely robbed of their goods (Mansi, XXVI, c. 1073). The actual text dates from 1408, but it may be based on previous instructions, or there may have still been some Jews in the country (Col. doc., *Chron. of S. Denys*, XIV, xvii, Vol. II, pp. 118 ff.).

[2] The accounts of 1299 show payments at this rate to converts in Touraine (L. Lazard, *op. cit.*, REJ, XVII, p. 215, n. 6).

IV attempted to extract after the Rhineland massacres of 1096 went into his own pocket, and were not devoted to re-building the Jewish communities. And when a similar outbreak of religious fanaticism led to the ruin of the communities of Spain in 1391, the fines which were imposed and in part collected, were for the purpose of recouping the royal losses through the non-payment by the ruined Jews of the many taxes imposed on them[1]. This action may sound —and indeed was—somewhat unsympathetic. But the position was no easy one when the revenue from the Jews was an important part of the royal income. The towns naturally objected to the fines, and the clergy were likely to assist them. But if, instead of severity, the king extended his pardon to those who had massacred, expelled or baptized his Jews, he was apt to find it very expensive. Thus, when John III of Aragon consented to excluding the Jews from Barcelona, after there had been some disturbances, he found the loss so great that within a few months he established a new Jewish community and granted it greater privileges than those enjoyed by the previous one—in particular, they were freed from the two distasteful obligations of providing bedding on royal visits, and keeping the king's menagerie![2]

In the second place it is tragic to observe how, as the period advances, the need for protection increases. Religious and economic hostility combined to embitter relationships. When the Jews were expelled from England, Edward I made serious attempts to ensure that they departed un-molested. The Wardens of all the ports were warned to protect them, the public was threatened with penalties if any rioting or looting took place, but these efforts did not secure the Jews a peaceful departure[3].

In Spain, after the middle of the fourteenth century, attacks upon the Jews were common, in spite of all the efforts of the various sovereigns to arrest them, and everywhere the same conditions repeated themselves. Embittered by the successive accusations of medieval superstition, the

[1] M. Kayserling, *Notes sur l'Histoire des Juifs en Espagne*; REJ, XLIII, p. 124.

[2] *Ibid.*, REJ, XXVIII, p. 113.

[3] B. L. Abrahams, *The Expulsion of the Jews from England*, JQR, VII, p. 445.

populace came to regard the Jews with such contempt and loathing, that royal or princely authority was quite incapable of preventing disorder.

XII. PROTECTION FROM JEWISH ACTION

So far we have been considering the protection of the Jews from various potential Christian enemies, whose action might lessen their value to their owner. But to make the picture complete it is also necessary to include various regulations by which the owner also insured himself against possible loss from the action of the Jews themselves. One such case has already been dealt with, that of the Jew who was converted to Christianity. Another case which troubled the kings of France and Spain was that of a Jew being excommunicated from his community. The right of excommunication was one which was highly valued by the Jews; but, obviously, if a person were excommunicated and compelled to leave the community, a loss ensued to the king, who could no longer collect taxes from him. The right was therefore allowed—on payment of a heavy compensation to the king.

In the question of the admission or refusal of new members the interests of the Jewish community and of its owner might also be in opposition. A small community would mean a greater share of the available business for each member, especially if the taxes were bearable[1]. On the other hand, the interests of both parties might be the same, as when the community of Palma in Majorca petitioned for the exclusion of various Jewish immigrants from Africa, on the ground that they were introducing various criminal or illegal practices, to the detriment of the royal finances and the reputation of the community[2].

It was also necessary to hold a balance between the advantage of rewarding a faithful servant with financial immunities and the disadvantage of losing some of the

[1] Cf. order of the Emperor Henry VII, to his lieutenant in Nuremberg, to admit any Jews who wished to settle in the town ' *contradictione qualibet Judeorum Nurembergensium non obstante* ' (MGH, LL, IV, Const. IV, ii, p. 1043).

[2] Cf. A. L. Isaacs, *The Jews of Majorca*, Index, *Jews*, *ad fin.*

income received from the community of which he had formed a part. For this reason tax exemptions were rarely granted in most countries[1]. But in Spain, where exemption from communal taxes was a common method of rewarding faithful service, political, financial, medical and scientific, the kings pressed to the uttermost the usual doctrine of the time that it was communities and not individuals who were assessed for taxes. But, as the assessments of Jewish communities were usually placed at the highest possible figure, it was not really possible to subtract from the list of a community its richest members, and then demand the same sum from the remainder. Protests were continuous, and on several occasions promises were made to cease such gifts, and existing immunities were cancelled[2].

XIII. LIFE BY BRIBERY

From the foregoing sections it is abundantly evident how powerless the Jews were in the presence of their owner. There was no custom, no tradition to which they could refer, as could the villeins or tenants, in the face of an autocratic master. Their owner could allow them to settle or reject them; could suddenly decide to alter the conditions of their residence, could as suddenly uproot them from one town and send them to another; or, if he so willed, expel them at a few days' notice from his dominions, or even kill them. As the charter of John of France puts it: ' they have no place of their own in all Christendom, where they can live and move and take up their dwelling; they can only live anywhere at the entire discretion and purely by the permission of the prince or princes under whose government they wish to settle as subjects, and who are willing to receive them as such '[3].

Confronted with this absolute power on the side of their owners, they could not reply by withholding from them the

---

[1] The volumes of *Constitutiones* of the MGH contain only one, that granted by Lewis the Bavarian to Jäcelin of Rothweil; Const. V, p. 702.

[2] E.g., Regné, *Catalogue*, Nos. 418, 3369 and 3437; REJ, LXI, p. 35, and LXXVIII, pp. 132 and 144.

[3] Laurière, III, p. 471.

money which was the object which those owners sought. Their loans were registered by a number of complicated systems and the amounts known to the authorities, and on loans which they did not register they had no legal power of extracting payment. The only way in which they could secure anything for themselves was by the offer of further money. In other words, they were compelled to live by bribes. It is, of course, true that bribes were extremely commonly accepted in the Middle Ages. But if the mere fact of offering bribes does not mark out the Jew from others, the fact that his bribery was a substitute for the minimum right which others possessed, and which he lacked, does constitute a real abnormality.

While at times rich Jews unquestionably offered bribes to evade the consequences of illegal acts or crimes which they had actually committed[1], such bribes offer no particular interest, nor can they be considered in any way as relevant to a specific study of Jewish-Christian relationships. There are black sheep in every community. But far more frequently bribes had to be offered to obtain the elementary rights of settlement, to secure physical protection in time of danger, to quash an accusation in which the recipient of the bribe himself did not believe, or even to avoid the consequences of an accusation specifically made to provide the opportunity for a little extra extortion. The offering and reception of bribes was so universal a custom that at times the Jews actually received the written privilege that ' a present ' offered to an official for some ' service ' was not to be taken either as a precedent by that official or as entitling other officials to similar ' presents '[2].

That charters of settlement were neither granted nor renewed without a cash payment became the normal procedure. Of the earlier charters there is no such record. But by the thirteenth century there are many such payments mentioned. The charter which the Jews of England and Normandy obtained from John cost them 4,000 marks[3]. The thirteenth-century Annals of Worms make frequent

---

[1] A good example of such cases is given in Matthew Paris, *Chron. Maj.*, V, p. 115.

[2] E.g., a privilege of Alphonso II of Aragon to the Jews of Tortosa in 1181 (Baer, *Aragon*, No. 48).

[3] J. Jacobs, *The Jews in Angevin England*, p. 215. See App. I, iii.

mention of the payments made by the Jews to both the bishops and the citizens for the protection extended to them[1]. The limiting of the number of years for which a privilege was valid was also a fruitful source of revenue, for a bribe had to be offered to allow of its renewal[2]. In Spain, where in many ways ' privileges ' were not merely the recognition of the minimum rights which would allow the Jews to indulge in the lending of money, but at times gave them a really privileged position relative to the rest of the inhabitants, the bribe received might be openly mentioned in the document as the reason for the grant[3]. At times the bribe was camouflaged. When Gaucher of Chastillon, Lord of Creçy, allowed Elias and Joya his wife to settle in the town in 1257, he did so on condition that they paid an annual tax of £20 tournois, and did not raise the question of any claims that they might already have against him[4]. The Archbishop of Trier in the thirteenth century had an amusing arrangement with the ' Bishop of the Jews ', which, while it enters into the same category by imposing irrelevant conditions to settlement, is relieved of the stigma of an extracted bribe by its mutuality. The Bishop of the Jews was bound to lend the Archbishop ten marks a year, and to charge no interest therefore; but in return the Archbishop presented him with ' a cow, a cask of wine, two measures of corn, and an old coat that he did not wish to wear any longer '[5].

The second great occasion for bribery was fear of massacre and the purchase of protection. As the Middle Ages progressed, the Jews became wary enough at times to take measures in advance for their security. Thus the Jews, in arranging their settlement in Hereford, explicitly stipulated that in times of danger from the populace they should be allowed to shelter in the castle[6]. But such foresight was not

---

[1] *Annales Wormatienses*, MGH, SS, XVII, pp. 57, 60, etc.

[2] E.g., Charles V in 1374 renewed the charter of 1361 for a payment of 3,000 gold francs, plus an annual tribute (Laurière, VI, p. 44).

[3] E.g., charter of 1383 granted to the Jews of Majorca by Pedro IV. The two reasons given are ' subvencione seu dono de certa quantitate florenorum auri pro nostris, quibus plurimum involvimur, necessitatibus ', and the abstention of the Jews of Majorca from ' actibus usurarum ' (Baer, *Aragon*, No. 356).

[4] Teulet, III, p. 373, No. 4366.

[5] Aronius, No. 581.

[6] I regret that I have lost the reference for this statement.

universal, and it more often happened that at the last moment they tried to bribe their protectors to take more urgent measures on their behalf, or even their persecutors to be satisfied with the spoliation of their goods. How common such efforts were at the time of the Crusades is revealed by the Hebrew chronicler who notes with wonder that the efforts of Bernard of Clairvaux on behalf of the Jews were made without his having been bribed.

In the same category as bribes to protect them from the mob can be considered the large sums at times extorted from them for no specific reason other than the temporary need of their owner. The method adopted was simple. On a prearranged day all the Jews of the kingdom or town were seized, and a huge sum demanded from them. Ignorant of the cause of their capture, and menaced with expulsion, death or torture, they were in no position to resist. For the danger was a real one. All with which they might be threatened, other communities had actually suffered. The easy security of the community of Mainz during the First Crusade, when they remained convinced until the actual catastrophe that, whatever might be happening elsewhere, nothing could happen to them, would have appeared inconceivable folly to most European Jews after the end of the twelfth century. An accusation of ritual murder, of poisoning wells, or of some economic crime, such as clipping or falsifying deeds, might be suddenly trumped up against them, or they might even be expelled or executed without any reason given. The town of Riquevihr in Alsace in 1420 suddenly expelled its Jews, unknown to its prince, and without any warning massacred those who were not sufficiently quick in escaping[1]. The Bishop of Strasbourg, on obtaining sovereignty over the Jews of Ruffach in 1308, without any reason given by the chronicler, executed the whole community[2]. It is therefore not surprising that when Philip Augustus in 1180, nine years after the massacres resulting from the first ritual murder accusation in France, suddenly, on a Sabbath, had all the Jews of France seized while they were peacefully worshipping in their synagogues, he did not find it difficult

---

[1] E. Scheid, *Histoire des Juifs d'Alsace*, p. 70.

[2] C. T. Weiss, *Geschichte und rechtliche Stellung der Juden im Fürstbistum Strassburg*, p. 7. E. Scheid, *op. cit.*, p. 22.

to extract from them an enormous bribe as the price of their freedom. According to one chronicler, he took all their gold and silver[1]; another, more plausibly, relates that they paid 15,000 marks ' as a kind of gift for their freedom '[2]. John of England was equally successful in obtaining large sums by this method. In 1210 he caused to be arrested all the Jews of the kingdom, and extracted from them the enormous sum of 66,000 marks. ' Extracted ' is *le mot juste* for this particular incident, since it was the occasion of the famous but tragic fate of the Jew of Bristol, who had a tooth extracted daily until he consented to redeem the rest by a payment of 10,000 marks[3]. Some of the victims of this enforced bribe were still in prison in 1217 after Henry III had come to the throne.

He also was no novice at discovering methods of enriching himself at the expense of the Jews, and one such occasion is worthy of mention in the present section as an example of the anxiety besetting Jewish life at the period. In 1236 there were massacres of the Jews throughout Brittany, Anjou and Poitou at the hands of collecting bands of Crusaders[4]. In fear lest it might spread to England, the Jews of that country asked the king to proclaim that no one was to do them any injury, and even paid him to make the proclamation[5].

The third use of bribes was to escape from a definite accusation made against them. Though the accusation remained unproved, even according to the justice of the time, yet it was a good occasion for the collection of a bribe. When the Jews were expelled from France in 1395, four were kept behind on the charge of having murdered a converted Jew, against whom the community was known to have made threats, and who had disappeared. Though his body was not found, and no proofs were discovered that he had been murdered by the Jews, yet they had to pay the sum of 18,000 gold francs to be allowed to leave the country, and were

---

[1] Rigordus, *De gestis Phil. Aug.*; Bouquet, XVII, pp. 5 and 6.

[2] R. de Diceto, *Imagines*, s.a. 1180; Bouquet, XIII, p. 204.

[3] A. Hyamson, *A History of the Jews of England*, 2nd edition, pp. 48 ff.

[4] *Chron. Britannicum*, cited in L. Brunschvicg, *Les Juifs d'Angers et du Pays Angevin*; REJ, XXIX, p. 233.

[5] Matthew Paris, *Chron. Maj.*, s.a. 1236, Rolls Series, III, p. 369; cf. a similar episode in 1239; *ibid.*, p. 543.

scourged into the bargain[1]. At times, however, the bribe was used to quash proceedings in which the guilt of the accused Jews was much more probable. Such a case, also concerning a convert, occurred in Aragon in 1331. Some Jews of Borja were alleged to have set about a couple of Friars in order to recover a boy who desired to be converted. In consideration of the payment of 2,500 solidi, the king absolved them ' whether they were guilty of the crime or not '[2].

The variety and the frequency with which the Jews owed their security to the giving of a bribe make it natural that the medieval chronicler came to assume that, whenever any document was issued in favour of the Jews, bribery had been at the bottom of it. The Popes were supposed to have received fabulous sums for the bulls prohibiting the accusations of ritual murder. Any prince or bishop who intervened to protect them from massacre or from false accusations was naturally assumed to have been bribed to do so. But, if the supposition was frequently true, it must be remembered that times have changed. To-day a man who attempts to bribe a judge is assumed by that very fact to be guilty. No such assumption can be made for the times with which we are dealing, for it was often the only way for the innocent to escape. But, even so, the psychological effect of such a life was deplorable. That the innocent continually made use of it for innocent purposes did not prevent the guilty from relying on it, often successfully, for guilty purposes. Much of the legend of the power of Jewish finance dates back to the age-long tradition that they were able to buy immunity from every accusation and for every purpose, and since the main right which they ' enjoyed ' was that of extracting money from the subject for the benefit of their owner, it is not surprising that the legend of Jewish bribery is a legend of a continual plot against the Gentile population. But what is forgotten is that it was their utter rightlessness and the cruelty of the time which forced them to adopt the only means in their power to secure a minimum of precarious security.

[1] Col. doc., *Chronique de S. Denys*, II, pp. 118 ff.

[2] Baer, *Aragon*, No. 195. The pardon, which, in the Spanish fashion, frankly states that it was accorded in return for a bribe, makes it pretty clear that the Jews had, in fact, been guilty of the assault.

CHAPTER FIVE

CHARTERS

I. THE BASIS AND PURPOSE OF THE CHARTERS

By the end of the fifteenth century the rightlessness of the Jew, which has been described in the last chapter, had proved his complete ruin. Successive massacres and expulsions reduced his financial value to his owners, his usury and successive superstitious accusations increased his unpopularity with the common people. There came inevitably a time to ruler after ruler when the disadvantage and the expense of protecting a Jewish settlement outweighed the diminishing financial returns which the presence of Jewish usurers might afford. Then came the moment when the unhappy Jews realised how little value was to be placed on the charters solemnly accorded them, on the protection of the citizens solemnly promised. Drained of their money, so that no respite could be obtained by bribes or presents, they could only bow their heads and seek elsewhere another temporary haven of refuge.

It is on this background of tragedy that the charters must be studied. Lacking though they were in all permanence or real security, they were the basis of protection against excessive demands from their owners and excessive violence from the clergy and the mob. Undoubtedly they created a feeling of temporary security, and humanity has an extraordinary capacity for living from day to day. During the war men came to think that they had always lived in trenches, and that their future would always be the same. In a curious fashion, custom outweighed the danger of sudden death on one side, and the memory of a different life at home on the other. So it was in the Jewries of France, Germany and elsewhere during this period. Again and again Jews returned to countries and to cities which had proved faithless, possessed of some faint hope that that would not happen to them which had happened to others. The feeling of security which possessed the community of Mainz up to the actual arrival of the Crusaders at the gates of the city, possessed other communities also in circumstances in which they had far less reason to believe that the storm would pass them by than had had their brethren of Mainz in 1096.

The story of the charters issued to Jews is, therefore, no record of

'Freedom broadening slowly down
From precedent to precedent'.

Other classes slowly won power and rights, and what they had won they were able to make the stepping-stone to further rights. For the Jews a past charter was no precedent for favourable conditions in a new one. They were fortunate if they did not lose something of what they had once possessed when the time came for a return to a land whence they had been expelled or for a reissue of a privilege which had lost its validity.

The earliest charters were freely given and freely received. Jewish merchants, travelling in uncertain times, found a need for a document of protection. They asked for it and got it. It is significant that other merchants followed their example and were given charters containing privileges 'similar to those given to our Jews'[1]. A Christian merchant of the fourteenth or fifteenth century would have wanted something much better than what was good enough for the despised and hated race.

Bishop Rüdiger of Speyer is the first to express the fact that a settlement of Jews could be of great value to the city to which they brought their industry and experience[2]; and granted them a charter which secured them a free and honourable position in his newly extended city. The emperor, Henry IV, in granting a second charter to the Jews of Speyer and a very similar one to the Jews of Worms, also uses terms such as would be natural in assuring a proper security to a valuable element in the life of the town[3]. That this particular element was an abnormal one only appeared when one of these charters was renewed by Frederick II;

---

[1] *Formulae Imperiales* of the Carolingian period; MGH, *Formulae*, pp. 311 and 315.

[2] Preamble to the charter of 1084, Aronius, No. 168.

[3] The charters of Worms and Speyer are given in parallel columns by Hoeniger, in ZGJD, I, pp. 136 ff.

it was then reissued because it was the special prerogative of the emperor to protect ' as a peculiar charge committed to him, those who did not accept the Christian Faith and who lived under his rule '.

This stage in which there appears a real sincerity in the protection extended to Jewish settlers soon passed. The rulers of the twelfth century first realised the financial value of their newly recognised property. Their charters of settlement abound in the most complimentary addresses to their beloved and faithful Jews[1]. But with a turn of the wheel the same prince is addressing the same Jews as accursed deicides whose presence is an intolerable affront to his Christian subjects. In the charters themselves the utter dependence of the Jews is rarely allowed to be too apparent. But once a charter was accepted, and Jewish settlers were actually resident under the giver of the charter, there was no need to preserve the fiction. If Jews presumed to settle in towns for which an express permission had not been granted, they were likely to find themselves suddenly removed[2]. In the beginning of his reign Henry III of England ordered his officials at the frontiers to give a cordial welcome to any Jews who wished to settle in the country; but those same officials were to watch carefully to see that none escaped from it[3]. During this reign the Jews made many efforts to quit the country. In 1244, when faced with the threat of banishment to Ireland[4], they tried to get their wives and children into safety, and in 1254 a solemn deputation headed by the arch-presbyter, Elyas of London, begged for permission for the whole community to leave the country, abandoning their wealth to the king[5]. But the king, who believed that there was still money to be squeezed out of them, refused his permission, and threatened with awful penalties any who were caught trying to escape.

On a few—a very few—occasions, the situation was completely reversed, and Jews were a rare commodity and highly sought after. But the reason for such a reversal of the

---

[1] Cf. *Patent Rolls*, 1216-25, p. 357.

[2] Cf. *Close Rolls of Edward I*, 1272-79, p. 130; and 1279-88, p. 256.

[3] Cf. *Patent Rolls*, 1216-25, p. 180; *Close Rolls*, 1254-56, p. 227.

[4] *Close Rolls*, 1242-47, p. 275.

[5] Matthew Paris, *Chron. Maj.*, Ed. Rolls Series, V, p. 441.

normal was in itself tragic. The continual massacres from which the communities of Germany suffered from the end of the thirteenth century up to the Black Death in 1349 were so destructive that it was several decades before the ranks could be again filled, and during this time Jews were scarce. In 1352 the Council and Gilds of Speyer, in inviting the Jews to return to their city, promised to take a solemn oath on behalf of themselves and their successors to protect in life and property, from all violence and injustice, all Jews who would settle within their walls. But, though the advantage seemed to lie with the Jews at this moment, they were not allowed to forget their rightlessness. For the document proceeded to lay down as one of the conditions of settlement that no question might be raised of the debts owing to the Jews at the time of the massacres in 1349[1]. The Archbishop of Mainz at the same period was even prepared to make the unusual concession that those who responded to his invitation might leave at any moment that they wished to, giving only a sufficient warning for the redemption of objects pawned with them[2]. Even at that period, however, conditions were not always favourable. It was only after humble petition from the Jews that the city of Strasbourg finally consented to allow them to return in 1369[3]. In France long negotiations took place before they consented to return in 1361, but the need for them was so great that they were able to obtain most unusual privileges.

II. THE DIPLOMATA OF LOUIS THE PIOUS

It has already been mentioned that the first charters of medieval Europe were the diplomas issued by Louis the Pious to Jews, individually or in groups, and that these in turn were similar in many respects to those issued to Christian merchants. Of the Jewish diplomas three exist, all dating from about 820. The first was issued to Rabbi Domatus and his nephew, the second to David and Joseph

[1] L. Rothschild, *Die Judengemeinden zu Mainz, Speyer u. Worms*, p. 9.
[2] J. Menczel, *Beiträge zur Geschichte der Juden von Mainz*, p. 24.
[3] E. Scheid, *Histoire des Juifs d'Alsace*, p. 51.

of Lyons and their family, the third to Abraham of Saragossa[1].

Just as a modern passport ' requests and requires in the name of His Majesty all those whom it may concern to allow the bearer to pass without let or hindrance, and to afford him every assistance of which he may stand in need ', so those of Louis informed ' all bishops, abbots, counts, prefects, governors, district officers, toll collectors, government commissioners, and all our faithful subjects ' that the Emperor had taken under his protection such and such a Jew and his family. They, their subordinates and their successors, were forbidden, under pain of imperial displeasure, to ' disturb the above-mentioned Hebrews on any unlawful occasion whatsoever or to bring them into disrepute, or to deprive them of any of the property of which they appear to be lawfully possessed, or to demand from them either tolls, post-horses, food and shelter for passing soldiers or officials, gratuities, contributions for the upkeep of road, river or bridge, transport dues or customs '.

The documents, however, went considerably beyond the requirements of a passport, in that they laid down also various conditions which implied both special commercial interests and settled residence. In the first place, the Jews were granted freedom in commerce, and permission to import and sell within the empire slaves acquired outside. This latter permission is given in a different form in each of the diplomas, illustrating the change of ideas on this question which was taking place at the period. Domatus and his companions are allowed complete freedom in the importation of slaves, and permission to sell them within the empire. Joseph is given the added protection that slaves whom he purchases for the purpose of sale may not be baptized without his consent. Abraham is allowed to import, but not to export slaves. He may sell them only within the empire. All three are allowed to employ Christians in their service, provided they do not require them to work on Sunday and Holy Days. But only Domatus is allowed the privilege, which raised the anger of Agobard, that he may refuse permission for the baptism of slaves in his own employment.

[1] Diplomata xxxii-xxxiv; Bouquet, VI, pp. 649 ff. No. xxxii is given in full in App. I, i.

The legal rights of the recipients were dealt with in several clauses. All received the fundamental right to ' live according to their own Law '; and this right was extended for Domatus and Joseph to exclude torture, in cases in which a Christian would have been exposed to it. Torture was only used in serious cases, and in the diploma of Abraham there was substituted for the clause dealing with the Ordeal an appeal to the judgment of the emperor. In cases between Jews and Christians, each side needed the confirmation of persons of the opposite religion in order to prove his case.

Finally, they were all given the general protection of living under the defence and authority of the emperor, and a heavy punishment was threatened those who did them violence.

III. THE CHARTERS OF SPEYER AND WORMS

The silence which follows the issue of the diplomas of Louis the Pious was finally broken by the appearance of three charters issued to Jews of the Rhineland at the end of the eleventh century.

In 1084 Rüdiger Huotzmann, the energetic Bishop of Speyer, extended his city by the elevation of a suburb, a *villa*, into an *urbs*, and explained that he considered that he ' would amplify a thousand times the dignity ' of the new settlement if he persuaded Jews to settle in it[1]. To do so he offered them a very generous charter[2] which, while reflecting conditions of Jewish life similar to those existing in the time of Louis the Pious, presents a number of new features. The most significant of these is his offer of a separate quarter for their residence, surrounded with a wall to protect them from the insolence of the mob. While references to the possibility of Christian violence are not absent from older documents, this is the first time that it is openly admitted that such serious protection as separate residence and a surrounding wall might be necessary.

The community which Rüdiger envisaged was to be a community of merchants. In their own quarter, on the

[1] Similar words are used 200 years later by Conrad von Hochstaden, Archbishop of Cologne, in informing the citizens that he had taken the Jews under his protection (Aronius, No. 588).

[2] Aronius, No. 168.

quays, and in the Christian city, they were granted complete liberty to carry on their commercial activities. They were also permitted to change money, an important matter when currencies were beginning to multiply and a knowledge of their relative values was an essential to business success. To encourage foreign Jews to come to the city for trading purposes, Jews from other centres were exempt from tolls.

In their relations with the Christian population they were treated with liberality. They might employ Christian nurses and servants; they might sell to Christians meat unfit for their own use; and Christians were explicitly authorised to buy the same. Lawsuits between Jews were naturally tried before the president of the Jewish community, but he could also try cases brought by Christians against Jewish defendants; an appeal in both cases was allowed to the Bishop or his chamberlain. Together with these precise details, Rüdiger offered them conditions as favourable as those which might obtain in any other German town.

In return for these privileges, the Jews were to pay an annual rent of three and a half pounds of the money of Speyer. They were also responsible for the watch and the upkeep of the walls of their own quarter, and had to include their servants in the defence of them. The fact that we have not the text of the charter, but only Rüdiger's account of it, may explain why he mentions that he gave them a cemetery, but omits any reference to a synagogue.

Six years after this grant, the Jews of Speyer obtained a further charter from the emperor, Henry IV. At or about the same time Henry made a similar grant to their fellows in Worms[1]. Neither of these two documents has come down to us in its original text. That of Speyer we possess in a late thirteenth-century copy in the episcopal archives, and that of Worms in a copy procured for the Jews of Cologne by the Archbishop in 1360. That in their main lines these two documents are authentic is unquestioned. But it is not possible to extend the same certainty to the wording of some of the clauses, and they must be accepted with a certain reserve.

For the purpose of obtaining the best text, the charter of

[1] The text is best studied in ZGJD, I, pp. 137 ff. The texts in Aronius are not complete. For the Worms charter see App. I, ii.

M

Speyer is usually regarded as the test by which that of Worms must be judged[1]. But from a more general point of view, that of Worms is more important, since it served as the basis for the subsequent status of the Jews throughout Germany. The chief point in dispute occurs in the first paragraph, which, in the Worms Charter, runs as follows:

Because we wish that, in all matters of justice, they shall depend only on us, by the authority of our royal Dignity we ordain that neither the bishop, nor the chamberlain, nor the count, nor the prefect, nor anyone else, shall presume to interfere in any judicial issue arising between Jews, or with Jews as defendants, but [such matters shall be treated] only by the person elected by them and appointed by us to exercise authority, for the special reason that they are *the serfs of our treasury*.

In this paragraph there is a definite statement of the 'servitudo camerae', and no similar statement occurs for nearly a century. The phrase is absent from the Speyer document, which replaces it by a quite general instruction that no official or citizen is to disturb the Jews in any unlawful fashion. The idea that Jews were the exclusive property of the emperor and the national kings only evolved slowly, and such words as early as 1090 are very suspicious.

Apart from this paragraph, the two charters are closely allied to the Diplomas of Louis. They envisage a community of merchants, engaged both in local and general trade, possessing their own laws and customs, and requiring a certain protection from members of the dominant religion. The differences between the two are very slight, and they are evidently based on the same formula, which in its turn is based on those of Louis.

The communities possessed property in land as well as in houses, within as well as outside the walls[2]. For the working of their properties and for domestic purposes, they were allowed to employ both pagan slaves and Christian men

[1] The existing copy was made from the original for preservation in the archives. We need, therefore, only expect the errors of a copyist: that of Worms was reissued as a fresh document in the thirteenth century, and the Middle Ages saw no reason against modifying such documents, even when they professed to be copies, in accordance with developments which might have taken place subsequent to the original issue.

[2] Clause ii.

and women servants. The pagan slaves were free to seek baptism, but could not, on this ground, be removed from the service of their Jewish masters. Their masters, in return, were to allow both slave and servant free exercise of their religion[1]. The merchants were free to travel where they would within the empire, and were completely exempt from all internal tolls[2]. The only restriction on their commercial activity was that they might not purchase Christian slaves[3]. Within the city they might sell their own products, especially wines and medicines (meat is mentioned in neither document), and act as changers of money. The Jews of Worms, however, might not compete with the Christian changers by setting up their tables in front of the Exchange or wherever else the Christian changers were established[4]. If, in the course of their commercial activity, they acquired an article which proved to have been stolen, they had to return it when they were paid the price which they swore on oath that they had paid for it[5].

The communities possessed their own judges for all disputes between Jews. In cases in which Jews and Christians were involved both Jewish and Christian evidence was needed by both parties to the dispute. Jews were not to be exposed to torture, and if their statements in court were challenged, they were to confirm them on oath after a delay of forty days[6]. It is not definitely stated before whom cases involving Christians were to be heard, but, should an appeal be made, it lay with the emperor for the Jews of Worms, and with the bishop for the Jews of Speyer[7]. Crimes

[1] Clauses viii-ix. If the baptism was made a pretext for removing the slave, the converter was to be punished. But there is no statement that the slaves were forbidden to be baptized, as in the Diploma of Louis. See above, p. 159.

[2] Clause iv.

[3] Clause x.

[4] Clauses iii and xv.

[5] Clause vi. This clause occurs in almost all the later usury charters, applied to articles pawned in return for a loan. Here there is no definite statement that the object had not been purchased outright, and the usual stipulations as to the disclosure of the real owner are absent. It would therefore be rash to see in the clause a proof that the lending of money had already assumed an importance in Jewish life in the two cities.

[6] Clause xii.

[7] Clauses xi, xii, xiv.

of violence against members of the communities were heavily punished, and for the theft of their property a two-fold restitution was ordered[1]. In order to protect them from the violence of disorderly elements, no troops or other strangers were to be billeted on them, and there was to be no requisitioning from their stables[2].

Of the religion of their servants mention has already been made. Should they themselves wish to be baptized, they were to wait for three days before they could be admitted to the rite, in order that their sincerity might be tested. Did they remain firm in their desire, then they were to be accepted into the Church, but they were to abandon their property[3]. As this clause occurs in both of the charters, it would appear excluded that it has been inserted by a later hand. It is therefore the earliest recognition of this particular implication of the Jews' status as property of their ruler. No statement is made as to who is to receive the property, but it is to be presumed that it went to the emperor or bishop[4]. If their children were seized by force, stolen or in any other way taken and baptized, the guilty party paid a heavy fine to the ruler, but there is no suggestion that the children were returned to their parents. Again it must be presumed that they were made to remain in their new faith.

IV. LATER CHARTERS OF THE SAME FAMILY

In 1157 their charter was confirmed to the Jews of Worms by Frederick Barbarossa; and in 1236 it was extended by Frederick II to all the Jews of Germany. This was done at the request of the Jews, and because it was the special responsibility of the emperor to protect those who were outside the Church. In 1260 Bishop Eberhard of Worms refers to its clauses as being ' neither abolished nor cancelled nor rendered void in any detail '. Finally, in 1360 the Jews of Cologne obtained a certified copy of it from the chancery, through the archbishop of that city. It was then issued as

[1] Clauses xiii and ii.
[2] Clauses v and xv.
[3] Clause vii.
[4] Clause vii.

still valid, and it is this copy which has survived—a certified copy issued by the Archbishop of Cologne of the certified copy issued by the Bishop of Worms of the extension to all the Jews of Germany by the Emperor Frederick II of the confirmation granted to the Jews of Worms by the Emperor Frederick Barbarossa of the original charter of Henry IV! It is therefore not surprising if it is impossible to guarantee the authenticity of any single clause of a so much copied document[1].

These successive confirmations show that this type of charter, based originally on the model of those of Louis the Pious, was still of value in fourteenth-century Germany, but it is fair to assume that it was only as a general statement of Jewish rights and of the imperial protection accorded them. For, concurrently with these imperial charters, the Jews obtained privileges from their direct rulers, civic or princely, in the different cities of their settlement; and in these a more detailed regulation of their economic status could be included. An interesting comparison of the two types can be drawn from the two charters issued to the Jews of Vienna in 1238 and 1244. The first, issued by the Emperor Frederick II, though not a confirmation of any previous grant, is based entirely on the old imperial model, whereas the second, issued by the Duke Frederick, deals almost entirely with questions arising out of the practice of moneylending.

A further charter of the same family, and one which possesses several features of interest, was granted in 1182 by Frederick Barbarossa to the Jews of Ratisbon. As this charter refers to previous privileges issued to the same community, it is possible that those issued to Worms and Speyer were not the only grants of Henry IV; but it is impossible to reconstruct the original grant out of the present charter[2]. That of 1182 possesses only a few clauses, but it is the first document of unquestionable authenticity which addresses the Jews as the property of the imperial treasury. They are granted the usual permission to live according to their accustomed ways. They may sell gold, silver and other metals, as well as every kind of merchandise;

---

[1] Text in ZGJD, I, p. 137.

[2] See article by E. Täubler in *Mitteilungen des Gesamtarchivs der Deutschen Juden*, IV, pp. 31 ff.

buy the same *after their ancient fashion*, exchange their property and goods as they will, and generally seek their living in the manner of their fathers. The one curious point about his permission is contained in the words in italics. One would expect simply ' buy and sell '. It is *possible* that this is a reference to the habit of making loans on the security of objects given in pawn, many of which, in fact, became the possession of the lender through the non-payment of the debt[1]. It is at any rate certain that the words are not an *authorisation* to enter the business of money-lending. For this something clearer would be needed. But if the business were already established, it was an oblique way of evading granting a definite sanction to usury. In any case, it dropped out of the subsequent confirmations of the charter. The first of these was granted by Frederick II in 1216. The actual clauses were confirmed without repetition, the new paragraphs dealing entirely with the heinousness of any official, lay or ecclesiastical, interfering with the Jew. In 1230 the Emperor's son, Henry VII, German king, confirmed it again, resuming all its commercial clauses in the single phrase that the Jews ' might buy and sell gold and silver in the city of Ratisbon '. In addition to this, he permitted them to refuse a summons before any judge other than their own. No case could be proved against them except by both Jewish and Christian witnesses. No one could disturb them in the possession of real estate, servants or goods which they had held for ten years[2]. The inclusion of ' goods ' is peculiar. Its explanation is uncertain, but it is possible that, like the clause discussed above, it indicates the beginning of the period in which pawnbroking played a considerable rôle in Jewish activities[3]. As long as it involved no more than that a merchant occasionally obliged a friend with a loan, taking some object of value as security, the question of unredeemed

---

[1] On this question see the article of Täubler referred to above, especially p. 41. The argument is not wholly convincing, but the words ' et antiquo more suo comparare ' are certainly curious.

[2] Aronius, No. 448.

[3] Täubler, however, thinks that the whole is merely a substitute for the ' jus hereditarium ' of the Carolingian documents (*ibid.*, p. 38). This may be so for real estate, but it is curious to demand a ten years' possession for ' res mobiles ' acquired by the ordinary method of purchase.

pledges would scarcely occur. Once the practice of lending on such objects became common, the question of the right of the creditor to dispose of unredeemed pledges would become important. That as long a limit as ten years was fixed shows that neither side had yet much experience of the needs of the profession. In any case, when Rudolf of Hapsburg, in 1274, granted a further confirmation of the charter of Frederick II, the special clauses, including the reference to ten years' possession, of the charter of Henry were dropped, and the phraseology reverted to that of Frederick[1].

The last important charter of this family is that granted by the Emperor Frederick II to the Jews of Vienna in 1238. In his war with Frederick, Duke of Austria, the Emperor had achieved the favour of the citizens of Vienna by the grant of a very generous charter in 1237. In it he had explicitly excluded the Jews from all offices, an exclusion not practised by his enemy, the Duke. Lest, however, the Jews should side with the latter, in the following year he granted them a charter in terms very similar to that of Worms, which two years previously he had extended to the whole of Germany. The texts possess a certain verbal dependence, based probably on the fact that the imperial archives travelled with the emperor. But the Viennese document is somewhat less liberal than its archetype[2], the charter of Worms. There are omissions in all its sections. In their relations with the official world, the Jews were neither given express protection from molestation, nor were they exempted from official requisitions. They were not permitted to employ Christian nurses and servants. They were granted no special exemption from tolls; and they were given no special permission to change money or to buy and sell every kind of merchandise. In fact, the only commercial privilege expressly granted was that they might state on oath what they had received for an object found to have been stolen, and return it only on receiving that sum. Another change for the worse is seen in the paragraph dealing with exemption from torture. The exemption was still accorded, but the punishment of those who transgressed it was omitted. It is

[1] Täubler, pp. 32 ff.
[2] The text will be found in Scherer, pp. 135-137.

in the light of this, the last original document of the Carolingian family of charters, that it is possible to trace the decline in the status and security of the Jews of Germany in the century following the First Crusade.

V. THE ENGLISH CHARTERS

The Carolingian tradition is unique in having lasted for more than four centuries, in a series of charters which are obviously mutually dependent. In England, though the whole period of settlement is shorter, there is also a single charter tradition, running from the time of Henry I to that of Henry III. The Jewish settlement in England differed from that in the Carolingian territories, in that it had no tradition behind it of civic rights going back to the protection of Roman Law. It is therefore probable that, even before Henry I, some written regulation of their position existed. They came into the country as merchants, but seem to have drifted into finance earlier than was common in the rest of northern Europe. Probably in the intense development which followed the Norman conquest the demand for cash expanded more rapidly than it did elsewhere and facilitated the change. Further, the accusation of anti-Christian murder (the earliest form of the accusation of ' ritual murder ') originated in England in the middle of the twelfth century, and emphasised the Jews' need of royal protection, and therefore of offering the *quid pro quo* which finance rather than commerce presented to the crown.

There are references to two charters earlier than the first which has survived to the present time. One is recorded to have been issued by Henry I (1100-1135), and it was either confirmed or replaced by Henry II (1154-1189). To this latter charter we have an indirect reference in a complaint addressed by the clergy to the king in about 1164. In this document they expressed their surprise that privileges granted to the City of London, and now proposed for the Jews, should be refused to themselves[1].

But while these two texts have perished, the two which have survived, issued by Richard I and John, sons of Henry

[1] J. Jacobs, *Jews of Angevin England*, p. 42.

II, both claim to be confirmations of those issued by their father and great-grandfather. Even if it is impossible to be sure that the actual lines of the former charters are exactly followed, and that they therefore reveal conditions as they were early in the twelfth century, yet these charters possess considerable interest in themselves. For, while they belong in their general form to the Carolingian family in that they envisage a community of merchants, they also recognise the special needs of a class devoted to the lending of money. This latter note runs all through the clauses. The charter of Richard I opens with a grant of freedom of residence, and possession of all lands, fiefs, purchases, gifts *and pledges* coming into their hands[1]. Their heirs have the right to inherit their property *and loans*[2]. They have freedom of passage in all the king's territories, both in England and Normandy, freedom from all tolls for their goods, as for the goods of the king himself, and freedom *to receive* and buy all that is brought to them except Church property and blood-stained garments[3]. They have the usual judicial privileges, with some additions in the same direction—*in cases concerning loans*, they are to prove the capital, the borrower the interest[4]. If the *debtor* dies, they are protected during a minority of the heir[5]. If they have held their *pledges* for a year and a day, they may sell them[6].

The charter of Richard is not granted directly to all the Jews of England, but to one Isaac, his sons and their men. It is, however, probable that, in effect, it applied generally to the Jews of the whole country. In any case, the charter of John, granted in 1201, is directed explicitly to the whole community. It is issued as a confirmation, not of the charters of Henry II or of Richard, but of that of Henry I. In the first paragraph, which allows them to hold all which they held in his day or had since reasonably acquired, the word 'mortgages' is added, indicating perhaps a new form of Jewish financial activity. Until the end of the twelfth

[1] Charter of 1190; Jacobs, *op. cit.*, p. 134; clause i.
[2] Clause iii.
[3] Clauses iii, vi and vii.
[4] Clauses ii, iv, and v.
[5] Clause vi.
[6] Clause v.

century mortgages had been a favourite method by which the monastic houses profited from their spare capital, but just at this period they were forbidden to use this method as being usurious[1]. It would therefore appear that the Jews had succeeded them in such transactions. The rest of the charter corresponds with that of Richard, with the addition that in a financial suit a Jew may use documentary evidence in place of witnesses[2].

From the fact that both John and Richard refer their charters back to their great-grandfather, Henry I, it is a reasonable assumption that his charter was in fact similar to theirs, and thus represents the earliest charter of which we have knowledge in which money-lending of one kind or another is clearly a major Jewish activity.

The latter half of the reign of John was one of the most miserable periods for the Jews of England, but the regent for the infant king Henry III seems to have been well disposed towards them. He released those whom John had imprisoned, and confirmed to English Jewry the charter of 1201. To strengthen it he placed the Jewries under the protection of twenty-four burgesses, appointed by the sheriffs, in each town where Jews dwelt[3]. This happier period was of short duration, for Henry III turned out to be as expert as John in extracting money from his Jews.

While at various times regulations were made affecting— generally adversely—their status, this confirmation of the charter of John is the last charter in Anglo-Jewish history before the expulsion of 1290[4].

VI. THE FRENCH CHARTERS

It is not until the beginning of the fourteenth century that we can find a full charter granted to the Jews in France. From other sources we can obtain information about their status at an earlier period, and the existing charters refer to

[1] R. G. Génestal, *Rôle des Monastères comme établissements de crédit*, pp. 78 ff., and below, p. 309.
[2] Jacobs, *op. cit.*, p. 212, the text is given in App. I, iii.
[3] Tovey, *Anglia Judaica*, p. 77.
[4] For the statute *De Judaismo* of 1275 see below, pp. 218ff. and App. I, iv.

earlier grants which have perished[1]. The regulation in considerable detail of their moneylending practices began at the end of the twelfth century; and treaties of agreement between the king and his barons about their respective Jews date from a few decades later. But it would appear that little systematic was done in the way of regulating legal and communal privileges until popular hostility to the Jews had reached a point at which the owners, if they were not to forgo the profit which they made out of them, were compelled to define strictly their rights and privileges, and to take effective steps for their protection. Our earliest real charter was granted by Louis X in 1315. It is in some senses a treaty with the Jews and gives the conditions on which they might return to France after the period of banishment to which they had been subjected by Philip the Fair in 1306; and it may be that the Jews were reluctant to return at all unless some such written statement of their position were granted them. In fact, the king gives as his first explanation ‘ the many causes ’ brought forward by the Jews for such a grant. Secondly, he admits that he was urged to it by the ‘ commune clameur du peuplę ’. Finally, he justifies himself by the thoughts that Saint Louis himself had both expelled and restored them, that Rome tolerated them in memory of the Passion, and that contact with Christians often led to their conversion. The second reason was probably the central one—the clamour of the populace, demanding opportunities for borrowing money. However, the Jews were soon to be reminded that it was possible for the public both to find a money-lender indispensable, and to be easily moved to violence against him.

The charter consists of twenty clauses, dealing both with their present settlement and with ‘ compensation ’ for their past expulsion[2]. The Jews were allowed to return for a period of twelve years, with the guarantee that if they were expelled again at the end of that period, they would be given a year’s

---

[1] Charter of Louis X, clause xviii, ‘ Leurs privileges, se ils sont trouvés, leur seront rendus, se il ne peuvent estre trouvé, et l’en treue les translas il leur seront renouvellés, excepté ce en quoy il seront contraires à ceste presente Ordenance ’ (Laurière, I, pp. 595 ff.). Cf. clause xxviii of the charter of 1361, *ibid.*, III, pp. 473 ff.

[2] Laurière, I, pp. 595 ff.

notice of it to enable them to wind up their affairs[1]. They might settle in any town which had previously possessed a Jewish community, but nowhere else. Baronial Jews, who moved to the territories of other barons, could not free themselves from all the rights and profits in them possessed by their previous lords. The crown, on the other hand, might retain any baronial Jew and incorporate him into a royal Jewry should it wish to do so[2].

All charters and privileges which they had previously enjoyed, except in so far as they were contradicted by the present grant, were to be returned if they could be discovered[3]. In the same way their synagogues and cemeteries were to be restored to them if it were practicable to do so. If it were not, they were to be allowed to purchase other suitable sites and buildings. If they recovered the ancient synagogue itself, they had to pay the owner the price which he had paid for it. Their religious books also were to be returned, except for such as had already been sold, and for copies of the Talmud, since in any case they were forbidden to possess it[4].

In contrast to the German cities, whose almost universal practice was to demand of Jews, on their returns after their frequent expulsions, that they should renounce the collection of any debts outstanding on their departure, Louis allowed them to collect one-third of all such debts for themselves. The reason for this generosity was not far to seek: they received this unexpected gift on condition that they collected the remaining two-thirds for the king. If they attempted to collect debts, which the debtor could prove to have been paid, they were to be punished. With this exception the past was to remain dead. They were not to be called to account for actions which had lain against them before their expulsion, for objects taken with them on their flight, or for financial transactions during their exile[5].

Two court officials were appointed as auditors of the Jews in order to protect their interests and to watch over the

[1] Clauses i and x.
[2] Clauses i and xi.
[3] Clause xviii.
[4] Clauses vii-ix.
[5] Clauses iv-vi.

observance of the Charter. These auditors were given authority to deal with all judicial matters, and to regulate issues concerning inheritance[1]. In their contact with the Christian population, the Jews were always to wear their badge; and they were on no account to enter into discussion on religious topics with any man, rich or poor, in public or in private[2].

The Jews who returned were to work with their hands, or to practise honest commerce. On no account whatever were they to practise usury. The king desired it to be definitely understood that he particularly did not wish them to practise such a trade. In fact, he expressly forbade them to do so, . . . but, if it *should* happen that *by accident* one of them did lend money, then . . . and the rest of the charter proceeds merrily to lay down the usual conditions granted to royal usurers![3] They might not refuse repayment when it was offered, but they could not themselves demand it until a year had passed from the time of the loan. They might only lend on objects deposited with them or on commercial stock. Church property and bloody or wet clothing might not be accepted. But the earlier intentions of the charter were not wholly forgotten. Though the Jews had official permission to charge usury, the royal courts were closed to them if they attempted to recover it from a recalcitrant debtor[4]. These curious inconsistencies reflect on one side the piety of the descendant of Saint Louis, and, on the other, the reason why the people clamoured for their return. The public were not moved by philanthropy or piety. They wanted money cheaper than they could get it from clergy, burghers or Italians.

The reign of Louis X was short. Only two years after this privilege was granted, his successor, Philip V, issued a further charter in which all pretences that the Jews would not practise money-lending were dropped, and adequate

---

[1] Clauses xix-xx. The word for inheritance might also mean 'real estate'.

[2] Clauses iii and xvii.

[3] Clause xii. ' Comme les Juis sont tenus a ouvrer et labourer de leurs mains, ou a marchander, si comme dessus est dit, nostre volonté n'est mie que ils puissent prester a usure, ainçois le deffendons expressement, et se ainsint estoit que il avenist par aventure que pretassent il ne porroient prendre plus de deux deniers pour livre par sepmaine.'

[4] Clauses xiii-xvi.

protection was given them to make the trade prosperous[1].
In addition, more effective religious and judicial safeguards
were accorded to them. They were, for example, not to be
fined more than ten pounds without being allowed to appeal
to the king; they were not to be submitted to the judicial duel
except in cases of murder, or tried in any courts except those
appointed for them; and, except in cases of flagrant crime,
neither they, their goods, nor their religious books were to
be seized by any official, secular or religious, without reference to the Crown officers.

In the beginning of 1322 Philip died, and his successor,
Charles IV, proceeded to expel the Jews in the same year.
The reasons for this expulsion are mysterious. They were
said to have plotted with the lepers to poison the Christian
population. The ' plot ' was accidentally revealed by the
discovery of a letter, and the Jews were first mulcted of an
enormous fine and then thrust out of the kingdom. But at
the same time it was also said that it was the insupportable
exactions of the usurers which led to it; and, in fact, the
Lombards were certainly expelled for this reason in 1330[2].
Whatever the reason, this expulsion of 1322 is a good example
of the insecurity of Jewish tenure. They were promised most
solemnly in 1315 that their settlement would not be disturbed for twelve years. The charter was confirmed in 1317.
Five years later they were compelled to leave the country.

With the exception of certain districts, the Jews remained
exiled from France until 1360 (1361). At the time of their
recall, John II (the Good), who had been captured at
Poitiers in 1356, was a prisoner in England. By the Peace of
Bretigny in 1360 he bound himself to pay the enormous sum
of three million gold crowns as ransom. Times were
exceedingly hard. The country was suffering from bad
harvests, and was preyed upon by armed bands of English,
German and Spanish mercenaries, the relics of the late
wars. The first instalment of 600,000 crowns proved almost
impossible to raise, and was only completed several months
in arrears of the appointed time.

It was in these circumstances that Charles the Dauphin
decided to recall the Jews, and to grant them a new charter

[1] Laurière, I, p. 646.
[2] *Ibid.*, II, pp. 59 ff.

for a period of twenty years[1]. Their return was negotiated on the Jewish side by Manecier of Vesoul, and the Jews were made to pay dearly for the privilege. On admission each head of a family had to pay fourteen gold florins[2] for himself and his wife, and one florin, two ' gros tournois ', for each child or dependant. Subsequently he had to pay an annual tax of seven florins for himself and his wife, and one florin for each child or dependant. This was to be collected by Manecier, who received a percentage for his pains. Louis of Etampes, a distant cousin of the king, was appointed guardian of the Jews[3]; and the details of their residence were elaborately laid down. Two changes from the conditions of their earlier settlements indicate at once that the crying need for money in the royal treasury was the cause for their recall. In the first place, all the Jews of the country were to be the property of the king, even if settled on baronial fiefs. All taxes were to be paid to him, apart from the actual rent of their houses[4]; and no baronial officials were to be allowed to requisition any goods, animals or other property of the Jews on any pretext whatever[5]. Secondly, they were allowed to charge fourpence per £ per week, or $86\frac{2}{3}$ per cent. usury on their loans[6].

This enormous rate was double what had previously been allowed in France, quadruple what Philip VI, during the period of distress in 1332, had permitted for loans to the peasants[7]. Needless to say, the extra was to go to the king in the form of heavy tallages, and not to the Jew, who by demanding, and being officially protected in demanding, so enormous an interest was putting himself in a position of considerable danger. Various Italians who were allowed to settle in different towns during the next twenty years were only allowed to charge 43 per cent.[8]

[1] Laurière, III, pp. 473 ff. The text is given in App. I, vi.
[2] A florin = 12 sols or shillings. In a charter of 1355 allowing a Jewish settlement in Dauphiné, Charles only demanded a poll tax of one florin per head. See below, pp. 193 ff.
[3] Laurière, III, p. 471.
[4] Clause iv.
[5] Clause xxi.
[6] Clauses viii and x.
[7] Laurière, II, p. 85, c. iv. This refers to Christian usurers, either Italian or native.
[8] *Ibid.*, VI, p. 336, c. ii; 478, c. ii; etc.

In return for the risk which they were running the Jews were able to obtain substantial advantages. For their actual settlement they were allowed to acquire houses, cemeteries and the land necessary for their livelihood[1]. There is no mention that they might only settle in cities where they had previously dwelt. They were given a greater internal autonomy than they had previously enjoyed. A rabbinic court of two rabbis and four others could excommunicate and banish any member of the community, without there being any appeal to the royal officials. But if any person were banished, a sum of one hundred florins was to be paid as compensation to the treasury for the loss incurred by the disappearance of a tallageable person[2]. Their books were not to be seized[3]; and they were not to be compelled to listen to Christian sermons[4]. They could appoint their own officials to collect tallages from individual members of the communities, and appeal to the nearest royal magistrates to enforce the collection[5].

They were also given extensive judicial protection. They were under the sole jurisdiction of the Count of Etampes, as guardian, and of the royal court[6]. They were given a complete amnesty for any crimes, even the gravest, committed during their previous residence[7]. If arrested, even on a criminal charge, they could be released on providing bail of suitable Jews or Christians[8]. They could not be submitted to a judicial duel, even on an accusation of murder[9]. No man could denounce them unless he were prepared himself to prosecute them, and no notice was to be taken of stolen objects found in their houses, unless they were in a locked chest or cupboard, since apparently a method of denunciation was to place suspicious objects, even dead children, in their houses, and then to lay an anonymous

[1] Laurière, III, pp. 473 ff. Clause i.
[2] Clause iii.
[3] Clause xxvii.
[4] Clause xxiii.
[5] Clause xxiv.
[6] Clause ii.
[7] Clause vii.
[8] Clause vi.
[9] Clause xxii.

accusation against them[1]. Even when accusations were made, due enquiries were to be carried out before they were arrested[2]. Every possible protection was given to them for the carrying on of their financial occupations, and for ensuring that all available wealth passed only into the royal treasury[3].

Not unnaturally, such extensive privileges aroused considerable opposition[4], and there exists in the Bibliothèque Nationale at Paris a draft of a complete alternative charter drawn up under clerical influence. While this will be considered in detail below[5], it is interesting to note that it entirely prohibited usury, without offering any other occupation, and was only interested in the complete and humiliating segregation of the Jewish from the Christian population, the conversion of the former, and the protection of the latter. Though this charter had no chance of royal acceptance, the clergy made their disapproval of the charter actually granted felt locally, in Languedoc going so far as to forbid Christians to sell any food or drink to Jews, and enforcing their prohibition so effectively that the latter were compelled to go to the governor for protection from imminent starvation[6].

With various revocations and modifications this charter remained valid until the final expulsion of the Jews from the kingdom of France in 1395. Jews still remained on various territories not directly under the crown, but there is only one further occasion on which a French king had to decide on his attitude to Jews. In 1482 Provence was united to the French crown, and the long period of Jewish prosperity under successive dynasties came to an end. With the approval of the king the Jews were expelled from one centre

---

[1] Clauses xix and xx. Cf. for such a case at Troyes, p. 138 above. Cf. also the charter of Bp. Hartmann of Augsburg of 1271 (Aronius, No. 751), by which the Jews were protected from the consequences of dead children being hidden in their houses or gardens.

[2] Clause xviii.

[3] Clauses viii, x, xi-xiii, xv-xvii, xxv.

[4] The subsequent history of this charter is given below, Ch. X, Sect. 9, The Jews and the Ransom of John II, pp. 371 ff.

[5] See pp. 216 ff.

[6] Laurière, IV, p. 440.

after another. By the beginning of the sixteenth century the small papal county of the Venaissin was their only refuge on what is now French soil.

VII. CHARTERS OF AUSTRIA AND EASTERN EUROPE

In a preceding section the development of the Carolingian family of charters was traced down to its final examples in Germany and Austria. The reconquest of Vienna by the Duke Frederick in 1239 nullified the imperial grant of 1238, and in 1244 the Duke issued his own charter to the Jews of his whole duchy. This abandoned for ever the Carolingian model, and was drawn up on entirely new lines. For it recognised that the primary occupation of the Jews was no longer commerce, but moneylending, a change which had taken place in England and France from a century to half a century earlier.

While the Frederician model was much better adapted to the actual circumstances of contemporary Jewish settlement than the imperial model, there is little evidence of new charters along similar lines in Germany itself. But in eastern Europe ' it formed the basis of the charters of Bela IV of Hungary in 1251 and 1256; of Premysl Ottokar II of Bohemia in 1254, 1255, and 1268; of Boleslav the Pious of Kalisch in 1264; of Bolko I of Silesia and Fürstenberg in 1295 (confirmed by Bolko II of Silesia and Schweidnitz in 1328); of Henry III of Glogau in 1299; of Casimir the Great of Poland in 1334, 1364 and 1367; and of the Grand Duke Witold of Lithuania in 1388. Further, it seems to have influenced the charters of Portenau of 1399 and of 1452; of Bishop Ulrich III of Brixen in 1403; of Duke Frederick IV of Tyrol in 1431; and the Capitula Judaeorum Pirani of 1484 '[1].

This universal use of the charter of Frederick as a model for the Jewries of eastern Europe gives it a very great importance. The Jews to whom it was granted by successive rulers over so wide an area were largely the refugees of the Crusades and the subsequent massacres in Germany. They

[1] Scherer, pp. 178-179.

were already accustomed to the specialised life of money-lending, and they largely followed this occupation in new countries in which they settled. But the backwardness of eastern European civilisation gave them more opportunities for following other trades than they possessed in the west. As merchants they could perform services in Poland and elsewhere which Christian gilds could perform in the countries which they had left. But this was only for a short while. History was not slow to repeat itself. The same kings who granted favourable conditions to the Jews found it also to their advantage to encourage German artisans and traders to settle in their territories, and the famous ' Magdeburg Law ', the Law of the Sachsenspiegel, was granted to municipalities in eastern Europe almost at the same time as charters were granted to the Jews. Gradually the same hostility to the Jews developed on the part of commercial rivals, and they were forced to devote themselves more and more exclusively to different financial occupations, money-lending and the management of the finances of the royal and noble estates.

Instead of the usual opening of an imperial charter, asserting the ' servitudo camerae ' of the Jews as the basis of their privileges[1], Frederick began only with a general philanthropic statement of his desire to do good to all his subjects, and consequently to the Jews[2]. But their direct dependence on him was implied in their exclusive relationship to the duke and his chamberlain in all legal matters[3], and the corollary of this dependence was the ducal protection implicit in the freedom granted them to travel throughout the ducal dominions, and their exemption from any special tolls on the part of municipalities or local authorities[4].

Religious toleration was to be deduced rather from a series of measures protecting them against violence than from any

[1] The fundamental charter of the Duchy of Austria was confirmed by the Emperors Lewis IV in 1330 and Charles IV in 1348. In both there is a general confirmation of the privileges of the Jews, but they are not called, as in similar confirmations in other parts of the empire, ' unsere Kammerknechte ' (MGH, LL, IV, Const. VI, i, p. 703, and VIII, pp. 599 ff.).

[2] The full text of the charter is given in Scherer, pp. 179 ff., and in App. I, vii.

[3] Clauses viii and xxix.

[4] Clause xii.

positive clause. Their synagogues and cemeteries were not to be disturbed[1]. Their children were not to be stolen— presumably for baptismal purposes[2]. No one was to be billeted in their houses[3]. They were to pay no tolls for the burial of their dead[4].

The greater part of the charter, however, deals directly or indirectly with the protection of their financial activities. A Jew might lend on anything brought to him, without enquiry as to its origin, except on bloody or wet clothes (Church property was omitted by Frederick, or, perhaps by an oversight, is omitted in the one copy of the charter which we possess, but it is included in other members of the family)[5]. If a Jew lent on either land or documents of value belonging to a baron, he was guaranteed protection in taking possession of the pledge[6]. Violent abstraction of the pledge by its owner, or assault on the Jew in his home, were to be punished as attacks on the Treasury[7]. After a year and a day a Jew might dispose of unredeemed pledges, on showing them to the magistrate, and if their value did not exceed that of the loan and its usury[8].

The rate which the Jew might charge for his loans was the astonishingly high one of $173\frac{1}{3}$ per cent. (eightpence per talent or £ per week)[9]; and, if a Christian repaid the capital of the loan and refused the usury, after a month's delay it was allowed to accumulate at compound rate[10].

Careful provision for the settlement of disputes about loans was made in a series of clauses. If a Christian plaintiff denied that a Jew had lent him money on an object in the Jew's possession, then the word of the Jew was accepted, on his swearing to the loan on an object of similar value. If a Jewish plaintiff asserted that he had lent a Christian money

---

[1] Clauses xiv and xv.
[2] Clause xxvi.
[3] Clause xxiv.
[4] Clause xiii.
[5] Clause v.
[6] Clause xxv.
[7] Clause xxviii.
[8] Clause xxvii.
[9] Clause xxx.
[10] Clause xxiii.

on a pledge, and the Christian denied it, then the word of
the latter was accepted on oath, provided that the Jew could
not produce witnesses to the transaction[1]. In a dispute as
to the amount of money lent on a pledge, the Jew was
believed on his oath[2]. In all cases where the Christian was
the plaintiff (except presumably that mentioned above) he
had to bring one Jew and one Christian to support his
claim[3]. If a Christian asserted that an object pawned with
a Jew was stolen from him, the Jew had to declare his ignorance of the theft on oath (and it will be remembered that he
was under no obligation to enquire into the origin of any
article brought him) and was obliged to hand over the object
only on payment of the capital and usury due on it[4]. If, on
the other hand, pawned objects were stolen or destroyed
by fire or riot while in the possession of the Jew, the Jew was
not bound to return the article if he made a declaration of its
loss. But it was a condition that the Jew's own property was
to be lost at the same time[5]. As pledges usually possessed
a value several times superior to the sum lent on them, this
was an advantage to the lender.

Finally, there were a number of clauses dealing with the
legal position in other than the financial cases. Jews could
only be tried by the duke or the special judge appointed by
him[6]. The judge could not take the initiative in proceeding
against any man, but could only act on complaint being made
to him[7]. Only in cases brought before the duke himself
was the Jew to take his oath solemnly on the Torah[8]. If a Jew
refused a summons, he was fined fourpence for the first and
second refusals, and thirty-six pence for the third[9]. A
Christian proceeding against him could not secure a conviction without Jewish as well as Christian evidence[10].

[1] Clauses ii and iv.
[2] Clause iii.
[3] Clause i.
[4] Clause vi. The French charters only allowed the Jew the capital.
[5] Clause vii.
[6] Clause xxix.
[7] Clause xxii.
[8] Clause xix.
[9] Clause xvii.
[10] Clause i.

A careful scale was inserted for acts of violence against a Jew. Murder was punished with death and confiscation[1]; serious wounding with a fine of twelve gold marks to the duke, and twelve of silver, together with the costs of cure, to the victim. This was a very high rate in the standards of the time. The unusual insertion of compensation in order to pay for the cure was apparently drawn from Jewish law[2]. If there were no bloodshed, the fine was reduced to four marks gold and silver to the duke and victim respectively. If the assailant could not pay, he lost his hand[3]. If a Christian raised his hand against a Jewess he also lost his hand[4]. If murder were done, but the murderer were unknown, then the relatives of the victim designated the person whom, on enquiry, they suspected, and the duke proceeded against that person[5].

Finally, there were two clauses dealing with violence between Jews. If a Jew wounded a Jew, the fine was £2, and was paid to the Jewish judge[6]. If a riot broke out in the Jewish quarter, the city justices had to call in the duke or the chamberlain, and could not act of themselves[7].

The other charters of the family differ from that of Frederick on a number of minor points. But they conform closely to the main lines of their model. One important variation lies in the amount of usury permitted. It is not always stated, and where stated at the Frederician figure, must be regarded as a maximum. It is difficult to believe that it was often possible in practice for the lender to exact, or the borrower to pay, the colossal usury permitted by Frederick.

VIII. CHARTERS OF CASTILE AND ARAGON

Four groups of charters have so far been examined. The oldest group is the Carolingian, extending from the Diplomas

[1] Clause x.
[2] Clause ix. See Scherer, pp. 219, 220.
[3] Clause xi.
[4] Clause xxi.
[5] Clause xx.
[6] Clause xviii.
[7] Clause viii.

of Louis the Pious to the Viennese grant of the Emperor Frederick II. These are charters to merchants, in which moneylending finds no place. Next comes the English group, granted to a new community half merchant, half moneylender. Then come two groups in which only money-lending is of any importance, that of France, and that of Austria, Bohemia, Poland and Hungary. The Spanish charters belong to yet a different set of circumstances and, in consequence, differ considerably from any of the groups considered above.

The three foundations out of which Jewish life evolved were all present. In place of the Roman citizenship of Gaul, there was the more recent citizenship within the Moslem kingdoms of the Peninsula; the memory of the Visigothic canons lived on in ecclesiastical circles, and was replaced only by the greater fanaticism of the Inquisition from the thirteenth century onwards; traces of Germanic custom lingered in the special dependence of the Jews upon the sovereigns. But the relations of these foundations to each other are different in Spain and elsewhere, largely because the Jewish population was itself different. In all countries in which they settled, and in which they received charters, they had some considerable financial value to their owners. But the value was not so great that other interests might not be set against it and prevail. This was the situation of the small Jewish communities in the north of Spain in the tenth and eleventh centuries. Then comes a change, and in the two succeeding centuries, the Jews were irreplaceable in the services which they could render to the Spanish sovereigns. Not only did they provide them with a large proportion of their revenue, but they also provided finance ministers; their industry and commerce contributed greatly to the prosperity of the whole country; their education made them suitable to serve as clerks and officers for the government, as scholars, scientists and doctors for the court. But in the end even these services were not proof against the fanaticism of Spanish Catholicism and the jealousy of the Christian population. And as their prosperity had been more brilliant than elsewhere in Christian Europe, so was their final downfall more catastrophic.

The few laws and other documents which have survived

from the period preceding the Re-conquest show that the treatment of Jews in Spain did not originally differ from that which they received elsewhere. In accordance with Germanic custom, the prince claimed the right of inheritance[1]. As the Jew was under royal protection, the wergeld for killing him was at least the same as for killing a Christian[2]; and at times it was higher, and equal to that demanded for killing a knight or a priest[3]. In a lawsuit, the rights of a Jew, being the rights of the crown, were the same as those of a Christian[4]. The general population did not view them with hostility. The Council of Oviedo in 1050 complained that Jews were living freely among the Christians[5]; and Gregory VII in 1081 warned the king to cease from allowing them to occupy posts of authority over Christians[6]. All the same, there were various petty restrictions in force, and in many ways the position of the Jews was inferior to that of the Christians. A Jew of Barcelona could make an oath to a Christian, but not receive one from him[7]. The inhabitants of Jaca could grind their corn where they would, but the Jews only in the royal mills[8].

The Jewish population of the early Christian kingdoms must have been much less important than that of the great cities in Moorish territory. Here in Visigothic times the Jews had been bitterly persecuted, but in the interval, under Moorish rule, they had been allowed to practise any profession and to occupy any position for which their wealth or capacities fitted them. The population of the Moslem kingdoms was an exceedingly mixed one. It contained not only Moslems of many different types and of widely separated geographical origin, but also important groups of Spanish Christians as well as Jews. The only intelligent way to rule such heterogeneous elements was to extend to all the widest possible toleration, and this was the policy generally adopted.

[1] Baer, *Aragon*, No. 2.
[2] Baer, *Castile*, No. 2; cf. *Aragon*, No. 5, clause xi.
[3] Baer, *Castile*, No. 11.
[4] Baer, *Aragon*, No. 5, clause cxxix.
[5] Baer, *Castile*, No. 8.
[6] *Ibid.*, No. 12.
[7] Baer, *Aragon*, No. 5, clause li.
[8] *Ibid.*, No. 6.

But outbreaks of hostility between the different groups were not unknown. Where each group preserved a large measure of distinction, jealousy of any group which secured a temporary prominence was natural. This led to occasional attacks against the Jews, but in spite of them they enjoyed a security which allowed of an extraordinary development in their religious, intellectual and economic life. While in the early days of the Moslem conquest they had possessed a certain military importance, in the later and more settled times it was as scientists, philosophers, and poets, as financiers, merchants and manufacturers, that they became prominent.

As the Christian kings pressed southwards from Leon and Castile in the north-west, and from Navarre, Aragon and Catalonia in the north-east, they came into this territory with its rich commercial and intellectual life. They left it as far as possible undisturbed. They ruled over Christians, Moors and Jews. The kings of Castile even called themselves ' Kings of the men of the two religions ', and only prejudice prevented them from calling it ' three '. But it was not easy to reconcile the different interests of these three sections of the population and, until his commercial and financial importance was fully realised by the authorities, the Jew was apt to suffer when either of the two other groups needed especial tenderness. If a prince wished to conciliate his ancient Christian subjects in order to obtain assistance in his campaign; if he wished to win over new Moslem subjects either because he had Moslem allies, or because he needed their loyalty while he attacked their still independent brethren, then he was likely to confer favours on these groups at the expense of the Jews.

In 1091 Alphonso VI of Castile and Leon was in desperate need of money to raise new armies to beat back the Almoravides, who had inflicted a crushing defeat on him six years previously. He therefore granted the people of Leon a very favourable charter. This included various advantages over the Jewish population. The latter might not give evidence against a Christian, either noble or peasant; cases in which Christians were involved with Jews were to be tried in any of the Christian courts, royal, baronial, or episcopal; the Jews were to accept trial by ordeal and, if their champion failed, the Christian received half the fine (if he succeeded, the king received the whole!); the Jew could not sue for assault unless he had been first attacked; no partiality was allowed him in matters of finance; if the Jewish creditor could produce evidence of the loan he received payment; if there were no witnesses, the matter was settled by the oath of both sides[1].

If in 1091 it was the Jews of Leon who were sacrificed to secure the support of the Christian population, in 1114 their co-religionists in Tudela were similarly offered up to secure the loyalty of the Moors in that city, which Alphonso I of Aragon and Navarre had captured. No Jew was to be placed in authority over Moors; no Jew of Tudela was to be allowed to purchase Moorish captives; no Jew was to insult a Moor, and if he did so he was to be beaten ' fort et dura-ment '[2]. It is not surprising that the Jews fled from the city. But Alphonso discovered that it was not possible entirely to neglect their interests, and recalled them with a grant of terms which would enable them to prosper, but which did not affect his grant to the Moors. [The Jews were given their own houses, into which neither Christian nor Moor might enter; they were given freedom of commerce in Tudela, and freedom from tolls entering and leaving the city; in judicial matters, they were given the same privileges as those inscribed in the 'Customs of the Jews of Najera ', a district to the west of Tudela[3].] At times, however, during the reconquest the easiest thing to do was to grant complete equality to all the population, Christian, Moorish and Jewish. This is the situation in the Customs of Carcastello (?1129), Caseda (1129), and Daroca (1142)[4].

The century which followed was the most brilliant and prosperous in the history of the Jews in Christian Spain. It coincided with a decline in the Moslem section of the country. A fanatical sect, the Almoravides, held power, and

[1] Baer, *Castile*, No. 14.

[2] Baer, *Aragon*, No. 569; cf. No. 27, a treaty between the Count of Barcelona and the Moors of Tortosa, which contains similar clauses.

[3] *Ibid.*, No. 570. It is one of the greatest losses to our knowledge of Jewish conditions at this period that the constantly quoted *Customs of the Jews of Najera* are unknown.

[4] *Ibid.*, Nos. 571, 572 and 22.

both Christians and Jews were bitterly persecuted by them; at times they were not even allowed to live under their rule at all. In Christian Spain, on the other hand, the Jews enjoyed every advantage. Ever since the capital of Castile had been transferred to Toledo in 1087 it had been a centre of Jewish culture. Jews were employed as ambassadors, as ministers of finance, as doctors and scientists. In Aragon their position was scarcely inferior. In such a period it is unnecessary to look for precise regulations as to the extent of their liberties. There were, of course, churchmen who viewed this situation with displeasure, but the time of their influence was still far off. While the reconquest was in progress the services of the Jews were indispensable even to princes who did not value their intellectual gifts. Not only did they provide able collectors of revenue, but they contributed from their own wealth, by their taxes and their loans, a large part of the resources needed by the crown. They even provided military assistance, and were reckoned no mean soldiers[1].

In the middle of the thirteenth century the active work of reconquest came to an end and, with more settled conditions, the more normal Christian attitude to the Jews began to assert itself. It is at this period that, both in Castile and in Aragon, lengthy regulations of the conditions of Jewish settlement begin to appear. In Castile there were a number of legal codes issued at this period in which the conduct of Jews was carefully defined. But they were still thought of as part of the general population, for references to Jews are scattered among other topics. In Aragon, on the other hand, definite charters were issued to separate Jewish communities, the collection granted to the Jews of Majorca being the fullest[2].

A detailed examination of these Spanish regulations would add but little to the descriptions already given of conditions elsewhere. The field covered is inevitably very similar, and, in general, the conditions granted are equal to the most favourable obtained in other countries. In all legal matters Jews and Christians possessed equal rights, except in the

[1] Cf. *ibid.*, No. 578, and *Castile*, No. 45.
[2] Cf. the list of documents given at the end of *The Jews of Majorca*, by A. L. Isaacs.

Laws of Estila[1] where the scales are slightly weighted in favour of the latter. As a general rule, each side needed to prove his case with witnesses who were members of the religion of the other. Among the most unusual points a few are worthy of mention. The basic status of the Jew is not always as clearly stated as it is in the charters of Germany. The *Book of the Customs of Castile* is quite definite that Jews, even those living on the lands of the nobility or religious orders, are ' the property of the king, and live under his protection and for his service '[2]. But the Customs of Ledesma place the Jews equally under the protection of the king and the city[3], and those of Salamanca more exactly define that they have no *lord* except the king, but that their protection is surrendered to the city, and their taxes collected through the city officers[4]. The fortunate situation of the Jews of Castile and the limitations on the property rights of their owners, are revealed in a clause in the *Fuero of Ledesma*, by which a Jew, who is assaulted in spite of a safe conduct granted him, received one-third of the fine himself, instead of its all going to his owner[5]. And the *Customs of Castile* allowed the Jews throughout the country to hold the persons of Christians for undischarged debts[6]. These particular *Customs* are also unusual in that, though they are a general law book not a special Jewry law, they include detailed regulations on matters concerning the internal life of the Jewish communities. Assault, abuse and especially the profanation of the Sabbath are dealt with in detail[7]. It is even prescribed that if a Jewess hangs her clothes out on the eve of the Sabbath the constable may confiscate them and hand them over to the royal officers.

In Aragon there is also frequent royal legislation on matters concerning the internal affairs of the Jewish communities, but it comes in special documents rather than in general law books. In their relations with the Christian

[1] Baer, *Castile*, No. 62.
[2] *Ibid.*, No. 60, clause cvii.
[3] *Ibid.*, No. 58, clause cccic.
[4] *Ibid.*, No. 57, clause cccxli.
[5] *Ibid.*, No. 58, clause ccclxxxviii.
[6] *Ibid.*, No. 60, clause xcvi.
[7] *Ibid.*, clause ccxx.

community, the Jews of Aragon received the same favourable conditions as the Jews of Castile. The most interesting special feature of the Aragonian grants is the early date at which protection was sought and given against excesses due to Christian fanaticism. Already in the second half of the thirteenth century a guarantee was given by James I to the Jews of Lerida that they would not be disturbed by Inquisitors denouncing their religious books. The king, not unnaturally, forbade them to possess books insulting the Christian faith but, even where such literature was in question, he would allow the matter to be judged only in his own courts[1]. In the same document he excused them from attending conversional sermons outside the Jewish quarter, although they could not refuse to listen to friars who entered their own synagogues accompanied by not more than ten Christians of good repute. As a consequence of the situation revealed by these clauses, the adequate protection of the Jewish quarter from invasion by hostile mobs became an issue in Aragon earlier than elsewhere. The Jews of Valencia were given a special street in 1273 and authorised to buy out all Christians dwelling within it, to close it with gates, and to prevent any house within that area passing into Christian hands[2].

In the fourteenth century the tone changed somewhat. The kings still desired to obtain the maximum advantage out of their Jews, and were prepared to grant them generous conditions in order to encourage them to settle. But the complaints of the Christian population, both commercial and religious, were growing continuously in intensity. When the Infante Alfonso of Aragon in 1320 granted a charter to encourage Jews to settle in Alcolea, he not only allowed them to build a synagogue, but expressly stated that within its walls they might sing their prayers in a loud or a low voice, by day or by night, just as they pleased. Complaints as to the services of the synagogue disturbing neighbouring churches go back to the days of Gregory the Great[3], but when such a matter needs to be mentioned in the foundation charter of a new community, it shows an extent of local

[1] Privilege to Jews of Lerida, 1268, see App. I, viii.
[2] Regné, *Catalogue*, No. 566; REJ, LXII, p. 52.
[3] Ep. II, vi; MGH, *Epistolae*, I, i, p. 104.

hostility unknown in earlier times. The same is true of the defiant tone in which the Jews are given permission to slaughter cattle in the Christian slaughter-house, ' whenever and as often as they like '.

But every time that a king met his Cortes he had to listen to petitions, begging him to restrict or abolish rights granted to his Jews. The importance and the power of the Cortes in the conduct of affairs in Spain greatly exceeded that of any similar body in the rest of feudal Europe. These complaints were, therefore, an effective weapon both of commercial rivalry and of clerical hostility, and they were rarely totally neglected by the sovereigns who received them[1].

The fourteenth century ended in Spain with a wild outbreak of religious violence against the Jews, due to the fanatical preaching of Ferrand Martinez. In 1391 there were widespread massacres in both Castile and Aragon, and thousands of Jews nominally accepted Christianity. Twenty years later a second wave of persecution spread through the country, owing to the preaching of another fanatic, Vincent Ferrer, and the results were again a host of insincere conversions. These two assaults upon the Jewries of the Peninsula led to unexpected results. The loss of revenue to the Crown and the great landowners was so great that at the beginning of the fifteenth century a number of privileges were issued in which every inducement was held out to Jews to resettle in their ancient quarters.

A single specimen of these charters will suffice to show the extent of the damage, and the lengths to which the Crown was prepared to go to re-establish its Jewries. In 1400 Martin of Aragon received a request for assistance from the relics of the great community of Lerida[2]. In 1391 over seventy members of the community had been killed and most of the rest had accepted baptism. The new community found itself completely bankrupted by its responsibility for the debts and taxes owing by the old one, and its quarter was a heap of ruins. The king cancelled all obligations based on the debts

---

[1] See ' Cortes ' in index to Baer, *Castile*. It should, perhaps, be added that as the Jews were expelled from England in 1290, a comparison between England and Spain on this particular subject would be irrelevant to the present study.

[2] Baer, *Aragon*, No. 472.

of the previous community. He ordered the houses of the
Jewish quarter to be rebuilt by their owners (who were
Christians), and in the meantime told the City Fathers to
rent houses to the Jews at a low rate. When the community
had thus re-established itself, it was to be free from all
taxes for six years, or until the settlement had reached the
number of one hundred families. Thereafter no member
was to receive exemption from his share of the communal
finances. (The community desired a promise from the king
that he would grant no moratoria to their debtors for ten
years, and that during the same period no proceedings should
be instituted against them for excessive usury. But here
they asked for more than the king was prepared to grant,
and all that they received was the promise that they should
be treated in the matter in the same way as the other Jewish
communities of the kingdom. If the royal caution on this
point—which did not directly affect his revenues—was
natural, it is curious that the Jews did not ask for, and the
king did not think to grant, any protection against the
activities of clerical fanatics, other than the general permission
to enjoy the privileges possessed by the previous community[1], in which such protection had been included.

In spite of this effort to reassure the Jews, their position
steadily deteriorated during the fifteenth century. Individuals still enjoyed authority which would have been
impossible in any other Christian country, and continued to
do so even under Ferdinand and Isabella themselves. But
the general Jewish population never recovered, either in
numbers, prosperity or security, from the tragic events
which had ushered in the century. The hostility of the
Christian public was kept alive by the clergy and intensified
by the dislike and suspicion with which both regarded the
'new Christians'. To the usual complaints against the
Jews were added those of assisting these 'converts' to
evade their Catholic duties, of aiding and encouraging them
to return to Judaism, and of fomenting in them a general
hatred and contempt for their nominal Christianity. The
security engendered by the completion of the reconquest
after a pause of more than two centuries ultimately emboldened the Church and the Crown to dispense with the

[1] Cf. above, p. 189.

services of the Jews altogether. A hundred years after the first serious blow to their security was delivered by Ferrand, the Spanish Jews were expelled from the country where they had dwelt for at least a millennium and a half, and to whose civilization they had contributed some of its greatest glories.

IX. NON-ROYAL CHARTERS IN FRANCE AND GERMANY

It is clearly impossible within the scope of a single chapter to examine or even to mention all the charters granted to Jews by different territorial authorities other than the emperor, and the kings of France, England, Spain and eastern Europe. The quotation of a few will be enough to illustrate the diversity and the arbitrariness of Jewish settlement. Two French groups may be selected from this point of view, the Narbonnais charters of the thirteenth century, and a series of charters of south-eastern France of the fourteenth.

In Narbonne there were from early times two separate Jewries, subjected to the two authorities between whom the city was divided, the archbishop and the viscount. At first both Jewries were submitted to arbitrary conditions, now favourable, now the reverse. But in 1217 the Viscount, Aymeri IV, granted important privileges to his own Jews. In return for a fixed sum of 1,000 sous, and an annual hearth tax of ten sous, the Jews were given permanent possession of their houses and properties, present or future, and—a very important point—they were promised that no other tax than the one mentioned would be imposed on them. Further, they might rent or sell their property as they willed, except to clerical or foreign sovereign owners. Nothing was said, and therefore no express limitations imposed, on their commercial or financial activities. The essential points were: security of tenure, and a precise definition of their financial obligations. This grant naturally attracted Jews coming to reside in Narbonne, or Jews residing already in the archiepiscopal division of the city, to the viscountal Jewry, and for more than fifty years the archbishop and his officers maintained a sullen struggle to assert their rights and to retain their Jews. It was not until 1284 that they could bring themselves to take the obvious remedy of issuing a charter, offering still more attractive terms, inviting Jews to settle within the district under the authority of the archbishop. This second charter, like the first, stressed a fixed limit to financial exactions, and offered not only security of tenure, but free permission to enter or leave the archiepiscopal Jewry at will. Since previously it had required five generations of residence to obtain permission to change from one Jewry to the other, this was an attractive bait. To what extent the archbishops might have succeeded in drawing away Jews from the viscounts by these terms, we cannot, unhappily, know, for in 1306 all the Jews of Narbonne were expelled by Philip the Fair[1]. In this case the rivalry of the two authorities contributed considerably to the prosperity of the Jews, and, even more, the presence of the other stayed the possible hand of oppression of each. The archbishop and the viscount were in perpetual conflict, so that a Jew in difficulties with one could often secure the protection of the other, not because his case was necessarily just, but because he afforded an opportunity for one rival to attack the other.

The permission—indeed, encouragement—to the Jews to return to France in 1361 has already been described. The actual negotiations were conducted by the Dauphin Charles, in the absence of the king in captivity in England. He was, perhaps, moved to appreciate the possible value of the Jews in the financial emergency which faced him by his own experience in Dauphiné. For five years previously he had admitted the Jews to settlement in a charter which recalls the terms offered to the Jews of France[2]. The Delphinal charter accords serious guarantees of protection and attractive terms for financial operations. But it reveals none of the urgency of the document of 1361. One of the striking differences is its insistence in three long clauses on the complete right of a Jew to leave all his property freely to whom he

---

[1] Regné, *Juifs de Narbonne*, REJ, LVIII, pp. 81 ff. and 210 ff.; see also Saige, *Les Juifs de Languedoc*, p. 155.
[2] Text in A. Prudhomme, *Les Juifs en Dauphiné*, in the *Bulletin de l'Académie Delphinale*, 3e Serie, XVII, pp. 217 ff.

O

willed, on the right of heirs to inherit under intestacy, and even on the right of the Jews to dispose of property when no obvious heirs could be found. The charter of 1361, on the other hand, is completely silent as to any liberty in this direction whatsoever. Seeing the close agreement on other points, it is a legitimate conclusion that the Crown wished to keep in its own hands the right to confiscate the property of deceased Jews if it found it profitable to do so. Another difference lies in the occupations allowed to the settlers. The Dauphin generously granted the Jews full rights to acquire every kind of property, houses, lands or forests, on condition of discharging whatever duties were imposed on such properties by the citizens of the locality where the property was situated. Such estates they might freely leave by will, sell or otherwise dispose of. Recalling the Jews to France, on the other hand, he only allowed them possession of houses and cemeteries, for revenues from land were less, and were obtained more slowly, than from moneylending. But in France he allowed them to settle wherever business was to be found, whereas in Dauphiné, though they might move about freely, they might only settle in the places allotted to them.

It is a sign of deterioration in the general estimate of the Jews when they needed especial protection from the menace of the population. This was granted in general terms in Dauphiné, but, lest timid Jews should not feel adequately protected, it was given in more specific language in 1361. In particular, Jews were excused attendance at conversional sermons and the inspection of their religious books.

The need of protection is even more evident in a charter which was granted by Philip the Good of Burgundy in 1374, and extended by him in 1379, 1381 and 1384[1]. This charter shows verbal agreement with the royal grant of 1361, in allowing the excessive interest of fourpence per week ($86\frac{2}{3}$ per cent.). It also agrees with that grant in two curious clauses. The Jews are permitted to ' practise speculative and mechanical arts '[2]; and they are not to be disturbed if

---

[1] Texts in Jules Simmonet, *Juifs et Lombards*; in the *Mémoires de l'Académie Impériale des Sciences, Arts et Lettres de Dijon*, IIe Série, XIII, pp. 264, 183, 269 and 189.

[2] French Charter, clause ix; Burgundian, clause iv.

objects, which should not be there, are found anywhere in their houses except in cupboards or chests of which the owner or his wife alone possesses the key[1]. But the most striking clauses of the Burgundian grant are those in which the duke solemnly and repeatedly forbade his own officers and the servants of his own household to violate the privileges which he granted.

The three charters are as curious in their omissions as in their agreements. They all date within twenty years of each other; they are issued within the same country; they are clearly mutually dependent; and yet in each the condition of the Jews is slightly different. Just according to the arbitrary will of the owner, the Jews received a privilege or the privilege was withheld from them.

In Narbonne Jewish privileges were determined by the presence of two Jewries within the same city; the examples from fourteenth century France illustrated the variety which might exist within the same period; a good illustration of yet a third possible determinant of Jewish conditions can be given from the changes which took place, from 1444 to 1455, in the Duchy of Franconia. In 1444 Franconian Jewry was given a most generous charter by the Duke, the Bishop of Würzburg. It contained unusual privileges, such as unlimited interest to non-citizens, freedom to refuse any form of repayment except gold, silver or minted coin, and liberty to leave the Duchy at any time that it pleased them[2]. The charter was granted for seven years, and in 1451 it was renewed[3]. But in the same year the Papal Legate, Nicholas of Cusa, appeared in Germany, with the express purpose *inter alia* of seeing that canonical legislation concerning the Jews was enforced, and that the Jews were compelled to wear the badge, a custom which had fallen into disuse. Nicholas was followed by the still more violent John Capistrano, and, as a result of the influence of the latter, in 1453 the Franconian Jews were given eight days within which to cease making any loans to Christians; and six months to recall outstanding loans (a limited interest included), sell their houses and quit the Duchy, since the bishop refused

---

[1] French, clauses xix and xx; Burgundian, clause ix.

[2] Wiener, *Regesten*, p. 197, No. 614.

[3] M. A. Szulwas, *Die Juden in Würzburg*, p. 77.

to tolerate any further Jewish settlement within his dominions[1]. That the arbitrary basis of Jewish conditions might turn to their favour as well as to their disadvantage is well illustrated in the next step in the story. For some unknown reason (probably not a bribe[2]) the whole order was cancelled, and in 1455 the Jews were allowed to leave off wearing the badge, renew their loans to Christians, and a special instruction was included in the new charter that past loans were to be fully paid[3].

X. THE JEWS IN THE GERMAN LAW BOOKS

In the beginning of the thirteenth century there appeared a compilation of the feudal and territorial law of Lower Germany, called the *Sachsenspiegel*. Its author was a knight, Eike von Repgow, and his purpose was not to create new laws, but to collect, arrange and clarify existing regulations. His work was of permanent value, and came to be considered a final legal authority in many parts of Lower Germany, and its author is considered the greatest German jurist of the Middle Ages. The particular interest in its references to Jews is that, though it gives explanations of laws, its author shows no knowledge of the Roman status of the Jews (he knew of Roman law only by hearsay), of their being serfs of the Imperial Treasury, or of their possessing a jurisdiction of their own.

According to Eike, the essential fact in the position of the Jews was that they enjoyed the King's Peace. According to him, this was originally granted them by Vespasian out of his gratitude to Josephus, who had cured Titus of gout; and it was this Roman grant which was confirmed by the Germanic Emperor in agreement with the princes. In virtue of the status thus conferred, assault upon a Jew who was not bearing arms was treated as a breach of the King's Peace. If the Jew was bearing arms, then he ceased to enjoy any privileged position, but—and this shows that Germanic custom affecting strangers was not the only basis of Jewish

---

[1] Wiener, *op. cit.*, p. 201, No. 630.
[2] M. A. Szulwas, *op. cit.*, pp. 79 ff.
[3] *Ibid.*, p. 80.

residence—he still enjoyed the treatment granted to a
Christian layman in similar circumstances.

While his treatment of Jewish settlement was not comprehensive, several points of detail were dealt with in a spirit
of complete toleration and objectivity. A Jew might not
act as guarantor for a Christian unless he was able to answer
for him in court. If a Jew killed or injured a Christian, he
was tried in the same way as a Christian. If a Jew bought,
or accepted as security for a loan, any Church property,
except in the presence of a guarantor, he was treated as a
thief. Any other property he might buy, by daylight and in
a public place. Transactions of this kind he could prove by
oath, and for his goods he must be paid, even if they proved
to be stolen. If the transaction were conducted without
witnesses, he could make no claim for payment[1].

Next in importance to the *Sachsenspiegel* is the Law Book
composed some fifty years later at Augsburg, the *Schwabenspiegel*. Its author was not an educated layman like Eike von
Repgow, but a cleric. Clerical conceptions therefore colour
the whole presentation of the situation of the Jews, and canon
law is inserted side by side with imperial. In the matters
covered by the *Sachsenspiegel* the author follows the same
line, but there are many additions, modifications and new
subjects treated. The author is aware of the idea of the
direct dependence of the Jews on the emperor, and it is this
dependence, and not the King's Peace, which he connects
with Roman tradition. According to him, the Jews were sold
to the Imperial Treasury by Titus, and thus became the
Emperor's men, but Josephus, by curing Titus of gout,
secured for them good conditions. The particular advantage
so accruing, according to the *Schwabenspiegel*, was that they
could not be convicted of an offence against a Christian,
except by Jewish as well as Christian evidence. But a Jewish
defendant might be convicted on Christian evidence, provided no Jew had been present at the time of the offence.
Presumably, if a Jew had been present, he either had to
support the prosecution, or it failed. A Christian defendant,
on the other hand, could not be convicted by Jewish evidence
alone, for the oath of a Jew was never valid against a Christian
denial.

[1] Aronius, No. 458.

In one respect, the author viewed conventional procedure with disapproval, for he refused to admit the protection granted in imperial charters to Jews who had unwittingly become possessors of stolen goods. Only if the transaction had been carried out in the open street, so that everyone could see what property was in question, was the Jew to receive the sum paid before being obliged to return such goods. Otherwise he, like any Christian, must return them without compensation. Curiously enough he allowed the Jews, under special authorisation, to receive Church goods in pawn, but if they were found with such goods and could not produce this authorisation, they were liable to be hanged.

He inserted canonical regulations on the following subjects: conversion, exclusion from the streets during Holy Week, social intercourse between Jews and Christians, common baths, Christian service in the houses of Jews, and the obligation of all Jews to wear a badge. He also ruled that a converted Jew might keep his property; and he allowed ecclesiastical as well as lay courts to exercise jurisdiction over the Jews. Finally, he appended a humiliating oath which the Jew had to take in court standing on a pigskin[1].

The *Schwabenspiegel* enjoyed an authority similar to that of its northern parallel, and was extensively used in southern Germany as well as in Austria, Bohemia and elsewhere. A third collection, which was of considerable importance in central Germany, was the *Meissener Rechtsbuch* or *Rechtsbuch nach Distinktionen*. It was composed in Meissen in the second half of the fourteenth century, and it is urban rather than territorial in character. At this time the protection of the Jews had largely passed from the hands of the emperors and great princes to the cities of their residence, and this book reflects the desire to protect them for the sake of the dignity of the city. It ignored the problem of usury, and assured the Jews and their property adequate security[2].

There are many similar collections of varying importance[3]. Some of them ignore the Jews; others—for example, the

---

[1] Aronius, No. 771.

[2] K. G. Hugelmann, *Das Judenrecht der Rechtsbücher*, in *Historisches Jahrbuch*, XLVIII, pp. 582 ff.

[3] G. Kisch, *The Jewry Law of the Medieval German Law-books*, I, pp. 101 ff.

Viennese law book—are violently hostile to them[1]. To examine all of them is not necessary. For the evidence of the three most important collections, which has already been given, confirms the situation revealed in the charters, that the treatment of the Jews was full of inconsistencies and uncertainties.

XI. 'CITIZENSHIP' IN GERMAN TOWNS

It has already been seen that there was far more variety in the treatment of the Jews in Germany than elsewhere. Unquestionably the ownership of the Jews was supposed to be ultimately vested in the Imperial Crown. How or when the Crown came to assume that this ownership was its sole and exclusive right is still obscure. But it is certain that in actual fact many other powers exercised all the rights which ownership implied, and that the Jews, on their side, turned to nearer and more effective authorities for a guarantee of their security. From these local authorities they received privileges very similar to those granted them elsewhere. But in the cities, especially those cities which possessed either autonomy under the Crown or special privileges from their overlords, the protection extended to the Jews came to take a peculiar form. By special deed the Jews were admitted individually to ' citizenship '; or, alternatively, the city was requested to or agreed to consider its Jews as ' citizens '.

There were good reasons for this development. It was due not to philanthropy, but to an intelligent and enlightened self-interest. In the first place, it united by ties of common loyalty the interests of Jewish residents and those of the rest of the inhabitants. Secondly, it gave the city fathers a status in defending the rights of the Jews which were very often their own rights. Finally, it enabled them to claim of the Jews a fair contribution to the budget of the city, most of which was expended on defence.

It is in the middle of the thirteenth century that it is possible to trace the first steps towards the grant of ' citizenship '. It is not surprising that in earlier times the owners of Jews, in inviting or permitting them to settle in any place,

[1] Scherer, p. 385.

did not take the attitude of the other inhabitants much into consideration. The cities themselves were only beginning to acquire autonomy and their own jurisdiction during the twelfth and thirteenth centuries, and by that time the tradition that Jews were the private property of kings and princes was already established. Since, before the towns had secured their own rights, the status of the Jews appeared to be fixed, it was only when other powers failed in practice that it occurred to the citizens to claim authority over the Jews for themselves.

A series of documents of the Archbishopric of Cologne will make this transition clear. In 1250, Archbishop Conrad received a request from the City Fathers of the Imperial City of Dortmund, asking him to take under his protection the Jews who were then, or who might in the future be, residing in the city[1]. Two years later the Archbishop decided that it would be greatly to the advantage of his own cathedral city if he encouraged Jews to settle in it. He therefore gave a very generous charter to those already resident, and opened the doors to any others who might wish to come. This grant he communicated to the city government, though he showed no signs that he was under any necessity to do so, or that he was acting at their request[2]. In 1259, in renewing the charter, he allotted to the city a certain sum of the tribute paid by the Jews, and again communicated his action to the fathers[3]. Seven years later, Engelbert II, the successor of Conrad, found that his Jewry had fallen on evil days. He renewed their privileges, but instead of communicating them to the burghers, he had them engraved on stone, and fixed to the walls of the cathedral, in the treasury of which they may still be seen[4].

A little more than a hundred years later, in 1373, the situation was so modified that the charter granted by Archbishop Frederick to the Jews of Cologne required the confirmation of the city, and the Archbishop was obliged to ask the City Fathers to take them under their protection, and to admit them as co-citizens with themselves (Sammt-

[1] Aronius, No. 575.
[2] Ibid., No. 588.
[3] Ibid., No. 644.
[4] Ibid., No. 718.

bürger)[1]. This the city agreed to do, and admitted them for
the period of ten years to all the rights enjoyed by other
citizens, in consideration of the archbishop granting to the
city the half of all taxes paid by the Jews, with the exception
of one particular tax which the archbishop was traditionally
entitled to receive. This grant was made to a new Jewish
settlement, and the city showed its temper by granting the
new settlers everything which their predecessors had received
from the archbishops. Moreover, they felt that they were
doing themselves a good stroke of business by their act, in
exactly the same way as Conrad had congratulated himself
on his charter of 1252. In celebration of the event, they
offered themselves a banquet, and charged their treasury
with ten marks as expenses for the occasion[2].

In many of the German cities similar actions were taking
place about the middle of the thirteenth century, showing
the growing interest of the city governments in their Jewish
neighbours. In 1252 the council of Goslar secured a promise
from King William that he would not ill-treat the Jews of
their city[3]. In 1258 the burghers of Worms secured the half
of a payment made by the Jews to the bishop[4]. In 1261 the
council of Halberstadt promised to respect the rights of,
and to grant protection to, the Jews belonging to the bishop[5].
Then in 1266 the first German town reaped the reward of
their efforts. The son of Conrad IV, Conradin, being in
possession of the city of Augsburg, definitely committed the
protection of his Jews there to his lieutenant, and to the
Burgomaster and Council[6]. As he was executed in Italy two
years later this situation may not have been very lasting, but
in 1271 the Bishop of Augsburg, who also possessed a Jewry
in the city, took exactly the same action, at the request of the
burghers[7].

[1] T. J. Lacomblet, *Urkundenbuch für die Geschichte des Niederrheins*,
III, No. 752, summary in C. Brisch, *Geschichte der Juden in Cöln*, II, p. 3.
The city had, in the interval, become an Imperial City, though the Arch-
bishop still possessed the Judenregal.

[2] C. Brisch, *op. cit.*, II, p. 5.

[3] Aronius, No. 585.

[4] *Ibid.*, No. 637.

[5] *Ibid.*, No. 676.

[6] *Ibid.*, No. 716.

[7] *Ibid.*, No. 751. Cf. No. 763, in which the Abbess of Quedlinburg
requests the city government to protect her Jews.

The earliest date at which the development is completed by the actual employment of the word ' citizen ' in relation to the Jews is probably impossible to establish. It occurs in the statutes of the city of Lucerne of 1252, but their authenticity is uncertain[1]. The citizens of Worms and Speyer in a treaty made between the two cities in 1297 certainly assumed full responsibility for their own Jews[2], but without mentioning the word ' citizen '. There exists a most interesting formula for the admission of a Jew as citizen of Worms, which is unfortunately undated. It is sufficiently important to quote in full:

' A Jew shall be accepted as a burgher in this manner:
' He shall first go before the Bishop of the Jews, and the Jewish elders, and they shall receive him according to their custom. When this has been done, the Jewish bishop, accompanied by the elders or by other Jews, shall bring him whom they have accepted before our Lord Bishop of Worms, and the City Councillors, and shall say that they on their part have received him as a citizen, and they shall receive him as a citizen, and (he shall swear) fealty to the Bishop, the Council and the City. He is then accepted as a citizen, and shall give the Bishop a quartern of wine, and a demi to each judge and the city clerk, and gratuities to the servers '.[3]

In Stendal, from 1297 onwards, a Jew who possessed ten marks of silver was automatically entitled to apply for citizenship[4]. In 1315 the Emperor, Lewis the Bavarian, granted a privilege to the city of Speyer, which included the right to receive as citizens (zû Buerger) such Jews as applied for admission, and fixed the very heavy penalty of fifty pounds of gold to be paid to the Imperial Treasury, and the same sum to the town, if anyone tried to interfere with its exercise[5]. From the middle of the fourteenth century onwards such grants are common. They are made in various forms. In Mulhouse, Göttingen, Frankfurt, Donauwörth

---

[1] Aronius, No. 590.

[2] MGH, LL, IV, Const. III, p. 544.

[3] J. Kohler, *Wormser Recht und Wormser Reformation* (*Die Carolina und ihre Vorgängerinnen*, IV), pp. 42 ff.

[4] W. Roscher, *Volkswirtschaft*, II, 3rd ed., p. 336.

[5] MGH, LL, IV, Const. V, p. 176.

Basel and Solothurn Jews were accepted as ' burghers '[1].
In Fribourg they were accepted as burghers, but on condition that they only lent their own money, not that of other
Jews or of Christians, and they were told that no guarantee
would be given them that other Jews or Lombards would
not be invited to settle. In the Archbishopric of Mainz, the
archbishop was careful to call them ' Judenburger ', to
distinguish them from Christians[2]. In Breslau, in the time
of Charles IV, the Council extended to particular Jews, at
the request of the emperor, ' the city peace ', and promised
to treat them in all respects ' like our own citizens '[3]. In
Rothenburg, each Jew was accepted individually, and
granted a sealed copy of his naturalisation. In return he
swore to observe the duties of a citizen, and a signed copy of
his declaration was held by the city[4]. At Colmar, where a
Jew was simply accepted as a citizen, he was given a copy of
the full conditions on which he was allowed to live in the
city and conduct his business. He had to return this copy
and surrender his citizenship if he quitted the place[5]. It is
interesting to note that this special Jewish citizenship was
revived in the nineteenth century in Frankfurt as a compromise between the complete emancipation enjoyed by the
Jews under the Napoleonic Primas and the reactionary ideas
of the Senate of the Free City at its re-establishment[6].

It is evident that the various titles and methods by which
' citizenship ' was conferred upon the Jews are but variants
of the same theme. In fact, whatever the language, the
Jewish citizenship was different from that of the Christians.
In the first place it was limited to a period of years; in the
second, it did not confer any right to rise to civic dignity;
and in the third, it could be arbitrarily withdrawn without

---

[1] S. Adler, *Geschichte der Juden in Mülhausen i. E.*, p. 36. Amiet, *Die franz. u. Lombard. Geldwucherer des M.A.* in *Jahrbuch f. Schweizer. Gesch.*, II, p. 199.

[2] Cf. J. S. Menczel, *Beiträge zur Geschichte der Juden von Mainz im XV. Jahrhundert.*, pp. 90, 94, 96.

[3] L. Oelsner, *Schlesische Urkunden zur Geschichte der Juden im Mittelalter*, pp. 61, 72, etc.

[4] H. Bresslau, *Zur Geschichte der Juden in Rothenburg a.T.*, ZGJD, III, pp. 320, 322, 324.

[5] E. Scheid, *Histoire des Juifs d'Alsace*, pp. 95 ff.

[6] I. Krakauer, *Geschichte der Juden in Frankfurt a.M.*, II, p. 514.

the Jew being able to secure any redress. But with all these limitations, it was an important step, and gave the Jews as much security as it was possible for them to obtain in their exceptional position, since it was granted by those with whom they lived in the closest contact, not by some distant prince, and since it identified the interests of the Jews with those who were most dangerous when hostile, and most powerful when friendly.

Finally it may be added, as an example of the contrast between northern and southern Europe, that in southern France, Jews were not only admitted as full citizens from the thirteenth century onwards[1], but were even admitted to the gilds. In lists of members of the gilds of cloth merchants and of tailors of Marseilles, Jews are shown, sometimes without any qualification, sometimes with the word ' Judeus ' added; but as on such rolls the word ' Christianus ' is also inserted, it shows that, for once, the word ' Jew ' implied neither inequality nor contempt[2].

XII. THE CHARTERS IN PERSPECTIVE

The foregoing pages reveal the extraordinary variety of the conditions under which the Jews lived in medieval Europe. There are obviously certain features common to almost all the charters, since they dealt with somewhat similar circumstances everywhere. It is probable that some of these common features are due to the knowledge possessed by the Jews themselves of conditions in different parts of Europe. For it would be natural for them to seek for their own community any special advantage which they had heard of or seen in the possession of another. But for all that, there was no fixed norm by which the value of a charter could be judged. In most cases the Jews had to accept what they could get, good or bad. For, as at the present time, emigration was not often a possible alternative. If to-day it is the country of immigration which closes the door, in those days it was

---

[1] See the articles in REJ of P. Hildenfinger on the Jews of Arles, XLI, p. 72; of J. Bauer, on those of Bédarrides, XXIX, p. 257; of A. Crémieux on those of Marseilles, XLVI, p. 4; and A. Mossé, *Histoire des Juifs d'Avignon*, p. 189.

[2] A. Crémieux, *loc. cit.*, p. 7.

more often the reverse. While there might be a certain
freedom of movement within a national community, and
while Jews of the Empire had considerable liberty up to the
fifteenth century to move from the territory of one prince or
city to that of another, it was not easy to cross national
frontiers. Jews were jealously guarded—up to the moment
where policy decided on their expulsion—and charters
allowing them to leave at will were rare.

If this is one explanation of what at first appears mysterious: why the Jews remained to suffer the appalling persecutions which medieval Christendom inflicted on them,
another explanation lies in the nature of the time. They
were not the only class to suffer injustice, though they
suffered more than any other, and during the periods of calm
life within a Jewish community was full of compensation
for the insults which might be received outside in the
streets.

While it is not possible to evade the fact that their position
steadily worsened throughout the period, and that they came
to appear more and more strange in the eyes of the Christian
population, it is important to realise wherein lay their
strangeness to the medieval mind. The facts that they
possessed special charters of residence, that they lived in a
special dependence upon a prince, would not in themselves
stimulate curiosity. It is possible to-day—with a little
exaggeration—to present the Jews as the single foreign
element in an otherwise homogeneous population. That was
impossible five hundred years ago. In every town, even in
ordinary villages, men lived under different jurisdictions,
were punished differently for the same crimes, paid different
taxes, wore different clothes, and owed different allegiances.
In any large centre there would have been other groups as
foreign in appearance and manner as the Jews, groups which
both possessed special charters setting them on a different
basis from the rest of the population, and lived apart from
the rest in their own streets and quarters.

The only difference between the Jews and these other
groups was religious. While hatred against them was often
economic and based upon their usury, they were not the
only chartered usurers. They were not even the only
usurers who were persecuted or who suffered sudden expul-

sion. But when hatred directed against the Jews broke into violence, there was always his religious otherness to lend it an air of respectability and even piety.

While it may not have occurred to the medieval mind as anything very important, one aspect of their situation contributed greatly to the ultimate tragedy. This was their basic homelessness. To call it ' statelessness ' is to introduce a modern conception which gives a false impression of medieval conditions. Lack of political power, though galling, did not distinguish them from large sections of the Christian population who were sometimes treated just as arbitrarily as the Jews. But it was only in southern Europe that the Jews were to be found in a city for the simple reason that, as far as history went back, they always had lived in that city. Everywhere in the north their term of residence was a limited one, and could only be renewed by a fresh act of their owner. It was this homelessness which made their rightlessness difficult to bear. In many parts of Europe serfs were rightless, and even when they received rights, these were far less extensive than those enjoyed by a chartered Jewish community. But the serf had his home, miserable though it was, and even if he was driven from it in war, no one challenged his right to return to it. The basic limitation of the charters, the last indignity in the position of the Jew as the private property of another, was that though ' rights ' might be conferred upon him, there was no medieval machinery which could give him a home[1]. Only real ' emancipation ' could do that, and such a state is only partially achieved even in the twentieth century.

---

[1] Cf. quotation facing title-page, and p. 149, n. 3.

CHAPTER SIX

REACTIONS TO THE CHARTERS

I. THE REFUSAL TO ACCEPT JEWS

The information given in the two previous chapters has shown that the peculiar status of the Jew and the discovery of his financial value resulted in a Jewish settlement becoming a benefit rather to its owner than to the people among whom it resided. As a result of this fact, the privileges which it was given often ran counter to the wishes of other sections of the population, in particular of the Church and of its Christian debtors. The inevitable result was that the value of a Jewish settlement needed always to be weighed against the disadvantages accruing from interested opposition.

The tactics employed by the opposing forces were many and various, and met with different degrees of success. The simplest of all tactics was obviously to make a straight request to be excused the presence of Jews altogether. Such a policy was adopted from time to time with complete success and, apart from general and national expulsions, there are a number of cases where the Jews were excluded or expelled from particular centres within a territory which they were otherwise allowed to inhabit. It is an interesting fact that it never became an official policy of the Church to solve in this way the problem created by the existence of Jews. The Church was certainly the motive power in a number of cases of general expulsion; but her official policy was rather to control their conduct, while leaving them to be a witness to the crime of deicide by their miserable condition, and hoping that contact with Christians would lead to their conversion.

What, however, the official policy of the Church might not demand, was sometimes granted at the request of individual piety. The case has already been quoted of the Abbess at Saintes who requested Saint Louis to remove his Jews, as she wished for no Jews on her estates[1]. Piety also seems to have moved Eleanor of Provence, mother of Edward I, to

[1] See above, p. 119.

request her son in 1275 to remove all Jews from the towns which she had received as her dower. As a consequence of this request the Jews were moved from Marlborough to Devizes, from Gloucester to Bristol, from Worcester to Hereford, and from Cambridge to Norwich[1].

A period of disorder might also lead to a request to be excused the presence of Jews. In the fifteenth century the towns of Alsace found themselves continually disturbed by the passage along the Rhine of Swiss mercenaries, who specialised in the sacking of Jewries. A town which possessed no Jewish residents was, therefore, in a favoured position. In 1468 the town of Colmar, weary of the expense and the continual anxiety involved in protecting them from these soldiers, informed its Jews that it would guarantee them protection only from attacks by disorderly elements among its own citizens[2]. In 1477 it decided to expel them altogether, and took the lead in a confederacy of Alsatian towns determined on the same policy[3]. While, when the danger was passed, some of the towns readmitted them, in others this exclusion marked the definite end of the medieval Jewish community[4].

But the commonest ground on which such an exclusion might be demanded was, unquestionably, economic necessity. Jealousy of its privileges, commercial rivalry and hopeless indebtedness played their part in leading a city to take such a step. When a whole province requested freedom from Jews, it was probably only the last argument which entered into consideration. In none of these cases was the request necessarily granted without compensation. In many—in fact most—cases it was not granted at all until the situation had become so serious that the ruler had to face actual riots if he refused to forgo his profit from the loans of his Jews. The semi-independent towns of Germany were particularly apt to take the law into their own hands, and decree the expulsion of their Jews with but the slightest reference to their prince, or with none at all. In the fifteenth century the

---

[1] *Select Pleas, etc., from the Rolls of the Exchequer of the Jews*, edited by J. M. Rigg, p. 85.
[2] E. Scheid, *Histoire des Juifs d'Alsace*, p. 99.
[3] *Ibid.*, p. 74.
[4] Further information on towns refusing Jews is given in Section 4 below.

troubled conditions of Alsace made such actions very frequent. In one case at least, popular hostility was such that the city fathers, having set a day for the departure of the Jews without any reference to their overlord, pursued them through the streets and killed those who did not leave quickly enough[1].

On the rare occasions where a ruler consented to the departure of his Jews earlier than absolute necessity warranted, he naturally expected payment from the beneficiaries of his generosity. Alphonse of Poitiers in 1249 charged four sous from every hearth whose owner possessed property worth twenty sous for acceding to the request of the mayors of Poitou and Saintonge that they might expel their Jews[2]. Alternatively, where the Jews paid a fixed tribute, the ruler might simply impose on the town the responsibility for making up the same sum in addition to their ordinary annual payments. This was done, for instance, by the King of Bohemia when he allowed the Jews to be expelled from Brüx in 1464[3], and by the Prince of Orange when he sanctioned their expulsion from that city in 1505[4]. Other cases in which the conflict with the towns over the presence of Jews ultimately led to expulsion will be more appropriately treated in considering the whole relation of the towns to the charters granted to the Jews. The examples already quoted are enough to indicate the situation.

Finally, a word should be said on the Jewish side of this question. It can easily be understood that the power of the Jews over their own movements was of the very slightest. In normal circumstances they could neither remain in a city in which the ruler was not willing to receive them, nor quit one from which he was unwilling to release them. At the same time, it is interesting to find that the rabbinical authorities did what they could to warn Jews against settlement in places where the ruler had seriously maltreated his Jews, in one case by forcing them to accept Christianity[5].

---

[1] E. Scheid, *op cit.*, p. 70.

[2] Teulet, III, p. 72, No. 3782.

[3] Bondy, No. 263.

[4] J. Bauer, *Les Juifs d'Orange*; REJ, XXXII, p. 239.

[5] Responsum of Rabbi Judah b. Samuel of Ratisbon, quoted in D. M. Shohet, *The Jewish Court in the Middle Ages*, p. 15.

P

This they did by placing settlement in such a territory under the ban of excommunication; but, in order to avoid creating unnecessary hardship, the ban was only valid during the lifetime of the offending ruler.

The community also had a limited power of rejecting new settlers. They could refuse to accept one, and actually expel him after he had taken up residence, if he refused to take his share in the communal taxes[1]. As their contributions to revenue were the main interest of their owner, it is not likely that he would interfere with the moderate exercise of this right. Apart from such specific points, they took the only step open to them to assist individual Jews to escape from impossible conditions, by declaring that an oath of allegiance exacted by force by a Christian prince was not binding if the Jew had taken to himself the maxim of Euripides that the ' tongue hath sworn, the heart remains unpledged '[2]. This was a reasonable permission in the circumstances, and must be set against the double background, that a Jew could not avail himself of the escape if another Jew would suffer from his action, and the general strict injunction of the rabbis that Jews must be scrupulously exact in their dealings with Christians for the sake of the ' sanctification of the Name '; in other words, for the honour of Judaism[3].

II. THE CHURCH AND THE CHARTERS

As the whole problem of the relation of the Church to the Jews will be dealt with in a subsequent volume, it will be enough at this point to indicate the main lines of her attitude, as it is revealed by the Papacy itself and the diocesan administration. Something has already been said of the struggle of the owners of Jews to preserve them from the activities of the Inquisition[4]. The complicated questions involved in the attitude of the Orders, the local clergy and the scholars must be left for later treatment.

[1] D. M. Shohet, *op. cit.*, pp. 23 ff. A. J. Zimmels, *Geschichte der Juden in Deutschland im* 13. *Jahrhdt.*, pp. 37 ff.

[2] D. M. Shohet, *op. cit.*, p. 14.

[3] *Ibid.*, Ch. IV *passim*.

[4] See above, pp. 136 ff.

It would appear that after a long period, in which her interest was concentrated elsewhere, the attention of the Church was again directed to the Jews by the massacres of the Crusades. The action of Agobard was local and temporary in its effects. From Rome itself there is almost complete silence between the letters of Gregory the Great and the letters of 1063 in which Alexander II dealt with the Crusade in Spain. After the more terrible events of 1096 Pope Urban concerned himself only with the uncanonical action of the emperor in allowing Jews, who had been forcibly baptized, to return to Judaism. In these two actions the limits of subsequent papal interest are disclosed, and they are expressly stated, in a quotation from a letter of Gregory the Great[1], in the bull *Sicut Judaeis non*[2] which was continually repeated by the medieval Popes: the Jews are not to be subjected to violence, but may enjoy no rights other than those permitted by law.

This bull was first issued, probably in 1120, by Calixtus II, at the instance of the Jews. The memory of the events of 1096 had vividly impressed the particular danger of religious enthusiasm upon their minds. It is only surprising that there is so long a delay before the bull appeared. It is possible that either Paschal II or Gelasius II may have made some pronouncement, but it is not very likely, for all subsequent bulls refer to that of Calixtus as the archetype. The bull of Calixtus has itself disappeared, and the earliest surviving text is that of Alexander III, which is based on that of Eugenius III, which, in turn, is based on the original bull of Calixtus[3]. The text of this important pronouncement runs as follows[4]:

Just as licence ought not to be granted the Jews to presume to do in their synagogues more than the law permits them, just so ought they not to suffer curtailment in those [privileges] which have been conceded them.

[1] Gregory, Ep. VIII, xxv; MGH, Ep. II, p. 27.

[2] Called also the *Constitutio pro Judaeis*.

[3] Text in Aronius, No. 313a. A later text, giving a formal denial of ritual murder, is given in M. Stern, *Die Stellung der Päpste zu den Juden*, No. 1.

[4] The translation is that of S. Grayzel in *The Church and the Jews in the Thirteenth Century*, p. 93, based upon the edition of the bull of Innocent III in 1199.

That is why, although they prefer to remain hardened in their obstinacy rather than acknowledge the prophetic words—and the eternal secrets—of their own scriptures, that they might thus arrive at the understanding of Christianity and Salvation, nevertheless, in view of the fact that they begged for our protection and our aid, and in accordance with the clemency that Christian piety imposes, we grant their petition and offer them the shield of our protection.)

We decree that no Christian shall use violence to force them to be baptized as long as they are unwilling and refuse, but that if anyone of them seeks refuge among the Christians of his own free will and by reason of his faith [only then], after his willingness has become quite clear shall he be made a Christian without subjecting himself to any calumny. For surely none can be believed to possess the true faith of a Christian who is known to have come to Christian baptism not willingly, and even against his wishes.

Moreover, without the judgment of the authority of the land, no Christian shall presume to wound their persons, or kill [them] or rob them of their money, or change the good customs which they have thus far enjoyed in the place where they live. Furthermore, while they celebrate their festivals, no one shall disturb them in any way by means of sticks or stones, nor exact from any of them forced service, except that which they have been accustomed to perform from ancient times. In opposition to the wickedness and avarice of evil men in these matters, we decree that no one shall presume to desecrate or reduce the cemetery of the Jews, or, with the object of extorting money, to exhume bodies there buried. If any one, however, after being acquainted with the contents of this decree, should presume to act in defiance of it (which God forbid), he shall suffer loss of honour and office, or he shall be restrained by the penalty of excommunication, unless he shall have made proper amends for his presumption.

This continually repeated bull was supplemented by the Third Lateran Council with a closer definition of the restrictions which should be enforced wherever Jews lived among Christians[1]. They were not to keep Christian servants; in cases where they might use their own witnesses against Christians, the latter might do the same against Jews; judges who showed partiality towards the Jews were to be anathematized; converts were to be allowed to keep all their property; where it had been confiscated, it was to be restored.

The councils did not take the trouble, which the Popes took, to ensure that the Jews were allowed to enjoy the rights indubitably theirs by the ancient custom of Roman and Canon Law, and this distinction remains valid all through the period. The reason may be that the members of the councils, being mostly diocesan and provincial administrators, were aware that the protection of the Jews lay in the hands of the secular princes, who were far more likely to err on the side of favouring the Jews than the reverse. The Papacy, on the other hand, regarded itself as a supreme authority with the duties of both protection and control.

The phrases in which the Popes extend their protection to the Jews recall those of the earlier charters, and may be meant to be reminiscent of them, but it is important to note that the Popes never disputed the claim of the secular princes that the Jews were their property. No Pope or bishop ever claimed Jews by virtue of his ecclesiastical position, and this recognition limited the interest of the Church in the Jews to the two points already mentioned. Her general position in regard to them was that they might be permitted to live among Christian people, as witnesses to the truth of Christianity, as the possessors of the Bible, and as possible converts[2]. This, however, was not the reason why the princes favoured Jewish settlement, and the conflicting motives of the two parties resulted in a continuous struggle between them. The princes did not want snivelling testimonies to the sin of deicide, but persons sufficiently protected to be able to contribute by their wealth and energy to the ever empty royal coffers. Their conduct was dictated by practical, not humanitarian motives. Any degradation which

---

[1] Canon xxvi; Mansi, XXII, c. 231.

[2] See the preamble to the bull of Innocent III confirming the *Constitutio pro Judaeis* in Grayzel, *op. et loc. cit.*, and the letter of Alexander II to the Spanish clergy, *supra*, p. 58.

was not likely to interfere with the financial value of the Jews they were ready to enforce. But on basic issues they stood firm. The point most grievous to the Church, the necessary legal protection of the Jews from courts whose whole feeling would have been weighted against them, has been already discussed. Even the Inquisition failed to make any real inroads into this legal fortress erected by the princes[1].

Foiled in her effort to undermine the favoured position of the Jews in the royal courts, the Church turned her attention to the protection of the Christian population from Jewish influence. The number of councils which launched ' omnibus ' canons following the example of the twenty-sixth canon of the Third Lateran Council is legion[2]. They come from every country, and from every century. Their result was probably extraordinarily slight. Without the co-operation of the princes, and unable to bring Jews into their own Courts Christian, the clergy had little power of seeing their canons carried out. It is partly for this reason also that their attempt to suppress Jewish usury was so complete a failure.

The only form in which they could make their disapproval at all effective was by excommunicating those Christians who consorted with Jews, but the latter could always rely on royal action to circumvent such excommunications. Two cases have already been quoted in which this was tried, one in the early days of Henry III of England, and one in the south of France after the return of the Jews in 1361[3]. But

---

[1] See above, pp. 136 ff.

[2] Such councils were: in France, Montpellier (1195), ix and x, Mansi, XXII, c. 669 f; Narbonne (1227), ii and iii, *ibid.*, XXIII, c. 21 f; Béziers (1246), xxxvii-xliii, *ibid.*, c. 701; Albi (1254), lxiii-lxx, *ibid.*, c. 850; Avignon (1279), vi, *ibid.*, XXIV, c. 237; Nîmes (1284), i, *ibid.*, c. 561 f; L'Isle (1288), xii, *ibid.*, c. 960; Anse (1299), *ibid*, c. 1219; Lavaur (1368), cxii-cxv, *ibid.*, XXVI, c. 536 f. In Germany, Aschaffenburg (1292), xviii, *ibid.*, XXIV, c. 1091; Mainz (1310), *ibid.*, XXV, c. 333. In England, *Constitutions of the Bishop of Worcester* (1229), xvii, *ibid.*, XXIII, c. 181; Exeter (1287), xlix, *ibid.*, XXIV, c. 830. In Spain, Zamora (1313), Baer, *Castile*, No. 133; Valladolid (1322), xxi, Mansi, XXV, c. 717; Tarragona (1329), xxxiii and lxxv, *ibid.*, c. 850; Tortosa (1429), xx, *ibid.*, XXVIII, c. 1156. In Eastern Europe, Vienna (1267), xix, *ibid.*, XXIII, c. 1175 f; Breslau (for the Province of Gnesen) (1267), x, xii-xiv, Aronius, No. 724; Ofen (1279), cxiii-cxiv, Graetz, *Gesch. der Juden*, VII, pp. 164 f; Prague (1346), Mansi, XXVI, c. 97 f.

[3] See above, p. 132 and p. 177.

in both cases the Church failed to accomplish her purpose. An alternative to excommunication was to secure the issue of legislation, of similar tenor to her canons, by pious or at least well-disposed princes. This was tried several times, but it also seems to have failed[1].

Action on the lines indicated by the *Constitutio pro Judaeis* and the canon of the Third Lateran Council may have been ineffective but, unhappily, Innocent III, or some of those whom he assembled for the fourth council at the Lateran in 1215, discovered a much more fatal weapon against the Jews in the institution of a badge to distinguish them from the Christian population[2]. The Jews struggled with all their power against the wearing of this mark, which was both considered degrading in itself and exposed them to the dangers of assault from Christian fanatics or robbers in search of loot. They succeeded in reducing its danger in Castile[3], and in ignoring it in Germany[4], at any rate for a considerable period, but in the end the Church prevailed, and the badge was almost universally enforced. With the later institution of the ghetto, it completed the degradation of the Jews. A Jewish quarter was originally established for their protection, or as a voluntary settlement. It first came to assume the air of a prison in legislation inspired by the Spanish clergy[5]. Its universal application dates from the council of Basel in 1434[6], but its general enforcement lies outside the medieval period.

The real weakness of the Church in her policy was her lack of any constructive idea as to how the Jews should be kept alive in the state of humiliation in which she wished them to live. It is true that there were always a number of occupations in every Jewish community other than usury,

---

[1] E.g. a mandate of Henry III of England, *Close Rolls*, 1234-37, p. 13; of Philip the Bold of France, G. Saige, *Les Juifs de Languedoc*, p. 212; of Ferdinand I of Aragon, P. Vidal, *Les Juifs de Roussillon*, REJ, XVI, pp. 6 ff.

[2] Lateran IV, canon lxviii, Mansi, XXII, c. 1055; see Grayzel, *op. cit.*, pp. 61 ff.

[3] F. Singermann, *Die Kennzeichnung der Juden im Mittelalter* (Diss.), 1915, pp. 22 ff.

[4] *Ibid.*, pp. 36 ff.

[5] Cf. Baer, *Aragon*, Nos. 293, 465, 483, 491, etc., and *Castile*, Nos. 275, 276, 290, 335, etc.

[6] Mansi, XXIX, c. 98 ff.

but the Church was not enthusiastic to see even these practised. She attacked the sale of victuals by Jews to Christians; the merchant and artisan gilds, under her inspiration, became religious bodies in which Jews could *ipso facto* not be members. Though she exacted tithes on what little land they owned, she was not anxious for them to acquire more. Her whole policy was negative. The practical proposals of the Fourth Lateran regulations were all negative. The efforts of Louis IX and Edward I, discussed in the next section, to divert the Jews from usury were a failure. Nor did she learn by experience. By far the most interesting evidence of the detailed conditions of settlement, which the Church would like to have imposed, are contained in a project for the recall of the Jews to France in 1361. Though the whole purpose of this recall was, in fact, financial, some cleric elaborated a charter in seventeen clauses, in which the only reference to usury was its prohibition. On the other hand, the social and religious life of the Jews was exactly regulated. No Jew was to have a Christian nurse or servant, since the former they seduced, and the latter they subverted. No Jewish butcher was to sell meat to a Christian, but if a Jew touched any eatable for sale in a Christian market, he was to buy it at once. No Jew was to eat meat on a Christian fast day. Jews were not to bathe in streams used by Christians. They were not to enter the Churches, cemeteries or houses of Christians, and no Christian woman was to enter their houses. No Jew was to sell drugs or teach medicine to a Christian. They were not to have more than one synagogue in any diocese (French dioceses are smaller than English ones, and almost every town of importance was the seat of a bishop); that synagogue was only to have one room, so that they might have nowhere to hide converts who wished to return to Judaism. With the same motive they were forbidden to shelter unknown Jewish strangers, lest they should prove to be renegade Christians. They were, of course, to wear a badge ' since they sometimes wear the dress of clerics or other Christians, and hear and see their secrets '. They were not to wear coloured clothes. They were not to discuss with a Christian except he be a theologian or a converted Jew, and they were to have no books except those allowed by the Church. They were to dwell apart in the lowest portions of the town. Finally, and most ingenious of all these regulations, they might not circumcise their children until they had reached a sufficient age to be able to answer a catechism on their religion[1]. It would be interesting to know whether the author of these regulations himself expected that any Jews would enter France in order to have the privilege of conforming to them.

III. ATTEMPTS TO DIVERT THE JEWS FROM USURY

At times the obvious evils of the medieval system of lending, coupled with Christian piety, caused the secular princes to make a serious effort to second the struggle of the Church against the usury of the Jews. Elaborate regulations were drafted for diverting the Jews into other and more ' honest ' occupations. They had not all the fatalistic attitude of the charter of Louis X of 1315, which first definitely forbade them to practise usury, and then made elaborate regulations as to what was to be done if they should happen to lend money to anyone[2].

It was through the influence of Saint Louis that the first move was made in this direction. Already in 1230 he secured a general agreement between his barons, forbidding any Christian to pay usury to the Jews, but he made no suggestion as to how else the Jews should live or the Christians obtain loans. In 1234 Archembaud of Bourbon, acting on his advice, forbade the Jews to practise usury within his dominions, and produced the alternative phrase that they were to live honestly by their own labours and by commerce[3]. Louis himself made use of the same phrase in an order for the reform of morals in Languedoc in 1254[4]. In 1268 he attempted to effect a similar reform of Christian usurers; and his successor, Philip III, repeated the attempt in 1274. But such efforts were doomed to sterility, unless they both provided alternative occupations for the Jew in a society which had a decreasing desire to see him competing as an artisan or

---

[1] M. Jusselin, *Projet d'Ordonnance concernant la situation des Juifs sous Jean II*; REJ, LIV, p. 145.

[2] See above, p. 173.

[3] Teulet, II, p. 264, No. 2284.

[4] Laurière, I, p. 75, cf. Council of Béziers, 1255; Mansi, XXIII, c. 882.

merchant, and at the same time offered more satisfactory conditions for Christians to obtain loans than those of unofficial Christian usurers. Louis, unfortunately, did neither of these things. Nor did his successor, who ' solemnly promulgated ' a similar edict in about 1272, in which the language of St. Louis is exactly repeated[1].

In 1275 Edward I of England made the first serious effort to provide alternative occupations for the Jews. To begin with, he made careful regulations for the winding up of their financial transactions, from which he honestly admitted that he and his predecessors had received much profit in the past. While the Jew was to forfeit his usury, the king was wise enough to guarantee him the return of his capital, in order that he might have the wherewithal to start on his new life. For this latter purpose he was allowed to purchase houses and property in the borough where he dwelt, and to hold such property directly of the Crown, though he could not alienate it without the Crown's consent. Possessed of property, he might engage in lawful commerce and trade, and the sheriffs and other officers of the Crown were ordered to protect him. His right of submitting himself only to the jurisdiction of the royal courts he retained in full. While these regulations do not essentially exceed the intentions of Saint Louis, they pay more attention to the necessary details of such a transformation. For Edward, who realised that still more was wanted, expressly allowed the Jews to buy agricultural land and to farm it themselves, holding the land of the Crown, and owing no feudal homage on it, but also receiving no such homage, and not exercising any advowson attached to the land. Unfortunately, Edward limited the period within which they might hold such land to ten years, and it had to be obtained within five years of the grant of the charter, to be held so long[2]. After a short period he discovered that the only consequence of the law had been to remove the close supervision of moneylending which had existed at the time when loans were legally made. Every kind of dishonest practice had crept in; under various guises enormous interest

[1] Laurière, XII, p. 323, cf. the will of Henry of Brabant, probably inspired by the action of Saint Louis, and including Caorsins; Scherer, p. 190, n. 1.

[2] *Statutes of the Realm* (Rec. Com.), I, p. 221, given in full in App. I, iv.

was charged, and no profit whatever accrued to the king from it. New usury laws were therefore made, and the statute of 1275 tacitly allowed to drop[1].

Many similar attempts were made in other places: in Burgundy in 1302[2], in Roussillon and Cerdagne in 1339[3], in Castile in 1348 (where also the experiment of allowing the Jews special facilities for obtaining land was tried[4]), and elsewhere. But there is no record of any having succeeded. On the other hand, it is worth remarking in this connection that one Jewish community was at any rate believed by its owner to have lived by commerce, without indulging in usury, and that was the community of Majorca, which received special privileges in 1383 as a reward for its virtue. As the owner, Pedro IV, admits to having received a handsome sum for the privilege, it is possible that this sum was also meant to cover the king's unusual faith[5]. But it is also possible that what is meant is the reasonableness of Jewish loans, for there is evidence that in 1391 the Jews of Majorca charged only ten per cent. as opposed to the usurious interest of Christians[6].

A problem which it is not easy to solve is whether, in actual fact, the intentions of Edward I were capable of realisation. The king was demanding that the Jews should live by commerce, handicrafts and agriculture. The Jews were not strangers to any of these occupations. In the first place, there never was a Jewish community in which every member was able to earn his livelihood exclusively by lending money. In many charters of settlement it is expressly stated how many members of the community might adopt that profession. The rest lived by other means. Secondly, even those Jews whose main occupation was finance were not able to avoid all relations with the world of commerce and agriculture. It was necessary to have a channel by which to sell unredeemed pledges of every description, from gold cups to sacks of corn

[1] Regulations of uncertain date, printed in Gross, *The Exchequer of the Jews of England*, in *Anglo-Jewish Exhibition Papers*, pp. 219 ff.

[2] J. Simmonet, *Juifs et Lombards*, in *Mémoires de l'Académie de Dijon*, 2e Série, XIII, p. 156.

[3] P. Vidal, *Les Juifs de Roussillon et Cerdagne*; REJ, XV, p. 37, n. 1.

[4] Baer, *Castile*, No. 178.

[5] Baer, *Aragon*, No. 356.

[6] L. Isaacs, *The Jews of Majorca*, p. 11.

or bales of wool; and, considering how much of the security of their loans lay in land, it is certain that they would be familiar with agricultural procedure, even if the actual working of the land was not frequently in their hands.

The royal proposal, therefore, did not demand of them absolute impossibilities. But there was another side to the question. While it is true that the Jews might have been able to live by the means suggested, the important question was whether the Christians concerned would easily allow them to do so. Medieval trade was an extremely close corporation. By the thirteenth century almost every occupation had its gild, to the membership of which Jews were unable to be admitted, and the king made no provision for altering this state of affairs. Both trade corporations and craft gilds would have made it impossible for a sudden rapid extension of Jewish activity along competitive lines to succeed[1]. Even greater difficulties would have beset the Jews who attempted to turn to agriculture. A sale or lease absolutely limited to ten years would not be likely to lead to the most profitable use of the land. But, apart from this, the suggestion itself invited the Jews to desert the communal life to which tradition had accustomed them, and which their religious loyalties required, and to live in isolation amidst the most ignorant, superstitious and hostile section of the Christian population. The squires, clergy and peasants of the countryside would scarcely provide congenial or even safe neighbours for a Jewish scholar-farmer or business man. It is this Christian hostility which provided the insuperable obstacle to the success of the experiment, for the king, whatever his own intentions and whatever the capacity or adaptability of the Jews, could not alter the general conditions of his time, or dissolve the prejudices and customs of his Christian subjects.

IV. THE ATTITUDE OF THE TOWNS

The complete failure of these experiments, and the development of medieval society, combined to ensure that Jewish

[1] See the article on ' The Expulsion of the Jews from England ', by B. L. Abrahams in JQR, VII, especially pp. 245 ff. That Abrahams very much exaggerates the incapacity of the Jews is shown by the list of occupations given in I. Abrahams, *Jewish Life in the Middle Ages*, first edition, pp. 245 ff.

life should become more and more exclusively urban in character. In such circumstances the attitude towards the Jews adopted by the inhabitants of the towns was of supreme importance. The goodwill of a distant prince could not permanently provide an alternative to the toleration of those among whom their lives were spent, and with whom a great part of their business was conducted.

In its simplest construction feudal society had no place for towns and the merchants who lived in them. While in the south of Europe the towns never ceased to be commercial centres of importance, in northern Europe urban settlements which were not mere dependencies of castles or abbeys were a growth of the eleventh and twelfth centuries. At first their inhabitants had no particular status but, as they acquired importance by their commerce and their crafts, they developed a desire for self-government. It is only as this took place that they became conscious of the fact that those townsmen who were Jews would not automatically come under their new jurisdiction. For, however vague and inconsistent the different elements in the status of the Jews, it is likely that they possessed some kind of recognition and licence from royal or baronial patrons before the Christian element of the population had become very conscious of its own needs.

The attack of the Crusaders in the Rhineland in 1096 was the first test of the attitude of the other merchants to the Jews. Without exception they and the civic authorities, where the latter existed, did all that they could to protect them. The Hebrew reports constantly distinguish them from the town rabble, which was simply interested in loot, and saw the opportunity to obtain it under the guise of religion. Later on the protection of the upper-class burghers became less certain. In the change which took place, religion and the increasing absorption of the Jews in moneylending both played a part.

It was probably in England that the change took place most rapidly, for it was there also that moneylending first became the characteristic Jewish occupation, and that the control of the Crown over them was strictest. As long as the Jews were merchants, individual jealousies could not obscure the fact that their interests were identical with those of Christian merchants. When they developed their trade in money they might still, as civic moneylenders, form a valuable, though unpopular, element in the population. But as chartered royal usurers their interests were likely to be diametrically opposed to those of the rest of the population.

The towns ' had bought at great expense, from king or noble or abbot, the right to be independent, self-governing communities, living under the jurisdiction of their own officers, free from the visits of the royal sheriffs, and paying a fixed sum in commutation of all dues to the king or the local lord; and yet many of them saw the king protecting in their midst a band of foreigners, who had the royal permission to go whithersoever they pleased, who could dwell among the burgesses, and were yet free not only from all customs and dues, and contributions to the ferm, but even from the jurisdiction of those authorities which were responsible for peace and good government '.[1] In England, where the central power was already strong, it was not possible for the citizens to hope to obtain for themselves the right, which many of their fellows on the Continent ultimately obtained, of including the Jews within their own taxation system and submitting them to their own justice. But, in addition to these reasons why they found Jews undesirable as residents, there were still greater grounds for dislike and opposition in their professional activities. However much individuals might profit by the loans they could contract with the Jews, this occupation not only brought no profit to the town itself, but was apt to drain money out of it. A large proportion of the money paid to the Jews in interest, or in repayment of their loans, found its way into the coffers of the king on one charge or another. Further, their deeds might for a number of reasons fall directly into his hands, and be collected for him by his sheriffs, whom, for this reason, the citizens were compelled to admit into their town. Even if the Jew was collecting the debts himself, he had the right to call in the king's officers to coërce a recalcitrant debtor. On the other hand, English towns did not profit much from the occasional cancellation of debts by which the king showed favour to his subjects. While, on the Continent, it was for the sake of

[1] B. L. Abrahams, *op. cit.*, pp. 87 ff.

peasants and merchants that these cancellations were often operated, in England Henry III, the only king who made any practice of this act of grace, did so on behalf of his courtiers or of the knights who followed him on his Gascon campaigns. From every point of view, therefore, the Jews were undesirable residents in English towns, and it is not surprising that there were frequent petitions to be allowed to dispense with them. Such requests could only be sparingly granted by the Crown. It was essential to the royal policy to ensure that Jewish settlements, each with its *archa*, the official chest within which the deeds of loans were deposited, should be widely distributed throughout the country. It was only those towns in which the Jewish settlement was unimportant, or in which some special circumstances made the application reasonable, that the king was likely to permit his Jewry to be closed. In Derby at the time when the application was made, only one Jew was resident[1]. For different reasons Bury Saint Edmunds obtained permission to expel its Jews as early as 1190; Leicester followed in 1231[2], Newcastle in 1234, Wycombe in 1235, Southampton in 1236, Berkhamsted in 1242, Newbury in 1244, and Derby in 1263[3].

So limited a recognition of what must have been a common feeling in the towns inevitably led to unhappy consequences. In 1189 an incident at the coronation of Richard I led to a massacre in London, and the flame once kindled spread right through the country. The initiative seems to have come primarily from the lesser baronage who were heavily indebted to the Jews, and from young Crusaders. But there is little sign of the citizens being on the side of the Jews, as they were a hundred years earlier in the Rhineland. When in 1203 there were again riots in London, the leading citizens seem to have been badly involved, and were held responsible to the king for what had happened[4]. In order to make the towns realise that the Crown intended to maintain its Jews, and that no sympathy would be shown to the citizens if evil befell them, in 1217 the Regents for the young

---

[1] *Close Rolls*, 1259-61, p. 381.

[2] The permission was obtained from Simon de Montfort, but Jews were never subsequently readmitted.

[3] B. L. Abrahams, *op. cit.*, p. 90.

[4] Rymer, *Foedera*, I, p. 89.

King Henry III ordered the sheriffs to choose twenty-four burgesses in every place where there was a Jewish community, and to make these men responsible for the safety of the Jews[1]. In spite of this riots broke out in 1234[2] in Norwich, and between 1262 and 1267 the Jewries of London, Worcester, Northampton, Canterbury and the Isle of Ely were sacked. In these riots the initiative was again taken by the barons, at war with the king, but the citizens participated in the destruction of the records and the pillage of the Jewries. How the conflict might have developed it is impossible to say, for less than thirty years later the Jews were expelled, not to return until long after the medieval period had come to an end.

In France much less is heard of the attitude of the cities. There were riots, inspired by the despair of urban debtors, but a conflict between urban authorities, jealous of their privileges, and the royal or baronial owners of the Jews does not seem to have been a feature of the French settlements. A few requests to be allowed to dispense with Jews are recorded[3], and at certain periods the Jews were not allowed to reside in small towns or villages, but this seems to be all.

In Germany the history of the relations between cities and Jews is longer and more complicated than anywhere else. The terms of the eleventh-century charters implied that a Jewish settlement would be thoroughly beneficial to the town which received it, and the ready protection accorded by the merchants to the Rhineland Jews during the First Crusade shows that this belief was justified. The failure of the protection does not contradict this. Even if human sympathy played a large part in the action of the burghers in 1096, yet they were also serving their own cause. One of the proofs of their worthiness to receive a charter of municipal liberties was their ability to keep order within the walls. A riot against the Jews was a disturbance of the peace of the town. Apart from the danger that the rioters might turn against themselves, the mere fact of a riot showed their impotence, and their need for the presence of the soldiers of

[1] Tovey, *Anglia Judaica*, p. 77.
[2] *Ibid.*, p. 101.
[3] E.g. the petition of the inhabitants of Villefranche to Edward I, c. 1290 (Col. doc., *Lettres des Rois*, I, p. 380), and the privilege of Eyrieu of 1328 (Laurière, VII, p. 318).

their overlord within their walls. The burghers were therefore anxious to include the Jews within the sphere of their
protection, and to see that no ill befell them.

If the need for preserving peace within the city identified
their cause with that of the Jews, the separate justice under
which the Jews lived also, paradoxically, created a link between them. In the twelfth and, in most places, in the
thirteenth centuries it was not possible for the burghers to
secure for themselves the rights of justice over the Jews.
But this did not leave them disinterested in the question.
If the owner of the Jews—who was usually the overlord of
the city—abused his rights with the Jews, two consequences
might follow. In the first place, this abuse might well be at
the expense of the burghers; and in the second, one abuse
might well lead to another, and they themselves be the next
sufferers. They were therefore as ready to support the Jews
in any conflict with their overlord, as to protect them in any
riot started by the populace.

Yet a third matter provided an important link between
them. The Jews followed many more occupations in the
German towns than they did in the English. During the
twelfth and thirteenth centuries, they were still merchants
of importance and, as such, contributed in many ways to the
various taxes imposed by the city for its own purposes, the
chief of which were defence and the upkeep of the walls.
Excessive exactions by the owner would lower the amount
which the Jews might contribute to the finances of the city.

With these three common interests no written guarantee
was required to assure the Jews a favourable reception from
the burghers of the towns in which they were settled. But,
as the autonomy of the towns increased and their complete
control of their own conditions developed, they came to feel
that they should control also the jurisdiction in matters
affecting Jews. They were, therefore, ready to make written
agreements with the owners of the Jews, in which they
guaranteed that they would assure them protection, and see
that the special tax claimed by the owner was paid; in return
they obtained authority to deal with questions affecting Jews
in their own courts. They also received the right to tax the
Jews, the financial claims of the owner being limited to
fixed payments. It is at this stage that the privileges to

Q

' Jewish burghers ' make their appearance. It was in such documents that, in return for definite obligations, the towns undertook the full protection of the Jews.

At the end of the thirteenth century, and in the fourteenth, the feeling of the populace towards the Jews steadily grew worse. A number of accusations of ritual murder and the profanation of the Host in the Rhenish regions and elsewhere had stirred up religious hatred, and it can be assumed that the steady growth of moneylending was creating a class of disgruntled debtors. In such circumstances it is natural that the prevailing disorders of the time should also manifest themselves in attacks upon the Jews, in which both religious and economic passions found satisfaction. These attacks the powers of the towns were unable wholly to repulse, and the difficulty of the city government was increased by the fact that the poorer classes in the cities were growing both more powerful and more hostile to the Jews.

It was in Alsace and south-west Germany that the Jews suffered most at this period, and in many cases the towns also suffered damage from the excesses of anti-Jewish riots. In the second decade of the fourteenth century a number of towns had been so wasted by civil disorder that they had to ask for special consideration from the king, and it is interesting that they included the Jews in their request[1]. But, thirty years later, the cities of Alsace were the scene of bloody riots started by the mercenaries of Eberhard, Duke of Württemberg, and, as this time a large proportion of the citizens took sides with the soldiers, the cities afforded very little or no protection to the Jews. The Jews complained bitterly to the Emperor, Charles IV, and reminded him that they were under his ultimate protection; they also claimed heavy damages against the cities. But it did not suit the Emperor, though he was not generally friendly to the cities of the south-west, to alienate them completely. The complaints of the Jews were therefore ignored, and the cities of Colmar, Schlettstadt, Ehnheim, Rosheim, Mülhausen, Kaisersberg, Türkheim, Münster and Oberehnheim were forgiven for all that they had done against the Jews, which the Emperor

---

[1] Cf. for various forms in which this request took place, the grants of Frederick the Handsome to Hagenau, Gmünd, and Constanz; MGH, LL, IV, Const. V, pp. 191, 209, 247, and 328.

promised ' to consider as though it had never happened '. The Jews were also forbidden to make any claims on their own behalf for their losses[1].

During this same period, from the latter half of the thirteenth century onwards, requests began to appear from German cities to their princes that they might be excused Jewish settlements, or that they might expel the Jews already resident among them[2]. From then onwards such requests were not uncommon, and were frequently granted—temporarily, at any rate. The alternative was to take advantage of the weakness of the emperor or other owner of the Jews to secure complete authority over them for the advantage of the city, and to reduce the right of the owner merely to the receipt of a small fixed tax.

A second change in the situation of the Jews, which began to be manifest about the same time, arose from a development with whose origin they were quite unconcerned. The German cities had been governed by the wealthy merchants and patricians; and the mass of craftsmen, organised in gilds, had little voice in domestic affairs. As they grew more important they realised that their interests and those of the patrician merchants did not completely coincide. They desired a strong policy of ' protection ' which would exclude all rival goods from their local market, so that, having the monopoly, they might keep up the price of their goods. At the same time they desired to buy food and drink from the peasants as cheaply as possible. The great merchants were quite uninterested in this kind of protection, since their commercial enterprises covered a far wider scope than the territory of their city. They were also much less affected by the prices charged by the peasants.

It was in the riots of 1348-9 which followed the circulation of the story that the Jews had caused the Black Death by poisoning the wells, that this conflict between patricians and gilds came to affect the Jews. The artisans saw in them only

[1] MGH, LL, IV, Const. VIII, pp. 367, 437, 455, and 459.

[2] E.g. Greifswald, 1264 (Aronius, No. 693); Colmar, 1285 (E. Scheid, *op. cit.*, p. 20); Breslau, 1319 (Bondy, No. 51), at the beginning of the period; and for the end, Stendal, 1453 (J. Landsberger, *Zur Geschichte der Juden in der Mark Brandenburg*; MGWJ, XXXI, pp. 37 ff.); Olmütz, 1454 (Bondy, No. 250) and Schlettstadt, 1479 (E. Scheid, *op. cit.*, p. 360). See also Section One of this chapter.

usurers to whom they were indebted, and did not realise
the advantages which had accrued to them from the presence
of a supply of money available for loans at an interest which
was lower than could be obtained from unofficial Christian
lenders—as they usually found out if they expelled the Jews.
In Strasbourg the patricians tried to protect the Jews from
the artisans, who clamoured for their destruction[1]. In the
panic created by the relentless spread of the Black Death,
there were few who kept their heads sufficiently to realise
the absurdity of this charge levelled against the Jews, and
it is to the honour of the patricians that they made this
effort. It proved not only unavailing in protecting the Jews,
but it led to a revolution in the city, and the overthrow of
the patrician government[2]. The same conflict was repeated
elsewhere, and it was extremely rare for the city fathers to
succeed in their effort to protect the Jews from the violence
of the urban proletariat[3]. It is not surprising that when
the Jews were re-admitted to Trier in 1362 they were
warned that, if riots broke out and the city was unable or
unwilling to undertake their protection, they might receive
a fortnight's notice to leave the town[4].

During the rest of the Middle Ages there is even less order
in the history of the Jews in German towns than there is in
the preceding centuries. The Jews themselves never recovered from the appalling destruction of life and wealth which
they suffered in 1349 and in the preceding half-century.
Some towns did not accept further Jewish settlements, in
others they were much smaller than they had been previously.
Their business also continued on a smaller scale, and their
importance to their owners consequently declined.

It is probably this reduction in their importance which
increased the confusion in their status, for they were not
sufficiently valuable to justify either side taking really
desperate measures to assert ownership. The history of the
Jews of Mainz in the fifteenth century admirably illustrates

[1] Even in the panic of 1349 superstition was reinforced by avarice.
Cf. the famous remark of the Alsatian Chronicle: ' Das bar gut das sü
hattent, . . . das war ouch die vergift die die Juden döttete ' (Königs-
hofen, *Strassburger Chronik.*, ed. Hegel, pp. 761-765).

[2] C. T. Weiss, *Die Stellung der Juden im Fürstbistum Strassburg*, p. 9.

[3] See J. Nohl, *Der Schwarze Tod*, Ch. viii, pp. 239 ff., *passim*.

[4] E. Hecht, *Geschichte der Juden im Trier'schen*; MGWJ, VII, p. 182.

this confusion. Between 1438 and 1471 the Jews were three times expelled from the town, each time by a different authority. The first expulsion was carried through by the Burgomaster and Council, without any reference to the archbishop to whom the Jews nominally belonged. In 1462 they were again expelled, together with other citizens, as a bye-product of a conflict between two rivals for the archiepiscopal throne. The third, and final, expulsion took place in 1470-1 at the order of the archbishop, without reference to the city[1].

In Spain history pursued a somewhat different course to the same end. Both in Castile and in Aragon the cities accepted the fact that the Jews were not their property. The absolute power of the Crown, limited though it was by the presence of the Cortes, never lost its authority as completely as did the Imperial power in the Empire. Moreover the Jews in Spain were much more important to the national economy than they were in Germany, so that the Crown was likely at any moment only to make the minimum concessions necessary to calm popular feeling.

Spanish history also presents features of special interest in the close alliance between the Church and the citizens to the disadvantage of the Jews. Already in the middle of the thirteenth century the Cortes began to demand sumptuary laws against them[2]. The grant of such laws could only have had an adverse effect on the interests of the merchants, since they would have reduced the trade in articles of dress and luxury, but they would have satisfied the clerical desire to make evident to everyone the fallen state of a deicide people. These demands continued steadily all through the period until, in the beginning of the fifteenth century, a new method of humiliating them was devised, and the Cortes demanded that they be forbidden to shave or cut their hair[3].

Apart from such measures of pure spite, or religious zeal, whichever the reader wishes to consider them, the main attack of the cities was threefold. The number of public offices, especially in the finances of the country, which were

---

[1] J. S. Menczel, *Geschichte der Juden v. Mainz im XV. Jahrhdt.*, pp. 42-58.

[2] Baer, *Castile*, No. 72, para. 26.

[3] *Ibid.*, No. 275, para. 18.

held by Jews caused considerable jealousy among Christians.
There was a continuous effort on the part of the Cortes to
persuade or compel the kings to promise the exclusion of all
Jews from such lucrative posts[1]. At times these efforts
succeeded—on paper—but in actual fact Jews continued to
hold office right up to the time of Ferdinand and Isabella.
In one case at least the Crown made the sensible reply to
this traditional demand, that the king had been perfectly
prepared to grant the farming of taxes to Christians at a
lower rate than they were farmed to Jews, but that as no
Christians had wanted or applied for the farms, it was not
his fault that the Jews had obtained them[2].

A second attack was directed against the special legal
procedure and the special courts which were guaranteed to
the Jews in their charters. This attack was gradually successful. In 1313 Queen Maria and the Infante Pedro,
guardians for the young king, Alphonso XI, made two
concessions; that the evidence of Jews alone should not be
valid against Christians, and that in criminal cases judgment
should be given according to the custom of the place, and not
according to the privileges of the Jews[3]. At the same time,
the regents abolished the right of the Jews to employ their
own bailiffs for the collection of their loans[4]. Emboldened
by this anti-Jewish policy of the Regency, the Church
proceeded to issue the most violent canons against the Jewish
population. In a council held at Zamora in 1313 all the
demands of Christian rivals in the matter of judicial privilege
were granted[5]. These successes of the anti-Jewish party
were only temporary for, less than half a century later,
matters had clearly returned to their former state. Pedro
the Cruel refused the request of the Cortes of Valladolid in
1351 that he should abolish the separate courts of the Jews[6];
and John I in 1385 similarly refused to change the laws
governing the evidence required in financial suits, though

[1] E.g. Cortes of Palencia (1313), Burgos (1367), Soria (1380), Valladolid
(1385); Baer, *Castile*, Nos. 138-139, 205, 228, 234.

[2] Reply of Henry of Trastamare, 1367; Lindo, *History of the Jews of
Spain and Portugal*, p. 152.

[3] Baer, *Castile*, Nos. 138 and 139.

[4] *Ibid.*, No. 139, para. 31.

[5] Lindo, *op. cit.*, p. 126.

[6] *Ibid.*, p. 147.

he admitted that the special privileges enjoyed by the Jews in respect of stolen goods were unwarranted and abolished them[1]. But in 1405 the cities gained their point about evidence, and Henry III allowed a Jew to be convicted on Christian evidence alone—with the weak proviso that the Christian was respectable[2]. In 1412, under the influence of Vincent Ferrer, the Queen Regent for the infant John II abolished the whole separate Jewish jurisdiction[3]. It would appear that on coming of age John II revoked this law, for the final abolition of Jewish legal privileges was the act of Ferdinand and Isabella in 1476[4].

The third line of attack of the cities was directed against Jewish commercial liberty. The struggle against the money-lender was so universal that it is not surprising to find traces of it also in Spain. But, apart from this profession, the Jews were prominent in many departments of commerce and industry and, as Christians grew proficient in these occupations, they began to include discriminating regulations against their Jewish rivals in their communal statutes. In Aragon, in the thirteenth century, it is fairly common to find the king ordering the royal officials to see that this or that Jewish business is not hampered by regulations which have been passed by the local authorities[5], and many of the express permissions granted by the Kings of Aragon to the Jews to carry on this or that trade suggest that there had been local opposition to their doing so. Sometimes the Christians secured royal approval of their efforts to limit Jewish business, but in one case at least they found that by doing so they had only damaged themselves by reducing the general prosperity of the town[6].

In the fourteenth century, as general hostility against the Jews steadily increased, it became possible for a town to restrict their enterprises, even in spite of the presence of a strong king on the throne. It was during the reign of

---

[1] Lindo, *op. cit.*, p. 167.

[2] *Ibid.*, p. 184.

[3] *Ibid.*, p. 198, Clause 7.

[4] Baer, *Castile*, No. 330.

[5] E.g. Regné, *Catalogue*, Nos. 1491 and 1670; REJ, LXVII, pp. 75 and 217.

[6] *Ibid.*, No. 1953; REJ, LXIX, p. 153.

Alfonso XI that the town of Seville included in its statutes a number of articles whose motive was simply to hamper Jewish business in the interest of the Christians[1]. At the beginning of the following century, during the period when the influence of Vincent Ferrer was predominant, much more serious and more general attacks on Jewish business life took place. The Regency was as ready to attack the commercial life of the Jews as it was to abolish their judicial privileges. In two ordinances, one issued by each of the two Regents, the Jews were excluded from almost every commercial and financial occupation[2]. During the chaotic reign of John many of the towns succeeded in making their own laws regulating Jewish conduct, but in 1443 John—or more probably Don Alvaro, his Constable—restored all their commercial rights to the Jews, while retaining some of the less important clerical restrictions in force[3].

Nominally, this restoration remained valid up to the time of their expulsion, and on several occasions Queen Isabella intervened on behalf of Jews who were being denied these rights by Inquisitors or local authorities[4]. But partial expulsions preceded the general edict of 1492, and the cities must have felt victorious in their struggle against Jewish competition many years before the final expulsion of the Jews.

V. JEWISH PERSONAL PRIVILEGES

We have so far been considering the reactions of Christian groups to the privileges granted to the Jews. But, while these privileges appeared excessive to the groups, clerical and civic, with which we have been dealing, it is equally true that they appeared burdensome to the Jews to whom they were granted. For it was the Jews who realised that the larger part of the profit went into royal and princely coffers, whereas the Christians only saw the large amounts which they themselves paid out in usury.

[1] Baer, *Castile*, No. 163.

[2] Ordinances of Valladolid; Baer, *Castile*, No. 275, and Lindo, *op. cit.*, p. 197; and of Cifuentes, Lindo, pp. 201 ff.

[3] Lindo, *op. cit.*, pp. 221 ff.

[4] Baer, *Castile*, Nos. 353, 356, 371.

As a consequence of this situation, much advantage was to be obtained by a rich Jew if he secured for himself a special privilege of non-solidarity with the other Jews of his community. It was in Spain that these personal privileges were especially common, and this is not surprising, for it was in that country that individual Jews were continually employed in important posts in the royal service. Farmers of the taxes, ambassadors, physicians and surgeons, and others of similar importance adopted this somewhat selfish method of securing advantages to themselves at the expense of their community. But withal they were but aping the Christians, and their privileges still fell far short of that which the nobility and clergy universally obtained in the medieval state at the expense of the unfortunate peasant.

The Jewish communities themselves deeply resented this action of those who were often their richest members. They placed the recipients of such favours under the ban of excommunication, and continually demanded of the king the promise that he would not exempt any single member of their Jewry from his share of the common burdens. The results of their efforts can be seen from three documents of Pedro II of Aragon of 1210 and 1212.

In February 1210 Pedro granted to the Monastery of Sigena a Jew, Master Vitalis, together with all his family and property. The gift was supposed to be an act of kindness to the monastery as well as to the Jews concerned. The latter were declared quit of any and every charge now or in the future to be exacted either by the Crown or by the Jewry of which Vitalis had formed a part. In addition they were exempted for all time from every road tax, toll or duty on themselves or their goods throughout the whole kingdom by land, sea, lake or river. No community, no civic authority, no royal judge or officer, nor any other official within the whole national administration, was to exact any charge whatever from them. They were confirmed in the full possession of all their property, or of any further property which they might acquire throughout the length and breadth of the kingdom, and of all privileges which they might have received from previous sovereigns or from others. They were at all times to have full right and authority to collect any debts without any hindrance (? in spite of any royal moratorium which might have been granted). They were not affected by any tax on merchandise which had been or might be created by the Jewish community where they had previously lived, or by any fine imposed for non-payment of this tax. Their new owners, the prioress and members of the community, were never to exchange them for other Jews, Christians or Saracens or otherwise dispose of them. Finally, the Jewish communities were strictly forbidden to show any sign of resentment against Vitalis and his family for the privilege which they had obtained. No Jew or Jewry was to excommunicate them, or impose any punishment on them whatever; nor to restrict their commercial rights; nor to expel them from the synagogue; nor to refuse to pray with them; nor to refuse them burial or circumcision[1].

While the advantages which accrued to Vitalis as a result of this privilege were undoubtedly great, it must not be imagined that his new owners received him out of pure philanthropy, for it is to be noted that there is not a single word as to any limitation imposed on *their* right to exact what they could from him. The profit of the monastery was, however, pure loss for the community of which he had once been a member. Hence the communities frequently pressed the king to promise that he would not grant such individual favours. In January 1212 Pedro granted such a promise to the Jewry of Huesca ' since burdens are borne more easily by many than by few, especially if they are fairly divided between all, and since those who undertake more of them than they can bear are crushed under their weight.' He cancelled all gifts of Jews to monasteries or to the knightly orders, and returned them to their communities. If a Jew refused to rejoin his community, he gave it licence to ex-communicate him and distrain upon his property; any Jew who in the future might seek to obtain such a privilege, the community might even, on payment of a compensation of one thousand solidi, stone. Their previous owners were required to hand over all property which the Jews had held while in their possession, and were refused any further claims in it. The king further promised that he would never again grant any privileges to individuals by which they

[1] Baer, *Aragon*, No. 74.

might be able to withdraw themselves from their share of the communal burden[1].

In March of the same year Pedro proceeded to give to the Knights of Saint John the Jew, Alazrach of Saragossa, together with his family, on terms even more favourable than those he had granted to Vitalis[2]!

All through Spanish history such promises were made to the communities, and all through they were broken; but the permanence of such gifts was also illusory. While the kings never regarded their promises as binding for the future, they were equally free in disregarding the promises of their predecessors. There are few grants that can be traced for any great length of time. It is, for example, unlikely that the gift of Alazrach of Saragossa to the Knights of Saint John in 1212 survived the cancellation of all such gifts of Jews of Saragossa by James II in 1325-6, even if it survived as long as that[3]. The indifference with which James himself regarded his promises is shown by the existence of a grant of non-solidarity to a Jew of Saragossa made by him in the very year in which he had promised to make no such gifts[4].

Equally frequent as the gifts of Jews to the great orders, were simpler privileges by which individuals were granted complete or limited independence of the communities. They might be exempted from additional contributions towards a deficit on the tribute[5]; their own percentage might be fixed, whatever increase might be demanded of the rest[6]; in very special cases they might be completely enfranchised from any authority of the community whatsoever, financial, judicial or religious, and placed directly under the protection of the king[7]. In addition to such financial privileges, various other curious advantages were eagerly sought by individuals. Undeterred by any fears of monotony in his diet, Cecri b. Moses Avendino of Saragossa obtained two pounds of

---

[1] Baer, *Aragon*, No. 78.

[2] *Ibid.*, No. 79.

[3] Regné, *Catalogue*, No. 3369; REJ, LXXVIII, p. 132.

[4] *Ibid.*, No. 3412, p. 139.

[5] E.g. Baer, *Aragon*, No. 174. Regné, *Catalogue*, No. 506; REJ, LXII, p. 44.

[6] E.g. Baer, *Aragon*, No. 99.

[7] E.g. *ibid.*, No. 47, and Regné, *passim*, from A.D. 1300 onwards.

mutton daily from the market of Saragossa, and his descendants obtained a renewal of the privilege from James II in 1291[1]. The grant of mutton seems to have placed this amateur Jeshurun in an envied situation, for there were many other candidates who obtained the same savoury favour, some one pound, some the coveted two[2]. One man, not satisfied with a mere couple of pounds of mutton, obtained a whole butcher as a privilege, with permission to obtain a second if the first ran away or got past his work, and with the right to secure his excommunication and to fine him one thousand sous if he dared withhold the profits[3]! Another obtained a front seat in the synagogue, to be placed between the seats of two other Jews who are named in the document[4]. It is not said that they were consulted. A third secured for himself and his family permission to wear clothes of any colour, even though *sub fusc* was the regulation of the community. Compared with these, to be excused office because of professional duties, or to be allowed to appear only in a Jewish court when defendant against either Jew or Christian, appears to indicate a lack of imagination on the part of either giver or recipient[5]. To be excused the wearing of the badge at a time when the rule was really being enforced must, on the other hand, have been a small but highly valued gift[6]. Even down to the days of Ferdinand and Isabella privileges of one kind and another continued to be given to chosen individuals[7].

In other countries such grants are very much rarer. The Carolingian Diplomas, and the charter of Richard I were indeed granted to individuals, but it is probable that they were in fact valid for the communities of which those individuals were the chiefs. Later, individual grants were

---

[1] Baer, *Aragon*, No. 64; Regné, *Catalogue*, No. 2406; REJ, LXXIII, p. 202.

[2] E.g. Baer, *op. cit.*, No. 37. Like the Scottish raiders, the Spanish Jews were discriminating in their taste for mutton; Jafia, the recipient in this case, preferred his from the Saracen market.

[3] Baer, *op. cit.*, No. 65.

[4] Regné, *Catalogue*, No. 459; REJ, LXI, p. 41.

[5] E.g. *ibid.*, Nos. 92 and 2820; REJ, LX and LXXVI, pp. 178 and 83.

[6] E.g. *ibid.*, No. 2813; REJ, LXXVI, p. 82.

[7] E.g. Baer, *Castile*, No. 364.

often merely passports for some special occasion[1], though exemption from tribute, or non-solidarity in the making up of deficits, occasionally occur[2].

VI. THE END

The Jews might secure for themselves charters which seemed to give them every security. Individuals might seek a still more sheltered position, enjoying the general toleration accorded to Jewish settlements and avoiding the burdens which they bore, but, in the end, the last word lay with public opinion and the mob. There is not a single national community which at some time of its existence was not the victim of mob violence. In England at the beginning of the thirteenth century, in France during the fourteenth, in Germany at intervals from the First Crusade onwards, but especially from the end of the thirteenth century up to the Black Death, in Spain from the end of the fourteenth century, everywhere the same story was repeated. With a mixture of religious and economic fury the mob fell upon the Jewries and massacred, burnt and pillaged. Sometimes these massacres were so thorough as to destroy whole communities. Especially during the Black Death were entire communities swept away. But, even if the results were less terrible or the community were immediately re-established, public opinion, supported by the Church, was usually ready to support any move for the expulsion of the Jews and the abolition of their charter. Royal piety or royal initiative was rarely the sole cause of the disappearance of a Jewish community, for as long as the people remained quiet, Jews were profitable. It was only when diminishing returns ceased to offset rising popular indignation that expulsion was decreed. In the last decade of the thirteenth century the Jews left England; a hundred years later they left France; yet a hundred years later they were expelled from Spain and Portugal. In Germany the nature of the political situation prevented any single expulsion, but from 1350

---

[1] E.g. Aronius, No. 468, or MGH, LL, IV, Const. VIII, p. 651.

[2] E.g. the grant of Henry III to Isaac of Norwich; *Patent Rolls*, 1225-32, p. 453; or that to certain Jews of Silesia; L. Oelsner, *Schlesische Urkunden zur Geschichte der Juden*, pp. 46-48.

onward the communities dwindled in number and importance. Principalities and great cities, which had banished and recalled them on many occasions in the earlier period, began to expel them finally before the end of the fourteenth century. They disappeared from Strasbourg in 1388, from Basel in 1397, from Cologne in 1426, from Breslau in 1453, from Mainz in 1473, from the Duchies of Mecklenburg in 1492, from those of Carinthia and Styria in 1496, from Nuremberg in 1499, and from Ratisbon, Bavaria, and elsewhere in the sixteenth century. By the end of the fifteenth century Jews still lived in Italy and in some towns of Germany, but outside these scattered centres they were mostly to be found in eastern Europe, especially in Poland. East of Poland they found a barrier limiting their penetration into Russia, and against this barrier they gradually piled up in ever-increasing numbers, until it came about that considerably more than half the European Jewish population was contained in the provinces stretching from the Baltic to the Black Sea, in what is now Poland, Lithuania, the Ukraine and Bessarabia.

CHAPTER SEVEN

THE JEWISH COMMUNITY WITHIN
THE CHRISTIAN SOCIETY

I. THE JEWISH COMMUNITY

It is not the purpose of this chapter to attempt any comprehensive picture of the life and conditions of medieval Jewry. Only certain aspects of its life, as they affected and were affected by the Christian societies within which it lived, need to be included. Even in these chosen aspects it is impossible to be comprehensive, for there was as much variety within Jewry as there was in the treatment meted out to the Jews by Christian masters. Moreover, one aspect of the question must remain always indeterminate, for the imponderabilia of a past age can never be precisely weighed. The Jews certainly formed an ' alien ' group in Christendom; but there are many degrees of ' alien-ness '. According to their desire to emphasise the intimate relation of Jewish to Christian history, or to denounce the presence of a foreign irritant in the body politic, writers will tend to minimise or accentuate Jewish distinctiveness.

Certainly the Jew exhibited many curious characteristics to the ordinary medieval man. He had often a strange name; he spoke a strange tongue, and wrote with a strange writing; he ate different food; he had different legal customs; he belonged to a different religion. Almost any of these peculiarities, taken singly, might be found in other groups, but there was no group so widely scattered amongst the general population which possessed them all; and no other group possessed so different a religion. All these were differences arising out of the will of the Jews themselves. In the thirteenth century the Jewish badge came to add another, which was imposed from without. But, on the other side, it must not be forgotten that strangeness is a quality which is not necessarily lasting. A newly arrived Jewish settlement, in a city which had never seen Jews close at hand, would certainly have provided gossip for weeks and months, but, as the years went on, as the Jews came to be part of the daily life of the citizens, it is natural to suppose that many of their strange customs came to be taken for granted and ceased to arouse comment. The populace would distinguish honest Jews from dishonest, kindly from unfriendly, good from bad. From a closed community they would have become a set of individuals with known and different characteristics. Yet they could never be completely absorbed into the population except by conversion to Christianity; as long as they remained Jews their Judaism, if nothing else, distinguished them.

But if their religion was the central point of their distinctiveness, it is a mistake to imagine that it was wholly a mystery. Unquestionably there was a sufficient element of the unknown in it to lend credibility to such charges as ritual murder. The Christian Church itself, when a very similar minority within the pagan Roman world, had been accused of precisely similar practices, together with charges of promiscuous immorality which were not alleged against the Synagogue. But at Jewish festivities, especially at weddings, Christians might be found, and the continual efforts of the Church to withdraw them proves the number of Christian servants who lived in Jewish families. Such servants were inevitably familiar with much of their religious ceremonial through the fact that various tasks, especially the lighting of fires and lamps, were performed by them on the Sabbaths and at festivals. But if the stories which such people told to their friends and families removed some of the mystery of the Jews, it would emphasise the differences, and especially the nonconformity of the Jews with religious practices which the simple Christian held to be divinely appointed as the only true way of life and regarded as essential for the winning of Heaven, and, even more important, the avoidance of Hell.

Some criticism was also probably directed against the solidarity which existed between Jewish individuals, for humanity is prone to forget that any group of individuals feeling themselves in a foreign environment will cling together. With the Jews, however, this solidarity has often been emphasised, for Jewish history has always been based on communities, not on individuals. In his travels through southern Europe in the twelfth century, Benjamin of Tudela sometimes found isolated Jews living alone in a city, and in the earlier settlement in northern France and elsewhere the Jews were evenly scattered through all the towns and villages[1], but such Jews were always linked to the nearest community. The whole development of Jewish life in Europe turned around the existence of organised and responsible communities, and it is important to realise that this organisation was no Christian or medieval creation. It is possible to trace the growth of European towns from their first confused beginning to the full flowering of their communal autonomy, and even independence. But Jewish organisation was already fully developed when it is first met with in the Carolingian Diplomata.

This fact is not in itself surprising, for there lay a millennium of experience of life in exile behind the European Jewries. With infinite patience and consummate skill there had been built up a system of life which yet challenged no non-Jewish authority with the menace of a divided loyalty. The Catholic Church, by the power of the Papacy, by the central organisation of the Orders, by its weapons of excommunication and interdict, by the collection of Peter's pence, and by the gift of rich livings to foreigners who never resided in the countries whence they drew their revenues, possessed many of the aspects of a super-state. In spite of unity of language, tradition and religion, in spite of the bonds of common sympathy and the close ties of business relationships, there was no central authority in the Jewish world, no single power which could issue orders to every community. Jewry never wore even the appearance of a super-state.

The place of external authority as a unifying influence in Jewish life was taken by the moral force of the judgments of individual rabbis. So long as the schools of Babylon lasted, it was to them that all the Jewries of the west turned for advice. But as they declined new scholars arose in Europe; the authority which they possessed was entirely moral; the communities which asked their advice on difficult matters of law and custom were at liberty to refuse it if they wished. It was only their learning that created the reputation of men

[1] Jacobs, *The Jews of Angevin England*, p. 382; L. Rabinowitz, *The Social Life of the Jews of Northern France*, Ch. iii.

R

like Gershom of Mainz, Rashi and his successors, Solomon ben Adreth, Meir of Rothenburg, Israel Isserlein, or Moses Isserles.

The basis of this community of thought, and the reason why Jews could turn to Jewish scholars in far-distant countries, was the common possession not only of the Scriptures, but of the Talmud. It was on the basis of the continual discussion of scholars in different rabbinical schools that Gershom and his successors were asked to decide on difficult points of practice. The common inheritance of this body of teaching was not, however, all that guided the life of the communities. In addition, there was local custom, which gradually formed its own body of tradition out of the necessities of life in a particular Christian environment, beneath particular political conditions, and under a particular climate. This custom was partly evolved by local rabbinical synods, and partly by distinguished local scholars. Great importance was attached to it, and on many questions it was held to override Talmudic precept[1].

It is the fact that the medieval communities already possessed this long and yet living tradition, which governed almost every aspect of their communal life, that accentuated their strangeness in Christian eyes. They did not evolve and grow to the same extent as the society around them. In Christian life new manners and practices were continually appearing; in the Jewries everything had already a background of centuries of thought and practice.

II. AUTHORITY OVER THE COMMUNITY

The fact that there was no tradition of a central authority in Judaism made the Jews the readier to accept the supreme authority of their Christian masters, and to obey the law of the country in which they lived. Already in Talmudic times it had been laid down that ' the law of the land is law ', so that it was no innovation when the early medieval rabbis insisted on this obedience as a religious principle. Their relation to the law of the land was expressed in the terms of the charter under which they lived, and in the nature of the

[1] Rabinowitz, *op. cit.*, Ch. v, 2.

supreme authority whose word was their final court of appeal, and who regulated their relations with Christian society.

Only in a few cases, either in early times when Jews were few, or when later a local baron was allowed to hold his own Jews, would the supreme authority be exercised by the actual owner of the Jewry. An ultimate appeal might lie with him, but all ordinary control was delegated to a special official. As to who this official might be, there was no single tradition. There is mention in Agobard of one Everard as ' Master of the Jews '[1], but the nature of his authority is only vaguely expressed, and he appears to have left executive action to the *missi* or commissioners of the emperor. In later times nobles of the highest rank are sometimes found as guardians of the Jews; Louis of Etampes, who held this office during the last sojourn of the Jews in France, was a second cousin of the king, and a man of considerable importance. In Germany this control was exercised in all kinds of ways, some of which have been seen in the previous chapters. It might be placed in the hands of the chamberlain of a prince bishop, the bailiff of the emperor, or the burgo-master of a city. In England it was vested in officers of the Exchequer known as the Justices of the Jews. In Aragon the king dealt directly with each Jewry, sometimes grouping them together for financial purposes, but retaining the main authority independently in his own hands. In all such cases the executive authority was Christian, but this did not preclude the existence of various forms of ' chief rabbi ', ' president ' or ' guardian ' being chosen or appointed from among the Jews themselves.

At certain periods in England and in France control of at any rate some aspects of the life of the community was vested jointly in Christian and Jewish hands. Under Louis of Etampes, whose main office was to control jurisdiction in cases affecting Jews[2], there were two commissioners to deal with all claims concerning taxes, and with their general division among the community. One of these was a Jew, and the other a Christian[3]. In England, two Justices of the Jews

---

[1] For the many views as to the position of Everard, see Scherer, pp. 252 ff.

[2] Laurière, *Ordonnances*, III, p. 471; IV, pp. 496 and 532.

[3] *Ibid.*, III, p. 487.

were first appointed by Richard I in 1198, and both were Jews[1]. Later, the Justices, who were considered to be officers of the Great Exchequer, were almost always Christians of the highest rank, but the ' Presbyter of the Jews ', who was a Jew, had a seat on the exchequer of the Jews, and an official residence there[2].

Even when supreme authority lay with a Christian officer designated by the ruler, it was customary for the latter to appoint or to ratify the appointment of the chief Jewish official, who might or might not be the religious head, the rabbi, of the community. The first Presbyter of the Jews in England was appointed by King John in 1199. He enjoyed a special safe conduct, and the king addressed him in the terms reserved for great nobles and officers of the Crown: ' dilectus et familiaris noster '[3]. This office continued to be a royal appointment until 1257, when, after some trouble had led to the deposition of the existing Presbyter, Elias le Evesk of London, Henry III conceded to the Jewish community full independence to elect their own head[4].

The English Presbyter was not as important a figure as the Justices of the Jews. In Castile, however, there was a court rabbi who held high authority, but even he was exceeded in dignity by the Chief Rabbi of Portugal, who was the most authoritative Jewish figure of the Middle Ages. Surrounded by officials, some of whom were Christians, he visited the Portuguese communities annually and administered justice. Certain documents he issued over his own seal as ' Chief Rabbi on behalf of the King ', and his general authority was equal to that of the greatest nobles[5].

In Germany centralisation was especially difficult. Local Jewries usually elected their own chief officer, with or without Christian ratification, but any higher authority was difficult to establish. In the later part of the Middle Ages ' Advocates of the Jews ' existed, and these were often chosen from among the Jews themselves. The most famous of these was Joselin of Rosheim, advocate of the Jews at the

---

[1] Tovey, *Anglia Judaica*, p. 44.

[2] *Calendar of Close Rolls*, 1234-1237, pp. 243 and 408.

[3] Tovey, *op. cit.*, pp. 55 and 61.

[4] *Patent Rolls*, 1247-1258, p. 570.

[5] M. Kayserling, *Geschichte der Juden in Portugal*, pp. 8 ff.

beginning of the sixteenth century[1]. In 1407, Ruprecht, the Roman king, attempted to create a chief rabbinate for Germany. A certain Rabbi Israel was thus appointed[2], but his authority was never recognised by the communities. The king considered the office necessary because of the confusion which prevailed within the empire and the consequent loss to the imperial treasury. The confusion, said the letter of appointment, had reached such a height that various persons styled themselves ' chief rabbi ,' and convicted or excommunicated Jews on the flimsiest grounds, even compelling some to flee from the country. But the innate congregationalism of Judaism rebelled against any such centralisation, and even ' district rabbis ' seem to have been rare. The letter of appointment of one such for the district of Bayreuth and Ansbach in the fourteenth century granted him all the rights and privileges enjoyed by other district rabbis, so that the appointment was not unique. It illustrates the situation which Ruprecht tried to alter by appointing a single chief rabbi for all Germany, that the Jews of Bayreuth and Ansbach needed to be ordered to take their instructions from their own rabbi and from no other without his permission[3].

While the conception of a chief rabbi as a Jewish archbishop was foreign to Jewish custom, and only rarely successful, another Christian institution was more readily incorporated into Jewish life. Difficulties of communication, the continual emergence of new problems, and the influence of the Christian organisation of councils, led the Jews to convene synods for the discussion of difficult questions. The communities of northern France were the first to inaugurate this movement[4]. This was natural, for the six Fairs of Champagne were the chief meeting places of travellers in northern Europe, and it was possible with little expense, and without exciting suspicion, to collect together scholars of many parts. The rabbis of Anjou record having attended a meeting at which not less than one hundred and fifty rabbis were present, from Troyes, Auxerre, Rheims,

---

[1] E. Scheid, *Les Juifs d'Alsace*, p. 85.

[2] Wiener, *Regesten*, pp. 71 ff.

[3] A. Eckstein, *Geschichte der Juden im Markgraftum Bayreuth*, p. 4.

[4] L. Finkelstein, *Jewish Self-government in the Middle Ages*, has a detailed discussion of these synods and their decisions.

Paris, Sens, Dreux, Lyons, Carpentras, Normandy, Aquitaine, Anjou, Poitou and Lorraine[1]. In the thirteenth century such synods were also held in Germany, and in England, where they were forbidden in 1242[2]. After the terrible persecutions of the fourteenth century in Spain, the Aragonese rabbis held a synod in 1354 with express consent of the king[3].

Synods never met with the frequency of Church councils but, when they did meet, they employed the same sanction for their decisions, the excommunication of the disobedient. The function of these meetings was manifold. Though, as has been said, the Jewries of Europe possessed their organisation and their faith, while Christendom was still struggling to find expression for itself, yet much of the Talmud was based on conditions so different from life in northern Christian Europe that modifications were continually necessary for the sake of preserving the religious principles which literal obedience to Talmudic law would have endangered[4]. A second function of these meetings was to consider the protection of their communities in a hostile Christian environment[5]. As a bridge between the two functions came many questions such as the treatment of Jews who, after forcible baptism, returned to the community. To preserve the good name of Jewry, Jews were forbidden to cite other Jews before Christian courts, unless they refused to appear before their own Jewish courts; they were forbidden to seek from Christian sources positions of authority over the community, for such should be obtained only by election, so that the internal autonomy of the community might be preserved; they were advised not to receive objects of Christian worship as pledges, because of the danger that the receiver might be suspected of misusing the article while it was in his possession, and of insulting Christianity thereby. In addition to such questions, innumerable points of purely

---

[1] L. Brunschvicg, *Les Juifs d'Angers*; REJ, XXIX, p. 230.

[2] *Close Rolls*, 1237-1242, p. 464.

[3] Baer, *Aragon*, No. 253; English translation in Finkelstein, pp. 336 ff.

[4] Cf. S. Zucrow, *Adjustment of Law to Life in Rabbinic Literature*, Chs. i, v, vi, etc.

[5] Cf. M. Güdemann, *Geschichte des Erziehungswesens u. d. Cultur der Juden in Frankreich u. Deutschland*, n. l. pp. 255 ff.

Jewish interest were thrashed out in the synods and accepted by the different communities. In this way a surprising degree of homogeneity was preserved in the development of Jewish life in different countries under very different conditions.

III. AUTHORITY IN JUDICIAL QUESTIONS

Even before the European Jews realised the need for special measures in a hostile Christian environment, they found it necessary to alter and to modify Talmudic prescriptions which were no longer applicable to their conditions. The Middle Ages did not possess the elaborate legal codes of imperial Rome, and, on the other hand, men were accustomed to the idea that a man should be tried by his peers. The Jews were, therefore, left with an even greater measure of judicial autonomy than they had possessed under late Roman authority, and with even more than the Talmudic rabbis had envisaged as existing in the Diaspora[1]. In the earliest charters cases which only affected Jews were left entirely to the Jews themselves to settle, and though a ' bishop of the Jews ' might be officially appointed by the prince, the whole procedure of trial was left in Jewish hands. This extensive liberty made it both possible and proper for the rabbis in both France and Germany to regard it as a serious offence if a Jew haled a brother Jew before a Christian court[2]. Not only was he ' washing dirty linen in public ', but it was much less likely that impartial justice would be done.

If inclusive jurisdiction in all matters between Jews was the rule in the earlier part of the period, exceptions began to appear in the thirteenth century. It was in England that Jewish judicial autonomy suffered its earliest and its most complete cancellation. Henry III appears to have completely abolished its executive power in 1242, and to have ordered Jews to appear before his own courts on all matters[3]. The Jewish court was left with a power of arbitration and

[1] D. M. Shohet, *The Jewish Court in the Middle Ages*, p. 126.

[2] Finkelstein, *op. cit.*, pp. 42 and 60; Shohet, p. 96.

[3] F. I. Schechter, *The Rightlessness of Medieval English Jewry*, JQR n.s., IV, p. 139.

no other. Less drastic was the action of Philip the Fair in 1291 in abolishing the special Justices of the Jews[1], for, as concerns cases between Jews, this would only have affected appeals from the rabbinical court, and such appeals were almost non-existent. A year before their final expulsion in 1395, Charles VI likewise abolished these special justices, who had been instituted in 1361[2]. A few years earlier, both in Aragon and in Castile, extensive limitations in the authority of the Jewish courts themselves were introduced by Pedro IV and John I. Pedro IV, in correcting and amplifying in 1377 the regulations of 1272[3] governing the community of Barcelona, excluded a number of crimes from its jurisdiction, even when both aggressor and victim were Jews[4]; and the Castilian Jewish jurisdiction in criminal cases was abolished altogether in 1380[5]. How extensive had been the authority of Jewish judges can be seen from the phrase which occurs in Aragonese documents, that they might try cases which arose out of ' Roman as well as out of Talmudic Law '[6], and how uncertain the general validity of regulations affecting the Jews, from the fact that this same Pedro of Aragon who introduced limitations into the rights of the Jews of Barcelona explicitly confirmed to the Jews of both Jativa and Majorca their full authority in criminal cases[7]. In Castile also the law of 1380 seems to have lost its validity by 1432, for the regulations of the Castilian communities of that year allowed to the Jewish judges jurisdiction in all criminal cases between Jews in which the rights of the Crown, the Church or the Nobility were not affected[8].

In Germany there was no consistency in the position in different communities. It varied from the situation in Zurich to that in Cologne. In the former city, the Jews possessed no jurisdiction of their own before the end of the fourteenth

---

[1] G. Saige, Les Juifs de Languedoc, p. 226.

[2] Laurière, VII, p. 643.

[3] Baer, Aragon, No. 106.

[4] Ibid., No. 317, especially pp. 462 and 466.

[5] Baer, Castile, No. 227, and Lindo, op. cit., p. 162, where the full text is given in English.

[6] E.g. Baer, Aragon, No. 367.

[7] Ibid., Nos. 348 and 367.

[8] I. Loeb, Règlement des Juifs en Castile, in REJ, XIII, pp. 200 ff.

century, when certain cases were surrendered to Jewish courts. Otherwise every case, civil apparently as well as criminal, was submitted to the civic authorities[1]. In Cologne, Jewish courts were allowed a wide jurisdiction, and Jewish judges were elected by the Jewish community. The universal desire of the Jews was that only appeals, or cases where one party refused the Jewish court, should come before non-Jewish judges[2].

It was natural that civil cases between Jews should have been left to Jewish courts, for the whole structure of Talmudic Law was entirely unknown to Christian judges, and they would have found themselves in a very difficult position had they had to decide questions of which Roman and Germanic Law took no cognisance. It is more surprising, in view of the general status of the Jew, to find that extensive powers sometimes lay with purely Jewish judges, treating a question according to Jewish law, to pass sentence on Christians. Needless to say, such extensive power was not universal, for there was no single principle governing the trial of mixed cases; but the most common practice was for a Jew to be cited before the Jewish court, and to cite in the Christian court, when the other party was a Christian. It was also common in all mixed cases to demand of each party that he should support his claim with both Christian and Jewish evidence[3]. But this is as far as agreement went in practice. In England mixed cases automatically came before the Justices of the Jews, who were generally Christian, and the question as to whether the Jew was plaintiff or defendant was irrelevant. In France it was usual for special judges to be appointed to hear cases in which Jews were involved on either side, but the system does not seem to have worked with the same smoothness as in England. Philip the Fair found it necessary to remove them throughout the south in 1291 because of irregularity in their letters of appointment, and handed over all cases affecting Jews either as plaintiff

---

[1] O. Stobbe, *Die Juden in Deutschland*, p. 141.

[2] *Ibid.*, pp. 141 ff. and n. 132a, p. 255; and Scherer, pp. 254 ff.

[3] There are exceptions to this on both sides. Jews could prove financial claims without Christian evidence by many charters, and occasionally Jews could not give evidence against Christians. Cf. J. Bauer, *Les Juifs de la Principauté d'Orange*, REJ, XXXII, p. 236; and A. Crémieux, *Les Juifs de Marseilles*, REJ, XLVI, pp. 25 ff.

or defendant to the ordinary royal courts[1]. During the last settlement in France, as has already been mentioned, there was also trouble with the Justices of the Jews. It would seem probable that such Justices had proved open to bribes—a temptation from which English Justices were not always free either—and that the easiest solution was to abolish the whole system.

Where there was no system of special Christian judges appointed to hear mixed cases, one of two things might happen: cases might be divided between Jewish and Christian ordinary courts, or all might be left to the latter. Both these solutions are common. There seems to have been no rule by which it is possible to foretell which way a privilege would go. The decision depended entirely on the financial interests of the Crown, and in any particular circumstances any of the different solutions might appear most favourable to those interests.

IV. EXCOMMUNICATION AND THE DEATH SENTENCE

The extent of the jurisdiction of a Jewish court did not necessarily correspond with its right of inflicting punishment. Just as the courts of the Inquisition, after sentence, handed the convicted person over to the secular arm, so the Jewish judges in serious cases remitted the guilty person to the royal or communal authorities for punishment. The nature of the punishments for which this remission was required varied according to the privilege enjoyed by the community. As a general rule, it was the Spanish communities which possessed the greatest authority for inflicting serious physical punishment themselves, although some German communities possessed the right of mutilation[2]. The most usual physical punishment was a beating in the synagogue, the severity of which varied with the nature of the offence. It was usually performed at the beginning of the evening service, in order that the congregation might offer prayers for atonement and forgiveness during the punishment[3].

[1] G. Saige, *Les Juifs de Languedoc*, p. 226.

[2] E.g. that of Nördlingen, cited in Stobbe, *op. cit.*, p. 255, n. 132a.

[3] Shohet, *op. cit.*, p. 140.

There is evidence that capital punishment was openly practised only by the Spanish communities. In 1304 Asher b. Yeḥiel, a German scholar and pupil of Meir of Rothenburg, became rabbi of Toledo, and, in a responsum to the Court of Cordova, he stated that with the exception of the Spanish communities he had never heard of any community practising the right, and he added that, though the Spanish communities enjoyed it by royal privilege, he himself had never sanctioned an execution[1]. The particular crime for which the Jews desired the possession of this power was denunciation[2]. Living as they did an extremely exposed life, they were perpetually at the mercy of informers. The extremely unsavoury character of many converts to Christianity, and their willingness to confirm the most baseless and beastly accusations against their late co-religionists, offer a horrible example of the type of warped individual which the strained life of the medieval Jewry was bound from time to time to produce. With an ever-empty treasury on one side, always ready to believe that there was still some wealth which might be squeezed out of the Jews, and a superstitious clergy and populace on the other, equally ready to believe anything against them, it is not surprising that the elders of the communities regarded betrayal to the Christian population or authorities as the most serious of crimes, and considered it permissible to stop the mouth of the informer, even by killing him[3]. A single specimen will be enough to illustrate the whole tribe of informers. Some of the sufferings of the Jews of England during the reign of Henry III have been already described. In his thirst for more and more money, the king in 1250 sent the Justices of the Jews on a special tour through the Jewries to make an exact exploration of their wealth. There joined himself to this mission a Jew, who rebuked those Christians who felt pity for the miseries of his fellows, who called the Justices lukewarm, who swore that the Jews could give twice what they had already given, and who promised that he could and

[1] Shohet, *op. cit.*, p. 137.

[2] It is granted to the community of Calatayud, for example, in a privilege of James I of 1229; Baer, *Aragon*, No. 88.

[3] Shohet, *op. cit.*, p. 136.

would reveal all their secrets to the king[1]. While this incident reveals that informers existed elsewhere, it was the wealthy and exposed Spanish communities which were most frequently concerned with them, and obtained the most liberal permission to deal with the offence as they would. The death sentence was decreed against them and, where the Jews themselves could not execute it, they could hand the criminal over to the bailiff, who was bound to see the sentence carried out. The Christian authorities themselves were sometimes required to hand over to justice any informer who was reported to them[2].

The crime of informing sometimes earned death, but the most serious punishment inflicted by the Jewish court for other offences was usually excommunication and expulsion from the community. While at the end of the period under review the Jewish ban fell into the same disrepute as the Christian, and was flung about with the same personal frivolity, it was a most powerful weapon when seriously employed. The menace of excommunication was the general sanction of communal ordinances and of the division of the communal taxes[3]. It could normally only be delivered in public, usually in the synagogue, and by the rabbi with the consent of the elders of the community[4]. The excommunicated person was treated as one dead, and completely cut off from all relations even with his own family[5]. The disadvantage to the community of both the ban and the death sentence was that it had to make good to its master the loss of a potential source of wealth. The cost of excommunication was generally one thousand sous[6], and though the value of the sou varied considerably, it was a sufficient sum to ensure that the full penalty was not inflicted except in serious cases. Nor could the community recoup itself for

---

[1] Matthew Paris, Ed. *Rolls Series*, V, p. 115. On informers in Spain see D. Kaufmann, *Jewish Informers in the Middle Ages*, JQR, VIII, pp. 217 ff.

[2] E.g. a privilege of the Jews of Barcelona from Pedro IV, 1377; Baer, *Aragon*, No. 317.

[3] J. Wiesner, *Der Bann*, pp. 66 ff.

[4] Shohet, *op. cit.*, pp. 33 and 51; Finkelstein, pp. 60 and 63 ff.

[5] This only refers to the greater excommunication. The various degrees of gravity in the punishment are discussed in Shohet, pp. 142 ff.

[6] As for example in the privilege of Pedro IV in note 2 above.

this expense from the property of the excommunicated person, for it was customary for this property to be temporarily or permanently confiscated by the royal treasury[1]. The cost would be sufficient to ensure that the full penalty of excommunication would be sparingly used; but, at least, the communities might have expected that all their members would be submitted to its sanction. In France the Christian authorities were not only not allowed to interfere with its pronouncement; they could not demand to know the crime for which it had been inflicted[2]. In Spain, however, it was common for personal privileges explicitly to include immunity from communal excommunication, and, apart from such there are a number of cases in which excommunicated persons appealed to the Crown, and the Crown cancelled the ban, informing the community that it had done so[3].

V. JEWS UNDER CHRISTIAN JURISDICTION

It will be obvious from the procedure in mixed cases already described that the Jews must frequently have had to appear in Christian courts. It was almost universally ordained that they could only sue a Christian in such a court, even if the Christian could not sue them except in a Jewish court. The nature of the cases in which a Jew was most likely to appear as plaintiff against a Christian explains why it was most satisfactory for the princes to establish their own Christian courts for all cases concerning Jews. For in the overwhelming majority of such cases the Jewish plaintiff must have been occupied with claiming repayment from a recalcitrant debtor. In such courts the Jew was very adequately protected. He was usually exempted from the necessity of providing any Christian witness to his claim, and either his bond or his oath was accepted as adequate proof of it. This favouritism, while inevitable from the royal point of view, roused, as we have seen, the indignation

---

[1] E.g. Charter of 1361, clause iii, Laurière, III, p. 473. Baer states that the same rule held in England and Germany, *Encyclopaedia Judaica*, VII, c. 195.

[2] From the clause referred to in the preceding note.

[3] E.g. Regné, *Catalogue*, Nos. 1234, 1235, and 2555; REJ, LXV, p. 208, and LXXV, p. 158.

of the Church, which at times went so far as to forbid a Christian lawyer to assist a Jew to plead, unless specially required to do so by the judge[1]. In matters which came before ordinary Christian courts, or where no special courts existed, the Jews seem to have been placed on the same footing as any other party[2].

To this equality there were two exceptions. In most cases the Jew had to take a special oath to confirm his statements. This oath was sometimes dignified, and the Jew swore on the Ten Commandments or the Pentateuch in the same way as the Christian swore on the Bible[3]. But it was not infrequent to find ridiculous and humiliating ceremonies attached to the oath[4], or even to find that the oath itself became a long-drawn-out invocation of maledictions[5].

If this exception was to the disadvantage of the Jew, the other was in his favour. Torture was an almost universal accompaniment of medieval trials on any serious charge, and the Jew was almost universally exempt from it; only in certain cases might it be permitted with the express authority of the prince[6], or in particularly flagrant offences[7]. In minor ways also the Jew was placed in an advantageous position. For civil offences he was readily allowed bail, and sometimes, when imprisoned, freedom to quit the gaol for the Sabbath and the Feasts[8]. But all these can have done little more than redress some of the balance of prejudice from which he inevitably had to suffer in a Christian court, where the first instinct of the judge would have been to free any Christian from the power of a member of the despised people.

---

[1] E.g. Statutes of Church of Liège, 1287, vii; Mansi, XXIV, c. 934.

[2] E.g. The Laws of Magdeburg, which were extensively copied in eastern Europe; Bondy, No. 45.

[3] E.g. Regné, *Catalogue*, No. 570; REJ, LXII, p. 53.

[4] *Ibid.*, No. 1232; REJ, LXV, p. 208.

[5] *Ibid.*, No. 1102, p. 76, the three alternatives were thus in existence in a single country, within a decade of each other. On forms of oath in Germany, see *Der Judeneid*, by H. K. Klausen in *Deutsche Rechtswissenschaft*, II, 1937. Other forms of oath are given in E. Ouverleaux, *Les Juifs de Belgique*; REJ, VII, pp. 253 ff.

[6] E.g. Privilege of James II to the Jews of Barcelona, 1302, *ibid.*, No. 2783; REJ, LXXVI, p. 77.

[7] Privilege of James I to Jews of Montpellier, *ibid.*, No. 356; REJ, LXI, p. 25.

[8] See Charter for the archiepiscopal Jewry of Narbonne, 1284, clause iv, in Regné, *Narbonne*; REJ, LXIII, p. 90.

The level of medieval justice was not always very high, even between Christians, and it is not surprising that Jewish authorities looked with disapproval on Jews having recourse to Christian courts. Their feeling was not based on any rejection of Christian law in itself for, as will be shown in the next section, they recognised it as binding in many cases, but on the painful experience that the Jew would be more likely to suffer from lawless violence, threats and extortion, than from any legal condemnation. It was not principles, but practice, which caused them to refer to Christian courts as dens of robbers, and to Christian justice as violence.

VI. CHRISTIAN LAW IN JEWISH COURTS

The facts that the ' Gentiles ' who are referred to in the Talmud were idolators, and that many pagan customs of those days justified the severest moral strictures, led to many laws being elaborated for the separation of Jews from the rest of the population, and to many derogatory and contemptuous remarks about the non-Jew being made in rabbinic discussions. In that most conservative of all formulae, the ritual of public worship, contemptuous phrases also occurred. The treatment which the Jews received from Christian priests and princes would have seemed to the ordinary Jew of the Middle Ages, as it does to the ordinary Christian of to-day, amply to justify all, and more than all, of bitterness or contempt towards non-Jews which he found in the pages of the Talmud. No one could expect that in his secret thoughts the ordinary medieval Jew could look on ordinary medieval Christianity with veneration or respect.

It is a great tribute both to the wisdom and to the sincerity of the rabbinical scholars of the Middle Ages that they withstood the temptation to endorse the popular view. In their wisdom they recognised the great danger to the Jews themselves in their repeating such phrases; and in their sincerity they accepted the fact that Christendom, however much it might persecute them, was not idolatrous[1], so that many Talmudic precepts were no longer valid, because no longer necessary. It might appear at first sight that this was

[1] Shohet, *op. cit.*, pp. 85 ff.

nothing more than that prudence which savours not a little of time-serving and cowardice, were it not for the fact that they combined their wisdom with an insistence on loyalty to Judaism and on the principle of ' the sanctification of the Name ' in the presence of the Gentile world, which did not stop short at martyrdom, and that in their sincerity they would not accept the validity of those acts of Christian authority which seemed to them to be but the demands of arbitrary violence.

The basis on which their policy was built they found in the statement of a rabbi of the second century that ' the law of the land is law '[1]. They needed, therefore, no reserve in their insistence that Jews must respect the law of the country where they dwelt. This historical justification of their attitude was reinforced by the obvious danger of the alternative. Canon and secular law, for example, forbade Jews to lend money on Church property. It was the utmost folly for a Jew to transgress this, and thereby expose the whole community of which he was a member to dangers which they could imagine too well. Such conduct was therefore discouraged by rabbinic law. The whole network of regulations covered by the acceptance of the law of the land could be further grouped under the central idea of the paramount importance of ' sanctifying the Divine Name ', that is, of giving the Christian no opportunity for levelling reproaches at the conduct or belief of the Jew. It was with this principle in mind that they held the defrauding of a Christian to be an even greater offence than to defraud a Jew[2]. An instance of the combination of the two in a single sphere is given by the attitude of the scholars to the presence of Jews in Christian courts. For a Jew to hale another Jew before such a court was a crime against the second idea; to refuse the evidence of Christians, or to forbid a Jew to give evidence for a Christian even against a Jew, offended against the first[3]. Further, to forbid the Jew giving his evidence would have been to sanction injustice being done in a court whose legality was

---

[1] Talmud, *Baba Bathra*, 54b; ed. Soncino, I, p. 222; for a discussion of the history and significance of the statement, see I. Herzog, *The Main Institutions of Jewish Law*, I, pp. 24-32.

[2] Shohet, *op. cit.*, pp. 86, 91, 92, 93.

[3] *Ibid.*, pp. 90 and 93 ff.

accepted, since without the evidence of the Jew the wrong man might have been convicted. But in this latter case their sincerity is also evident, for a Jew might not give his evidence in a court which would have accepted it without confirmation, since Jewish law forbade conviction on the evidence of one man alone. Only in courts which required two witnesses to establish guilt might the Jew testify[1]. The balance and care which such an exact attitude imply may well explain the fact that, though there must have been many cases in which Christian plaintiffs had to sue in Jewish courts, there is no evidence anywhere of any outcry, either of layman or cleric, against the justice administered by Jewish judges. This is all the more remarkable in that the Church absolutely rejected *the principle* that Jews might judge Christians, and yet could not produce any evidence that Christians so judged suffered unfair treatment. The complaints against injustice in questions of indebtedness do not affect this statement, for the judges in such cases were normally the Christian ' Justices of the Jews '.

Not only was respect for Christian laws imposed on Jews, but in many cases Jews themselves had to be judged according to Christian law by Jewish judges. The body of case law which grew up in Talmudic times, and which was enormously expanded in the immense collections of the Responsa of the Rabbis[2], makes continual use of the principle that ' the law

[1] Shohet, *p. cit.*, p. 94.

[2] As an example of a Responsum dealing with the law of the land, cf. the following of R. Meir of Rothenburg, in *Responsensammlung R. Meirs*, Ed. Prague, p. 131 (translated from the German text in Zimmels, p. 97, n. 165): ' You ask me about the taxes which for many years the Jews of the whole Empire used to pay corporately. But the king has handed over part of his empire to his son and now ceases to collect taxes from the Jews living in the towns of his son, saying: " They are no concern of mine, they belong to my son." Now the communities situated in the king's territory demand the taxes from those which belong to the king's son, just as before, when those, too, had been immediately subject to the king. *Reply*. It appears to me that, if the king has entirely renounced those towns, and if the revenues which they produce are paid not into the royal treasury, but to the son or to the son's administrator, that it then goes without saying that the royal communities have no right to force the other communities to pay taxes together with them. . . . But if the king has given his son only the towns proper and the revenues accruing from them only in time to come, and the king continues to regard the towns as his property and to collect taxes from them, then the union between the communities has not ceased to exist and they pay their taxes together as before.'

S

of the land is law ' in its decisions. In questions affecting tenure of property, payment of taxes, government decrees of all kinds, the judge could not but try the case according to it. Any other basis would have been completely unreal. Almost every privilege granted to the Jews, after finance had become their chief occupation, laid it down that unredeemed pledges might be sold after a year and a day. The Talmud[1], which only envisaged temporary loans between neighbours, allowed sale after thirty days, but Jewish courts followed the instructions of the privilege. Similar cases must have been constantly occurring, so that it is not surprising that Jewish judges were sometimes explicitly authorised to try cases by different laws.

This Jewish recognition of Christian law was not purely one-sided, for every Jewish settlement inevitably demanded of the Christian authorities, and received from them, legal sanction of Jewish customs. They almost universally enjoyed immunity from any disturbance on the Sabbath or during Jewish Festivals. It might be inconvenient for a Christian litigant to have to wait for his case against a Jew to be heard, but if the season was one in which the Jews performed no business, he had to wait until it was over. Judaism demands the killing of meat by a particular method. By the law of the land, the Jews were entitled to their special meat markets, or their special place in the municipal abattoirs. They were even entitled to sell to Christians meat which they found ritually unfit for their own use. Even on points which affected Christians, account was taken of Jewish traditions. There is no more curious case of this than the privilege granted to Jews who were found in possession of stolen goods. Their right to demand that the real owner should pay for their return moved, as we have seen, the author of the *Schwabenspiegel*[2] to indignation, for a Christian, in similar circumstances, was compelled to return the article, and could only obtain compensation from the man from whom he bought it. The right is based on Talmudic law[3], and, as explained in that law, is not without justification, but it is easy to understand that it would have irritated the

[1] *Baba Mezia*, 113a; ed. Soncino, p. 644.
[2] See above, p. 198.
[3] *Baba Kamma*, 114b, ed. Soncino, p. 679

original Christian owner of the goods in question to have to pay for their recovery, if their temporary possessor happened to be a Jew rather than a Christian[1]. But apart from the protest of the *Schwabenspiegel* and the Castilian case already quoted[2], there is no sign of action to remedy this situation except an act of the Parliament of Bohemia of 1494, by which the onus of recovering his money was laid on the Jew, and the owner was allowed to receive his pledge back free, and, moreover, to receive compensation if its theft had involved him in loss[3]. The principle by which mortgage replaced vif-gage, and the debtor instead of the creditor retained the use of the property mortgaged, was also based on Talmudic precedent[4], for Christian practice had always assumed the enjoyment of the property by the creditor. The fact that occasionally compensation for injury was paid to the injured person instead of to his owner, is another example of the incorporation of Jewish custom[5]. In Spain this Christian recognition of Jewish law and custom took another form, and it was common for the different communities to receive the royal sanction of all their communal statutes, and even for purely Jewish regulations to be embodied in the general codes of Law[6].

VII. COMMUNAL RESPONSIBILITY

In spite of the various exceptions which have been mentioned from time to time, Christian authority regarded ' the Jews ' of any country or city as a single corporate entity. Duties were allotted, taxes imposed, and crimes imputed to the Jewry as a whole.

[1] See the review by M. Eschelbacher of H. Meyer, *Entwerung und Eigentum im deutschen Fahrnisrecht*, in MGWJ, 1903, p. 181.

[2] See above, p. 231.

[3] Bondy, No. 288.

[4] I. Herzog, *op. cit.*, pp. 361 ff.

[5] *Baba Kamma*, 83b, ed. Soncino, p. 473. Compensation is granted in the privilege of Duke Frederick to the Jews of Austria, clauses ix and xi; Scherer, p. 181. In this case the injured person is treated as a free man; rabbinic treatment of compensation for slaves was extremely harsh; cf. S. Zucrow, *Women, Slaves and the Ignorant in Rabbinic Literature*, pp. 175 ff.

[6] E.g Fuero of Castile, Baer, *Castile*, No. 60.

In matters of taxation this communal solidarity was an advantage rather than a grievance, provided the community could arrest—or at least control—the grant of charters of non-solidarity to its richest members. Jewish taxes were allotted in two ways. In some cases the community was simply ordered to find a certain amount, in others it was ordered to impose a poll tax on each member. In either case, the final amount was handed over in a single sum, either by a specified individual to whom the right of farming the tax had been conceded, or by specially constituted officers of the community entrusted with the power of making enquiry into the incomes of individual members. In both systems it was a definite advantage that the collection was not made from individuals by Christian officials, for it enabled the communities to conceal the poverty of some of their members, who would certainly have been expelled had it been known that they did not possess the requisite capital to pay their taxes[1].

A second duty which was naturally undertaken by the community as a whole was that of sharing in the cost of defence. A European city in the Middle Ages was surrounded by walls, and the upkeep and extension of its fortifications was the most responsible task of the city government. Every citizen was expected to share in defence in case of need. This responsibility was not always allotted individually to the citizens, but corporately to the gilds and companies of which the individuals were members. The most natural action to take in regard to the Jews was to allot them also their particular place in the defences of the city, charge them with the upkeep of that section of the walls, and see that they provided trained soldiers to defend it. This policy was followed in the earliest German charter, that of Speyer[2], but it very soon dropped out of use. The privileged position of the Jew, together with clerics and women, in the various Land Peaces depended on his being unarmed, and it is common to find the Jewish community making a payment instead of undertaking actual share in defence[3]. This custom

---

[1] Cf. the Responsum of Meir of Rothenburg on this subject in *Geschichte der Juden in Deutschland im 13. Jahrhundert*, by H. Z. Zimmels, p. 30.

[2] Aronius, No. 168.

[3] Cf. H. Fischer, *Die verfassungsrechtliche Stellung der Juden*, pp. 98 ff ·

was not, however, universal. It is related that in time of danger the Bohemian Jews in the thirteenth century had to carry arms, and perform their share of the watch, even on the Sabbath, and in many German towns the sharing in guard duty remained into the same century[1]. In cases of need, even in later centuries, Jews were summoned to the walls, so that it is unlikely that they were entirely strange to military exercises[2]. In England the Assize of Arms of 1181 definitely ordered them to surrender their weapons, an indication that they had previously possessed them[3]. In Spain the Jews remained up to the end responsible for bearing arms; communities took their share in defence, and individual Jews made reputations for themselves as bold and skilful soldiers[4]. But here also there are examples of the opposite custom, that they paid a contribution in lieu of personal service[5].

The application of the principle that a whole community might be held responsible for a crime committed by one of its members was neither confined to the Jews, nor to the Middle Ages. In certain cases it is still employed to-day. But it affected the Jews with a particular severity, both because of the general precariousness of their position, and because of the nature of the accusations which were fastened officially on the community as a whole. Omitting for the moment the general arrest of the Jews for the purpose of extracting money, these mass arrests were the consequence of the wild accusations of medieval superstition, ritual murder, the poisoning of wells, the profanation of Hosts, or the plotting against Christendom. Such crimes were considered to be the actions not of ' some Jews ', but of ' the Jews ', and nothing was more pernicious for their future in Europe than the creation of this imaginary picture of Jewish

---

[1] Zimmels, *op. cit.*, pp. 21 and 36; cf. also p. 97, n. 177, where a number of examples and references are given.

[2] E.g. at the siege of Erfurt in 1309, *Chron. S. Petri Erford. Mod.*; MGH, SS, XXX, i, p. 442.

[3] Cap.v; Roger of Hoveden, *Chron.*, s.a. 1181; ed. Rolls Series II, p. 261.

[4] Baer, *Castile*, Nos. 45 and 320; see also article, ' Army ', in *The Jewish Encyclopaedia*; and *Les Juifs et l'art Militaire au Moyen Age*, by M. Ginsburger; REJ, LXXXVIII, p. 156.

[5] E.g. the Jews of El Frago in 1295-6, Regné, *Catalogue*, No. 2614; REJ, LXXV, p. 168.

official activity. Elaborate tales, which remained deeply embedded in the popular imagination, were told of official instructions now to this community, now to that, to procure the Christian blood necessary for ritual purposes; bags of poison were believed to have been distributed from Jewry to Jewry; the stabbing of wafers was related to be a solemn communal act. The presence of Jewish travellers in any important centre lent credence to the idea that such men passed from country to country as emissaries of some secret central authority. These supposed activities prepared the imagination of the nineteenth century, bewildered by the fact of the Rothschild fortune, for the acceptance of the legend of a secret Jewish government and all the fantasy which culminates in the ' Protocols of the Elders of Zion '.

VIII. INHERITANCE AND THE TENURE OF LAND

In descriptions of European Jewish life language is often used which implies that the medieval Jew was entirely separated from the land and from any knowledge of the processes of agriculture. Agriculture being ' production ' *par excellence*, the consequence is drawn that the Jew was equally divorced from productive occupations. Part of the confusion of thought which underlies such language is due to the transplantation of the modern city into medieval times. In so far as the urban life of the Jew is concerned, it is not he who has withdrawn from the land, but the land which has withdrawn from him—as from all other dwellers in cities except those who are rich enough to own estates in the country. But the medieval Jew was not confined, in his relation to agriculture, to the fact that he might easily as a townsman have grown his own vegetables and cultivated his own vines. At times he was freely permitted to own agricultural estates; he was extensively engaged in the trade in agricultural and viticultural products; and the security for much of his loans was land. In so far as the two latter are concerned, while it is true to-day that a man may deal in wheat or in landed estate all his life and be ignorant of the appearance of a cornfield, since, in fact, he is merely speculating in financial markets, it is improbable that in the Middle Ages such complete detachment could have been common.

It is not until the thirteenth century that any ' public opinion ' came into existence which saw any problem in Jewish land-ownership. The Church had been troubled much earlier over the question of tithes, but, provided she received her tithes, did not, up to that time, see any further ground for protest[1], so long as ownership did not imply the right to receive or the duty to pay homage[2]. But in the second half of the thirteenth century it became impossible for Jews to hold land in England[3]; the thirteenth century expulsions led the Jews themselves to abandon agricultural occupations in France, though they continued them in Dauphiné and the south. In Germany it was in the four- teenth century only that the Jews and the land really became separated[4], though agriculture must have become rare much earlier[5]. At the same time as it came to be felt that Jews ought not to own land, scruples arose as to their farming land which they held on mortgage, or on which they had fore- closed.

To give any precise date at which Jews were everywhere forbidden to hold land is as impossible as it is to define pre- cisely when the Jews themselves tended to abandon agri- culture; and the difficulty is increased by the uncertainty in so many references of the meaning of the word ' land '. Obviously there is no implication of rural occupations in a Jew holding the land on which his house is built. It is safer to assume a gradual and almost unnoticed disappearance of the Jews from this occupation. Fear of the peasants, and the worthlessness of land to a community under order of expulsion, would both have been motives for a change. Yet another motive deserves fuller treatment.

[1] Nearly all the papal letters, canons, etc., dealing with this question date from the twelfth and thirteenth centuries. In the south, as might be expected, fourteenth-century references may be found. E.g. Council of Avignon, 1326, canon lvii; Mansi, XXV, c. 773.

[2] Cf. Council of Westminster, canon xii; Mansi, XXII, c. 143; cf. also canon xix on ownership of houses and land.

[3] Cf. Walter of York and Godfrey of Winchester, Letter to Richard Stanes, De ant. leg. lib., Camden Soc., p. 234; and Letter of Archbishop Peckham, No. 674, Rolls Series, III, p. 937.

[4] E.g. Strasbourg, where they are first forbidden to own land in 1322; M. Ephraim, Histoire des Juifs d'Alsace; REJ, LXXVII, p. 158.

[5] See p. 341 for Eliezer b. Nathan on twelfth century conditions in the Rhineland.

The Jew had absolutely no certainty that he could bequeath property to his son, so that there could not be with him, as with the ordinary Christian possessed of a certain competence, the hope of rooting and securing his family in permanent property. The facts about inheritance, in so far as Jews are concerned, are as uncertain and contradictory as almost every other fact of medieval Jewish life. If the maxim be stated that the Jew could not bequeath property, there is ample evidence to support it; if it be replied that the average Jew obviously did bequeath his property to his children, and they as obviously enjoyed it without disturbance, this also can be amply proved. The one fact which emerges from this contradiction is insecurity, and this would be much more evident when the inheritance was land, which could not be concealed, than when it was goods, which might be hidden or whose value might be reduced for ' probate '.

In England the rule seems to have been that if a Jew had led a blameless life, never receiving any condemnation in the royal court, he possessed complete testamentary rights[1]. Had he committed some crime, or died as a result of a death sentence, his whole property was forfeited to the Crown, and the heir had to buy it back—if he were allowed to do so at all—by the surrender of a considerable proportion of his inheritance. In Germany, on the other hand, there seems to have been no connection between the conduct of the Jew and the disposal of his property. Gifts of the property of Jews have already been recorded[2], and many others can be found in the Constitutions of the emperors and elsewhere. Even if such cases were exceptional, they indicate a complete absence of certainty. In Spain, to offer yet a third alternative, it never became an established principle that Jews might not bequeath their property, or that the Jewish community might not decide of its disposal if there were no natural heir[3].

If this study were concerned with the life of the Jewish communities of the Middle Ages, it would be necessary to

[1] E.g. *Calendar of Inquisitions*, Henry III, No. 747; Edward I, Vol. II, No. 143, III, No. 26.

[2] See above, pp. 111 ff.

[3] E.g. instructions of the Infante Pedro to the secretaries of the community of Gerona on the property of the deceased Boneta; Regné, *Catalogue*, No. 2310; REJ, LXIX, p. 211.

pass in review the many other occupations with which the Jews were concerned, but from the standpoint of Jewish-Christian relations they can be omitted. Even the fact that all through the period there were Jews in some parts of Europe holding public offices of more or less importance does not affect the general situation. It is the life of the communities, not of the exceptional individual, which determines Jewish history.

IX. THE DECLINE OF THE COMMUNITIES

In the multiplicity and variety of Jewish conditions during a period of five centuries, in the continual contradictions which are to be found, not merely from country to country or from decade to decade, but existing side by side in the same country and at the same time, only one consistent note can be discovered, the note of steady decline. Around the fringes of the countries which determine the colour of Jewish history, England, France, Spain and, above all, Germany, the decline may have been postponed for centuries. Italy in the south and Poland in the east saw prosperous communities still expanding when those of western Europe were sinking into ruins. But it would be to falsify history to concentrate on them, in order to obtain relief from the general gloom of the colouring. A single fact will illuminate this statement. Their prosperity was powerless to relieve the tragedy of the western and central settlements. On the contrary, the tragedy spread to them also; it was delayed, but the contagion existed already in their systems, and the disease needed but a few more centuries to develop. The ghetto of the Papal city of Rome survived into the nineteenth century with all the barbarities which northern Europe had known centuries before, and for centuries abandoned. The ghetto of eastern Europe was only shattered by the revolution of 1917, and its effects are with us still. The accusations of ritual murder and the profanation of the Host disappeared from the west to return thither from Russia, Poland and the Balkan countries in the nineteenth century.

In the political history of Jewry which has been traced in this and the previous chapters the course of the decline has been evident, but political history does not explain its reasons. With one of the reasons this book is not concerned. The study of the growth of superstition, the steadily increasing popular hatred of the Jew, the smashing blows delivered at Jewish intellectual life by successive expulsions and the destruction of their schools of learning, these must be left for the following volume. But one central reason still remains to be studied, the fatal rôle allotted to the Jew in the economy of the time, the rôle of royal usurer. It is only by an artificial separation of inextricably interwoven motives that it is possible for a historian to say that the hatred of the Jew was *exclusively* religious or *exclusively* economic. As a complete explanation either is untrue by itself. The background of political and religious history and tradition prepared the stage for the Jew to appear in his new character. The part given him to play was one which would inevitably make of him the enemy of the people among whom he lived. So much is true. But, had it not been for the subjection of the Jew to a particular political development, and the subjection of the Christian to a particular theological picture of the Jew, he would never have played the part allotted to him at all.

PART III

THE ROYAL USURER

BIBLIOGRAPHICAL INTRODUCTION

The reason for the change in substance from the Carolingian to the later groups of charters was the discovery by the princes that much profit was to be made out of the encouragement of moneylending in their Jewries. But they were only able to secure this profit by the particular structure of contemporary economic society. It used to be believed, and it is still continually asserted, that the determining factors leading the Jews to become usurers were a hereditary aptitude for the profession on their part, and the canonical prohibition of usury as a profession for Christians. The conclusions are drawn from these beliefs that all usurers were Jews and that, conversely, all Jews were usurers. The facts were entirely different; usury, both among Christians and Jews, grew out of economic needs, and the action of the Church never secured more than partial and temporary successes.

For this reason Chapters Eight and Nine deal first with the struggle of the Church, then with the general growth of the trade in money. Only with this background is it possible to approach the special position occupied by the Jews in the profession. In the list of books it will be seen that some deal with the general problem of usury. The work of Génestal, dealing largely with Normandy, is important for an understanding of the situation before usury became primarily a profession of merchants. Tawney's *Religion and the Rise of Capitalism* is especially valuable. Others deal with Christian usurers. To give a comprehensive bibliography on this subject would clearly be beyond the needs of this volume, but Amiet, Neumann, Mirot and Simmonet are sufficient to give an excellent general picture of different types of Christian usurer. Amiet contains some representative documents concerning usury in the Swiss commercial cities. For the Jewish usurer the best study is that of Hoffmann. Most of the other books are included because they contain sections dealing with the question. Detailed studies of Jewish usury in France are lacking, as is any adequate study of the group of usurers known as ' Cahorsin '.

LIST OF BOOKS

AMIET, J. J.

Die französischen und lombardischen Geldwucherer des Mittelalters, in *Jahrbuch für schweizerische Geschichte* I, II. Zürich, 1876, 1877.

ASHLEY, W. J.

An Introduction to English Economic History and Theory. Revised edition. Two vols. London, 1901.

BERNFELD, I.

Das Zinsverbot bei den Juden nach talmudisch-rabbinischem Recht (*Das Licht,* No. viii). Berlin, 1928.

CARO, G.

Sozial- und Wirtschaftsgeschichte der Juden im Mittelalter. Two vols. Leipzig, 1908, 1920.

FUNK, F. X.

Geschichte des kirchlichen Zinsverbots. Tübingen, 1876.

GÉNESTAL DU CHAUMEIL, R.

Rôle des Monastères comme établissements de crédit. Paris, 1901.

HAHN, B.

Die Wirtschaftliche Tätigkeit der Juden im Fränkischen und Deutschen Reich bis zum 2. Kreuzzug. Diss. Freiburg i.B., 1911.

HOFFMANN, M.

Der Geldhandel der deutschen Juden während des Mittelalters bis zum Jahre 1350. Leipzig, 1910.

LAMPRECHT, K.

Deutsches Wirtschaftsleben im Mittelalter. Four vols. Leipzig, 1885, 1886.

LOEWE, H.
ABRAHAMS, I.
STOKES, H. P.

Starrs and Jewish Charters preserved in the British Museum. Three vols. Printed for the Jewish Historical Society of England, Cambridge (Vols. II and III: London), 1930-1932.

MIROT, L.   *Etudes Lucquoises*, in *Bibliothèque de l'Ecole de Chartes*, Nos. LXXXVIII and LXXXIX.

NEUMANN, M.   *Geschichte des Wuchers in Deutschland*. Halle, 1860.

ROSCHER, W.   *Die Stellung der Juden im Mittelalter betrachtet vom Standpunkt der allgemeinen Handelspolitik. In Ansichten der Volkswirtschaft*. Third edition, Vol. II. Leipzig, 1878.

RABINOWITZ, L.   *The Social Life of the Jews of Northern France*. (In the press.)

SCHERER, J. E.   *Die Rechtsverhältnisse der Juden in den deutsch-österreichischen Ländern.* Leipzig, 1901.

SIMMONET, J.   *Juifs et Lombards.* In *Mémoires de l'Académie Impériale de Dijon*, IIe Série, tome 13e. Année 1865.

STOBBE, O.   *Die Juden in Deutschland während des Mittelalters, in politischer, socialer und rechtlicher Beziehung.* Third edition. Braunschweig, 1866. Repr. Berlin, 1923.

SÜSSMANN, A.   *Die Judenschuldentilgungen unter König Wenzel.* Berlin, 1907.

TAWNEY, R. H.   *Religion and the Rise of Capitalism.* London, 1926.

WILSON, THOMAS   *A Discourse upon Usury.* With an historical introduction by R. H. Tawney. London, 1925.

ZIMMELS, H. J.   *Beiträge zur Geschichte der Juden in Deutschland im 13. Jahrhundert, insbesondere auf Grund der Gutachten des R. Meir Rothenburg.* Wien, 1926.

CHAPTER EIGHT

MEDIEVAL THEORY OF USURY

I. NATURE OF MEDIEVAL BORROWING AND LENDING

When the modern citizen has money lying idle in the bank he thinks of investing it in some kind of industrial or other securities. When he is short of cash he negotiates an overdraft with his bank. He would not ordinarily think either of employing the spare capital in loans to his friends on interest, or of going to a professional moneylender to tide over a temporary shortness. Shops allow credit to regular clients even in humble circumstances; and payments can be made in instalments for nearly every object of domestic use.

The man who wishes to develop an industry forms a limited liability company by which, technically at least, those from whom he ' borrows ' the money to start his industry share in the control of the enterprise. They have no claim upon his personal property for interest upon their loan, or even for the capital.

Apart from these regular transactions, banks cope with most of the ordinary necessities of the middle and professional classes, and the casual needs of most classes are met by friendly loans from their acquaintances. It is only when some unusual or unproductive loan has to be secured, to cover some special extravagance or unexpected shortage, that recourse is had to a moneylender or a pawnbroker. Such lending is therefore in the nature of a speculation, and it may almost be said of a rash speculation since, if there were not something abnormal in the situation, there would be other, and cheaper, ways of meeting it. When such an emergency arises the middle and upper classes go to kindly gentry prepared to lend on ' note of hand alone ' sums ranging from five to five thousand pounds. Since their operations possess a certain scope, they can be to a considerable extent controlled, and their interest limited to 48 per

T

cent. or less. The poorer and less fortunate approximate more nearly to their medieval ancestors; they pawn some possession, though they would not like to do as did their ancestors, conduct the transaction either before anything up to ten witnesses, or in the open street. The pawnbroker is even more strictly controlled than the moneylender, and his interest, which is not allowed to exceed 48 per cent., is usually about 25 per cent. Finally, there is, especially among workers in factories and similar groups, the individual who himself lends or who, more often, has a relation who is kind enough to help a man out of difficulties insoluble by ordinary means. Here there is, naturally, no control of interest, and a single example may illustrate the heights to which it can soar. A case was recently reported in which a woman without a licence lent to her poor neighbours. Her practice was to lend £1 on Saturday and to receive £1 1s. 8d. on the following Saturday. This amounted to interest at the rate of $433\frac{1}{3}$ per cent. per annum[1].

To understand the medieval situation it is necessary to abandon this entire set of facts. Conditions were totally different and money itself, the inevitable basis of 'money-lending', was not the natural form in which a man's wealth was estimated, but a relatively rare commodity. To-day it would be easier for the average man to lend his neighbour a couple of shillings to buy milk than to lend him a goat. So far as Europe is concerned, it is only in eastern Europe and the Balkans that a situation similar to the medieval conditions of western Europe can still be seen. There, in bad times, such as the present (1937), the only actual coin which a peasant may handle in a whole year may be the coin required to pay his taxes. For all other purposes he arranges his life without coin.

A further difference is that to-day we make a sharp distinction between honourable finance, and money transactions which are felt to be dishonourable. A man feels quite differently about asking for a bank overdraft and going to a moneylender. He does not consider that he is committing any religious or civil crime in investing his surplus. It is only the shame which the poor feel in going to the pawnshop and the secrecy of the private lender that recall the earlier

[1] *Evening Standard*, April 28, 1937.

situation; and these survivals explain one of the differences between those centuries and to-day. Even the controlled rate of interest of a pawnshop is so high that it is evident that only dire necessity makes people willing to pay it. To be seen entering the shop of a pawnbroker is therefore an admission of extreme poverty. Similarly, the hole-and-corner method of lending among the poor, even when the legal rate of interest is not exceeded, is a recognition of the social disapproval with which such transactions are known to be regarded.

From the standpoint of medieval Christendom, the term 'usury' covers every transaction in which profit out of money is concerned. In the earlier part of the period, even commercial profit out of buying and selling was considered in the same way. The greatest financiers, such as the Bardi and Peruzzi, who financed Edward III, and the little village usurer were on the same footing. Usury at seven per cent. and at two hundred were equally condemned. We make a distinction to-day between profit and usury, and allot the latter word only to those cases in which we consider the profit immoderate. In other cases we speak of interest. From the medieval standpoint, the distinction is different. 'Interest' might be extremely excessive—in fact, often was[1]—but in a loan at 'interest' a delay existed, however short, within which the original sum could be repaid without any addition. 'Usury', on the other hand, was an automatic increase on the capital lent from the actual day of lending.

II. THE CHRISTIAN VIEW OF USURY

In its starkest form the medieval doctrine of 'usury' condemned every way in which more was received than had been paid out. The increase might take place in various ways. In a 'mortgage' the creditor only received the sum of money back which he had lent; but the usury consisted in his enjoyment of the estate in the interval. In transactions with peasants a loan might be made in coin and repaid in crops. This was usury unless the lender took a risk that the crops

---

[1] On the theory of 'interest' see below, pp. 294 ff.

might bring in less than the sum loaned[1]. It was usury to demand back the loan in a different currency, since the relative values might change in the intervening time. In the strictest interpretation it was even usury when merchandise was sold in the ordinary way of business at a higher price than that at which it had been bought.

The bases from which this rigorous doctrine evolved were multiple. In the first place, there was the authority of Christ. It is interesting that the Parable of the Talents was entirely ignored. The Church never made use of the fact that the servant who had buried his master's talent was reproached for not putting it out to profit, so that his master might receive it back with interest[2]. The essential passage of the Gospel was held to be the phrase which is now translated ' lend never despairing ', but which the Vulgate renders ' nihil inde sperantes '—expecting nothing in return[3]. Equally important were three passages from the Old Testament, which were still more explicit.

If thou lend money to any of my people with thee that is poor, thou shalt not be to him a creditor, neither shall ye lay upon him usury[4].

Thou shalt not lend upon usury to thy brother; usury of money, usury of victuals, usury of anything that is lent upon usury; unto a foreigner thou mayest lend upon usury; but unto thy brother thou shalt not lend upon usury[5].

If thy brother be waxen poor and his hand fail with thee; then thou shalt uphold him: as a stranger and a sojourner

---

[1] Cf. Decretal. Gregor. IX, V, xix, De usuris, c. vi.

[2] Matt. xxv, 27, A.V., usury; Vulgate, usura; Greek, τόκος. Jerome, in his commentary on the passage, sets the fashion: ' pecunia ergo et argentum praedicatio Evangelii est, et sermo divinus, qui dari debuit nummulariis et trapezitis id est vel caeteris doctoribus (quod fecerunt et apostoli per singulas provincias, presbyteros et episcopos ordinantes) vel multis credentibus qui possunt pecuniam duplicare et cum usuris reddere, ut quidquid sermone didicerant opere explerent.' The medieval commentators followed suit.

[3] Lk. vi, 35; for its application see e.g. Decretal. Gregor. IX, V, xix, De usuris, c. x.

[4] Ex. xxii, 25.

[5] Deut. xxiii, 19-20.

shall he live with thee. Take thou no usury of him nor increase; but fear thy God: that thy brother may live with thee. Thou shalt not give him thy money upon usury, nor give him thy victuals for increase[1].

Each of these passages comes from a different Pentateuchal source. The first, from the earlier period of the kingdom, is contained in the oldest collection of Hebrew laws which we possess, ' The Book of the Covenant '; the second is from the Deuteronomic Code of the later days of the kingdom; the third comes from the ' Code of Holiness ', an early collection of the Book of Leviticus, later than the Deuteronomic Law, but earlier than the Exile. As all these sources belong to a period when the Israelites had very little contact with commerce, it is evident that in their original setting they envisaged nothing so formal as medieval moneylending, or the complicated developments of medieval society. They presupposed a simple agricultural community, and dealt with the inevitable borrowing and lending which goes on between poor neighbours—that very class of uncontrollable indebtedness which is as much a curse to-day as it was in the days of the Jewish kingdoms. They dealt with showing kindness to a neighbour in need, and were not even primarily concerned with money—' usury of money, usury of victuals, usury of anything that is lent upon usury '; certainly their author did not imagine that the borrower was going to make the loan the basis of commercial profit, or that the lender was lending as a profession.

Of great popular importance is the concession in the Deuteronomic passage, *unto a stranger thou mayest lend upon usury*, which was interpreted in such a way that Jews were considered to be permitted to lend upon usury to Christians, while Christians might not so lend to their fellows. Needless to say, this is not what the passage meant. What it refers to would be called to-day ' security ' rather than ' usury '; for whereas if a man lent to a neighbour living next door, he knew that he would still be there the following day and had no need to demand security, it was not unreasonable to ask it of someone who was simply passing through, and might at any time depart, leaving no trace behind. But while this

[1] Lev. xxv, 35-37.

text was *popularly* used as a sanction for Jewish money-lending, it is at least to the credit of the theologians that they did not accept this compromise. Innocent III in 1198 refused to allow Jews as well as Christians to charge usury if they had lent money to men who undertook a Crusade[1]; and Raymond de Pennaforte adduced a text of Ambrose alleging that usury could only be exacted with intent to injure, and pointed out that the Christian could not desire that anyone should be injured[2]. Jew and Christian both, therefore, committed mortal sin in lending on usury.

Not content with attacking any profit on money as a mortal sin, the Church at first applied the same absolute standpoint to almost any kind of commercial profit. The Constitutions of Theodulfus and the Capitulary of Charlemagne, two of the earliest European regulations of ' usury ', are both concerned with goods as well as coin. Charlemagne quotes the case of a man who buys corn cheap at the time of the harvest, and later sells it at a higher price. If he does this out of avarice, then this is a desire for ' filthy lucre ', and sinful; if he does it because of necessity, this is to be considered lawful business[3].

To go into the details of this aspect of the question is not necessary, for in the distinction drawn by Charlemagne the essence of the doctrine of the medieval canonists is contained. The western Church grew up in an agricultural community of little wealth, and of few commercial needs, and it was the relatively great wealth of the merchants, whether Jew or, more commonly, Christian, which convinced her that something was wrong about their business. She regarded commerce entirely from the standpoint of its service to the community, and not from that of its provision of wealth to the individual. She was concerned with *motive* above everything, for on motive depended salvation. She was perfectly willing to allow the merchant a ' just price ' which would permit him to live and support his family reasonably according to his status in society. But she quickly observed

[1] Grayzel, *op. cit.*, pp. 86 ff.

[2] *Summa*, II, vii, 9.

[3] *Cap. of March*, 806, vii; in MGH, LL, I, p. 145. Cf. Canon 10 of the Council of Trier, of 1227, where this question of the harvest is dealt with, as it is in many other canons of the same period.

that a very different desire animated the merchant. He desired to get rich, and that was the sin of avarice[1]. The necessity of literal obedience to the Scriptures, just because they were the Scriptures, cannot, all the same, be entirely overlooked. A question was remitted to Alexander III, the Pope under whom the problem came to a head, from the Archbishop of Palermo which illustrates this. The Archbishop desired to ransom poor Christians from the Saracens, and asked the Pope whether profits might not be made from usury for this purpose, but the Pope replied that authority could not be given for *any purpose* for the practice of actions condemned by the Scriptures[2]. Here it is clear that no question of avarice can enter, but that did not affect the Pope's decision. Whatever may have been the practice, the secular courts took, in principle, exactly the same attitude as the canonists. Gild courts and citizens alike attacked any attempts at monopolies and corners. Even in the great commercial cities of Italy 'usury' was regarded with theoretical abhorrence, and 'usurers' were fined by the justices.

If it be asked why both Church and society strove to enforce literal obedience to these passages of the ancient Law, while so many of its other prescriptions were ignored, it may be answered that early European society was sufficiently similar to the Hebrew kingdoms for these prescriptions to appeal as much to common sense as they did to theories of Biblical inspiration. The lending and borrowing which existed was mostly to satisfy the needs of the poor—whether temporarily or permanently so—and since money was a rare commodity, the possessor of it was continually tempted to an anti-social exploitation of his monopoly. The relieving of the necessities of another with money should have been merely one form of the exercise of that charity which was a fundamental Christian duty.

It may readily be admitted that the Church took too narrow a view of the problem, but it would be gravely unjust to the immense struggle, which she waged for centuries against the sin of usury, to dismiss it simply with censure or contempt. In the first place, she was moved with a very

---

[1] Cf. R. H. Tawney, *Religion and the Rise of Capitalism*, pp. 36-55.

[2] *Decretal. Gregor. IX*, V, xix, *De usuris*, c. iv.

genuine feeling of responsibility for the miseries of the poor, and there is not the slightest doubt that the poorer classes, who needed money not for any cause which would bring them profit, but to meet urgent necessities, did suffer cruelly from the monopolies of the usurers, and were frequently ruined by their legal or illegal exactions. While princes might sometimes confiscate the debts owed to Jewish or Italian usurers simply for their own profit, the number of occasions on which they had entirely to cancel them is an index of the real social menace of the profession. For such cancellations represented a considerable loss to the prince, and could only have been forced upon him by the fear of serious famine or disorder if he refused to take this drastic and personally unprofitable step.

Secondly, although the most unsatisfactory side of the work of the canonists and scholastics was their slowness to distinguish the emergence both of loans for commercial purposes, and of a social need for professional moneylenders, yet even here much can be said in their defence. Medieval society did not believe in a policy of *laissez-faire*. It was a whole into which each part fitted according to its own competence. It was unfortunate that they did not recognise that men followed moneylending as a profession, because society needed to be able to borrow money, and that many of their loans were made for the profit of the borrower; but the glaring fact about usury, as it was practised, was the pitiful plight of the borrower, powerless to repay the capital because the mounting usury by itself reduced him to ruin. Here, clearly, was something which destroyed the balance of society. In concentrating their attention on these victims, for a long time they saw nothing else.

Moreover, it was this sight, and not mere theory, which lent force to the continual insistence on the deadliness of the sin of avarice, and they had ample grounds for the belief that it was not a desire to serve the weaker brethren, but a desire to make profit out of them, which determined the conditions of the loans granted by the usurer. Spiritually, he also needed salvation as much as his victims.

Thirdly, it is not possible to understand this particular activity of the Church without relating it to the general spirit of the time. It is not merely on the question of usury that the Church made, and men acknowledged, far greater demands than would be expected even of enthusiastic churchmen to-day. The medieval man readily accepted the activities of the Inquisition, and infuriated laymen spontaneously burnt heretics in horror at their offence some time before the clerical Inquisition was organised. The idea that men may be made good by coërcion and by threat may be a fallacious one, but it was universally accepted. It would seem strange to-day for a bishop, accepting into the Anglican communion one who had previously been a Baptist, to impose upon him any penance for his past ' errors ' at all. But then an Albigensian or other heretic who made his peace with the Church took it for granted that he should do penance for the rest of his life, perhaps, even eat nothing but bread and water until the end of his days. A society which accepted that the Church should say, ' you shall not be heretical ', did not in theory reject her precept, ' you shall not be avaricious '. Both attempts failed, but in the manner of thought of the time it was natural that both should be made.

III. THE ATTEMPT TO ENFORCE IT IN CANON LAW

It is out of the general conflict with avarice that the Christian attack against making a profit out of money originally opened in the fourth century. In a number of sermons and tracts the great writers of that and the succeeding century dealt with the subject. Ambrose of Milan, Gaudentius of Brescia, Salvianus of Marseilles, Basil of Caesarea and Gregory of Nyssa all devoted time to the denunciation of avarice[1]. Canons of both eastern and western councils reinforced their appeals with stern punishments. The Councils of Nicaea and Laodicea in the east, the Gallic collection known as the ' Canons of the African Church ' in the west, threatened the clerical usurer with degradation and the layman with excommunication[2]. Leo the Great found that it was a

---

[1] Ambrose, *De Tobia Admonitio*; Gaudentius, *Sermo xiii, contra avaritiam Judae (Iscariot) et pro pauperibus*; Salvianus, *Contra Avaritiam Lib. IV*; Basil, *Homily on Ps. xiv against usurers*; Gregory of Nyssa, *Contra usurarios*.

[2] Nicaea, xvii; Laodicea, iv; Carthage III, xvi; VI, xvii, etc.

scourge in Campania[1]; Gregory the Great refused to accept a candidate for a bishopric because he had heard that the man in question was a usurer. Finally, Theodulfus of Orleans at the end of the eighth century not only forbade it, but defined precisely what he meant by it in the most uncompromising terms[2].

In the Roman world the attack had been clerical, and not reinforced by law. It had also been mainly, though by no means exclusively, directed against usury amongst the clergy. With Charlemagne, the secular arm came to reinforce the spiritual. It must be admitted that the reinforcement was a mild one, since no penalties were attached to the offence. But at least Charlemagne issued a statement confirming the main contention of Theodulfus that anything beyond the principal lent was to be considered usurious, and therefore sinful. That the step was a novelty he recognised by giving various simple explanations of his meaning[3].

During the next few centuries the Church leaders were mainly occupied with the reform of general ecclesiastical conditions and with the development of their own social organisation. But the old canons against usury remained in force, and were recalled to mind by the various collections whose compilation were a feature of the period. Attention was next drawn to the matter by the immense increase in trade and general activity in the twelfth century. At the General Council held at the Lateran in 1179, Alexander III referred for the first time to people who made usury their whole profession, and to the general prevalence of this sin. In order to suppress it usurers were excluded from communion, their alms were rejected, and they were refused Christian burial. Any clergy who condoned their offence were to be suspended until the Ordinary had dealt with them[4]. Similar action was being taken at the same time in local councils[5], and the Pope himself stressed the seriousness of the issue in repeated letters to different dioceses[6].

---

[1] *Ep. ad Ep. per Campaniam, etc.*; Harduin, *Concilia*, I, p. 1753.

[2] Cap. II; Mansi, XIII, c. 1016: 'Quisquis per quodlibet ingenium magis accipit quam praestat, sciat se usuram fecisse.'

[3] *Cap. of* 806; MGH, LL, I, p. 144.

[4] Lateran III, xxv; Mansi, XXII, c. 231.

[5] E.g. Westminster (1173), xiii; Mansi, XXII, c. 143.

[6] E.g. Mansi, XXI, cc. 922 and 1196.

Both clerics and laymen came under the same condemnation, and there was evidence of both being extensively engaged in the practice.

For the next hundred years local councils continued everywhere their effort to enforce the decisions of the Lateran Council. It was dealt with in France in councils at Avignon in 1209, Paris in 1212, Montpellier in 1214, Narbonne in 1227, Château Gontier in 1231, Béziers in 1246, Le Mans in 1247, Albi in 1254, and Sens in 1269. From the British Isles canons survive of a Scottish Council of 1225, and of a council at Worcester in 1240; German prelates dealt with it at Trier in 1227 and 1238, and at Vienna in 1267[1]. Though such a list is in no way complete, it is enough to indicate both the seriousness of the effort put forth by the Church and the extent of the practice which she was attempting to suppress. Hints of the failure of the effort appear in an ever-increasing severity in the penalties. Usurers were classed with various obviously reprehensible persons to indicate to the general public how they were to be considered: with witches, incendiaries, evil-doers and highway robbers by one council[2]; with fornicators, keepers of concubines and adulterers by another[3]; and with gamblers, speculators and publicans by a third[4]. The sin of usury was classed with homicide, sacrilege, perjury, homosexual offences, incest and parricide and, like them, could not be remitted by a priest in the Confessional[5]. Public warnings were to be given of the nature of the sin by every priest, once a year, quarterly, monthly, or even weekly[6]. The children of usurers were warned to make restitution out of their inheritance, and to surrender what had been so gained, even if they did not know the owners to whom it should be restored[7].

---

[1] All to be found in Mansi, Vols. XXII-XXIV. Many similar canons are to be found in other works, but these are enough to show the gravity of the conflict.

[2] Conc. Scoticum, lxviii.

[3] Narbonne, xxiii.

[4] Trier, viii (1227).

[5] Ibid., iv.

[6] E.g. Scot., lxviii; Narbonne, viii, etc.

[7] Le Mans, Mansi, XXIII, c. 742. Half a century earlier, in a letter to the Bishop of Piacenza, Alexander III had insisted on this restitution; Decretal. Gregor. IX, V, xix, De usuris, c. ix.

The centre of the effort during this period seems to have been France. Extensive campaigns against the Jewish usurer had been conducted there during the latter half of the twelfth century, and they had been expelled in 1180, to return in 1198. But side by side with the Jews there appeared at the beginning of the thirteenth century ' communes ' of usurers who behaved with an aggressiveness impossible to their Jewish rivals. It is against these that the canons of the French Councils are directed. The Council of Paris in 1212 thus describes them:

' In almost every city, town and village of France the ingrained malice of the devil has firmly established synagogues of usurers and extortioners, commonly called communes; and these diabolical institutions, forbidden by ecclesiastical constitutions, are completely wrecking the ecclesiastical system of jurisdiction.'

The Council complained that they had established their own courts, in defiance of the bishops; and that, with the connivance of the king and barons, whom they had bribed, they were causing their victims to be imprisoned and fined if they attempted to carry a case into the ecclesiastical courts[1].

This report of their activities reads extremely like Matthew Paris's description of the establishment of the Cahorsin in England twenty years later[2]. That they should have established themselves throughout France first is natural.

The rapid increase of the problem corresponded to increasing commercial activity. The demand for money grew continually. The excommunication of the usurer could not arrest the tide. The Council of Paris was equally unsuccessful when it ordained the excommunication of any lawyer who prevented a case concerning usury from coming before the courts Christian, where the usury would have been cancelled automatically. But when the direct attack failed to awe the moneylender into submission, there remained several ways in which the Church might make difficulties for him. If he were a Jew an effort could be made to prevent the Christian population from providing him with food, until he was starved into obedience; or he could be prevented from

[1] Paris, V, 8, Mansi, XXII, c. 851.
[2] See below, p. 285.

entering the churches, which were often the safest place in which to keep deeds. These methods were more difficult when the usurers were nominally Christian. Two additional weapons were, therefore, employed. In many places the deed registering a loan needed not only the seals of borrower and lender, but also that of some public official appointed by the princely or civic authorities for that purpose. Such officials were almost inevitably *clerici*, and as such amenable to ecclesiastical discipline. The Council of Sens, therefore, forbade ' any ecclesiastical person whatever to affix his seal to any document which explicitly or implicitly contained a demand for usury '. If this canon had been obeyed it would have also prevented any cleric or ecclesiastical corporation from making or accepting a loan on usurious terms, since as either debtor or creditor they would have had to sign the document. The same council also adopted another indirect method of attack. The ecclesiastical corporations were extensive landowners. In not a few cases entire towns belonged to the church or abbey around which they had originally grown, and, in every town, the churches and monasteries possessed extensive property. The council, therefore, also ordered that no house in the possession of the Church should be leased to anyone for the conduct of a moneylending business, and forbade any tenant of church property to indulge in usury[1].

Such was the power of the usurers that the same council made elaborate provisions to protect any bishop who attempted to carry out their canons from molestation, libel and specious litigation on the part of the usurers against whom he proceeded; and, realising that these steps were empirical, the council concluded by asking that a report on their efficacy should be presented before the next general council, which, if they had failed of their effect, should evolve fresh measures for dealing with the scourge[2]. Matthew Paris proves to us that these fears of the Council of Sens were not illusory. In 1235 the Cahorsin settled in London and began to practise their business. Their voracity and cunning were such that they soon had a large section of the population in their toils. Moved to indignation, the bishop

---

[1] Sens, ii; Mansi, XXIV, c. 4.
[2] *Ibid.,* iii.

attempted to protect his flock by expelling them from the
city. They laughed at his order of expulsion and boasted
that they enjoyed adequate protection at the Roman court;
and when the bishop attempted to enforce it, they succeeded
in involving him in a lawsuit which compelled him, at an
advanced age, to make a journey to Rome to defend his case[1].

The next General Council, held at Lyons in 1274, adopted
the proposals of Sens and carried them a stage further.
Nobody, whether layman or cleric, no individual or corporation, of whatever rank or office, was to lease, or allow to be
leased, any property to a foreigner wishing to practise, or
practising, usury. Excommunication, interdict and other
ecclesiastical penalties were the punishment. The motive for
this indirect attack, which demanded considerable sacrifice
on the part of innocent house owners, was quite openly
admitted[2]. Since there was very little hope of persuading the
usurer to renounce his business of his own free will, it was
necessary to place every possible obstacle in his path. Nevertheless, the council did not completely accept defeat at the
hands of the usurer himself. If he was indifferent to excommunication and the refusal of Christian burial, which
penalties the Lateran Council had already laid upon him,
there was a chance that he might be moved by the disinheritance of his family. The Council of Lyons threatened
this by declaring his will to be invalid[3] and, since at this time
testamentary questions were mainly dealt with in ecclesiastical courts, the Council had decreed a penalty which the
Church was competent to enforce.

In studying the canons which have so far been discussed
a certain development can be traced. The earliest of all
dealt only with clerical usury; then usury as practised by
Christian laymen came under consideration; then every
kind of usurer, clerical, lay and Jewish, was condemned; and
finally the Council of Lyons, while reminding the faithful
of the Lateran canons, devoted all its own effort to suppressing the usury of ' foreigners '; in other words, of those
called either ' Lombards ' or ' Cahorsin ', the chief moneylenders of the Middle Ages.

[1] *Chron. maj.*, Rolls Series, III, p. 331.
[2] Lyons, xxvi; Mansi, XXIV, cc. 99 ff.
[3] *Ibid.*, c. xxvii.

In the succeeding period steps were continually taken to bring the decrees of the Councils of the Lateran and of Lyons before the general Christian public. They were ordered to be read and expounded from every pulpit. In some dioceses they were to be publicly affixed. The people were to be reminded every Sunday that the penalty for usury was excommunication. But still the Church failed to make headway, and successive councils seized now on one point, now on another from which they hoped for success. In Cologne in 1280 the method of forbidding any notary to inscribe the usurer's deeds was tried again[1]; in Noyon in the same year the bishops were urged to increasing severity, and authorised to summon to their presence both persons accused anonymously, and even persons against whom there was no evidence but a strong presumption that they were guilty of the offence. In such cases the bishop was to impose certain penances and, if the person concerned refused to purge himself by accepting them, he was to be adjudged guilty and excommunicated. Further, any advocate who undertook the defence of a usurer was first to swear that he himself was convinced that his client was innocent, and only in such cases was he to defend him. If he was not so convinced, he was to retire from the case or be disbarred[2]. In other words, the alternative defence that the practice of his client was legitimate was disallowed in advance. The Council of Avignon in 1282 allowed anonymous accusations[3]. Four years later the Council of Ravenna allowed a notary to make a will for a person suspected of usury only in the presence of the vicar of his parish, who would ensure that proper restitution was made[4]. In the next year a Council at Würzburg added a fresh humiliation to the life of the usurer. If his sin was discovered after his death, the cemetery in which he was buried was to be placed under an interdict until his corpse was dug up and thrown out[5]. In Cologne, in 1300, executors who discovered any unjust profit in a will were ordered to make restitution out of the property, even

[1] c. xiv; Mansi, XXIV, c. 359.
[2] Noyon, iii and iv; Mansi, XXIV, c. 375.
[3] c. i; Mansi, XXIV, c. 439.
[4] c. vi; *ibid.*, c. 621.
[5] c. xxiii; *ibid.*, c. 859.

though there was no authority for such action in the will itself[1]. Even in one of the main homes of the Italian bankers, the local church attempted to enforce the canons of Lyons and the Lateran. A council at Lucca in 1308 dealt with the matter at great length, and hopefully added detailed instructions for the reception of dying and repentant usurers[2].

In Germany conciliar ingenuity was not exhausted by the decisions of Cologne. A council at Trier in 1310 forbade the wives and children of usurers to accept the products of the labours of their husbands and fathers. The wife, where possible, was to live on her dowry. If that failed, she was to appeal for assistance to her relations. Even if that did not succeed, she was not to rest content, but to earn her living by begging. Only if she and her children were actually dying of starvation was she to accept money from her husband[3]. In the same year, at Mainz, similar efforts to make conditions more unpleasant for the usurer were put forward. The dying usurer was not to have his confession heard unless he had previously made restitution. Refusal of burial did not free his heirs from the duty of returning his property to its rightful owners. Further, if a usurer remained obstinate for one month after excommunication, then it automatically fell on his wife, children and servants, and they were refused all the rites of the Church except baptism and extreme unction.

In the following year (1311) another important step was taken. Usury was officially identified with heresy, and placed under the control of the Inquisition. The association was not in itself new. Under the influence of Bishop Fulk, the close friend of Saint Dominic, a group had been founded in Toulouse as early as 1209, whose task was ' to drive out heretics and to combat usurers '[4]. And Matthew Paris, in speaking of Milan, called it ' a home of all heretics— Paterines, Luciferians, Publicans, Albigenses and *usurers* '[5]. But the formal identification, with its tremendous implication that it lay with the Inquisition to combat it, dates from

---

[1] c. x; Mansi, XXV, c. 20.
[2] Lucca, xxviii, xxix, lvi and lxx; *ibid.*, cc. 181 ff.
[3] c. cxli; Mansi, XXV, c. 289.
[4] J. Guiraud, *Histoire de l'Inquisition*, I, p. 399.
[5] *Chron. maj.*, ed. Rolls Series, III, p. 375.

the time of the Council of Vienne summoned by Clement V. A number of reasons may have contributed to this decision of the Pope. He was a Gascon, and therefore familiar with the work of the Inquisition in its original home, the south of France; he was the first Pope to reside at Avignon, and may therefore have been more independent of the Italian usurers than were the Popes in Rome; and he was much influenced by Philip the Fair, whose greed for money exceeded that of the Pope, and who was making a drive against the Lombard usurers at about this time.

In any case, at the Council of Vienne, whose main purpose was the suppression of the Templars, or at some immediately subsequent date, a ' Constitution ' was promulgated which, after referring to the prevalence of usury and the wiles of usurers in evading detection, excommunicated all civic authorities who failed to revoke all laws authorising usury within their jurisdiction, and added that anyone who dared to defend the practice as legitimate should be treated as a heretic. Those suspected of usury were bound to produce their accounts on demand. On this basis both the regular ecclesiastical courts and the courts of the Inquisition were explicitly authorised to punish those accused or suspected of the offence[1]. What result this action produced it is extremely difficult to assess. References to Inquisitions on the subject of usury are very rare; but it is impossible to tell whether this is simply because public attention has been concentrated on their pursuit of heretics, until some historian has made a detailed survey of the available evidence[2].

Though the Inquisition was thus introduced into the field, ordinary ecclesiastical methods were not abandoned. In the fourteenth century a determined effort was made in successive councils to deal with the problem at its source— that is, in the commercial cities of northern Italy. A Council of the Province of Milan, held at Bergamo in 1311, opened the campaign. The old canons excommunicating usurers, and refusing them Christian burial, were confirmed, and notaries who drew up documents which contained usury

[1] *Clement. Const.*, V, v.

[2] R. H. Tawney, *op. cit.*, p. 50, tells of an Inquisitor at Florence who collected 7,000 florins in two years from ' usurers and blasphemers '. But even this leaves the question open, for we do not know how much was collected for each offence.

U

were placed under the same penalties as usurers themselves. The Council then proceeded to compile the most elaborate rules for ensuring the genuineness of any expression of repentance on the part of usurers, and refused to accept them as penitents except under the most stringent safeguards[1]. The potential victims, with their accustomed skill in evasion, replied to this new campaign by bribery. Feigning repentance, they made a payment to the parish priest in earnest of their intention to restore their fortunes to the rightful owners, and, obtaining absolution, continued their wicked ways. The priests seem to have been prone to the temptation to retain this advance payment, and then to have condoned the offence. Thus challenged, the Church replied at a Council at Perugia by making still more stringent regulations as to the conditions under which an advance payment might be accepted[2]. This also failed of its effect, and the Church looked round for fresh weapons. Armed now with the powers of the Inquisition, she demanded the production of deeds, accounts and records; and the Constitutions of the Diocese of Ferrara—which rather weakened their position by being compelled to devote considerable space to the suppression of usury among the clergy themselves—both re-enforced all the methods and penalties which had already been prescribed, and provided, for the assistance of those who had to deal with the matter, a list of the tricks by which usury was concealed within seemingly innocent contracts[3]. This simply tempted the enemy to more ingenious forms of evasion; and the Constitutions of Aquileia of 1339 not only ordained that the Bishop, or a special deputy appointed for the purpose, should alone be entitled to judge of the sincerity of a confession of usury, but also, in despair at the wiles of their opponents, declared forthright that *any* contract made with *any* member of a group, family or company believed to be occupied with usury, was to be deemed to be usurious, however innocent it appeared[4]. It is in such sweeping assumptions that it is possible to see the influence of the

---

[1] Bergamo, rubrics xxiv and xxv; Mansi, XXV, cc. 498 ff.

[2] Mansi, XXV, c. 643.

[3] Const. of Ferrara, 1332, Nos. 32 and 46; Mansi, XXV, cc. 917 and 923.

[4] Mansi, XXV, cc. 1120 ff.

Inquisitors who dealt not otherwise with those suspected of heresy.

In the same year the Church of Padua also published a book of Constitutions in which the detection of usury found its place. In these the priests were given guidance as to how to detect those who carried on their business under a different name. It would also appear that the usurers had met the demand for the production of their accounts and records by the bland statement that they were not in business, and had no records. Where there was suspicion that the accused person had been guilty of usury a statement that he possessed no records was never to be believed, and he was to be held guilty of having concealed them, since by law some written statement of any financial transaction was obligatory[1].

After Padua, the Church of Florence carried on the struggle. In a comprehensive ' Constitution ', the whole ground was gone over again. All foreign persons engaged, or suspected to be engaged, in usury were to be refused admission to the city, or, if already admitted, to be expelled with little delay. No notary was to write any contract in which usury was contained. No citizen of Florence was to engage in usury and any case which was discovered was to be reported immediately to the clergy for their action. No conscience money was to be accepted except before a competent official whose duty it was to ensure that full restitution was made before the usurer was received as a penitent[2]. Next Padua in 1350 returned to the attack along its chosen line of inspecting the records of suspects. The statement of the suspect that he was not in possession of records was to be flatly disbelieved unless trustworthy persons could be produced to swear that there had been records, but that they had been destroyed either by fire, or by some other means. If this could not be proved the inquiry was to continue until records were produced[3]. Finally a Council at Benevento completed the series by giving two new weapons to the clergy. The bishop received authority to impose fines on those who did not repent after one month under the penalty

[1] Const. xx; Mansi, XXV, cc. 1139 ff.

[2] Const. Synod. v; Mansi, XXV, cc. 61 ff. On the effects of this, cf. Tawney, *op. cit.*, p. 37.

[3] Mansi, XXVI, cc. 229 ff.

of excommunication; and immediate denunciation of all
known or suspected usurers was made an obligation on every
citizen[1].

Other countries had not been completely idle while the
Italian Church was putting forth this supreme effort. In
Prague in 1355 an effort had been made to attack ' usury '
as it affected illegitimate profit in commerce, and various
methods of securing such profit were carefully explained for
the benefit of the clergy[2]. In France, at a council of the
three southern provinces of Auch, Narbonne and Toulouse
held at Lavaur in 1368, at the time when the government
was disposed to sanction every method of usury in the hope
of raising money[3], the delegates decided to excommunicate
any judge who dared to enforce in court a usurious contract.
In the Empire, a council at Salzburg in 1420 began with the
modest opening: ' let the bishops prohibit usury *as far as they
are able* '[4], and then went on to re-state the existing canonical
prohibitions: usurers were to be excommunicated three
times a year; they were to be exposed by public denunciation; evasions were described and condemned; statements
to this effect were to be read in all churches before Lent;
usurers, and those who rented houses to usurers, were to be
excommunicated by name; those suspected of usury on the
word of two or three reliable witnesses were to be denied
Christian burial; clergy in whose cemeteries usurers had been
buried were excommunicated until they secured restitution;
the canon of the Lateran Council of 1179 was to be strictly
observed; owners of land, of every rank and quality, who
allowed foreigners to lease houses and practise usury, were
to be punished with excommunication and, in the case of
corporate owners, placed under interdict; the territories of
bishops or princes who remained obdurate for one month
were similarly to be placed under interdict; suggested
restitution was to be most carefully scrutinised; wills of
usurers were invalid; those who buried them were to be
excommunicated; usurers were to be solemnly warned of

---

[1] c. viii-xi; Mansi, XXVI, cc. 622 ff.

[2] c. lix; Mansi, XXVI, cc. 405 ff.

[3] See below, pp. 373 ff.

[4] Salzburg, x; Mansi, XXVIII, c. 987.

their fate; and all those whom public rumour and obvious appearances accused were to be reckoned manifest usurers[1].

During the fifteenth century, under the influence of Italian thinkers, considerable modifications of this intransigent attitude took place[2], but in the period with which we are mainly concerned, canon law did not soften in rigour. Only when the lending of money involved also sharing in the risks undertaken by the borrower was it not reckoned to be usury, and allowed to make a profit. If, for example, a man lent money for the fitting out of a ship to acquire merchandise for sale, he was not to be considered a usurer, provided he risked the loss of his money and only obtained a profit if the merchant who actually sailed in the ship succeeded in his venture[3]. Annuities also were lawful, for the giver did not know how long the receiver would live[4]. But such cases only touched the fringe of the main problem.

IV. SYSTEMS WHICH TRIED TO EVADE DEFINITION AS 'USURY'

That the regulations of the Councils were continuously evaded is already evident. The evasions took innumerable forms but two of them need special examination, that by which the money was not lent directly, but through a Jew or other moneylender, and that which arose out of the theory of 'interest'.

It appeared an admirably simple method of evading the canons to lay the mortal sin on the shoulders of someone else, and at times both clerics and laymen took this action. Sometimes the money was lent to a Christian usurer, sometimes to a Jewish[5]. The latter case seems to have been the more frequent, since, whatever the theological position, popular opinion inclined to the view that the Jew might make his profit from it without committing mortal sin. Alternatively, if he did commit mortal sin, it did not matter since he was damned anyhow. In the early centuries of

---

[1] *Ibid.*, c. xviii–xxiii.
[2] Cf. Tawney, *op. cit.*, Ch. I *passim*.
[3] Cf. G. Coulton, *An Episode in Canon Law*, in *History*, July 1921.
[4] Cf. Tawney, *op. cit.*, p. 42.
[5] Cf. Trier (1277), ic; Mansi, XXIV, c. 201.

Christianity there was nothing to prevent partnerships for any kind of business purposes between Jews and Christians[1], and in those times it was only where the Christian partner was a cleric that the arrangement was prohibited. As the Jews became more distinct from the general community it is probable that such partnerships would become much rarer, and that the placing of money with Jews for the purpose of profit would be not merely the extension of an established habit of commercial intercourse, but a new departure, expressly devised to evade the usury laws. Anyhow, the Church treated it as such, and as soon as she became aware of it, prohibited it[2]. The illegality of the action was so obvious that there could be no defence.

The other evasion is somewhat different and it proved much more difficult to decide for or against its legality—at any rate, as it existed in practice. While it was never questioned by the scholastics that it was unlawful to claim any profit out of the loan of a sum of money, it was possible to consider the making of a charge for the loan from another point of view. If a man lent money, which was due to be paid back in ten days' time, then, if the debtor failed to pay, the lender might lose an opportunity of legitimate and profitable investment which he had planned to seize upon that day. Whether this subtility grew out of a desire to evade the rigidity of canon law or not, does not matter. In any case, once this justification of a charge for a loan came to be adopted, it set a new problem for the scholastics. That a man was entitled to claim compensation for loss, when that loss had arisen through the failure of another to keep his contract, could scarcely be challenged, and was accepted as early as the beginning of the thirteenth century. This compensation was called ' interest ' from a phrase in the code of Justinian, *that which is between* (in Latin, *quod interest*) or ' *the difference* between the creditor's present position, and what it would have been had the bargain been fulfilled '[3]. But the lawyers, defining the matter further,

---

[1] Cf. *The Conflict of the Church and the Synagogue*, pp. 269, 332, and 341.

[2] Cf. Worcester (1240), lviii; S. Pölten (1284); Mansi, XXIII, c. 543 and XXIV, c. 510.

[3] Ashley. *op. cit.*, II, p. 399.

claimed that the loss was of two kinds, for both of which the right to compensation existed. There was the *damnum emergens*, the loss actually sustained by the creditor through the debtor's default; but there was also the *lucrum cessans*, the certain profit which had failed to materialise for the same reason. This latter the church could not so easily accept, for it undermined the basis of her whole position, that money could not and should not make a profit. The schoolmen seem to have modified their teaching in favour of interest as the period advanced[1], but in this they were out of harmony with the more practical churchmen of whom the councils were composed, whose battle against this system of lending continued unabated.

The essence of the method was that a delay must occur between the granting of the loan and the beginning of compensation, for the legal claim to compensation only began when the lender failed to repay the money at the time appointed. From the schoolmen's point of view, the time allowed needed to be a reasonable one and, in the case of failure to repay, the loss incurred had to be a real one, or one whose actual probability could be proved. In practice the lenders fixed their time limit at a point at which they were as certain as it was possible to be that the borrower could not repay, and, as the amount of compensation which would become due after the delay expired was already fixed in the original bond, it is obvious that they were not really concerned with any definite use to which they proposed to put their money on repayment. It was a legal fiction, such as lawyers have loved in every generation, and while the men of the cloister succumbed largely to it, the administrators of the Church would have none of it. Matthew Paris, who viewed it with great disapproval, gives a specimen of the form of bond which it involved[2]. The ' compensation ' was usually a sum equal to the sum lent or to half that sum, and as it became due the day after the period of grace expired, it was often much worse than the old ' usury '.

[1] On the whole question of *damnum emergens* and *lucrum cessans* see Ashley, *op. cit.*, I, pp. 197 ff., and II, pp. 399 ff.

[2] *Chron. maj.*, ed. Rolls Series, III, pp. 329 ff.; cf. *ibid.*, V, 404. See also J. Amiet, *Die französischen und lombardischen Geldwucherer des Mittelalters*, in *Jahrbuch für schweizerische Geschichte*, I and II, where a number of such bonds are described.

Further, it was customary to add to the compensation a number of other onerous terms. The debtor had to lodge himself, his sureties, or even his servants, in some place accessible to the creditor, and he or his substitutes had to remain there, at his expense, until the debt was paid. Alternatively, he might have to bear the expenses of the creditor and his servants until the debt was paid, presumably because they were losing time waiting for the payment, and so entitled to compensation. It must have been somewhat disheartening that this one attempt to allow for reasonable compensation which the Church permitted should have produced, not the cheap money desired, but the most heartless of all the usurious exactions of the Middle Ages.

V. INTERNAL REASONS FOR THE FAILURE OF THE CHURCH

In spite of the immense effort put forth by all the councils, it has to be admitted that the results were purely illusory. In view of the immense power of the Church, such a result is surprising, until the causes of it are analysed. They are manifold.

In the first place, throughout the conflict, the Church was a house divided against itself, not from one, but from several points of view. Up to the end of the period individual clergy indulged in usurious practices. Even in the great ecclesiastical corporations, where it should have been easier to eradicate the abuse, it was only suppressed in one form in order to appear in another. The reasons for this are discussed in the following chapter. Through the hands of the clergy and of the monasteries coin passed in a society which was permanently short of coin. In many forgotten cases, probably in the immense majority of cases, both lent freely and, in obedience to the laws of Scripture and of the Church, asked and received no profit from their loans. The lives of the medieval saints and bishops often refer to their charity to the poor and, if we have to recognise that clerical usurers were never eradicated, yet it would be foolish to assume that all parsons, monks and friars were possessed of such avarice that they deliberately courted excommunication,

More serious was the fact that so many of the upper clergy were also secular princes. Every cathedral and great abbey possessed some degree of territorial independence, and certain bishops and abbots were semi-independent rulers. As such they followed the traditions of their times, and granted charters to Jews, Lombards and Cahorsin similar to those issued by their secular neighbours. Had they refused to do so, they would have been involved in perpetual conflict with their citizens. But if many bishops and abbots were also princes, this applies even more to the Papacy itself. For the financial interests of a bishop were limited to his diocese. The financial interests of the Papacy were conterminous with Christendom. A papal merchant could defy the thunders of a local bishop, as we have already seen. The luxury and splendour of the Papal court, and the ambition for the aggrandisement of themselves and their families which possessed so many of the medieval Popes, caused them to be in continual need of money, and they who provided it could make their own terms. In 1311 Clement V took the great step of identifying usury with heresy, and submitting it to the Inquisition. But fifty years later Clement VI took a very different line. A pious Dauphin, in obedience to the canons, expelled the Lombards from Dauphiné. His Governor, himself an Archbishop of Lyons, wrote to the Pope to consult him as to whether this step was really necessary; and Clement VI replied that the Dauphin might well tolerate that which the Pope himself tolerated, and that it was a pity to expel either Jews or Lombards when it was possible to make a profit out of them[1]. In a dialogue between a cleric and a knight of the same period, the most that the cleric can say in defence of either Pope or King is to distinguish between toleration and approval[2].

Another reason for the failure was the very basis of the attack. The *absoluteness* of the prohibition corresponded so little to the needs of a developing society that it doomed itself to sterility. Even if all question of acquiring wealth be omitted, the lending of money took the time of the lender,

[1] A. Prudhomme, *Les Juifs en Dauphiné*; Bulletin de l'Académie Delphinale, IIe Série, tome xiiie. 1883, p. 154.

[2] *Songe du Vergier,* quoted in Simmonet, *Juifs et Lombards,* loc. cit. pp. 175 ff.

and payment had to be made for the deeds recording the transaction; expensive lawsuits might be necessary for its recovery; the debtor might move, and the creditor undergo considerable costs in finding him; a hundred causes involved the creditor in expense before any net profit from which he and his family might live could be obtained. Yet, if he reckoned any of these expenses in making up the total to be repaid, the Church declared him to be no better than a parricide or an adulterer.

But a more serious charge still can be laid against the Church for adopting so unpractical a standpoint. Within her ample bosom were to be found all the intellectuals of the time. Whether it be a treatise on agriculture or a dissertation on the doctrine of the Trinity, its author was almost certain to be a clerk; and within the Church alone could have been found the men who might have evolved a reasonable theory of usury. The only results of the *non possumus* which she opposed to the discussion of what was fair profit in moneylending were that she made the whole profession disreputable, attached a stigma to every kind of business loan, destroyed all attempts to put the profession on the rational basis on which it could have rendered immense services to the community, and, by adding to the normal risks of the profession excommunication, the disinheritance of his children and other penalties, justified the usurer in increasing his charges. Further, since the usurer was but human, he naturally retaliated on the society which ostracised and outlawed him by employing every device discoverable to outwit his enemies and ensnare his debtors. Hostility accentuated his avarice, and finally produced the finest example which history offers of the principle that it is better to be hanged for a sheep than a lamb.

VI. THE FAILURE OF SUBSTITUTES

The two most unhappy results of the slowness of the Churchmen to distinguish between a reasonable and an unreasonable return on the lending of money were that, while their influence on the great Italian and other companies was negligible, they often succeeded in preventing citizens from lending money to each other at moderate interest, and they destroyed their own efforts to provide a substitute for the professional usurer to minister to the needs of the poor.

The ordinary citizen was no more anxious to pay the enormous interest demanded by the Lombards and others than were the Churchmen to allow it to be paid. But as private or local lending lacked the influence and power of the great banks, it was not difficult for the local clergy to suppress it. An effort was made in Bavaria at the end of the twelfth century to establish a local loan bank with reasonable interest, but it was still-born. A more serious effort was made in the Franche Comté in 1363. The communities of Salins and Bracon opened a communal credit system, by which loans were made to fellow-citizens at the rate of seven per cent. on the security of all kinds of property existing within the communes, and so under their control. It struggled to exist for a few years, and then failed, although the communities had previously expelled the Jews and Lombards, and so attempted to give their own institution a monopoly[1].

In Switzerland, where the influence of canon law seems to have been less, and the battle over usury raged with less fury, there are many cases in the fourteenth and fifteenth centuries of citizens lending at interest varying from five to ten per cent.[2]; but they did it in defiance of the law, and only rarely succeeded in eliminating the Lombards or other foreign usurers.

As the Church did not approach the question from the angle of providing cheap money on a commercial basis, the only substitute which could be offered for the immense burden of professional usury and interest was the provision of free charitable loans. Where actual cash was not in question, the charitable activities of monasteries, parishes and gilds probably provided for the greater part of the popular wants of society, but sometimes actual coin was essential to the would-be borrower. Evidence of efforts being made to meet this necessity also is somewhat meagre. As early as 1251 the Bishops of Salisbury and of Bath and Wells obtained money from the burgesses of a number of

---

[1] Morey, *Les juifs en Franche-Comté*. REJ, VII, pp. 33 ff.
[2] Amiet., *loc. cit.*, pp. 204 and 260.

towns, which was to be used, under the supervision of trust-worthy persons, for lending to the poor without usury. This action they communicated to Pope Innocent IV, who ex-pressed his approval of the scheme, gave it his blessing, and authorised them to take all necessary action to prevent anyone from interfering with its operation[1]. In other places similar schemes are occasionally to be found. Money was sometimes left by will for this purpose and, naturally, much was done privately without any particular organisation. But such work was inevitably fragmentary, and could not assist more than a small proportion of those who from time to time needed a loan of money.

It is not until the fifteenth century that any systematic attempt was made to attack the problem. Then the Fran-ciscans, who were especially conscious of the troubles of the poor, began to organise in different Italian towns pawnshops, known as *montes pietatis*, where no interest was charged on the loan. Unfortunately, such an experiment was doomed to failure from the beginning, unless new charitable gifts could be constantly procured, not only to replace the losses due to bad debts, but also to cover the actual expenses of adminis-tration. Had such a system been evolved a couple of cen-turies earlier, then, since they were mostly practical men and not merely Utopian visionaries, the schoolmen might have come to some theory of reasonable usury. But, in fact, it was not until the sixteenth century, when the whole field of economic life was undergoing radical transformation, that Pope Leo X was finally prevailed upon to allow a small charge to be made to cover the administrative expenses of the loans.

VII. THE CONFLICT WITH THE ROMAN VIEW OF USURY

A final reason for the failure, both of the denunciations of the Church and of her tentative alternative systems, was the presence within Christian society of a different conception of money which possessed so respectable an authority that it was impossible entirely to ignore it.

[1] *Calendar of Papal Letters*, ed. W. H. Bliss, I, p. 267; cf. Tawney, *op. cit.*, p. 54 and notes.

Medieval civilisation did not grow out of nothing. The inheritance of the Roman Empire was still with it, and Roman law had approached the whole subject of money and gain from an entirely different standpoint. The lending of money for gain had been accepted as natural. It was considered a commercial and not a charitable activity, and the interest allowed was regulated according to the risks involved. Maritime business, which carried the greatest risks, was left to arrangement between the parties. Other loans carried a maximum interest of twelve per cent. during the first centuries of the empire, until Justinian forbade compound interest, limited maritime loans to an interest of twelve per cent., other commercial loans to eight per cent., and fixed the general level at six per cent.[1]

Not only did Roman society allow the lending of money for interest, but it also admitted gain as a legitimate motive for commerce. It was not interested in the morals of the question, or the eternal salvation of the merchant. It considered that in any business transaction it was natural that the parties should try to over-reach each other, and left it to the intelligence of each to look after his own interests[2]. Further, Roman law recognised an absolute right to the private possession of property, and to unlimited freedom of contract, two ideas which were not present in the custom of the Germanic societies which formed so large a proportion of the membership of Christendom.

While, therefore, the Church in the north of Europe could construct her doctrines, either on virgin soil or against a background in which some of her ideas of corporate responsibility were to be found, the Vatican, as an ancient Roman and primarily Italian power, and the Italian cities, were traditionally accustomed to quite other standards.

At the end of the eleventh century the importance of this dual tradition was emphasised by the renewed interest in Justinian which characterised the Italian universities, and this interest spread to France and England in the next hundred years. Scholars became so deeply engrossed in the study of Roman law that they tended to neglect canon law altogether; and the natural result was that the doctors were

[1] Scherer, pp. 186 ff.
[2] Ashley, *op. cit.*, I, pp. 131 ff.

continually to be found defending the usurer. Hence the continual threats in the canons against those lawyers who dared to say that usury was lawful, and who undertook the defence of those who practised it. Churchmen could, indeed, refer to ' the Philosopher ' as a voice in their favour from the ancient world, for Aristotle had said, or was believed to have said, that money was barren; but the final authority of the lawyer was not Aristotle but Justinian, and Justinian had said the opposite.

Where the Church was right, and the lawyer wrong, was that the Roman conception of the matter had been linked to an entirely different society. If unlimited right of contract was a part of Roman society and justified therein by the general state of commercial life and the safeguards against abuse existing in other sections of the Roman code, northern medieval society offered a completely different picture. In the commercial cities of Italy interest rose from the Roman level to twelve and fifteen per cent., because security was certainly less than it had been in Roman days. But it did not rise higher, because the borrower both knew his business and had a choice of methods of raising cash before him. It was useless for one man to demand fifty per cent. when fifteen could be obtained next door. The general state of society provided a natural check on avarice. But in the north, where money was scarce, the usurer often a local monopolist and the potential debtors less experienced, the Roman system opened the door to appalling abuses.

The story of the conflict of the two positions is the usual story of a moral idea foolishly presented struggling with a practical point of view foolishly abused. Naturally, neither side won. No Church can secure perfection both of action and of motive by coërcion; and no group can ruthlessly exploit another without ultimately ' somebody doing something about it '. In this particular case, the position of the opponents ensured in advance that neither side could win; for the Churchmen were not visionaries of the cloister, but responsible administrators in society as it was, and the merchants were not economic machines, but believing Christians, whose settlements throughout Europe prided themselves on the wealth of their religious foundations and the extent of their works of piety.

In so far as the question of principle was concerned, the merchants won that particular battle. With the Reformation and the wealth of the new capitalism, many of the medieval restrictions on trade and finance came to be considered the fantasies of a forgotten world. In the present age scholars have come to realise that there was much common sense and understanding of the needs of the weaker sections of society behind the Churchmen's position; and men of business themselves have begun to doubt whether unrestricted competition and the right to exploit whatever can be exploited is really the wisest form of business. In so far as practice was concerned, the battle was more evenly divided. The Church modified her doctrines of fair business considerably between the twelfth century and the fifteenth; but during that period she also convinced a number of secular princes, lawyers and scholars that moneylending as practised by medieval merchants was more a scourge than a blessing.

VIII. THE CONFLICT AND THE JEWISH USURER

It will have been evident in all the previous discussion of usury that the Church in fact, if not in theory, was concerned with the practice of that profession among her own flock, and even her own officials. The penalties which she continually decreed would have only affected those who accepted her scheme of salvation. To this there is one exception. Excommunication was pronounced on various occasions against Jewish communities, and was capable of producing considerable effects upon them, since it involved the breaking of every contact with the Christian population[1]. But it is not possible to separate this punishment, which could affect the Jews, from those which could not, and the fact that it was Christians and not Jews that she had in mind remains unvitiated by this exception.

For this fact two reasons are possible. It might have been that the Church saw no objection to the practice of usury by Jews, and therefore abstained from attacking it. Or, alternatively, it could be argued that her hands were so full with the greater evil, since her first responsibility lay towards her

[1] See above, pp. 131 ff.

own members, that she perforce postponed attacking the Jews until the day when she had set her own house in order, a day which never came.

There is a certain amount to be said for both views. It is probable that in the centuries preceding the commercial development of Europe, she had not thought of any discrimination. In those centuries, in fact, it was mostly her own servants who were responsible[1], and her clients corresponded most closely to those to protect whom the original Mosaic prohibitions had been devised. But the real struggle began in the twelfth century, and by that time the chief usurers were the merchants, Jews and Christians alike. Jews are first referred to by the Church as the creditors of Crusaders, and usury due to them by the latter was cancelled —or, to be more accurate, the Church desired that it should be cancelled[2]. While this may be taken as toleration of usury exacted from those who were not Crusaders, it would be straining the argument of silence too far to claim that such was consciously sanctioned. Moreover, the passage already quoted of Raymond of Pennafort clearly indicates that it was avarice itself, and not the particular group which committed that sin, which the Church attacked[3].

In the following centuries the conditions must be taken to be the same, except where positive proofs exist to the contrary. The general attitude to the Jews implies disapproval of anything which puts Christians in their power, and this indebtedness certainly did. It was particularly important that churches and religious institutions should be free from such domination, and canons to this effect abound, but no point of principle differentiates clerics and laymen on such a matter. It was only a question of greater urgency. Further, the Church on various occasions urged or secured measures by which the Jews should be turned from moneylending to agriculture and trade. All these arguments justify the general conclusion that the Church did not in principle make any exception to her rules in favour of the Jews.

On the other side can be produced certain evidence from Germany, showing that, at a certain period at any rate, there

[1] See below, p. 308.
[2] E.g. Paris (1188); Lateran IV, 1215; Mansi, XXII, cc. 578 and 1003.
[3] See above, p. 278.

was a tendency to justify an exception. The grounds of this exception were the impossibility of the Jews earning a living in any other way, or the necessity of money being available for loan, and the prohibition of Christians lending it for profit. Thus a diet at Mainz in 1255 bluffly takes the second view[1]. The fuller edition of the *Sachsenspiegel* (ca. 1225) takes the first, prefacing its remarks quaintly with the phrase that ' by the Law of God no Jew shall take usury; but their station in life has ordained it otherwise '[2]. The Emperor Frederick II, in his Constitutions of the Kingdom of Sicily, boldly stated that usury was not forbidden to the Jews by the divine law, and therefore permitted it[3], but Frederick II cannot be quoted as an authority on canonical principles. A synod at Breslau in 1266 referred to ' burdensome and immoderate usury ', and excommunicated Jews who demand such, until they have made restitution; and possibly implied thereby that a profit might be made which could not be so described, and which Jews might therefore legitimately acquire[4].

From such actions it might be assumed that the Church sanctioned Jewish usury, provided the interest was not ' burdensome and immoderate '. Undoubtedly, in practice those who authorised usury, whether secular or ecclesiastical princes, attempted to limit its evil by various measures tending to prevent it from becoming ' burdensome '; but it would be difficult to produce evidence that any distinction in principle existed between light and heavy usury. The development of scholastic thought in the matter of profit, and of ' interest ', did not affect their intransigence on ' usury ', and the basis of Jewish moneylending was ' usury ', that is a charge for the loan, beginning from the day on which the loan was made, calculated in the bond usually as a fixed sum due on the day appointed for repayment, and, if the debt were not then repaid, continuing to grow at the same rate. The distinction, therefore, was one which might be observed in the realm of statecraft, but it had no validity in that of theology, and this must be taken as the norm of the medieval

[1] MGH, LL, II, p. 372.
[2] Neumann, *Geschichte des Wuchers in Deutschland*, p. 305.
[3] *Ibid.*, p. 307.
[4] Aronius, No. 724.

X

situation. Whatever may be charged against the Church for her treatment of the Jews during these centuries, it cannot be said that she officially sanctioned permission being given to the Jews to commit what she believed to be a mortal sin. by whoever it was committed.

CHAPTER NINE

THE MERCHANT AND THE USURER

I. THE BEGINNINGS OF EUROPEAN MONEY-LENDING

It has been necessary to give in some details the struggle of the Church against the sin of usury, because it is so often assumed that the Church contented herself with a simple prohibition which was generally successful, and that, in consequence, all or almost all medieval usurers were Jews. Instead of this simple and successful assertion the records of the councils reveal a long and arduous struggle, a stern chase in the wake of the wily moneylender, whose continual evasions demanded an ever-watchful attitude on the part of those who would enforce their canonical regulations.

And in the end the Church failed of her object; failed, for four reasons. She failed because it is impossible to achieve a standard of perfection by methods of coërcion, and she demanded, not moderation in the profit to be made out of the lending of money, but that no profit should be made out of it whatever. Secondly, she failed because her own practice as a wealthy corporation in no way accorded with what she tried to enforce upon Christian laymen. Thirdly, she failed because men at times are forced to borrow, and she offered no adequate alternative to the moneylender. Finally, she failed because throughout the period there existed a different and quite respectable tradition by which interest was lawful, the tradition of the Roman empire, embodied in the practice of the Italian cities and confirmed by the study of Justinian in the law schools of Europe.

The measure of her failure can be gauged from the fact that throughout the period the chief moneylenders were Christian, and that, apart from short periods and particular localities, the Jew never played more than a specialised and subordinate part. He lacked both the wealth and the permanence to take the whole responsibility himself, even had he wished to. Nor did he compensate for these lacks by any temperamental or inherited aptitude for the profession. In the Roman empire he had been little concerned with finance; in medieval Europe he took his part among the lenders of money hesitatingly and empirically, and for the same reasons as his Christian rivals.

For the determining factor was not aptitude, but opportunity. It has been said already that the central difference between the medieval and modern situations is that in these days actual coin is the easiest thing to lend, whereas in the creative centuries of European moneylending, the tenth to the twelfth, coin was a rare commodity, only to be found in a few groups within the community. When, therefore, the rest of society needed it, they had to go to these groups to get it; and, in the measure of their opportunities, each of four classes lent the money which they possessed or which passed through their hands. The four groups were: the monasteries, the secular clergy, the merchants, and the tax collectors.

The earliest lenders of money seem to have been the monasteries. From rents and tolls, from the offerings of the faithful at their shrines, and from the sale of the produce of their lands, they received a considerable revenue in money. Apart from the upkeep of the monastery itself, a good deal of this was spent on the services which it performed to the countryside, in feeding and tending travellers, in caring for the sick and in similar purposes. But the monks were also keenly interested in extending their property, and in such matters they looked for profitable investments for their surplus in the same way as any other proprietor. The main investment of the period was land, and it became their ambition to acquire more and still more land. The fact that they had money which could be lent opened many doors to its acquisition.

There was only one method by which they could lend their money in a way which was not called usury, and there is very little evidence of its being practised. By this method, a man borrowed a sum of money, leaving his land as security with his creditor. The creditor farmed the land until he had recovered from the crops a sum equivalent to that which he had lent, and then returned it. This was called *vif gage*, for the security itself created its own redemption. From the standpoint of canon law this was a proper way for a religious corporation to use its spare money. But it did not appeal to the monasteries, and in practice one of two things happened. Either the loan was nominally made at *vif gage*, but the creditor, with or without the consent of the debtor, continued the enjoyment of the estate until he had made a nice additional sum as profit, or he only agreed to lend on *mort gage*. By this latter system, the borrower had to repay in coin the sum lent, without usury, but the creditor retained the property until he did so. The pledge itself remained ' dead ' and contributed nothing to its redemption, for all the profit on its use was retained by the creditor.

Alexander III, the Pope who summoned the Lateran Council of 1179 which first attacked the problem of usury, set his face against these two evasions[1], and appears to have had sufficient success in suppressing the mortgage system and the evasions of *vif gage* for the monasteries to look to other methods of investing their revenues. Doubtless one reason for his success was the fact that mortgages themselves possessed certain disadvantages from the standpoint of a monastic treasurer. In a large number of cases, enjoyment of the land became permanent, because the original owner, having borrowed for some unconstructive purpose, was never in a position to redeem it; but if the loan were repaid, the treasurer had to start again to look for another investment. The new ways which were evolved had the advantage of permanence, and, in consequence, the monasteries ceased to enter into consideration with a borrower who did not wish permanently to alienate his property.

It is extremely difficult to estimate the extent of the practice of usury among the secular clergy. The sums which they lent would have been small, and on short term loans. In most cases there was probably no record in writing of the loan at all. Even if there were, the archives of an individual are not as likely to survive as those of a permanent institution. But the continual insistence of the earlier canons, and the scattered references in the later canons which dealt primarily with the professional usurer, are adequate evidence that clerical usurers were to be found in every country. Other

[1] *Decretal. Gregor. IX*, V, xix, *De usuris*, cc. i, ii, and viii. Cf. above, p. 170.

references show that the 'clerici' referred to were not merely government clerks or persons only nominally in orders[1], but the actual holders of benefices, living in their cures. In fact, as the parochial system developed, and the countryside came to be covered with churches in the charge of resident priests, such men were the most accessible sources of supply for thousands of humble borrowers.

It was the development of commercial life throughout north-western Europe in the twelfth century which brought the third class of lender into prominence. The spread of commerce, and the consequent growth of towns, enormously increased the radius of activity of the merchant. Whereas in the tenth century merchant settlements were rare and small in northern Europe, in the twelfth they were to be found everywhere. A travelling merchant was little use as a lender. He was not likely to travel with large supplies of spare coin, and, in any case, a piece of land in a district through which he happened to be passing offered him an entirely valueless exchange for his loan. Nor, on the other hand, even if he was able to obtain an object of value as security, would he desire to transport about with him such objects. It was only as centres of settlement increased that the money in the possession of the merchant came to be a potential source of relief to the immense majority of needy clients.

The merchant of the early period is, therefore, only to be considered as a valuable source of credit for very small and restricted areas dotted throughout the country. The special significance of this fact is that it is only on the very threshold of the Middle Ages that it is possible to speak of anything approaching a Jewish monopoly of certain trades. And in so far as it existed, this monopoly covered only a few branches, and those branches involving long journeys. In this way Jews travelled all across Europe, but a completed voyage must have lasted a period of years. The terms of medieval moneylending, however, were almost always short, so that, apart from the considerations already advanced, it can be safely assumed that the Jewish merchant only served as lender in the district in which he actually lived, and at this

---

[1] Cf. E. E. Power, *Peasant Life and Rural Conditions*, in *Cambridge Medieval History*, VII, pp. 742 and 744, and the Ordinance of Philip II of ca. 1183 in Laurière, XI, p. 231.

period Jews were not to be found as settled residents in more than a few dozen cities north of the Alps and the Loire. Elsewhere he appeared only as a traveller.

The fourth class which had access to money was that of tax collectors. Tolls and duties of one kind and another formed a large proportion of the income of a medieval baron, and the collectors of these tolls and duties mostly paid for the privilege of collecting them, and expected to make a profit out of the occupation. Here, as with the clergy, it is difficult to produce actual evidence that they lent money at an early period, but since we know that they did so later[1], when, in fact, there were alternative possibilities for raising a loan, there seems no reason to believe that they should not have done so earlier also, when they must have had the monopoly of fluid cash in many scattered settlements.

For the earliest period, then, it is safe to say that the main sources from which a man in need of money could obtain relief were the monasteries, and to a lesser extent the clergy and the collectors of tolls and taxes. The merchants, who with the development of commerce and security came to be the wealthiest class of the community, were of little use until the twelfth century because they were known to the immense majority of the population merely as travellers, and land, the normal security which the potential debtor could offer, was of little use to them.

II. THE RISE OF A MERCHANT CLASS

Though the significance of the merchant as moneylender only dates from the twelfth century, it is necessary to trace his rise in the earlier period in order to set the financial activities of Jewish merchants in their proper perspective.

In the few market centres of northern Europe which existed in the Carolingian epoch would have been found four possible types of merchant. Of these the wealthiest and best organised, though also the rarest in their appearance in any but the largest centres, were the merchants of Byzantium. There was no other city in the European world which could compete with Byzantium in either wealth or organisation,

[1] Philip VI of France forbids the practice in 1331. Laurière, II, p. 67,

and though the links which bound her merchants to north-western Europe were tenuous, they were never wholly broken. Next in importance would have been the Jewish group, and they would have been both more regular and more ubiquitous in their activities than the Byzantines. The centres in which they were resident to the north of the Alps and the Loire were still few, but they were beginning to settle as residents in the basins of the Seine and the Rhine. Of almost equal importance to the Jews must, even in the ninth century, be reckoned the merchants of the Italian cities. Ravenna, Venice, Amalfi, Florence, Lucca, Rome and other cities as well were already commercial and industrial centres, small though they might be compared with that which they subsequently became. The last class was more heterogeneous but the most numerous of all. To a large extent it consisted of persons who, while classed as *mercatores* or *negociatores* in charters, were not wholly so occupied. Within this class the most important group were the agents of the monasteries coming to dispose of the surplus of their properties and the products of their artisans. Their range would have been only local, their visits mostly confined to the fairs and markets nearest their houses, but in those fairs much of the buying and selling of the routine necessities of life must have been in their hands, and in the hands of others of this class. These others were also but temporary merchants, coming to sell the wares of the fields, the looms or the workshops of the surrounding villages. It would be a fair division of the field to state that the first three classes of merchants, the Byzantines, Jews and Italians, dealt primarily in articles of luxury, produced abroad, and that the last class dealt with the larger though cheaper section of the market, food, wine, ordinary cloth, leather goods and such-like. To this division one reservation must be made. Local famine frequently necessitated the importation of corn from other regions, and there was always a certain long-distance trade in wine and in articles of food which grew in one region rather than another. This inter-regional trade was largely carried on by Jews.

The Jew was thus the only regular and, so to say, professional merchant who competed with the local and part-time merchant; but in this period he had an advantage also in relation to the others of his own class. Up to the sixth century the greater part of the commerce of France had entered by Marseilles and the valley of the Rhone. The commercial routes of the country spread out as ribs of a fan from the Mediterranean littoral. The depredations of the Vandal fleet in the fifth century and, still more, the Moslem conquest of the south, east, and much of the west shores of the Mediterranean in the seventh and eighth caused the southern French ports to be practically closed to Christian commerce. Genoa and Pisa were still leading a struggle against Moslem pirates in the eleventh century, and the Crusades themselves owe much of their appeal to the desire to recover the security of the Mediterranean trade. But in the days before the Italian maritime cities gained sufficient strength to defend themselves against these pirates, the Jews, who were more friendly with the Moslems, enjoyed a considerable immunity, and much of the sea-carrying trade from Asia to Europe passed into their hands. Thus in the Carolingian period the Jew enjoyed two great advantages over other merchants. If we look at the picture again a couple of centuries later, we find that he has lost or is losing them both.

In the first place, the Northmen, who had spread terror along all the littoral of northern Europe and even in the Mediterranean, discovered in the tenth century the great advantages, first of combining trade with piracy, and later of substituting the former for the latter. In the year 1000 it is said that the town of York was full of traders of all nations, but especially of Danes. The Norman kingdom of Sicily was, next to the Angevin, the most highly-developed trading monarchy in Europe. But even before this they had secured the monopoly of the profitable trades with Russia and the Baltic and, penetrating to the Black Sea, had provided an alternative route for the passage of the merchandise of Asia into northern Europe. During this same period Venice, Genoa and Pisa, but especially the first of these, deprived the Jewish merchants of their preponderating influence in the Mediterranean trade, for by the tenth century Venetian merchants were trading slaves in Egypt, and visiting with their wares all the ports of the eastern Mediterranean.

At the same time as they were losing their long-distance

carrying trade between Asia and Europe, the Jews also lost their importance in the large-scale trading in local centres. The part-time merchants without capital of the ninth century gradually formed themselves into ' gilds ' and ' hanses ', developed their capital, stabilised their conditions, and founded a cluster of commercial cities along the navigable rivers falling into the North Sea and the Channel. Industry developed with commercial possibilities, and many goods which Jews and others had been accustomed to bring from afar came to be produced and traded by Flemish, German and northern French merchants. By the time of the first Crusade the significance of the Jewish merchant was inevitably diminishing. It is not that in actual volume Jewish trading interests became less, but that the total volume of trade was greatly increasing, and that the new trading interests were not Jewish.

This development had an important effect on the situation of the Jews from another point also. Two further advantages, which the Jews had possessed in the eighth and ninth centuries, they now had to share with others. In the earlier period they alone had been able to pass from country to country, finding all along their routes communities of their own people. They could arrange credits at a distance, receive information of far-away conditions, and find everywhere interpreters through the common medium of Hebrew. They also possessed their own judicial autonomy and extensive privileges specially designed to assist their commercial activities. The rise of the maritime cities of Italy, and later of the northern Hanse, gave others the advantages for distant trade that the Jews alone had formerly possessed. Italian and other Christian merchants had agents throughout Europe. Wherever they settled they formed their own communities, linked with their mother towns, and, in the independence of the latter, they possessed an advantage which the Jews lacked.

The merchants of the north were slower to obtain these advantages enjoyed by their Italian rivals, but in another field they also secured conditions which set them on a footing more than equal to that of the Jews. The settlements of the merchants had mostly grown up under the protection of the walls of the old princely, monastic or episcopal ' cities ' of

Carolingian times. These were little more than fortresses, and had no special communal life, and the merchants looked to them only for protection. In origin these merchants must have been largely of the class of serfs, but, having come from the unknown, they were presumed to be free. Personal freedom was, however, not enough to supply their needs, and the judicial conditions within the fortress walls were of no value to them at all. In their joint travels—for they mostly travelled in companies like the eastern caravans of to-day—they had built up a system of commercial practice which became the ' Law Merchant ' of later times. As the importance of their settlements increased, they demanded written charters of privileges allowing them to apply similar laws in their settlements. Since their presence brought wealth to the owners of the burgs around which they lived, they secured these without great difficulty. Once possessed of them, they enjoyed at least the same privileges as their Jewish rivals, and often much greater ones.

III. THE EMERGENCE OF INTERNATIONAL CHRISTIAN MERCHANTS

If the eleventh century saw the disappearance of the few special advantages the Jewish merchants had enjoyed, the twelfth and thirteenth saw the beginning of their disadvantages *vis-à-vis* their Christian rivals. This does not mean that any simultaneous change in their position took place throughout Europe. The change was a very gradual one, similar events producing similar results centuries apart. Thus the ability of the Venetians to develop their trade without the assistance of the Jews appears already in an order of the year 945 by which Venetian ship captains were not allowed to carry Jewish merchants as passengers[1]. In Poland, on the other hand, Jewish merchants were being given every encouragement to develop their trade in the charters of Casimir the Great of the middle of the fourteenth century. But while in Italy the change comes in the tenth century, and in Poland hundreds of years later, the setting of the critical period in the twelfth possesses a general

[1] W. Roscher, *System der Volkswirthschaft*, II, p. 335.

validity, for this is the moment of the rise of medieval commerce and industry in western Europe.

It is not necessary for the purpose of the present study to relate in any detail the appearance of a class of Christian merchants possessing characteristics similar to those which in the earlier period had marked out the Jews. There was no unique centre from which this class sprang, for while the most numerous certainly came from northern Italy, and passed under the general title in northern Europe of ' Lombards ', a second group which was almost as important went by the name of ' Cahorsin ', ' Cawerschen ' or variants of these two forms. Who these merchants were is still a debated question. For while it would appear that these two titles linked them definitely with Cahors, the capital of Quercy in south-west France, yet there seems no adequate reason why from this relatively small and unimportant town merchants should have spread all over Europe. Others therefore seek an Italian origin for the name, and derive it from either a place or a family of northern Italy. In any case, it became simply a synonym for a foreign usurer and at times the same group are called alternatively Lombards and Cahorsin[1].

These two groups are those most commonly met with, but there are others of lesser importance. Matthew Paris refers to the merchants of Sens as possessing a widespread and evil reputation[2], and the Flemish cities also sent out their merchants far and wide[3]. Finally, there was the powerful and wealthy group of German merchants with whom the name of Hanse—common, in fact, to many merchant groups of northern Europe[4]—came to be especially associated.

All these groups developed a network of trading connections throughout Europe in the course of the twelfth and the first half of the thirteenth centuries. Matthew Paris refers to the presence of the Cahorsin in England in 1235[5]. The Lombards were already ripe for expulsion in France in 1268, and Philip III in 1274[6] hastened the going of those who had

---

[1] E.g. Amiet, *loc. cit.*, I, p. 233.

[2] *Chron. maj.*, ed. Rolls Series, IV, p. 8.

[3] Matthew Paris gives them the same reputation as those of Sens. *Ibid.*, p. 16.

[4] E.g. the merchants of Paris and Burgundy are referred to as *Hanses* in charters of 1203 and 1220. Laurière, XI, pp. 290 and 309.

[5] *Chron. maj.*, ed. Rolls Series, III, p. 328.

[6] Laurière, I, pp. 96 and 298,

escaped the order of Louis IX. In Germany, where the
earliest reference to Lombard traders actually dates from the
tenth century, they were settled in many towns by the
beginning of the thirteenth[1]. In Burgundy and the Swiss
cities references to Lombard settlers begin about the same
time. The great meeting place of these merchants was
Champagne, where a series of fairs had been established in
the middle of the twelfth century. There were in all six
such fairs in the year, each lasting six weeks. Merchants met
there from all over Europe; commercial transactions and
private debts were settled; payments were made from northern to southern European lenders and borrowers, and it is
in connection with these transactions that one of the earliest
attempts at separating private and commercial loans was
made by Philip the Fair who, in 1311, distinguished loans
made at the fairs from all other loans, and allowed the rate
of two and a half per cent. to be charged from one fair to
another, while elsewhere only one penny per week per £
was allowed[2]. This represented an interest of five twelfths
per cent. per week, against two and a half per cent. for a
period varying from two weeks up to eight.

Of the activities of these merchants during the twelfth
century we have little detailed information[3]. It is the period
in which the foundations of their prosperity in northern
Europe were laid, and in which they spread not only to the
great commercial centres, but also, like the Jews in the same
epoch, to many smaller cities and even villages. During this
century also their activities developed at, perhaps, a slightly
slower speed, along the lines followed simultaneously in
Jewish business. The persecutions accompanying the
Crusades, and some of the conditions of Jewish settlement,
turned the mind of the Jewish merchants of the twelfth
century already to finance. Evidence of Italian usurers at

---

[1] Amiet, *loc. cit.*, I, p. 210.

[2] Laurière, I, pp. 484 and 494 ff.

[3] Many documents of one particular firm of Christian usurers of the
middle of the twelfth century have survived. The leader of the firm
was one William Cade, whose activities were such that he left the sum of
£5,000—enormous for those days—in outstanding loans. See M. T.
Stead and H. Jenkinson, in *English Historical Review*, XXVIII, pp. 209 ff.,
and *A moneylender's bonds of the twelfth century*, by the latter, in *Essays
in History, Reginald Lane Poole Tribute Volume*, pp. 190 ff.

this period is common. Elsewhere it is still rare[1], but in the first half of the thirteenth century financial activities at the side of commercial are universal, and by the second half, Lombards and Cahorsin had come to be regarded exclusively as usurers whose terms of business were harder and whose conduct was more unscrupulous than that of the Jews. When the Lombards were expelled from France in 1268[2], it was exclusively as usurers that they were expelled, and it was as usurers solely that Matthew Paris regarded the Cahorsin thirty years earlier in England[3]. In the thirteenth century, in both countries, serious efforts were made to suppress their usurious activities. Even Henry III of England, in spite of his continual shortage of money, decided to expel the usurers of Sens, and only gave up the idea when offered a bribe sufficient to convince him of their value[4]. The efforts of Louis IX and Philip III in France were followed by further efforts of Philip IV, who after having extracted what he could from the Lombards, first attempted to suppress their dishonesty, and then, having failed in this, expelled them in 1311[5]. The period of expulsion cannot have lasted very long for, though we do not know the date of their return, they had so impoverished France less than twenty years later that in 1330 Philip VI had them all arrested, cancelled all the interest on debts due to them, and confiscated the capital for the benefit of the Treasury[6].

Experiences of this kind, which were not peculiar to France, may have decided the Lombards to seek regular charters similar to those issued to the Jews, and authorising them to practise usury. The earliest charter of this kind was issued to the Lombards of Cologne in 1332, for a period of eleven years[7]. Similar charters were issued in Bingen (1363) and Oberwesel (1376)[8]. Between 1378 and the end of the

[1] The beginning of the Church's intensive campaign against usury is the Lateran Council of 1179.

[2] Cf. Laurière, I, p. 96.

[3] Chron. maj., ed. Rolls Series, III, pp. 328 ff.

[4] Ibid., V, pp. 245 ff.

[5] Laurière, I, pp. 484 and 489. Cf. also 490, where they are given permission to appeal.

[6] Ibid., II, pp. 59 ff. Cf. XII, p. 35.

[7] Amiet, loc. cit., I, pp. 212 and 221 ff.

[8] Ibid., I, p. 218.

century a number were issued to settlers in various towns of France. To the same period belong charters regulating their activities in various Swiss towns; for example, Solothurn (1377) and Biel (1397). The similarity in both dates and features of these charters suggest that they were part of a common Lombard policy at the time, and this is confirmed by the fact that it is sometimes expressly mentioned that their terms were suggested by the Lombards themselves. They also closely resemble the contemporary charters given to the Jews, though there are differences, mostly in favour of the Lombards. A comparison of the conditions under which the Jews returned to France in 1361, with privileges issued to the Lombards to settle in various French towns during the following decades will make this clear. The privileges in question refer to the commercial centres of the north, Amiens, Abbeville, Meaux, Troyes and Paris[1].

The first great distinction is that the Lombards were free to leave the country either by selling their rights to others or as soon as the term of the privilege had expired; but after they had announced their intention to depart, they might still remain for two years without paying taxes, in order to settle up their affairs, provided that during this period they did not make fresh loans[2]. If, in his campaign against usury, the Pope or any other person urged the king to expel them, and the king felt bound to do so, he promised to give them suitable warning[3]. In various forms they were allowed to sell their privileges to other Christians if they wished to do so; and, on the other hand, they might receive from the Treasurer further privileges, and these would be deemed of equal validity with those given by the king[4]. All these were privileges not enjoyed by the Jews. On the other hand, both parties had to give public notice of departure, in order that their pledges might be redeemed[5].

In the definition of their legal situation there were few

---

[1] All the documents are to be found in Laurière—settlement in Abbeville, Amiens and Meaux (1378), VI, p. 335; Troyes (1380), *ibid.*, p. 477; Paris (1382), *ibid.*, p. 652; Troyes, etc. (1392), VII, p. 787. The documents are quoted by their dates.

[2] 1378, clause xxiv; 1380, clause xxvii; 1392, clause xxvi.

[3] 1380, c. xxvi; 1382, c. xxi; 1392, c. xxv.

[4] 1378, c. xxii; 1380, c. xxi; 1382, c. xxvi; 1392, c. xiv.

[5] 1361, c. xv; 1378, c. xiv, etc.

differences, but such as there were favoured the Lombards. Both possessed the right of inheritance[1]; both were immune from arrest for crimes committed before the issue of their charters[2]; both were subject only to the royal courts, except by their own consent, and the justices could only proceed against them on complaint being made and properly supported[3]. Once a case against them was opened, they were given extraordinary advantages over the prosecution, since, if the Lombard could give a clear defence, the case was dismissed without the prosecution being heard. In financial cases the Jews were similarly believed on their oath, and contrary statements were inadmissible[4]. Both were exempt from duels[5]. On the other hand, the Lombards possessed an important privilege, in practice nearly always withheld from Jews, that only the accused person could be held responsible for his crime, and his community could not be involved in it[6].

In their civic obligations, they enjoyed similar rights: exemption from military requisitioning[7] and from war and defence service. Here the Jews actually enjoyed a privilege denied the Lombards; neither performed military service, but the Lombards had to pay special war taxes if such were imposed, whereas the whole financial effort of the Jews was devoted to paying the ransom of John II[8]. Both, if they lived in baronial territories, paid no more than the rent of their houses to the baron concerned[9]. But in their relations to the royal finances, the Lombards possessed a fundamental advantage over the Jews. Both were exempted from tolls[10];

[1] It is a presumption that the Jews possessed this right in 1361, since they enjoyed it in the charter of 1317, c. v, and received in 1361, c. xxviii, the general right to all liberties previously enjoyed if not in conflict with the actual text of the charter of 1361. For Lombards, see 1378, c. xxi, etc.

[2] 1361, c. vii; 1382, c. xvii.

[3] 1361, cc. ii, xviii-xx (the special royal court of the Guardian of the Jews); 1378, cc. vii, xi, xii, etc.

[4] 1361, c. xi (this was modified in 1372, in cases where the prosecution could produce proof); 1378, c. xii, etc.

[5] 1361, c. xxii; 1380, c. xxii, etc.

[6] 1378, c. xvi, etc.

[7] 1361, c. xxi; 1378, c. xxiii, etc.

[8] 1361, c. xvi; 1378, c. xvii, etc.

[9] 1361, c. iv; 1378, c. viii, etc.

[10] 1361, c. xvii; 1378, c. xviii, etc.

but the Lombards were also explicitly exempted from all special exactions of the privy purse, and the king explicitly denied himself the right to ask them for presents for himself or for anyone else[1].

When we turn to the specific object of their settlements, the trade in money, two rights enjoyed by the Lombards still further emphasised their advantage over the Jews. They were allowed to change money[2], and in northern Europe, from the twelfth century onwards, this right had been almost universally denied to the Jews. The immense confusion of medieval currency made the changing of money a highly skilled profession, and one which was indispensable in every centre where merchants congregated. And the exercise of the profession allowed large opportunities for profit, for there were many different currencies existing at the same place and at the same time, often with no fixed relation between them. Thus when Philip VI issued an edict on the coinage in 1332—an almost annual event in fourteenth century France—he fixed the rates of the florin and Parisian sou in one series, and the money of Tournai in another, but he gave no indication at all of the relationship between the two sets of currency[3]. Secondly, in the actual towns for which their charters were given them, the Lombards were given a monopoly of all moneylending, and as these towns were among the most important commercial centres of France, this excluded the Jews from most profitable fields of activity[4]. The Jews possessed no such monopoly either against other members of their own community, or against Italian or other Christian rivals.

In the actual conduct of moneylending the privileges granted to the Jews were so extensive that it is difficult to imagine the Lombards discovering ways of extending them. In fact, they were not allowed to charge so high a rate as the Jews, for the latter could demand fourpence in the £, while the former could only ask between twopence and twopence-farthing[5]. This seems to have galled the Lombards, for when

---

[1] 1378, c. xix; 1380, c. xxiii, etc.

[2] 1378, c. iv, etc.

[3] Laurière, II, p. 84.

[4] 1378, c. xx, etc.

[5] 1361, c. viii; 1378, cc. ii, iii, etc.

Y

the privilege of 1380 granted to those of Troyes was renewed in 1392, they secured the insertion of the toothsome morsel that they might include in the terms of their loans any conditions whatsoever to which they could obtain the consent of their unhappy debtors[1]. It is curious that history records no violent protests among the churchmen and inquisitors of Champagne at this epoch. No Jew in all the Middle Ages— legally, at least—entered into such a paradise of unlimited possibility. In the handling of pledges, there was little difference between them, except that the Lombards were protected in the somewhat hypothetical case of a servant bringing a pledge to obtain a loan for his master, and being subsequently dismissed. In such cases the master could not disclaim liability on the ground that the servant had stolen the object[2].

One last privilege enjoyed by the Lombards only reflects credit on the Jews by its omission, for the Lombards demanded and obtained legal protection from accusations of rape made against them by their own private, or by public, prostitutes[3].

Finally, the Lombards possessed a general clause that obscurities in the charter were to be interpreted in their favour, which corresponds roughly to the privilege of the Jews that any advantage they could show that they had ever possessed which was not inconsistent with the charter of 1361, they might claim to enjoy[4]. But the Lombards of Troyes again had the last word for, after obtaining all their specific privileges, they also secured the general encouragement that they might carry on their business in whatever way might seem to them to offer the greatest profit[5].

The German and Swiss charters also offer many points of interest, but it is, unfortunately, not possible to compare them so exactly with contemporary charters granted by the same authorities to Jews. Certain parallels, however, can be discovered between them and the Frederician family of Jewish charters. The charters of Solothurn and Biel, for

[1] 1392, c. iii.
[2] 1378, c. x, etc.
[3] 1380, c. xxv; 1382, c. xx.
[4] 1361, c. xxviii; 1378, c. xxv, etc.
[5] 1392, c. ii.

example, granted the same protection against the disappearance of pledges in a fire as was given by Duke Frederick to the Jews of Austria. There are also parallels between these charters and the French charters to Lombards, on such questions as the immunity of the community from responsibility for offences of individuals, the acceptance of their word unless it could be disproved by three witnesses, and protection from prostitutes. All these occur in the German group; in the Swiss group there are similar parallels. They enjoyed the same consideration if they left the town on the expiration of their privilege. They were promised protection against the Pope or any one else—here the Swiss towns were bolder than the French kings, who admitted that they might be unable to give such protection, and promised only to give them notice if they were compelled to expel them—and they were guaranteed against molestation if there happened to be a war or a quarrel between the town in which they lived and the Lombards of Lombardy.

These parallels are enough to show that those who drew up the different privileges were well acquainted with the most favourable conditions elsewhere, and certain of them also suggest a direct relationship between the German and the slightly later Swiss group. In particular, both give the unusual period of a year and six weeks, instead of a year and a day, as the time after which pledges may be sold. As to the other clauses, those which are necessary in order to carry on the trade at all may be ignored, but there are a number of points in both groups which indicate that the Lombards in Germany obtained a more favourable position than that commonly enjoyed by the Jews. The Lombards were granted the following special privileges: masters might sue their servants, giving no proof other than their own statements; when they sold their pledges after a year and six weeks, they might pocket the difference between the price realised and the sum owed; claims made by the Lombards on the property of debtors were to be given priority over all other claims; in a war between two towns, each possessing a Lombard settlement, the latter were to be allowed to move under safe conduct freely between the belligerents. This is in direct opposition, not only to the common sense of the situation, but also to the conditions allowed to both Jewish and native Christian merchants. In the Convention of Worms, for example, made between the cities of the Rhineland in 1254, it is explicitly laid down that neither Jewish nor Christian merchant may in any way assist the enemies of the parties to the convention[1].

Various paragraphs in the Swiss documents also emphasise the extraordinarily favourable terms these moneylenders could impose upon their hosts. They were not responsible for the depreciation of pledges through mice or moth; a court had to meet immediately if a Lombard presented a complaint; disputes between them and the town were to be settled by a board of seven members of the town council, to be chosen by the Lombards, and their decision was final; that the pressure of the Church and the Inquisition was not completely negligible they admitted in demanding written guarantees that they should not be liable to prosecution in either secular or ecclesiastical courts if their wealth increased as the result of their usuries.

IV. THE APPEARANCE OF THE CHRISTIAN MERCHANT BURGHER

It has already been shown how the administrative and ecclesiastical burgs of north-west Europe tended in the eleventh century to attract merchant settlers by the opportunities they offered of protection. Around the burg grew the fauburg (forisburgus) with its own walls. As it developed it desired its own constitution, and this it obtained in many places during the twelfth century. The movement for the establishment of ' communes ' has a far wider interest than that of commerce, but it was natural that those settlements which were primarily settlements of merchants should seek for the establishment of a commune which assured to them, not merely a relative independence, but commercial security and privileges. On two very important points the merchant communes present a close resemblance to the Jewish communities which obtained the charters of the Carolingian group. The merchants were not part of the local feudal society. Whatever their individual origin, they, like the Jews,

[1] MGH, LL, IV, Const. II, p. 582.

had been brought together by a common interest which replaced their original status. They might have been serfs of many different owners; as merchants they were treated as free men and a corporate group. Secondly, as merchants they were subject to the justice and taxation of the prince and not of the local authorities, and here again their situation was parallel to that of the Jews. On the other hand, these merchant communes presented one important difference from the Jewish communities. Their merchant gild preceded the granting of their privileges, and comprised the whole governing population of the place in question. As they were not a minority group within a larger local society, various communal rights could be conceded to them which would have been inapplicable to the Jews.

The parallels and distinctions can be most easily seen by a comparison of the charter granted to Saint Omer in 1127 by the Count of Flanders[1] with those issued to the Jews. In the first place, the charter is issued to the inhabitants of Saint Omer ' sicut meos homines '—as to the count's men. Their former status is ignored, and a new status given them. In the same way in the Carolingian charters the tattered relics of Roman rights are replaced by the Jews being taken under the direct protection of the prince as ' his men '. In both cases, as the men of the prince, the recipients of the deed are subjected to his justice. The Jews were totally exempt from the jurisdiction of courts Christian: the burghers of Saint Omer were totally exempt from such courts outside Saint Omer and within the city were only subjected to them in matters of sacrilege (breaking into a church, or assaulting the clergy) and of rape. In both cases also a wide liberty was allowed to the jurisdiction of their own courts in internal matters: for the Jews to the rabbinical courts, for the burghers to the customs of their gilds. In both cases also they were exempt from trial by duel. The burghers were given rights of taking justice into their own hands in matters of assault, if the justice of the count's governor failed them. Similar rights appear in Jewish charters of the Frederician group, but not in the Carolingian.

There are also close parallels in the rights of each in relation to defence, war, and the presence of a local garrison.

[1] Giry, *Histoire de S. Omer*, pp. 371 ff.

The precise details differ with the differing circumstances, but the principles, that merchants wished to be free from the exactions of troops billeted in the town and from the interruptions caused by foreign wars, were the same in each case. Another matter of the greatest importance was the relation of merchants to the ordinary feudal taxes and to the tolls levied on goods entering and leaving the territories of the prince. The burghers of Saint Omer received in this matter even fuller liberties than those ordinarily enjoyed by the Jews, for in addition to the most generous treatment of their goods, they secured immunity from those tallages and arbitrary exactions which no Jewish community could permanently escape.

It is probable that the lending of money formed even then an activity of merchants, for there are regulations according to which they could imprison and distrain on a defaulting debtor; but as with the contemporary charters issued to the Jews, the small attention given to the question shows that it was not yet a matter of great importance.

Finally, the burghers of Saint Omer received rights which emphasise their distinction from, and their superiority over, the communities of Jewish merchants—the rights of coining and of protecting the stability of their own currency.

Similar charters, with variations in the details, were obtained during the twelfth century by almost all of the great commercial cities of the north. These the cities of Flanders obtained most readily, the burghers of episcopal cities with the most difficulty. But all alike ultimately obtained them, and with them abolished any advantage which the Jewish merchants might previously have possessed over their Christian rivals.

V. THE LOCAL MERCHANT TURNS USURER

The traditional sequence of events in medieval Jewish history is a very simple one. At the threshold of the Middle Ages, in the Carolingian epoch, the Jew held the monopoly of commerce. Later on, Christians took to commerce, but were forbidden to indulge in financial operations. The Jew therefore deserted commerce and entered on his second monopoly, moneylending. It has been shown already that the first of these monopolies was so limited in both time and scope that ' monopoly ' is much too strong a word to describe it, and that the second has only existed in the imagination of historians. In the previous chapter the actual course of events was examined from the standpoint of the Church, and her struggle against Christian usury. In the previous sections of the present chapter the natural origin of borrowing, and the emergence of a class of cosmopolitan merchants who lent money, have been described. To complete the picture, and to set the Jewish usurer in his true perspective in the whole, it only remains to explore the situation of the Christian merchant-burgher, and to discover the part which he played in the development of the profession.

Like all others who lent money, the merchant burgher came to the profession naturally and, as it were, unconsciously. The inclusion of regulations for the recovery of debts was no accident in the charter given to Saint Omer in 1127. Seven years later the merchants of Paris appealed to Louis VI for assistance in the same matter, and the king's reply illustrates the chaos of jurisdictions of the time. He ordered the Prevôt to assist the merchants by distraining on the property of their debtors, but he ruled that this could only apply if the property in question was under the jurisdiction of the Crown[1]. It is to be presumed that the creditors would need in each case the authorisation of the overlord before distraining for debt.

Throughout the whole of the Middle Ages the lending of money by the resident Christian merchant, mostly to his fellow citizens or to nobles of his vicinity, continued. In the Swiss cities there is frequent reference to individual lending by the merchants, and one case at least of corporate efforts to free the city itself from foreign indebtedness by sharing the liability among the inhabitants, and paying interest to them instead of to outsiders. But the delicacy of such transactions appears in the law passed at the same time, forbidding anyone calling such public-spirited lenders ' usurers ' or ' extortioners '[2]. Since the interest paid in this case was in the neighbourhood of eight per cent., it is a pity

[1] Laurière, I, p. 6.
[2] Amiet, *loc. cit.*, I, p. 242; cf. II, p. 163.

that such intelligent methods of ' conversion ' were not more
frequently followed. Normally, where the city excluded
foreign usurers, whether Jew or Lombard, the interest itself
did not diminish. Thus neither were allowed to settle at
Saint Omer throughout the whole period, and indebtedness
seems to have been a rare phenomenon at any time within
the city. But the interest allowed was the common rate of
twopence in the £, or forty-three and one-third per cent.[1]

The lending activities of merchants, while they continued
up to the end of the Middle Ages, were on a very small scale
compared with those of a chartered usurer. They were not
protected as were those of the latter, and were consequently
an easier mark for the zeal of any local cleric. He could
triumph over an honest merchant, who may have lent at
from five to ten per cent., while the Lombard or Jew who
lent at ten times that rate escaped his clutches.

VI. THE RIVALRY BETWEEN CHRISTIAN AND JEWISH USURERS

The expulsion of Christian usurers from the thirteenth
century onwards, the fourteenth century charters, the provision made by the burghers for their own financial activities,
all emphasise that the Jew by no means had the field to
himself. The rivalry between Lombard or Cahorsin, burgher
and Jew, extended over the whole field and the whole period.
The basis of the conflict was both the need of the profession,
and the profits which could be made out of it. When the
heavy hand of Henry III of England fell upon the Cahorsin
in 1251, and many were imprisoned and others fled from the
country, Matthew Paris tells us that the Jews rejoiced to see
it; when, two years later, the piety of Louis IX chased the
Jews out of France, the same chronicler remarks that ' the
Cahorsin eagerly took possession of the places and offices of
the expelled Jews '[2]. Jews, when they had the opportunity,
were ready to take the place of Christians; Lombards and
Cahorsin tried to squeeze out Jews; burghers tried to expel
or dispense with both. Meanwhile, the monasteries and the

[1] Giry, *op. cit.*, p. 296.
[2] *Chron. maj.*, ed. Rolls Series, V, pp. 245 and 361.

clergy quietly continued to find profitable investments which would either escape the eyes of the authorities or, if detected, appear innocent of any taint of the crime ' detested on the pages of both Testaments '. And each of the professional usurers, when he saw the possibility, was ready to exact the most unscrupulous conditions from the power from whom he received his licence, or from the debtor who was unable to resist his demands.

In the conflict between the Jews and their different Christian rivals all the advantage lay with the latter, and neither council nor inquisitor succeeded in deterring them from exploiting it. The only real burden which the Church imposed was on their imagination and their ingenuity, and those seem to have been equal to their task. So far as straight loans on security were concerned, the Jew rarely altered his system of lending on ' usury ', which accrued from the day of the loan. His possibility of making illegal profit did not come from some hair-splitting about the nature of the transaction, but from a simpler trick. He commonly did not inscribe capital and usury separately in the bond, but simply stated that a certain sum would be due on a certain day in a certain currency. It was in this way that he concealed the amount which he had lent, and could, on enquiry being made, claim that far more of the sum mentioned represented capital than was actually the case. But he made this extra profit at the risk of his head, or of a heavy fine. The Christian was more subtle. His dishonesty was mental: it lay in the system itself. But so long as the system was accepted as not being usurious there was no limit to his profits. He observed the letter of the law by allowing a period to elapse within which the repayment might be made without any additional charge. But after that the charges were far greater than those of the Jews. As he was careful to fix the time within which repayment might be made without interest at a date on which it was extremely improbable that the debtor would be able to take advantage of it, he was able to claim that his practice was both legal and moral.

A second great advantage which the Christian possessed was his ability to rely on the smouldering hostility of the populace against the unbelievers as a means of securing the discomfiture of his business rivals. An irrelevant issue could easily be raised and, even if an outburst against the Jews began with a direct attack upon their economic conduct, it was easy to turn it into channels safer for the Christian usurer who might otherwise appear to the public as equally detestable.

Amongst the many accusations of ritual murder, of profanation of the Host, and of poisoning of wells, there were certainly some where the jealousy of Christian rivals fanned the fires, even if it did not light them. To establish the proofs of such a statement is practically impossible, for the motive put forward was religious, whether we are considering the motive which aroused the crowd who acted or that which interested the chronicler who reported. Moreover, the merchants themselves may well have been convinced that religion and commercial profit both pointed with equal sincerity to the same line of action[1], and even were they not so convinced they would certainly have kept their scepticism to themselves.

While the fanning of the fires of religious fanaticism might profit either group of Christian merchants, each group had also its own special advantage in the struggle against the Jewish rival. The prime weapon of the different Italian bankers was their vastly superior wealth and the power which that wealth brought them. It is certainly true that there were a number of expulsions of Italian usurers in France during the fourteenth century, but there is little evidence that such expulsions affected the small group of great capitalists whose services were indispensable in a dozen different ways to the court[2]. On the other hand, the expulsions of Jewish colonies usually involved the wealthiest as well as the poorest, and it is only on rare occasions that privileged individuals were long able to evade general restrictions on Jewish life.

Yet even with the weapon of superior wealth the struggle was a slow one. At first the authorities and the public tended to regard the two groups with equal favour or equal suspicion, for the friendship and protection shown to a few royal furnishers did not necessarily cover the whole group of

---

[1] S. Schweinburg-Eibenschütz, *Le Livre des chrétiens et le livre des Juifs*, in REJ, XXVII, p. 108.

[2] Cf. Mirot, *Etudes Lucquoises*, in *Bibliothèque de l'Ecole de Chartes*, Vols. 88, 89. The merchants of Lucca were in the specially fortunate position after 1334 of being theoretically subjects of the King of France.

which they were members. In the fourteenth century there were many cases where Jews and foreign moneylenders were put on the same footing. A regulation made in Zurich in 1351 treated Jews and Cahorsin alike in their lending activities[1], and the same was done in fourteenth-century Burgundy and in many other places. How evenly balanced the power of the two combatants might be is revealed in the two following situations, though in each the Christians had a slight advantage. In Dauphiné in the middle of the fourteenth century each obtained the right of settlement in return for an entrance payment and an annual tax. The Lombards paid 1,500 florins for the first and 1,750 for the second; the Jews were clearly somewhat less wealthy, for they requested permission to pay for their entrance in two instalments, although the sum was only a thousand florins, and their annual tax also was two hundred and fifty florins less than that of the Lombards[2]. In 1391 the Jews returned to Berne and obtained the right of citizenship for a period of years. Certain privileges were granted them in excess of those enjoyed by the local Lombard community. The Lombards protested, and the city felt itself obliged to inform the Jews that when the Lombard charter was renewed it would either contain these additional privileges, or the Jews would themselves be deprived of them. As a matter of fact, equality, when it came, was of a different order, for both were expelled in 1427[3]. Whenever possible, a Christian group which received a charter asked also for a monopoly in their profession. Sometimes they obtained it, sometimes they failed. Six Lombard families obtained permission to settle in Mouzon in the Ardennes in 1381, and secured the clause that during the period of the charter no Jew or other Lombard would be allowed to settle there[4]. The Lombards settling in Biel in 1397 obtained the same right, although their charter was based on that granted to the Lombards of Solothurn, who did not. The latter succeeded in excluding other Lombards, but the town retained its liberty in the matter of Jews[5].

In Germany the duel followed along the same lines. The

[1] Amiet, *loc. cit.*, I, p. 227.
[2] Prudhomme, *Les Juifs en Dauphiné*, p. 154.
[3] Amiet, *loc. cit.*, I, p. 244.
[4] Laurière, VII, p. 717.
[5] Amiet, *loc. cit.*, I, p. 254.

Lombards settled there later than in France, but, when they did, they immediately became dangerous opponents. It was apparently a habit in the Rhineland, in contracts of sales, to stipulate that if the buyer failed to pay the money by the time agreed, the seller might recoup himself by borrowing the same amount, and the buyer accepted responsibility for the payment of the interest. In earlier documents, it was expressly stated that the seller might borrow from the Jews[1]. In later ones the common phrase is ' from Christians, Lombards or Jews '[2].

Though the struggle of the Jews against Christian professional moneylenders was long drawn out, it is clear that the Jews were fighting a losing battle. It is only rarely, and for short durations, that they scored a victory. Against the burgher they were even less successful. The Crown might impose Jews on secondary commercial and industrial centres, and the town be too weak to resist; but nothing shows more clearly the limitations of their activities than the absence of Jews in the three chief centres of medieval European commerce. In the great industrial and commercial centres of Flanders and northern Italy Jews played no rôle of any importance. In the German Hanseatic cities they played no part at all, though they obtained their greatest power and their nearest approach to monopoly in some of the other German towns.

It has already been said that the efforts of the Church to combat Christian usury were more successful with the local burghers than with the great international companies. This was particularly true in Germany in the thirteenth century and after, so that there were a number of places where the only pawnbrokers were Jews, and where even more important finance was also in their hands. When the clergy were expressly permitted to borrow money from Jews, as they were in various German dioceses in the thirteenth century, there is certainly a strong presumption that money was not available from any other source. Moreover, the alternative occupations open to the German Jews were few, and in some towns Jews were expressly excluded from all trade. But lest

---

[1] Kuske, *Quellen z. Gesch. des Köln. Handels*, I, p. 18, Nos. 60, 62; F. Lau, *Geschichte der Stadt Düsseldorf*, II, No. 174.

[2] Kuske, *op. cit.*, pp. 150, 152, 157.

it be thought that such a situation permits of a generalisation, it must not be forgotten that many privileges which have been already discussed explicitly state that only a fixed number of persons within the invited community may act as usurers.

In fact, the monopoly and the exclusion from other occupations were both of short duration. The change over of the Jews from trade to moneylending produced a new trading necessity, that of disposing of unredeemed pledges— or, when repayment was made in kind, of disposing of that. New Jewish trades sprang up, many of which became special Jewish interests for centuries. It is in this way that the Jews of Alsace and western Germany became associated with the trade in horses and cattle, for the noble or the farmer, who had no object of precious metal or jewel at his disposal, could more easily pawn his beast than anything else. In the same way trade in agricultural produce fell into Jewish hands from the land or crops given by peasants as security for their loans. In the wine country of the Rhine and Moselle, wine was also a frequent form of security, and Jews are found trading in that. Cloth, too, provided a common object of pawn for artisans. Last, but by no means least, it is from this cause that Jews, even up to modern times, have come to be so closely associated with the traffic in old clothes. But all these commercial activities were but involuntary by-products of the main occupation, the lending of money[1].

While thus pawnbroking became the prime occupation of many Jews of Germany, it must still not be thought that all moneylending had fallen into their hands. Leaving aside surreptitious loans by generous-seeming but avaricious neighbours, and the exclusion of the Jews from the stronghold of German medieval commerce, the towns of the Hanseatic League, we find that even in other towns, while they dealt with the ordinary day-to-day loans of different classes, the Jews handled only rarely the ' high finance ' of the cities and governments[2].

[1] For an example of this change in the Jews of a single town, cf. I. Kracauer, *Aus der Inneren Geschichte der Juden Frankfurts*, pp. 26 ff.

[2] A summary of city lending is given in M. Hoffmann, *Der Geldhandel der deutschen Juden während des Mittelalters*, pp. 46 ff.

VII. THE DEBTOR'S CHOICE

The behaviour of Jewish usurers drew forth deep and continuous complaints from all classes during the Middle Ages, and there is not the slightest doubt that much of their unpopularity was justified, even if the payment which they received, murder and arson, forced baptism and expulsion, was grossly in excess of the crime which they were supposed to have deliberately committed. What is too frequently ignored is that the complaint against the Christian usurer is no less bitter, even if he rarely paid for his exactions with his life. The language in which the French kings described the activities of Christian usurers in the edicts of their expulsions is exactly the same as that of similar edicts affecting the Jews. Both, for example, were expelled by Philip IV in 1311. In explaining why it was necessary to expel the Jews, the king gave the reason that:

> they harry and oppress widows and orphans with their irrelevant accusations; they persecute and molest innumerable innocent persons with false charges; by threats and terror they compel persons secretly to sign obligations which contain hidden implications, and then fraudulently demand their fulfilment; they make usurious contracts; they exhibit intolerable conduct, and dishonour Christian customs and behaviour in innumerable ways which it is impossible to mention openly[1].

In the edict of expulsion against the Lombards, he said that:

> the Italians are expelled because of the insupportable havoc and destruction [which they create]; because of the scourge of the usury which they exact from the citizens of our kingdom; because of the destruction of our currency; because of the infringement of our edicts, and because the operations of our exchange and our laws are completely upset by them[2].

And lest it be thought that the fabrication of wily and illegal contracts was a specifically Jewish misdemeanour, when the Lombards were arrested again, less than twenty years later, it was because:

[1] Laurière, I, p. 488.
[2] *Ibid.*, p. 489.

they are so cunning and malicious that they have their contracts drawn up in their own terms, with such skill that it is almost impossible to take exception to them; then they bind the debtor by a specific oath of renunciation in so wily a manner that, before he knows where he is, he would be involved in greater legal charges in getting out of their net than the profit which he could make out of the cancellation of their usury[1].

If we turn from royal edicts to popular condemnation, the complaints of Villefranche and Beaucaire at the end of the thirteenth and the beginning of the fourteenth centuries afford an excellent comparison. The inhabitants of Ville-franche petitioned Philip IV to expel the Jews *because they are absolutely and utterly destroying the town and district*[2]. The inhabitants of Beaucaire petitioned the seneschal to remove certain Christian usurers, *because there is widespread fear that the whole community may suffer irreparable harm from their activities*[3].

A single actual case taken, not from popular imagination but from the report of the Commissioners appointed to clear up the situation left by the Lombards in the middle of the fourteenth century, will show that these fears were not exaggerated. In 1334 a certain Guillaume Lord of Drace, in the Bailiwick of Mâcon, borrowed the sum of 140 florins. His son-in-law took over the debt, and in 1347 signed a document recognising his liability for 1,300 florins. He still made no payment, and in 1350 signed a further obligation for 900 florins in addition to the 1,300 already owing. He then succeeded in paying off 400 florins, and at the same time made an arrangement to pay off the remaining 1,800 florins in yearly instalments of 200 florins for nine years[4]. Similar cases can be discovered in the records of Jewish usury, but that is of less interest than to compare the general opinions

---

[1] Laurière, II, p. 60.

[2] *Col. doc., Lettres des Rois*, I, p. 380.

[3] S. Kahn, *Les Juifs de la Senechaussée de Beaucaire*; REJ, LXV, p. 187.

[4] Taken from the inquiry into Lombard usury, 1351. Laurière, IV, p. 81. An even more extensive story of the consequences of Christian usury is unfolded by Matthew Paris in the effort of Henry III to secure Sicily and Apulia for his son. *Chron. maj.*, ed. Rolls Series, Vols. V and VI, *passim*, especially V, pp. 347, 459, 552 and 581 ff.

of medieval writers themselves on the relative severity of the two scourges, Christian and Jewish.

In view of the fact that all the writers are Christian, and most of them ecclesiastics, it is surprising that they are unanimous in preferring the Jewish usurer to the Christian. This is not due to the feeling that Christian usury is the greater sin, though that view is also expressed, nor is it due to any affection for the Jews, for these same writers accept as facts ritual murder and all the other accusations launched at medieval Jewry. The basis of their preference is that the Jewish usurer is fairer and more merciful to his debtor than the Christian. This claim is made in England, France, and Germany alike. The Barons at Melun in 1230 urged on Louis IX that the country needed possibilities for borrowing money, and that, this being so, it was better to encourage Jews rather than Christians to take up the profession, since their interest was lower[1]. In 1253, Bishop Grosseteste of Lincoln, complaining against the Pope's merchants, said that the Jewish method of charging usury was more reasonable for the debtor than the Christian[2], and yet Grosseteste vigorously disapproved of the way in which the Jews exploited and ruined the Christian population[3]. In 1306 a Norman chronicler reported that the Jews were expelled from France,

' . . . which would have been a good thing, had the government provided against one inconvenient result. For there are many occasions on which people, however well-off they may be, have a sudden need of money, and if they cannot produce it, either lose an inheritance, are excommunicated or are punished; or else they fall into some great misfortune because they cannot rapidly collect the rents or debts due to them; whereas if they could raise the money for a little usury, they would escape. But after the expulsion of the Jews, they could not find any money, except by borrowing it through agents from certain Christians, both clerics, and laymen, who lent at such an

[1] William of Chartres, *De Vita et Miraculis Sancti Ludovici*, Bouquet, XX, p. 34.

[2] Matthew Paris, *Chron. maj.*, ed. Rolls Series, V, p. 405.

[3] Letter to the Countess of Winchester; *Epistolae*, ed. H. R. Luard, Rolls Series, pp. 33 ff.

enormous rate of interest that it was more than double
what was charged by the Jews, and who did it in such a
way that the debtors did not know the lenders who were
in possession of their pledges. This was a dangerous
situation, for if the agents died or gave up the business,
they did not know where to recover them.'[1]

Even more striking are references to Jewish and Christian
usury in such poems as ' le Patenostre de l'Usurier '[2], and in
the rhymed chronicle of Geoffrey of Paris:

> Car Juifs furent débonnères
> Trop plus en faisant tels affaires
> Que ne furent ore chrestien . . .
> Mais si li Juifs demouré
> Fussent au réaume de France,
> Chrestien moult grant aidance
> Eussent en que ils n'ont pas . . .
> Car por po trouvoit on argent[3].

In 1480, in a draft reply to his States which appealed for
the expulsion of the Jews, the son of the Elector of Brandenburg, acting for his absent father, stated that ' at one time
the Jews were forbidden to stay in Brandenburg, but that
in that period the people were worse oppressed by the
Christians than they had been by the Jews, so that the latter
had been readmitted '. Wherefore he refused to expel them
again[4]. Finally, in his famous ' Ship of Fools ' written in
1493, Sebastian Brant writes:

> Die wuochrer füren wild gewerb,
> Den armen sind sie ruch und herb,
> Nit achtens, dass all Welt verderb.
> Ich will vom übernütz nit schriben,
> Den man mit zinss und gült duot triben,

---

[1] A Norman chronicle of the fourteenth century quoted in Barabé,
Tabellionage Royale et Sigillographie Normande, p. 488.

[2] *Fabliaux et Contes des poètes français*, ed. Meon, IV, p. 99; cf. *ibid.*,
III, p. 87.

[3] Geffroi de Paris, *Chronique Rimée*, verses 3121-3123, 3162-3165, 3169.
Bouquet, XXII, p. 119. Quoted in REJ, XLVIII, p. 224, ' for Jews
were excessively generous in such matters, more so than any Christian.
But if the Jews had stayed in France, the Christians would have greatly
profited by it, which profit they now lack, for where can they find
money? '

[4] A. Ackermann, *Geschichte der Juden in Brandenburg a.H.*, pp. 27 ff.,
which corrects Bernfeld, *op. cit.*, p. 13.

Z

Mit lihen, bläschkouf und mit borgen,
Manchem ein pfunt gewinnt ein morgen,
Me, dan es tuon ein jor lang solt.
Man lihet eim jetz münz um golt,
Für zehen schribt man eilf ins buoch.
Gar lidlich war der Juden gesuoch,
Die Kristen-Juden sie vertriben;
Mit Judenspiess die selben rennen—
Und schwigt darzuo all recht und gsatz[1].

It says much for the unsatisfactory nature of medieval finance that there existed side by side the continuous complaint of the extortion of the Jews when they were present, and this desire for their return when they were absent, for that there is truth in the accusation that even Jewish usury was ruinous for the poorer classes is evident from innumerable sources.

The usurers practise a brutal trade.
They are hard and harsh on the poor,
Not caring that everybody perishes.
I shan't write of compound interest
From capital plus interest,
Of lending, faked sales, and borrowing.
Some earn one pound of a morning,
More than they ought to in a whole year.
Small coin is borrowed and gold repaid,
Eleven is written into the book for ten.
Really tolerable was what the Jews had asked;
The Christian-Jews drove them out.
They practise the art of the Jewish cut-throat
And all justice and laws are silent over it.

Narrenschiff, tit. xc. On the expression ' Judenspiess,' see M. Güde-mann, *Geschichte des Erziehungswesens in Deutschland während des XIV. und XV. Jahrhunderts*, pp. 276 ff.

CHAPTER TEN

THE JEWISH USURER

I. THE BEGINNING OF JEWISH USURY

In the two previous chapters the general framework, within which Jewish usury can be seen in its proper proportion, has been discussed. It has been seen that the attitude of the Church did not result in a monopoly of the whole profession falling into the hands of a group supposedly well adapted by temperament and history to assume it. It was no question of aptitude that created moneylenders, but the fact of possessing cash to lend. Four classes lent, regular and secular clergy, tax-collectors, and merchants. Each class exercised the profession as long and as widely as it could. The limited victory of the Church reduced the lending powers of the first two classes during the very period in which the fourth came into prominence and acquired immensely enhanced facilities for practising this profession. It is as members of this fourth class that the Jews came also to practise this activity and, during the whole period of the Middle Ages, they were never without rivals in its pursuit.

It remains now to examine in greater detail the Jewish share in moneylending, and to disengage the particular characteristics which distinguished it from the activities of Christians and, indeed, caused its great extension in most of the countries of Europe at different periods.

If it is difficult to obtain full information about early Christian usury in Europe, it is equally difficult to secure details of Jewish operations. In both commerce and money-lending the two groups are mentioned together in the casual references which occur. Charlemagne associated Jewish and Christian merchants together when he forbade Church goods to be taken by them[1]. Anno, Archbishop of Cologne, who died in 1075, left directions in his will that his creditors, both Christian and Jewish, should be paid[2]. At the end of

[1] *Cap. of* 806, V, v.
[2] Aronius, No. 164.

the eleventh century references to financial dealings become more frequent. The charter of Rüdiger of Speyer and the two charters of Henry IV all granted to the Jews certain privileges as money-*changers*. The charters of Henry also contain the first references to what became a standing problem for the pawnbroker, his liability if objects deposited with him proved to have been stolen. We cannot tell whether it was as pawnbrokers or as merchants that the Jews of Speyer obtained such goods. In any case, these documents are silent about a number of questions which came to be of capital importance, both to creditor and debtor, once money-lending became a whole-time occupation. When could the creditor sell his pawns? What rate of interest could he charge? How was the whole transaction proved, if challenged from either side? What were the limitations to be imposed on the objects which the pawnbroker might receive? At a period where none of these questions had become sufficiently insistent to demand regulation we may be sure that the whole business had but a minor importance.

In the period following the massacres of the First Crusade the change began to take place. But though the massacres are the single most important incident in producing the change, at the time they did little more than create a predisposition among Jews to seek occupations which did not involve travel. That the occupation came so often to be moneylending was due to those reasons which fostered the trade also among Christians—the immense increase of commercial activity in the century following the Crusade.

It must also be realised that the change was not one immediately acceptable to the Jews themselves. After all, the original prohibition of usury came from Jewish law, and was considered valid for themselves by the Jews of post-biblical times. According to the Mishnah, ' one may borrow from and lend to them (heathens) on interest. The same applies to a resident alien '[1]. This straight permission, however, displeased the rabbis of the Talmudic period, who set against it the prohibition of usury in the Psalms and Proverbs[2], and hedged it about with conditions of which the essence was that money might be lent on usury if the profit

---

[1] Talmud, Nezikin, *Baba Mezi'a*, 70b, ed. Soncino, p. 407.
[2] *Ps.* xv, 5; and *Prov.*, xxviii, 8.

was necessary for a livelihood, but not if the object was to acquire riches[1]. The ideal still remained not to take it under any circumstances[2]. In any case, the Talmud as clearly forbade Jews to take it from Jews as the Canonists forbade Christians to take it from Christians. The first evidence that it had become necessary to modify this attitude appears in a twelfth-century collection of rules. In them it is laid down that ' a man shall not lend to Gentiles for interest, when he is able to get a livelihood in any other way '[3]; if any alternative occupation were possible, the profession of usurer was to be abandoned[4]. In the same century Rabbi Eliezer b. Nathan of Mainz issued a judgment of a similar character: ' by this we understand that in the present time, where Jews own no fields or vineyards whereby they could live, lending money to non-Jews for their livelihood is necessary and therefore permitted '[5]. When this is contrasted with the curt statement of Rashi (1040-1105) that ' whoever lends money to a foreigner on interest will be destroyed '[6], this is a further confirmation that it is not until after the Crusade that the change occurred.

The earliest evidence of moneylending as an occupation of sufficient importance to need charter regulation, is to be found in the north of Spain. In the charter granted in 1120 to all the inhabitants of Funes in Navarre are several references implying this activity among Jews. In all financial transactions a Jew had to draw up a deed in favour of a Christian, and a Christian a deed in favour of a Jew; and a Christian had to take an oath (? of possession or payment) before he could recover his pledge from a Jew[7]. In 1171 the Jewish community of Funes itself acquired statutes, which also included several clauses dealing with usury. The king promised never to cancel debts due to a Jew; and a Jew was not liable for the return of a pledge after one year[8]. The

---

[1] *Baba Mezi'a*, 70b, ed. Soncino, pp. 407 ff.

[2] Nezikin, *Makkoth*, 24a, ed. Soncino, p. 171.

[3] *The Book of the Pious*, quoted in I. Bernfeld, *Das Zinsverbot*, p. 10.

[4] *Ibid.*, from the same source, p. 19.

[5] *Ibid.*, p. 19. Cf. the defence of moneylending by a thirteenth-century Jew in Grayzel, *op. cit.*, p. 46, n. 24.

[6] *Ibid.*, p. 10.

[7] *Jewish Encyclopaedia*, art. Funes.

[8] Baer, *Aragon*, No. 579.

particular interest of this latter document is that it is modelled on the privilege issued to the Jews of Tudela in the previous year; but the two clauses dealing with moneylending do not appear in the Tudelan grant. While this was not a region much affected by the gathering of Crusaders in 1096, it had been the scene of a preliminary crusade against the Moors in 1063, a fact which again connects the adoption of this profession with insecurity.

If we possessed any actual texts of the privileges granted to the Jews in Norman England, it would probably be possible to prove that opportunity attracted as much as insecurity compelled, for it seems that it was the English Jews who were the first to develop into an important money-lending community. Unfortunately, though we have references to privileges of Henry I, their texts have not survived. On the other hand, English archives are exceptionally rich in twelfth-century documents, and these provide a good substitute. When it is found that in 1130 an Englishman can owe the considerable sum of 200 marks of silver for the help which the king had given him in regard to his debts to the Jews, or that a group of Jews owe the king ten marks of gold for his help in aiding them to recover their loans to Earl Ranulf[1], it is obvious that they were dealing in loans of considerable size, and that they were doing so under royal protection and control. Further, in the same year the Jews of London were fined £2,000 for a murder, a sum equivalent to about five per cent. of the king's annual revenue, and though there is no evidence that more than half was paid, even that is an enormous amount. We know nothing on the Continent to indicate the possession of wealth in coin on such a scale at this date, and the probable explanation lies in the special nature of English Jewry. Jews came over in large groups as a new element in the population at a time of intense national development. The immense impetus given to building, and the general demand for luxuries resulting from the close union with the Continent, consequent upon the Norman conquest, created an unprecedented demand for money. The Jews, who were both newcomers and merchants, could more easily change their occupations than could their better established brethren on the Continent. Further,

[1] J. Jacobs, *The Jews of Angevin England,* pp. 14 f.

though many Flemings came over at the same time, there were as yet no Italians in the country, so that they and the Flemings could alone supply the demand.

In any case, by the end of the twelfth century, extensive regulations were already needed for the control of the profession. The immense property which the treasury received at the death of Aaron of Lincoln, and the corresponding losses caused by the massacres at York and elsewhere, may have been the immediate cause of these regulations, which are more complete than anything hitherto issued. The charter of 1190 had recognised the profession of moneylender, but had gone into few details, and those only such as concerned the security of the Jew. The regulations of 1194, which concerned exclusively the interests of the treasury, show the importance of the profession for the national economy. A complete registration of all Jewish property was to be made. A few cities throughout the country were appointed where offices were to be set up for the control of bonds, and elsewhere no formal contracts could be made. Copies of the bonds were to be kept at these places under lock and key; in addition, they were all to be entered on a roll kept by the king's clerks[1]. By these regulations the profession first explicitly assumed the form it was to keep throughout the period, of a royal as much as, or even more than, a Jewish interest.

The next region in which the profession became common was northern France, where the commercial importance of the Champagne Fairs probably aided its development. In his attack on the Jews in about 1146 Peter of Cluny accused them of commercial dishonesty but not of usury[2], but two statutes of Philip Augustus of 1206 and 1218[3] provided a relatively complete set of French rules for moneylending, and also considered the Jew only as a moneylender, without making provision for any other form of activity. This confirms a remark of Innocent III in a letter to the Count of Nevers in 1208, that certain secular princes actually encouraged Jews to settle in different towns of their kingdoms for the purpose of lending money at usury, and enforced the

---

[1] Jacobs, pp. 156 ff.

[2] *Ep. ad Ludovicum Regem:* P.L., CLXXXIX, c. 366 ff.

[3] Laurière, I, p. 44 (the date is given *ibid.*, XI, p. 291), and I, pp. 36 f.

payment of it through the judges of their courts, even to the extent of allowing widows and orphans to be despoiled of their property, and the Church to be robbed of her tithes[1]. In fact, moneylending had become the most important Jewish occupation in France, in spite of all the efforts of Louis VIII, and still more of Louis IX, to suppress all lending for profit, which, of course, means all commercial lending whatever. A canon of the Council of Poitiers in 1280 confirms this by complaining that nearly all the Jews in the city and diocese of Poitiers were openly occupied with it[2].

In the Rhineland the profession appeared at the same time as in northern France; in the rest of Germany and in central Europe the change seems to have been much more gradual. Wealthy Jewish merchants are found already in the eleventh century in Prague[3], Ratisbon[4], and elsewhere, and doubtless they indulged in pawnbroking also. But the earliest evidence of moneylending as a main occupation is the charter of Frederick of Austria in 1244. This set the model for all the subsequent charters of eastern Europe, although the 'merchant charter' of Henry IV could still be employed as a basis of settlement for the Jews of the Empire in the fourteenth century. In 1255, eleven years after the issue of the Austrian charter, the laws of the Rhineland Confederation carefully fixed the scale of usury allowed to Jews, adding the explanation that it was 'necessary to do so because Christian usurers were excommunicated'[5].

In Italy the situation was entirely different. There the Jew never gained anything approaching a monopoly of moneylending, and had neither the wealth nor the power to compete with the commercial cities of the north. It was only at a later date and under special conditions that he was needed[6].

---

[1] *Ep. Innocentii*, X, 190, ed. Baluze.

[2] Mansi, XXIV, p. 384.

[3] Cosmas, *Chron. Bohem.*, MGH, SS, IX, p. 98.

[4] *Ibid.*, p. 112.

[5] Aronius, No. 618.

[6] E.g., in the fourteenth century Jews were invited to settle in San Marino, to provide fluid capital; REJ, XLVIII, p. 242. In Florence they were invited to establish loan banks in 1437 (*Encyclopaedia Judaica*, Vol. VI, article *Florenz*).

It has been seen already that moneylending was neither an invention nor a monopoly of the Jews. If to some extent they replaced the monasteries and the clergy, as canonical prohibition gained power over the latter and specialised the operations of the former, they at best divided the profits with Italian usurers and native citizens, but, subjected as they were to royal exactions from which Christian usurers were largely immune, they collapsed before the end of the Middle Ages, and there was little Jewish wealth in northern Europe to share in the immense developments which accompanied the discovery of a new world. In England they flourished as moneylenders from the beginning of the twelfth to the middle of the thirteenth century, but they were ruined before their expulsion in 1290. In France they flourished at various periods from the end of the twelfth to the end of the fourteenth century, but frequent expulsions prevented this from being called a period of continuous prosperity. In Germany they do not appear to have become important until the thirteenth century, and they were probably completely ruined by the beginning of the fifteenth.

II. THE SCOPE OF JEWISH OPERATIONS

In *Puck of Pook's Hill*, Kipling tells an effective story of how, by withholding gold from John, a Jew secured the signature of Magna Carta[1]; and in the story he recounts how, ' doors shut, candles lit ', the Jews would put off their rags and their cringing, and decide the fate of nations by their knowledge of the movement of ' that mighty underground river ', gold, and by their power to give or to withhold it. There are many reasons for not accepting the picture, attractive though it be. The first is that it was only on rare occasions, and for limited purposes, that the owner of the Jews had need to borrow from them. If they had money to give him he took it, and if he was compelled to borrow, he borrowed because he could not exact any money from his Jews, and he had to borrow from Christians. The power to decide the fate of nations rests with those who have the

---

[1] *The Treasure and the Law*, p. 283.

power to give or to withhold, not with those whose wealth is carefully registered with their owners, and who can with impunity be tortured, killed or exiled.

The different conditions under which Jews lived in different territories, and the changes in different epochs in the same territory, make it impossible to indicate with precision any general conditions of Jewish finance[1]. At one time or another their debtors included persons of every walk of life, from emperors or kings, down to the humble peasantry. Individuals of wealth comparable to that possessed by the great Christian bankers emerged from time to time in different countries, and were not infrequent in the Jewries of Spain; for brief periods communities achieved almost dazzling prosperity; before the spread of violence and massacre in the second half of the thirteenth century, most of the Jewries must have been comfortably prosperous. Nevertheless, the typical Jewish business was petty rather than high finance, and the bulk of the clients poor and middle-class Christians, rather than bishops, abbots, and nobles.

In its prosperous days English Jewry produced two persons who could be considered ' millionaires ', Aaron of Lincoln and Aaron of York. The wealth of the former was so enormous that when it was confiscated after his death a special department of the exchequer had to be created to deal with it. At the end of the thirteenth century there appeared a great French banker and merchant in Burgundy, Elias of Vesoul[2], whose commercial and financial relations extended to Germany and brought him into contact with all classes in France and Burgundy. The return to France in 1361 was negotiated by another Jew of great wealth, Manecier of Vesoul. In Germany, in the fourteenth century, there were a few ' court Jews ' who acted as bankers and even farmers of taxes for their princely owners[3]. Some of the Spanish and Portuguese Jews were even wealthier right up

---

[1] G. Caro, *Sozial- und Wirtschaftsgeschichte der Juden im Mittelalter*, I, p. 221.

[2] *Ibid.*, II, pp. 72 and 291 ff.

[3] *Ibid.*, II, pp. 138 ff. and 152 ff.; M. Hoffmann, *Der Geldhandel der deutschen Juden*, pp. 110 ff.; Lewinsky, *Der Jüdische Hofbankier der Magdeburger Erzbischöfe*, in MGWJ, XLVIII, p. 457,

to the end of their sojourn in the Peninsula, and Don Isaac Abrabanel was appealed to by his late sovereign to assist him in negotiating financial agreements, even after he had been driven into exile. But even he had little political power, and his English, French and German predecessors probably had even less.

The fact that the bulk of surviving Jewish deeds are concerned with loans on land does not mean that these formed the majority of the transactions of the Jews. They have survived through the accident that they were registered in a permanent form. The lesser transactions, based on some object deposited with the creditor, were not so carefully recorded. This is confirmed by the terms of the many charters on which their activities were based, all of which deal in detail with the depositing of pledges, but most of which are completely silent about the more complicated questions involved in the mortgaging of land.

The scope of Jewish operations must also have been intimately linked with the failure or success of the campaign against Christian usury, and the presence of Italian rivals. Where foreign Christian usurers were absent, Jews and burghers would have divided the more as well as the less important transactions; on the few occasions where the Church was successful, noble as well as peasant had to turn to the Jew.

A final point, which possesses considerable interest, is concerned with the source of the funds which the Jew had available for his loans. Towards the end of the period, the poverty of the Jews is in itself a proof that their transactions were modest, but at various moments of their career there is proof that Christians, observing the canonical prohibitions for themselves, placed funds at the disposal of the Jews, and collected the profits therefrom. As such arrangements were by their very nature secret, it is difficult to estimate their extent. Various councils, as far apart as Worcester and St. Pölten, referred to the practice in the thirteenth century[1], and even churches and individual clergy seem to have been guilty of this evasion of Canon Law[2].

---

[1] Worcester, lviii, 1240, and St. Pölten, 1284; Mansi, XXIII, c. 543, and XXIV, c. 510.

[2] Neumann, *Geschichte des Wuchers in Deutschland*, p. 521.

III. LIMITATIONS

The situation described in the previous paragraph indicates sufficiently clearly that it proved impossible to limit the scope of the business by any hard and fast rules, and even that where such rules existed they were not observed. Such as they were, the limitations on Jewish activity fell easily into two classes, those imposed by the Church, and those imposed by secular authorities.

The prohibitions of the Church were based both on the sinfulness of usury as such, and on the special dishonour involved in the Body of Christ being under the financial yoke of His murderers. The first heading includes the continual and academic prohibitions of usury, and the specific attempts, already discussed, to divert the Jews to agriculture, artisan occupations, or 'loyal' commerce. Under the second come the canons forbidding clerics, in need of a loan, to obtain it from Jews. While the first can scarcely be called a ' limitation ', since it is a total prohibition, the second is properly dealt with under the present heading. For there is a general recognition that there were times when, in order to carry on their complicated existence, the monasteries were obliged to borrow ready money[1], and the same might well happen to the secular clergy. This was no new problem. Even in the time of Charlemagne laws had to be passed to prevent Church property from falling into the hands of Jews or other merchants.

The first desire of the Church was, naturally, to prevent the monasteries from getting into debt at all. As this was very rarely achieved, the alternative was to control the extent and the nature of the indebtedness which might be permitted[2].

---

[1] The indebtedness of even wealthy abbeys is explicable sometimes by incompetence or dishonesty, but also by the system by which they met their expenses. The revenues of the abbey were not usually collected in a central chest from which the infirmary, the kitchen, the almsgiving, the church and other departments drew what they needed. Each department was allotted a portion of the property and drew its income therefrom direct. Thus a building programme in one department might create a large deficit in that section of the budget. In the records of the Abbey of Bury Saint Edmunds, for example, all kinds of different monastic officials separately contracted debts with the Jews. Jacobs, p. 59.

[2] The council of Oxford in 1222 forbade all monastic borrowing, either from Christians or Jews, ' nisi ingens necessitas id exposcat ' (Mansi, XXII, c. 1179).

In the twelfth century the creditors of the monasteries were often Jews. Aaron of Lincoln is famous for the number of great abbeys and churches which were in his debt. In the thirteenth it was usual, side by side with regulations as to the amount of indebtedness permitted, for Church councils to specify that the debt might not be contracted with a Jew[1]. This seems to have worked in France, where the action of the councils was supported by the royal owner of the Jews, for as early as 1206 Philip Augustus forbade his Jews to lend money on the security of Church lands[2]. In Germany the matter was not so simple. It has already been seen that at various times conditions made of the Jews local monopolists of usury, so that the Church was obliged to turn to them if there were need of a loan.

In many cases churches did not mortgage their lands in order to raise money, but pawned some of their valuables. Even relatively poor establishments must have had some property in precious objects, due to the gifts of the faithful, which could easily be spared, so far as actual use was concerned. Side by side with the protection of landed property, the councils did their best to prevent these objects from falling into the hands of Jews, who might be tempted to dishonour them in order to show their contempt for the Christian faith. But this was a much more difficult matter, for the transaction could be carried through so much more easily and quietly. While it would be exaggerated to accept the implication of Peter of Cluny, made at the time of the Second Crusade, that any such objects found in the possession of Jews must have been stolen[3], it is perfectly true that their acceptance was illegal from both the Jewish and the Christian point of view, for, as has already been said, the rabbis discouraged Jews from accepting such articles with the same vigour as the princes or councils[4]. In Germany, however, in the thirteenth century it was recognised that the

---

[1] Council of Melun, 1216, iv; Rouen, 1231, i; Paris, 1248, ix; Bayeux, c. 1300, lxxxviii; Mansi, XXII, c. 1088; XXIII, cc. 213 and 766; XXV, c. 76.

[2] Laurière, I, p. 44, clause v.

[3] *Ep. ad Ludovicum VII*; P.L., CLXXXIX, c. 368.

[4] Such transactions are forbidden in almost every privilege, and, e.g., in the Constitutions of Odo, xv, and the Councils of Tarragona, lxx; Lavaur, lxxxii, etc.; Mansi, XXII, c. 681; XXV, c. 871; XXVI, c. 520.

need might be so great, the difficulty of finding a Christian moneylender so considerable, that the bishop was authorised to permit such transactions in case of dire necessity[1]. In the diocese of Würzburg, the object pawned had to be placed in a locked box, so that it might not be profaned or insulted by Jewish touch[2].

While the Church, when obliged to recognise the need of moneylenders, distinguished Jews from others on religious grounds, the state guided its policy only by self-interest. It had to keep a delicate balance between two competitors. The Jews were its property, therefore they were the most profitable usurers to license; but they were also the most exposed to popular dislike, and to protect them was sometimes dangerous. On the other side of the scales had to be set the much greater wealth of the Christian usurers, their ability to provide loans when the Jews were drained dry, and the powerful protection which they enjoyed in high quarters; they were, therefore, people whom it was not wise to offend. Certain plums seem always to have fallen to the Christians, especially the minting and changing of money, neither of which were commonly permitted to Jews[3], though both were closely connected with the possession and lending of money. The great Christian banking houses, however, were not so interested in the local activities of pawnbrokers, and this field was shared between Jews and ' Lombards '. But, even here, prudence often secured better conditions to Lombards than to their Jewish rivals. A Jew was usually forbidden to hold the actual person of a Christian for debt, while a Christian Lombard could do so without insulting the sacrament of baptism[4], and evidence has already been given that Lombards more easily secured monopolies than their Jewish competitors.

A second motive which caused their owners to limit the activity of Jewish financiers, was fear of popular resentment.

---

[1] E.g. Trier, 1227, viii; 1277, lxxi; Mansi, XXIII, c. 32; and XXIV, c. 199; Gnesen, 1285; REJ, LXXVIII, p. 77, n. 4.

[2] Würzburg, 1298, vii; Mansi, XXIV, c. 1191.

[3] Cf., for example, Mirot, *Etudes Lucquoises*, in the *Bibliothèque de l'Ecole de Chartes*, LXXXVIII, p. 73, and LXXXIX, p. 348.

[4] Cf. Laurière, I, p. 36, clause viii; p. 54, clause ii; VII, p. 589. The rule was not universal, and Innocent III complains of Jews holding Christians, in his letter to the Count of Nevers; ed. Baluze, Ep. X, 190.

It is curious to contrast the limitations by which French and Spanish kings protected the peasants, sometimes forbidding their implements to be taken from them in pawn, sometimes setting the usury they were to pay at a lower rate than that paid by other sections of the population, with the common practice in German towns of limiting the usury which might be charged to burghers, but allowing any rate obtainable to be exacted from the peasants.

Towards the end of the period a new limitation began to make its appearance. This time it would seem that it was neither the need of conciliating Christian rivals nor fear of the populace which brought it into being, but the steady decline of the Jewries themselves. Jewish tenure was so uncertain, Jewish financial power so reduced, that it became dangerous to allow them to deal with important loans, or loans which could only be slowly repaid. In Alsace, Jews were excluded from dealing in mortgages in the fifteenth century[1]; in Moravia, at the end of the century, their loans to the landed gentry were restricted. In England, before the expulsion, they had been made to dispose within a year of land on which they had foreclosed; in Frankfurt, a century later, the same regulation was introduced[2]. It may be that the extreme difficulty of clearing up the affairs of expelled usurers[3] contributed also to this limitation, for so much of feudal society was built upon the services and duties owed by land, that it might be a serious inconvenience to have its title uncertain, or its ownership in the hands of one who was excused its ordinary duties.

IV. RATES OF USURY

The continuous hatred with which usurers were regarded, and the frantic efforts of the Church to suppress them, were largely due to the enormous rate of ' usury ' or ' interest ' which prevailed. Looking at the question from the stand-point of the debtor, it is easy to understand his indignation. When the question is examined from the side of the creditor,

[1] E. Scheid, *Les Juifs d'Alsace*, pp. 70 ff.
[2] I. Kracauer, *Geschichte der Juden in Frankfurt a.M.*, I, p. 109.
[3] Cf. Laurière, I, pp. 85, 443, 470.

and particularly the Jewish creditor, it is at first sight surprising that the charges were not lowered. The usurer was
never very secure, and such an action would appear to be
both prudent and obvious. That it was neither obvious nor
even practicable, was due to conditions, only some of which
were economic.

The Jewish usurer was never secure; at any moment one
of five things might happen to him: he might be murdered,
or his house sacked by a mob on some fantastic charge or
simply out of religious enthusiasm; he might be expelled
by his owner; his owner might suddenly decree the cancellation of his loans, either in whole or in part, either usury or
capital; the owner might equally well proclaim a moratorium
of several years for all his debtors; finally, the owner might
divert the repayment of the loans to his own coffers.

All this added enormously to the risks of the profession,
and as it is also an inevitable rule in business that the man
who pays must cover the losses arising out of the default of
the man who does not, the rates of usury were inevitably high.
There is, however, a point which is frequently overlooked.
A modern usurer continues to collect his interest until his
debt is paid. If the interest is not paid, it is added to the
capital and accumulates further profit; and all this time the
usurer himself is legally and socially secure. His immense
charges are largely due to greed. His medieval ancestor had
to deal with a number of limitations. He was very rarely
allowed to charge compound interest; at times his usury
could only run for one year, whatever its rate, and however
long repayment was deferred; and it was common to stipulate
that once the usury had reached the total of the capital, it
could not increase further. A fifteenth-century scribe of Basel
worked out the terrifying consequences of borrowing a
guilder at the rate of two hellers a week, and not repaying it
for twenty years. By that time the ' wicked Jewish hell-
hound ' would claim 2,496 guilders for the one guilder he
had lent. To verify the writer's mathematics is less important
than to obtain evidence that the hell-hound got it; and this
he does not give[1]. It is, of course, possible that at that
particular moment, in that particular city, he might have

---

[1] E. Fuchs, *Die Juden in der Karikatur*, gives an illustration of the
Broadsheet between pp. 16 and 17.

been legally entitled to it, but no ordinary debtor ran any such risks in borrowing a guilder, and it is very doubtful whether at any time a Jew could have enforced a claim for such payment in any court.

Nor is it necessary to assume such colossal augmentations of the sums borrowed to understand the havoc which usury caused, or the extent of the indebtedness of every class of society. Most people who have borrowed money for other reasons than commercial or industrial development, have experienced the difficulty of repayment in a single sum. The recognition of this fact lies at the basis of the whole development of the ' instalment system ', and on several occasions a similar repayment by instalments was ordered in medieval times.

Finally, not only were there official limitations as to the amount to which, or the length of time during which, usury might be added to capital, but the majority of medieval transactions were repaid in less than a year. One of the earliest existing collections of records of loans, the rolls of William Cade, a Christian usurer of the middle of the twelfth century, contains no single mention of the year. The loan is contracted on one saint's day, and is to be repaid on another, within the same year[1]. If debtors had not usually paid within these terms, lenders would certainly have always included the year of the loan in their record.

For this reason medieval rates of interest were always stated at weekly rates, although there is no standard rate between one country and another. In the earlier charters the commonest figure was a penny in the pound ($21\frac{2}{3}$ per cent. per annum); later it varied from this figure up to eightpence ($173\frac{1}{3}$ per cent.)[2]. It is not possible to give any economic reason for these variations. When the Jews returned to France in 1361 they were allowed to charge fourpence, although thirty years previously the rate had been reduced from twopence to one penny[3], because of economic distress, and times had certainly not improved in the interval. This particular instance reveals the whole situation. It was neither the interests of the creditor or of the borrower, nor

---

[1] See above, p. 317, n. 3.
[2] For the different levels in different countries, see Scherer, pp. 185 ff.
[3] Laurière, III, p. 473, clause xiv.

AA

the ordinary law of supply and demand, which fixed the rate of usury, but the fact that the profits of a Jewish usurer were part of the budget of the medieval state. An astonishingly frank example of the consequences of this situation is provided by Vladislav of Bohemia in 1497, who authorised the Jews to charge twice the rate of interest allowed to Christians, because the enormous taxes which they had to meet would otherwise absorb the whole profit, and leave them nothing on which they could feed themselves and their families[1].

It is a great mistake to imagine that the Jews became permanently wealthy by their operations. If very large sums passed through their hands, an enormous proportion made but the briefest stay on their premises, for the end of two centuries largely devoted to this profession was the ruin of the Jews of Europe. The princes who passed laws to suppress the extortion of usury, who cancelled debts or portions of them, may not have been conscious of hypocrisy in their expressions of horror at the wickedness of the usurers, but at times, at any rate, they realised that the net result of their generosity was a reduction of the royal revenue[2].

The rate of usury and the advisability of protecting it thus depended on a double combination of circumstances. The princes had to balance their financial profit against the discontent of their subjects, and tended only to give weight to the latter when riots and violence made patent the ruin they had created. The Jews had to weigh their personal security and their permission of residence against the necessity for continually finding considerable sums to satisfy the exactions of their owners.

It is, however, pertinent to ask how it came to be possible to persuade the public to pay these enormous rates. For it would be useless to-day for a bank suddenly to charge twice as much for a loan as was charged by a neighbour. The only result would be the loss of all its more important customers. The main reason why it was possible in the Middle Ages has already been given: money was a scarce commodity, so that he who had it could obtain such rates from people whose desperate situation forced them to borrow at any rate

---

[1] Bondy, No. 292.

[2] Ordinance of Philip IV, 1303, Laurière, I, p. 545; and Ordinance of Charles VI, 1387, *ibid.*, VII, p. 171.

obtainable. Difficulty of movement still further restricted the freedom of the borrower, for there was not likely to be much choice in any but the largest cities. The ordinary client was forced to accept what he was offered locally.

At the same time, it must not be assumed that the maximum interest was always charged. For example, the legal maximum interest in Burgundy at the end of the fourteenth century was 87 per cent. But records remain of charges at every level from 25 per cent. upwards[1]. The same banker would also vary his rates according to the security offered, or his knowledge of his client. In the middle of the twelfth century an Englishman, Richard of Anestey, was forced to borrow from different Jews in order to sustain his claim to his uncle's estate. On two occasions Jacob of Newport lent to him at fourpence per week; when Richard returned for a third loan, he lowered the rate to threepence. Dieulacresse of Canterbury and Comitissa of Cambridge lowered their interest on a second loan in the same way. Hakelot, who had at first lent at threepence, later lowered it to twopence; and one Jew, Brun of Windsor, lent to him at a penny halfpenny. Altogether, the usury which he paid varied from fourpence to three halfpence, and the average was about twopence three farthings, or just under 60 per cent.[2]

V. THE RECORDING OF THE TRANSACTION

Even though the average rates of usury were enormous, they often failed either to cover the risks involved for the lender or to satisfy his cupidity, for evasion was common. In these circumstances the proper recording of the debt became a matter of considerable importance for the debtor. It was also of importance for the prince, since a public record of the financial transactions of his Jews enabled him at any time to assess the amount he could collect from them.

The earliest attempts to regulate the records of debts are to be found in England at the end of the twelfth century. In 1194 the *Capitula de Judaeis* were issued as a result of the destruction of Hebrew deeds during the riots of the preceding

[1] L. Gauthier, *Les Juifs dans les deux Bourgognes*; REJ, XLIX, pp. 244 ff.
[2] Jacobs, *op. cit.*, pp. 38 ff.

years[1]. Special centres were appointed for registering deeds of loans, and both Jewish and Christian officials were put in charge of the chests in which they were contained. From this the Exchequer of the Jews ultimately came into being. In France, in 1206, it was ordered that in every town one notary should be appointed to record all Jewish debts, and it was not until 1361, when the Government was anxious to do all it could to encourage Jewish usury, that permission was given to any notary to perform this function. In Spain official notaries also appear at the beginning of the thirteenth century[2]. In France additional precautions were taken, in that specially trustworthy citizens were deputed to hold seals whose attachment to the deed alone gave it validity[3]. In Germany Jews seem to have been left free to write and seal their own documents[4]; and in the beginning of the fourteenth century, in Aragon, Jews were allowed to act as official notaries[5]. But both in England and in France a document not properly sealed and drawn up by Christian clerks invalidated the claim of the Jew to repayment.

It is interesting to note that in its losing battle against usury the Church attempted to reduce the ill by forbidding clerics to record Jewish debts[6], and also by forbidding the chests containing the records being housed in churches, often the only places of security[7].

In spite of the fact that it was well known that many usurers exceeded the limit of interest allowed, there seems to have been no effort to circumvent this practice by prescribing the actual phrases in which debts were to be recorded. If a case actually came into court, the Jew might be unable to claim the excess, for the common practice was for the creditor to state on oath the capital, and the debtor the interest, but the actual deed almost universally recorded only a single sum, and the usurers themselves only recorded

---

[1] Jacobs, *op. cit.*, pp. 156 ff.; see section 1 above.

[2] Regné, *Catalogue*, Nos. 5, 131, etc.; REJ, LX, pp. 163, 186, etc.

[3] Charter of Philip Augustus, clause viii, Laurière, I, p. 45.

[4] Charter of Frederick of Austria, clause xxv, see App. I, No. vii.

[5] Regné, *Catalogue*, Nos. 2556 and 3081; REJ, LXXV, p. 158, and LXXVII, p. 183.

[6] Poitiers, 1280, vi; Mansi, XXIV, c. 384.

[7] Oxford, 1222, xi; Mansi, XXII, c. 1172.

the same in their own accounts[1]. The usual statement was that such a sum was due on such a day, and in this sum both capital and usury were confounded.

VI. THE SECURITY AND PROTECTION OF THE CREDITOR

Nowhere is the royal interest in the whole business more apparent than in the contrast between the judicial protection accorded to the creditor, and the lack of provision for the safeguarding of the debtor. It was customary in various chanceries of Europe for specimens of letters in common use to be preserved. In such a German collection is to be found a specimen of a letter to the debtors of a Jew, ordering them to pay immediately what they owe or make a satisfactory composition with him of their debt, and threatening them with the direst penalties should they refuse or fail to do so[2]. There is no evidence that there was any such routine preparation for the defence of a debtor. In almost every case the evidence of the creditor was accepted in preference to his. As early as 1208 Innocent III complained that the Count of Nevers and others like him refused to allow the most reputable witnesses against a Jew[3]. The debtor could only summon the creditor in a court belonging to the guardian of the Jews or the king, and could not bring him before the ordinary magistrates of his city. In the French charters of 1361 and the following years, the protection of the Jews was extended to such a point that even these special magistrates were expressly refused the power even to allow a delay in the time appointed for repayment[4].

The main reason for the insistence with which charters promised complete judicial security to the Jewish moneylender was fear, not of the debtor, but of the Church. She could be guaranteed always to be on his side, and to do all in her power to prevent him from being legally obliged to

[1] See the books of Elias of Vesoul; REJ, IX, pp. 33 ff.

[2] A. Warschauer, *Mitteilungen aus einem mittelalterlichen Formelbuche*; ZGJD, IV, p. 277.

[3] *Ep. Innocentii*, X, 190, ed. Baluze.

[4] E.g. Laurière, IV, p. 237; cf. Petition of the Jews of Lerida in 1400 (Baer, *Aragon*, No. 472).

pay the interest of his debt. A good example of the conflicts which thus arose occurred between Philip Augustus and Innocent III, over the Crusade against the Cathari. Philip received a letter from the Pope ordering that the property of Crusaders should remain intact and under the protection of the Church during their absence; that the clergy should protect them from usury; and that the secular arm should compel Jews to disgorge any profits which they had already made out of them. Philip wrote to Odo, Duke of Burgundy, and asked his advice on the matter. Odo strongly advised him to resist the Pope since, if he yielded, he and his barons would lose the just profits of their own property[1]. In the same spirit, and with even more directness, Blanche, Countess of Champagne, arrested Erard of Brienne on his way to the Crusade because he owed money to her Jews[2]. Four years later the Pope was still insisting that the clergy must compel by ecclesiastical penalties the barons to cancel the interest due from Crusaders to their Jews[3]. But the king would not give way, and in 1214 firmly ordered that Crusaders, before leaving their homes, should pay all their taxes and settle any debts 'hominibus nostris', that is to his Jews, or leave adequate security for their payment from the revenues of their lands[4].

The Church did not admit herself beaten, and the princes did not intend to make concessions. In the diocese of Auxerre the quarrel reached the point where the bishop excommunicated those who obeyed the Count, and laid their land under an interdict, and the Count replied by imprisoning those who obeyed the bishop[5]. In the royal demesne the officials, only a year after the death of Saint Louis, were busy carrying out the policy of Philip Augustus. A council meeting at S. Quentin in 1271 bitterly complained that:

> . . . a reading of the constitutions of the Church makes it quite clear that laymen have no authority to decide in Church matters, but we have clear evidence from many

[1] Teulet, I, No. 768, p. 292.
[2] Ibid., No. 1474, p. 526. For the settlement of the question, see No. 1479, p. 532.
[3] Ibid., No. 899, p. 340.
[4] Laurière, I, p. 32.
[5] See above, p. 357, n. 3

sides that the audacity of certain secular princes has reached such a pitch that, if Jews complain that any ecclesiastical person is indebted to them, forthwith, without even asking leave of the Bishop, without proof and without confession, his goods are seized for the compulsory payment of his debts. Since this is contrary to both canon and civil law, and since it is also unreasonable in itself that the enemies of the Crucified should be better placed than Christians, we ordain that any prelate, in whose jurisdiction such behaviour occurs, shall proceed to inflict ecclesiastical penalties until restitution is made both for the pecuniary loss and for the insult offered[1].

In England, in the reign of Henry III, the protection of the royal courts was extended still further; the Church was unable even to secure the trial of Jews in cases where they were accused of ecclesiastical offences[2].

In the examination of the implications of the Jew being private property, in the review of the charters, and in the discussion of the situation of Jews and Christians in legal cases, ample evidence has been given of the universality of the struggle of which the thirteenth-century conflict in France is a single example. Throughout, the owners of Jewries made but the minimum concessions, and these only temporarily, to the needs of the debtor, whether they were brought to their notice by riots, by petition or by the action of the Church. No permanent readjustment of the scales was ever secured. The barons who compelled John to sign Magna Carta included a clause protecting the estate, the widow and the heirs of deceased debtors, but they did nothing for living ones[3]. German towns did something for their own citizens, but they ignored the needs of peasants[4]. The kings of Spain made a concession to one town, but they ignored it in dealing with another, even when they were not bribed to withdraw it from a town which had already received it.

All that can be pleaded on the other side is that revenue

---

[1] Mansi, XXIV, c. 20.

[2] Merton, 1258, and Lambeth, 1261; Mansi, XXIII, cc. 980 and 1067.

[3] Magna Carta, clause xi.

[4] Cf. Scheid, *op. cit.*, pp. 96 and 53; and Weiss, *Die Juden in Strassburg*, p. 4, n. 2.

from the Jews was an important part of royal income. Figures do not exist for anything like a detailed study of the amount contributed by the Jews to the revenues of different states, but in particular circumstances it might be more than one-third of the total received from a single tax[1]; and it must often have been between a tenth and a twentieth of the annual revenue. Further, in addition to such regular sums, the presence of Jews always offered the possibility of a special tallage in emergency.

In such circumstances it is easy to understand that sovereigns who were perpetually in debt were not likely to forgo this income. They protected their Jews unscrupulously against the Church, the towns, and the peasants, and when public clamour rose to too high a pitch, and they were obliged to yield, they affected complete innocence and expressed their Christian horror at the monstrous iniquity of usury. Perhaps, with their ignorance of scientific economics, they rarely did connect themselves with the results which they produced, and really thought it a heroic sacrifice when they yielded some of their income for the common good. But a system whereby a considerable proportion of the royal revenue was drawn not from the prosperity, but from the indebtedness of the subject, remains a monument of curious incompetence.

VII. THE RUINOUS EFFECT OF USURY

Nowhere is the difference between the modern and the medieval situation more striking than when usury is considered from this aspect. For it meant that it was not the prosperous farmer who was taxed most heavily, but the farmer who could not make both ends meet; not the successful squire, but the waster; the peasant, not when his crops were good, but when they failed; the artisan, not when he sold his wares, but when he could not find a market. Not unnaturally, a century of such a system was more than any community could stand, and the story of Jewish usury is a continuous alternation of invitation, protection, protestation and condemnation.

[1] Cf. the figures in Zimmels, *op. cit.*, p. 34, and Stobbe, pp. 51 ff.

Jewish moneylending reached important proportions in England in the middle of the twelfth century; in 1189 and 1190 there were massacres throughout the country, beginning in London and extending to Dunstable, Lynn, Stamford, Norwich, York, Bury St. Edmunds, Colchester, Thetford and Ospringe[1]. The classes which were primarily responsible for the riots were those most deeply indebted, the lesser baronage, the knights and the burghers; and the rioters often made their purpose perfectly clear by carefully seeking out and destroying the Jewish records of their indebtedness.

The earliest surviving French moneylending charter dates from 1206, and it is unlikely that the profession became important much before the second half of the twelfth century. By 1223 Louis VIII had to cancel all usury, and allow debtors three years to pay off the capital[2]. Saint Louis, when he came to the throne, found the evil just as great as before, and actually expelled the Jews in 1253. But before the end of his reign he readmitted them, while not allowing them to practise usury. The command was so effectively obeyed that in 1291 Philip the Fair had to exclude them from access to the peasants, whom they had ruined[3]. They were expelled from France in 1306 and returned in 1315. By 1322 usury had to be reduced to a penny because of the utter ruin of the poor[4]. In Spain the same history was repeated, though moratoria took the place of expulsion; and the cities of Germany, Austria and Bohemia had the same tale to tell.

But the lesson seems never to have been learnt for, after the first movement had completed its evolution, it was only to repeat itself again. The expelled Jews were allowed to return. Their exactions again ruined their debtors. More riots; a new expulsion; and all the time the princes clung up to the last possible minute to the profit which they drew from the hated presence of the usurer.

However much emphasis be laid on theoretical considerations or Biblical verses, the Church had no need of such props in her fight against the evil. She was right in her

---

[1] Hyamson, *op. cit.*, pp. 31-41.
[2] Laurière, I, p. 47.
[3] G. Saige, *Les Juifs de Languedoc*, p. 223.
[4] Laurière, II, p. 84.

statement that once the principle were allowed ' in a few years ' the wealth of the Christian was exhausted[1].

The Church recognised that the princes were largely responsible, and implored them not to show themselves enemies of their Christian subjects, but rather to keep their Jews within bounds. But it is doubtful if the princes realised their responsibility, or that it lay in their power to mitigate the evil, not by refusing to permit moneylending, but by abating their demands upon the profit. The step which they took was a futile one. They made concessions to reduce usury, but the demand for enormous tallages continued, and, in addition, the Jew was still expected to purchase every privilege which he was able to obtain.

The mere formal statement of the maximum usury allowable was of little value, though the charters of England, France and Spain all continued to state a maximum, whether one, two, three or fourpence per pound per week, or, in Spain, $33\frac{1}{3}$ per cent. per year. In France two other methods were employed in the thirteenth century. In the earliest charter of the kind which we possess[2] is the definite statement, made in such a way that it implied that it was already an established practice, that ' a debt cannot accumulate usury during more than one year '. The rate allowed in the same charter is twopence per week, so that the maximum which a man could be called upon to pay for a debt of £1 would be £1 8s. 6d., however long he took in his payment[3]. Unless debts were promptly paid, this was not a very profitable return for the creditor, and it is not surprising to find that this system met with little success, especially as the same charter also allowed the debtor a certain time after the debt was contracted to repay it without usury at all[4]. What the length of time was we have no means of knowing, but even if it was only a few days, it operated to reduce the net gain on the transaction.

Concurrently with this system there was another in force,

---

[1] Lateran IV, c. lxvii; Mansi, XXII, c. 1054.

[2] Laurière, XI, p. 315. See App. I, v.

[3] In Strasbourg, in 1375, it was only allowed to accumulate for six months. The rate was twopence per week. Scheid, op. cit., p. 53.

[4] This was probably an attempt to legalise 'usury' by assimilating it to ' interest '. See above, pp. 295 ff,

by which the usury, at whatever rate it accumulated, was
never allowed to exceed the capital[1]. Inasmuch as these
systems did not distinguish between honest inability to pay,
and mere unwillingness to do so, but penalised the creditor
in regard to both, it is natural that the latter proceeded to
discover methods of evasion. Evasion on paper seems at
this period to have been difficult. Special notaries had been
set apart under public control for the registration and writing
of IOU's, and they required the seal of a public official in
order to have their validity. In neither case could the Jew,
therefore, enforce in a court of law a claim to more than one
year's usury by the first system, or a sum of usury greater
than the original loan by the second. The evasion consisted
in making a verbal agreement with the debtor. The simplest
way was for the lender to give him less money in cash than
was actually stated in the deed[2]. To overcome this device,
both creditor and debtor were made to take an oath that the
sum given and received corresponded to that inscribed by
the notary; and *both* were liable to punishment if the statement was found to be false. Another method practised by
the usurer was to make a private agreement about the rate of
interest, the creditor refusing to make the loan at all unless
the debtor paid him a higher rate than the law allowed or he
was able legally to enforce. Traces of this may be seen in
the frequently repeated order that a creditor must accept
repayment, and surrender his pawn, when the debtor tenders
him the capital together with the interest inscribed in the
bond. It is difficult to explain in any other way the unusual
spectacle of a debtor desiring to pay and a creditor refusing
acceptance[3].

As the pressure of royal exactions increased, and the goodwill between the Jews and their neighbours diminished,
cunning and unscrupulous evasions became commoner and,
as the bias of judicial protection became more and more
impossible to maintain in the face of popular resentment,
they became more necessary if the royal demands were to be
met. Already in 1228, when usury was only beginning in

[1] E.g., Customal of Montpellier, 1204, clause cxvi; Teulet, I, No. 721,
p. 264.

[2] Cf. Laurière, I, p. 44, c. 6.

[3] E.g., *ibid.*, clause ii,

northern Europe, and when the Jews in Aragon were still receiving extensive privileges, the inhabitants of the Aragonese Province of Roussillon were protesting so vigorously that James I ordered the courts to discountenance any Jew's statement as to his loans, even made on oath, unless it was supported by documents or absolutely reliable witnesses[1]. How long the inhabitants of Roussillon retained their privilege we do not know, but in 1317 those of Montpellier were complaining that whenever there was a dispute as to the interest due—and they complained bitterly of the rate allowed—the Jew was allowed to settle the question by a statement on oath which the Christian could not challenge[2], and this in spite of the fact that a council at Montpellier had forbidden Christian judges to hear any case brought by a Jew against a Christian, and had ordered them to accept the statement of a Christian, on his simple oath, that the whole amount which the Jew demanded of him was usury[3].

It is easier to understand these Utopian canons, when examples exist to prove that, when they had the power, the owners not only ignored the laws governing the maximum interest, but even gave legal protection to the Jews in their evasions. The classic example of this occurs during the last sojourn of the Jews in France, when, in response to their complaint that it was difficult for them to collect their loans, and that they had lost heavily in the riots which their exactions had caused, the Crown in the first place forbade any royal judge to hear cases against Jews for ten years, even if they had not only exceeded the legal maximum, but were charging that which medieval law hardly ever allowed, compound interest, and, in the second place, cancelled all cases already determined against them[4].

But such magnificent complaisance was rarely to be relied on, and the normal situation was that, as royal or ecclesiastical action made one method of evasion difficult, another was immediately invented. A neat dodge in a period where dozens of currencies ran side by side, with different values

---

[1] P. Vidal, *Les Juifs de Roussillon et de Cerdagne*; REJ, XV, p. 40; cf. Customal of Carcassonne, clause liv, Teulet, I, No. 743, p. 278.

[2] Laurière, XI, p. 447.

[3] Canon v; Mansi, XXIII, c. 992.

[4] See Ordinances of 1387 and 1388; Laurière, VII, pp. 171 and 225.

for coins bearing the same name, was to inscribe in the deed payment in the currency of Tournai, Paris, or some other coin at that moment of value, but to give the debtor his loan in a less valuable coinage with the same name[1]. Much could also be done by employing dishonest notaries, since the majority of debtors could not read[2], and in Dauphiné at the end of the fourteenth century this evasion was said to have reached such perfection with such disastrous results that ' a large proportion of the population has had all its property foreclosed upon, is unable to pay its land and other taxes to the Dauphin, or support any other public charges, and numbers have had to leave their homes and earn their livings as mercenaries, or go into exile from their country '[3].

Another favourite method was to disguise the loan as a sale. The debtor sold the creditor some article for a low price, and signed an obligation to repurchase it at a much larger one. This method became so commonplace that no actual object changed hands whatever. But the commonest method of all was simply to state in the deed that a certain sum would be due on a certain date, so that it was impossible to tell what loan had actually been granted, and what proportion was interest.

The effort to control the evil by limitation was thus an obvious failure. It only bred ever more skilful evasions. A more direct method, and one which was more favoured by the Church, was the direct cancellation of all usury whatever. There is nothing which shows more clearly how little normal economic considerations enter into the history of medieval moneylending, especially when it directly profited the privy purse. For while it may be possible to evolve a form of society in which needy citizens obtain temporary loans without paying interest, it is obvious that the making of such loans at their own expense cannot be a whole-time profession for individuals within that society. By this menace, however, the Jew, who was almost excluded from every other occupation, who was expected to pay extensive taxes both to the Crown and the Church, who was allowed,

---

[1] See the efforts of Philip IV to deal with this in 1311. Laurière, I, p. 484, clause v, and p. 494, clause v.

[2] *Ibid.*, VIII, p. 57.

[3] *Ibid.*

indeed compelled, to lend money to those who asked for it, was not to be allowed to make any charge for the service[1]. For usury was *everything* which was added to the original sum lent.

Throughout the thirteenth century the Church struggled to insist upon the impossible. General and provincial councils included the Jews again and again in the prohibition of all interest and menaced the secular powers with excommunication if they failed to assist[2]. Christian judges were forbidden ever to enforce the payment of usury to a Jew[3]. The debtors themselves were threatened with the same penalty if they dared to pay it[4]. Jews who attempted to charge it were to be excluded from any kind of contact with Christians[5]. In France the Church had also the support of the secular power in the persons of Louis VIII, Louis IX, and Philip IV, all of whom passed ordinances against it[6].

After the thirteenth century, much less is heard of this method of coping with the evil. It reappears in Dauphiné in 1339, and again in 1342, but this time with the modification that with the permission of the Dauphin usury might be charged[7]. And when for a moment Charles V of France thought of expelling the Jews in 1367, he issued an order that the capital of all debts should be paid, but no interest[8].

The cause of the failure of these efforts is seen in one of the last canons dealing with the subject. The Council of Poitiers in 1280, after forbidding Christians to pay usury to the Jews when they borrowed from them, is compelled to add ' *but if necessity compels the Christian*. . . . [9]' Beggars cannot be choosers, and to go to a moneylender and say

---

[1] Paris, 1212; Mansi, XXII, c. 851. Lateran IV, *ibid.*, c. 1054 f. Avignon, 1209, *ibid.*, c. 786. Bordeaux, 1214; E. Gaullieur, *Notes sur les Juifs à Bordeaux*; REJ, XI, p. 82. Beziers, 1246; Mansi, XXIII, c. 701, and 1255, xxiii; *ibid.*, c. 882, etc.

[2] Beziers, 1255, xxviii; Mansi, XXIII, c. 883, etc.

[3] Innocent III, *Ep. ad Fideles Moguntiae*; Mansi, XXII, c. 958. Albi, 1254, lxiii; *ibid.*, XXIII, c. 850; Montpellier, 1258, v; *ibid.*, c. 992, etc.

[4] *Odonis Stat.*, add. 1; Mansi, XXII, c. 685, etc.

[5] Innocent III, *Ep. ad Fideles Moguntiae*; Mansi, XXII, c. 958.

[6] Laurière, I, pp. 47, 53, 333.

[7] Prudhomme, *Histoire des Juifs en Dauphiné*, p. 147.

[8] Col. doc., *Mandements de Charles V*, p. 216.

[9] Poitiers, vi; Mansi, XXIV, c. 384.

' lend me five pounds, but I will pay you no interest ', was as Utopian in the thirteenth century as it would be in the twentieth.

VIII. THE CONFISCATION AND CANCELLATION OF DEBTS

Limitation was a failure. The prohibition of interest proved Utopian, whether decreed by kings or councils. There was, however, a drastic way of enforcing it. This was to seize all the Jews on a prearranged day, confiscate all their papers, appoint commissioners to survey their operations, and then to collect as far as possible the sums originally loaned. The ultimate destination of such sums was more likely to be the treasury than the coffers of the Jewish creditor, but at least it brought some relief to the debtor. The method was tried in various countries, and at various times. What is difficult is to discover whether popular or royal necessity dictated it.

In England in the first half of the thirteenth century the seizure of the Jews was certainly entirely a financial measure dictated by the needs of the royal party in the conflicts of John and the Barons, and later in the struggle around Simon de Montfort, who himself, as a counter move, cancelled all debts owing to the Jews in 1264[1]. It is more difficult to be sure as to the cause of the contemporary events in France. In 1223 Louis VIII and his barons made an agreement on the subject of the Jews, of which one clause ran that no interest was to be collected, but that the debtors were to pay the capital of their debts in three instalments, not to the Jewish creditors, but to the barons to whom they belonged[2]. In theory the baron then handed it over to the Jew, but in practice part or all of it is likely to have remained in his coffers.

The confiscation ordered by his successor, Saint Louis, was certainly not conditioned by any financial motives, for the king not only remitted a portion of the capital[3], but

---

[1] Hyamson, *History of the Jews in England*, 2nd ed., p. 75. The authority is unfortunately not given.

[2] Laurière, I, p. 47.

[3] *Ibid.*, p. 54.

repaid from the royal coffers interest that had already been paid[1]. He would not even retain sums for which no owners could be found, and continued the search for them until both the Pope and the Archbishop of Paris assured him that the money could be spent on charity without sin—and the archbishop was very willing to undertake the responsibility of so spending it[2]. These first experiences of confiscation on a large scale proved very slow and costly affairs. Ten years after the edict of Louis, Alphonse of Poitiers, the king's brother and governor of all the west of France, was still occupied with sorting out the property of royal and baronial Jews, with giving instructions for the digging up of all the cellars in the houses where they had lived, and with calming indignant owners either of Jews or of pledges[3]. When in the fourteenth century the process was several times repeated with both Jewish and Christian usurers, the difficulties seem to have occupied special commissioners for most of the century[4].

The violent confiscation of records, and the collection of the capital of the loans recorded, was not only a failure, but involved a costly administration. There remained still one arrow in the quiver of uneconomic methods of dealing with an economic problem—the cancellation of the debts, in part or in whole. Needless to say, this was a still more expensive measure, unless the debts were owing to the Jews of someone else. It was therefore a popular measure with rebels and pretenders. When Simon de Montfort generously cancelled debts owing the Jews in 1264, it was Henry III, and not himself, who would suffer from his act. Henry of Trastamare, claimant to the throne of Castile, also cancelled the debts owing to the Jews but, on obtaining the throne, found that it meant an empty treasury, since the Jews made it clear to him that no recovery of loans meant no payment of taxes. He therefore immediately cancelled the cancellation and,

[1] E.g. £600 were paid out of the treasury to debtors in Touraine in 1260. See L. Lazard, *Les Juifs de Touraine*; REJ, XVII, p. 213, n. 4.

[2] Letter to Louis of Reginald, Abp. of Paris, and Bulls of Alexander IV; Teulet, III pp. 473 and 401.

[3] Col. doc., *Correspondance d'Alphonse de Poitiers*, Nos. 646-650, 888, etc.

[4] See, e.g., Laurière, I, pp. 443 (1306), 470 (1309), 489 (1311), 553 (1315), 604 (1315); XI, p. 435 (1315); II, p. 59 (1330), etc.

when the outcry from the country ruined by the civil war made some retraction inevitable, he reduced but did not cancel them again[1].

The French authorities resorted to cancellation as opposed to confiscation on three occasions. Philip Augustus cancelled the debts owed to the Jews when he expelled them in 1182[2]; Saint Louis finally cancelled debts after some years of attempting to settle the difference between capital and usury[3]; and in the final expulsion, after the Crown had done all it could to maintain its revenues from the Jews, it had to resort to the same expedient[4]. On one occasion at least even the French Church attempted to enforce the cancellation of debts. In 1280, the year in which the Council of Poitiers was trying to prevent the payment of usury, a council in the neighbouring province of Saintonge excommunicated any judge who enforced any payment of a debt to a Jew, even though the Jew produced full documentary evidence of the obligation[5].

But the classical country of debt cancellation is Germany. The earliest known example is given by Rudolf I, who in 1290 cancelled all the debts owing to Salmon of Mulhouse, ' owing to his enormous extortion '[6]. In other cases individual debtors secured the cancellation of their debts from German princes as English debtors had from Henry III. In the fourteenth century, when the possession of Jews was a right enjoyed by many princes and cities, a considerable traffic in cancellations took place[7]. In 1385 King Wenceslas, in agreement with thirty-eight important cities, cancelled all usury on debts owing to Jews, and a quarter of the capital. For this concession the king received 40,000 guilders[8]. Finding this a profitable course, in 1390 he conceded to the Duke of Bavaria and to other Bavarian, Swabian and

---

[1] M. Kayserling, *Note sur l'histoire des Juifs en Espagne*; REJ, XXXIII, p. 148.
[2] William the Breton, *Philippide*, I, verses 367 f.; Bouquet, XVII, p. 126.
[3] Col. doc., *Correspondance d'Alphonse de Poitiers*, No. 817; cf. No. 1027, where at one and the same time Alphonse orders pledges to be returned on payment of capital, and forbids courts to take up any complaints of Jews re non-payment.
[4] Laurière, VIII, pp. 64, clause xi, and 181.
[5] Saintes, c. xiii; Mansi, XXIV, c. 379.
[6] S. Adler, *Juden in Mülhausen*, pp. 5 ff.
[7] A. Süssmann, *Die Judenschuldentilgungen unter K. Wenzel*, pp. 44 ff.
[8] *Ibid.*, pp. 32 ff.

BB

Franconian authorities the right to stop all repayment to Jews, in return for the payment of a proportion of the debts to himself; the local authorities were also entitled to take a share of them[1]. From Regensburg alone he received 15,000 guilders for this grant[2], but when some cities withheld his commission he refused to allow them to profit by the cancellation[3]. All that the unfortunate Jews could do in return was to plead that this made the payment of the ' golden penny ' impossible[4].

It is curious to contrast the frequency with which the princes and cities of northern Europe, when cancellation had failed, resorted to expulsion, with the continuous period of Jewish settlement in the Spanish Peninsula. One reason for this is certainly the greater variety of Jewish occupations in Castile and Aragon. The Jews were always active in many occupations other than moneylending, even if the latter played an important rôle from the twelfth century onwards. But the main reason is the system of moratoria which was continually applied. Though the Jews complained bitterly against them, they were obviously never completely ruined by them, and for this the variety of their occupations, already referred to, was responsible. Even though the normal usury under James I of Aragon was only twenty per cent.[5], moratoria of several years' duration were sometimes granted to Christian debtors. On one occasion this did lead to the flight of considerable numbers of Jews from the country[6]; but they soon returned, for, with the greatest skill, moratoria and promises to grant no moratoria were so evenly distributed that the inhabitants were preserved from ruin and the Jews from flight. Further, the sovereigns were readier than their northern cousins to remit portions of the taxes due to them from their Jews, when they were convinced that the alternative was likely to be serious[7]. The result of this

---

[1] A. Süssmann, op. cit., pp. 109 ff.
[2] Wiener, Regesten, No. 360, p. 156. This was supposed to represent 15 per cent. of the debts.
[3] Ibid., No. 363.
[4] Cf. ibid., No. 370, p. 157.
[5] Cf. Regné, Catalogue, Nos. 4, 10, 37, etc.; REJ, LX, pp. 162, 164, 169.
[6] Ibid., No. 94; p. 179.
[7] Regné, Catalogue, gives so many documents dealing with this question that it is useless to quote them. They will be found on every page.

finesse was that, though complete cancellation was not resorted to, there was very little actual violence shown against the Jews until the end of the fourteenth century, and it was then due to religious rather than economic hostility.

Elsewhere, violence remained the last resort of the debtor who was ruined, or who considered himself to be so; and the bankrupt was ably seconded in his actions by the mass of debtors who merely disliked paying their debts. The terrible massacre of York in 1190 culminated in the destruction of the archives of the York Jewry[1]; the riots against the Jews which accompanied the outbreak of the war between Henry III and his barons in 1262 were the result of indebtedness. The Jewries of London, Worcester, Northampton, Canterbury, Lincoln and Ely were all sacked, and everywhere the records were destroyed[2]. In France the riots of 1380 were due to the same cause, and the German cities record countless instances of the debtors' resorting to violence.

A further point of interest in the riots in England during the thirteenth century may be noticed. The destruction of the deeds and property of the Jew had a political as well as an economic motive. Not only were debtors anxious to avoid payment, but the barons were anxious to cut off supplies from the king, whose ability to collect money out of the Jews was notorious. By destroying this source of wealth, they were able to reduce his power of opposing them. Their predecessors in the days of John had behaved in the same way, and the first act of the struggle which led to the signing of Magna Carta was the destruction of the rich Jewry of London, and of all the wealth which might have assisted their royal adversary.

IX. THE JEWS AND THE RANSOM OF JOHN II OF FRANCE

So far the various efforts to deal with the evils of usury have been considered without reference to any one particular time or place. To give the same picture from the standpoint

[1] William of Newburgh, *Historia*, in *Chronicles of the Reign of Stephen*, etc., ed. Rolls Series, I, p. 322.

[2] Tovey, *Anglia Judaica*, pp. 159 ff.

of a single situation will show with what rapidity the different forces came into play. From the many which might be chosen, the period from 1361 to 1395 in France offers various advantages, since the documents available are somewhat comprehensive. In 1358 John, who had been captured at the battle of Poitiers, accepted a treaty, ratified the following year, by which *inter alia* he undertook to pay a ransom of four, later reduced to three, million gold crowns. The country had fallen into an unhappy condition; jacqueries of peasants were common, and suppressed with much bloodshed; from 1360 to 1364 the harvests were bad, and there were outbreaks of plague. In 1361 the Jews, who had for two generations been excluded from France, were re-admitted—for a consideration[1],—allowed to lend money at 87 per cent., which was double the rate previously valid in the country, and were given the fullest protection by the authorities.

By 1363 the protests against the behaviour of the Jews caused the king to issue ordinances compelling them to wear their badge[2], and depriving them of their special courts, ' because of the awful abuses to which they have given rise '. They were also deprived of the right to imprison their debtors[3]. Emboldened by these concessions, the public, especially in the south, refused to pay their debts at all. This, however, the Crown did not intend to accept. Its concessions were only intended to make the way of the moneylender easier, by making him less unpopular. Officials were ordered to compel people to pay their debts, in spite of any document they might produce granting them remission or delay[4]. The clergy replied to the enforcement of this order by excommunicating the Jews, and forbidding any Christian to sell them any of the necessities of life. They are also said to have encouraged their parishioners to violence against them and, whether due to the clergy or not, riots broke out in various places. As a result the revenue which the Crown expected to draw from the Jews of the south disappeared. In great indignation the king ordered

---

[1] See above, p. 175.
[2] Laurière, III, pp. 603 and 642.
[3] *Ibid.*, p. 642.
[4] *Ibid.*, IV, p. 237.

THE JEWISH USURER 373

his officers to enforce the payment of debts[1], and to proceed with the utmost severity against both laity and clergy if they were interfering with Jewish business and security.

For two years this policy succeeded, but at such a cost that in the third year the king was compelled to yield to his subjects. The expulsion of the Jews was ordered; all interest due to them was cancelled; only the capital might be collected[2]. Neither the order of expulsion nor the order cancelling it have survived, nor do we know whether heavy bribes, or increasing expenditure, led to its revocation. The Jews remained, but for some years their status seems to have been undefined. Then in 1370 the charter of 1361 was re-issued[3]. But in a very short time, 'for certain and just causes', it was suspended, and the Jews were cited before the Prévôt of Paris by the Royal Procurator, to answer for the crimes 'committed against their privileges to the harm and damage of the state and of our subjects'[4].

In 1372 they obtained a new grant of the privilege of 1361, and a general order to royal officials to protect them in their lawful business. But certain limitations were imposed. The badge was to be worn. They might travel through, but not conduct business in, places where they did not reside. Above all, their oath was not to be valid against proved evidence to the contrary[5]. For a couple of years they prospered, and the wealthier ones were able to buy from the king personal privileges, releasing them from their share in the communal tallages. But again tranquillity was short lived. War and internal difficulties necessitated heavy taxation, and by 1375 the people began to get restive. Certain taxes were abolished to calm the public temper. The deficit was probably demanded from the Jews, for the next document in the series is a complaint that they are unable to bear the increased burden, and a request for the cancellation of all exemptions granted to individuals. The latter was acceded to[6]. But it would

---

[1] Laurière, IV, p. 440.
[2] Col. doc., *Mandements de Charles V*, p. 216.
[3] Laurière, V, p. 490.
[4] *Ibid.*, p. 497.
[5] *Ibid.*, p. 498.
[6] *Ibid.*, VI, p. 173.

appear that Jewish prosperity was beginning to decline[1], for there began about this period a steady influx of Lombards, with permits to settle and to establish monopolies in various cities[2]. Important commercial centres of the north fell into their hands, Amiens, Abbeville and Meaux in 1378, Troyes in 1380; and in 1382 they were allowed to establish themselves in Paris. As a result, the Jews began to lose their business at the Champagne fairs, the most important financial centres of the country, and appealed to the king for protection against what they considered to be unjust discrimination[3]. But this was not their only grievance, for they complained that they had to suffer from the accusations and denunciations of converts from Judaism, and that they required special protection from arbitrary arrest, imprisonment and menaces[4].

At this time Charles V died, and Louis Duke of Anjou, acting as regent for the boy king Charles VI, granted the Jews an extension for six years of their original privilege of 1361; and especially urged their protection upon his officials, in order that they might make sufficient profit to pay up the arrears of their debts to the Crown[5]. This, however, was not a fortunate moment to extend any special protection to so unpopular a trade; public opinion was in a state of ferment owing to the general misrule and the extortion of tax-collectors, and in Paris and elsewhere there were serious riots throughout 1380. In this disorder the Jews suffered severely; many were killed, the houses of more were sacked, their pledges were stolen, their deeds were burned[6].

Their unpopularity with their debtors was not likely to be lessened by a concession which they immediately secured to protect themselves. By a new grant they had only to state on oath that a pledge deposited with them had been destroyed in the riot, and they were quit of any obligation to make

---

[1] When required to make a loan of 20,000 gold francs and a payment of 200 gold francs per week, they were only able to do so by the remission of all other taxes (Laurière, VI, p. 339).

[2] *Ibid.*, pp. 335, 477, etc.

[3] *Ibid.*, p. 439.

[4] *Ibid.*, p. 340.

[5] *Ibid.*, p. 521.

[6] Col. doc., *Chron. de S. Denys*, I, vi and vii, pp. 45 ff.

compensation for its loss[1]. In spite of this, six years later the Jews of the royal demesne found themselves entirely unable to meet the heavy demands made upon them, and appealed to the king for permission to secure from the Jews of Languedoc, who had suffered less from murder and pillage in the riots, contributions for the payment of tallages and taxes imposed on the whole community. This the Crown, anxious for its revenues, naturally granted[2]. But by itself it was not enough, for the Jews complained also that the debtors were given such facilities for delaying or refusing payment, that it was impossible for them to get in enough money to live on, even apart from the taxes which they loyally tried to pay[3]. The judges were therefore ordered to allow no one, except those who were actually engaged in military service, remission in their payments. Even this proved inadequate to produce the sums required by the Crown, for the judges were solidly on the side of the debtors and discovered so many infringements of the law committed by the Jews, and fined them so heavily for exceeding their legal maximum of interest or for charging compound interest, that their businesses were ruined[4]. At this point the Crown came down so firmly on the side of the Jews that royal judges and officials were forbidden to accept proceedings against them for any infringement of the laws which limited their usury or forbade compound interest. Unless the fabric of justice was to collapse entirely, so monstrous a concession could not long remain in operation, but the determination of the king to preserve his revenues resulted in an order in the following February (1389) quashing all proceedings against the Jews for crimes connected with usury[5].

Emboldened by such extraordinary complaisance, the Jews had made hay while the sun shone. They rented for their ' guardians ' a mansion at the gates of the Paris Jewry, and compelled all Christians to bring any cases against them to this court, where justice was administered at their

[1] Laurière, VI, p. 563.
[2] *Ibid.*, VII, p. 169.
[3] *Ibid.*, p. 170.
[4] *Ibid.*, p. 171.
[5] *Ibid.*, p. 225. The King of Aragon, Martin, acted in a similar way in the resettlement of the Jews at Lerida in 1400 after the riots of 1391 (Baer, *Aragon*, No. 472, clause xii; cf. No. 553, clause v).

convenience and in their favour. The guardians were even salaried by the Jews. This was going too far even for the revenue-seeking Crown, and only a week after they had succeeded in quashing all proceedings against themselves, this pleasant little family arrangement was suppressed *in toto*, the office of guardian abolished, and the Jews submitted to the ordinary royal courts[1].

The pendulum movement now demanded some concession to the Jews and, accordingly, when they again complained that they were unable to meet their obligations through their lack of power to enforce payment by their debtors, they were permitted to imprison them—a right rarely conceded[2] and explicitly refused a few months earlier at a time when the king was favourably inclined to their victims. It is to be imagined that the Church, which had already, twenty years previously, taken the lead in the south in opposing the extensive privileges originally granted, was aroused by this subjection of the persons of Christians to Jewish arrest, for the permission only lasted six months, and was then again cancelled[3]. In the north reaction was also rising. In 1393 the Jews complained that the populace was ' shouting insults and opprobrious remarks after them, was assaulting them, laying violent hands on them, knocking off their hats in the road, and attacking them with knives and sticks '. Royal officers were therefore ordered to publish anew the privileges under which they lived, and to see that they were strictly observed[4].

But to demand that the Jews should be left in peace, and at the same time to extort enormous sums from them, was to allow them the liberty to exploit their debtors unmercifully. It was time for the next swing of the pendulum. It came again from the south. Taking advantage of the privileges offered them, the Jews evaded the regular licences prescribed for their judicial proceedings, and secured various illegal privileges through their guardians. This abuse had already caused trouble once, but this time the king was quite clear that the practice must be stopped; the abuse in question was paid for, not by the debtors, but by the Crown, since the

---

[1] Laurière, VII, p. 226.
[2] Referred to *ibid.*, p. 589.
[3] *Ibid.*, p. 589.
[4] *Ibid.*, XII, p. 182.

chancery lost the revenue which it was accustomed to receive from the issue of licences[1]. Further, the Jews, relying on ancient immunities, had begun again to augment their usury above the legal maximum, and to charge compound interest as well. Thereupon the Prévôt of Paris proceeded to seize and imprison the wealthiest among them, and to arrest many others. Proceedings were started against them in the summer of 1394. For the sum of 6,000 francs, together with a promise to pay all the regular taxes imposed on them, the Jews succeeded in getting them quashed, and an amnesty granted for any irregularity of which they might have been guilty[2]. At the same time, and at their request, their special guardians and courts were abolished. Apparently they had been peculiarly venal, alternating between undue favour and excessive harshness towards both sides. The budgetary aspect of the question was very visible in the terms of the amnesty granted them, in that the king ordered no proceedings of any kind to be allowed against them until sufficient debts had been paid them back to provide the 6,000 francs—a fact which also reveals that by this time the Jews were simply living from hand to mouth.

It is therefore legitimate to assume that the sacrifice was not excessive when, three months later (September 1394), the king, ' moved by piety and fearing the evil influence of the Jews on Christians ', and objecting also to their many grave offences against the pockets of his subjects, decided to order their expulsion. A short delay was allowed for the settlement of debts, and then the Jews were to leave the country[3].

In the first order nothing was said as to whether the repayment of the debts was to include usury. The delay expired, and much money was still outstanding. This would not have moved the king but for the fact that the Jews of Languedoc still owed him money, and owed his cousin, Philip of Bar, 10,000 francs. Lest his cousin should lose this sum, the Jews were allowed a delay to collect that amount, and the seneschals were ordered to assist them, using force to the debtors if necessary[4].

[1] Laurière, VII, p. 580.
[2] Ibid., p. 643.
[3] Ibid., p. 675.
[4] Ibid., VIII, p. 32.

But before his unhappy cousin had succeeded in recovering the sum owed him, the king issued a further order cancelling all the debts outstanding, both capital and interest[1]. This naturally made it even more difficult for Philip to collect the money, so that the king was forced to issue an order allowing 10,000 francs' worth of debts to be collected to pay him. How the unfortunates were selected who were to be made to pay debts which had been already cancelled, the king did not say[2]. There must have been great relief when, the following year, the king ordered all deeds which could be discovered, and which might be considered to be still outstanding debts, to be collected and burnt[3].

So ended the last settlement of the Jews in medieval France.

X. THE RUIN AND EXPULSION OF THE USURER

Just as it is rarely possible to attribute a riot or massacre *exclusively* to a single motive, so also with the expulsions which were a recurrent feature of the period is it rarely possible to attribute any particular case exclusively to the single motive of usury. There are, however, many cases in which hatred of the usurer and popular indebtedness played a very predominant rôle.

The history of the Jews in France, from their recall in 1361 to their final expulsion in 1394-5, provided an admirable illustration of the rise and decline of a single period of settlement. The same country also provides the best example of successive cycles of settlement and expulsion over two hundred and fifty years. It has already been suggested that the period at which moneylending became a really important occupation lies somewhere in the second half of the twelfth century. Peter of Cluny does not refer to usury among the crimes of the Jews in 1146[4]; but in 1182 Philip Augustus, who had ascended the throne in 1180, decreed their expulsion. The incident is dealt with at length in a number of

---

[1] Laurière, VIII, p. 64, clause xi.
[2] *Ibid.*, p. 70.
[3] *Ibid.*, p. 181.
[4] See p. 343.

chronicles, and is variously explained[1]. It was only ten years after the ritual murder accusation of Blois[2], and Philip is said by Rigordus and his chaplain, William of Britanny, to have enquired whether the Jews really did murder and eat Christians, and being told that it was true, to have decided to expel them. Gislebert ascribes the expulsion to an enormous bribe offered by the Christians—presumably rival merchants. But three of the best accounts stress the enormous wealth which the Jews had acquired from their moneylending—the anonymous Chronicle of the Kings of France going so far as to say that they had obtained possession of half Paris —and the consequent distress of their Christian debtors. It is therefore legitimate to consider this an expulsion in which usury played the principal rôle. Their loans were cancelled, their land and houses confiscated to the king, and they were allowed to take with them only the proceeds of the sale of their furniture and merchandise. The first cycle was thus closed in the royal demesne.

In 1198 Fulco, a priest of the diocese of Paris, conducted a mission in Isle de France and the Nièvre, denouncing the luxury of the age and, in particular, the sin of usury. With this programme, he naturally fulminated against the Jews and, with the consent of the bishops, secured the cancellation of half of all the debts owing them and a short moratorium on the payment of the other half. Influenced by him, some of the barons actually expelled their Jews[3], and so completed the cycle in their territories also.

The second cycle opened with the refugees from the baronial territories, and those who had been ruined by the destruction of their profits, taking refuge in the royal demesne. They were allowed by Philip Augustus to remain there, to the great disapproval of the clergy[4]. It is probable that purely financial motives dictated this permission. Philip

---

[1] Gislebert, *Chron.*, s.a. 1180, MGH, SS, XXI, p. 529; Rigordus, *De Gestis Phil. Aug.*, s.a. 1182; cf. *Chron. S. Denys*, I, iii, Bouquet, XVII, pp. 8 ff., 350, and 352 ff.; William the Breton, *Philippide*, pp. 66 and 126; *Chron. Reg. Franc.*, s.a. 1180, *ibid.*, XII, p. 215.

[2] Ephraim bar Jacob in NS, pp. 199 ff.

[3] Robert of Auxerre, *Chron.*, s.a. 1198; MGH, SS, XXVI, p. 258.

[4] *Ibid.*, and Rigordus, s.a. 1198; Bouquet, XVII, pp. 48 and 49. William the Breton softens the condemnation expressed by Rigordus, *ibid.*, p. 73. Cf. also *Chron. of S. Denys, ibid.*, p. 385.

was no longer the boy of sixteen who had impulsively expelled them. He needed money to further his policy of extending the royal territories; and the charter which he granted them on their return was exclusively connected with their financial dealings. After a dozen years of usury the first signs of distress began to appear, and in the revised privilege of 1218 the peasantry were excluded from the sphere of Jewish operations and were allowed to pay their existing debts in three annual instalments. In 1223 Louis VIII, who had just come to the throne, took the familiar next step of prohibiting usury altogether. At the same time he expelled the Jews from Normandy, and made a treaty with his barons that neither would ever receive the Jews of the other. The attempt to regulate the relations of royal and baronial Jews dominated the policy of the thirteenth century, for vexatory measures were useless when territories under different authorities lay so close together[1]. Louis IX completed the second cycle in the royal demesne by expelling the Jews from it in about 1253[2] while he was on his return from his first crusade. Meanwhile, they had already been expelled from Brittany, and their loans cancelled, by Duke John, who acted from a mixture of religious, crusading and economic reasons[3]. In 1249 Alphonse de Poitiers, brother of Saint Louis, expelled them from Poitou and Saintonge[4], and in 1269 from Carpentras[5]. In 1288 they were expelled from Anjou and Maine[6]. In 1290 the English Jews, who had taken refuge within the French dominions, were expelled by Philip IV[7], and in 1291 they were expelled by the same king from all small towns and villages[8].

In all these expulsions it is to be presumed that the Jews moved no farther than was necessary, and did not leave the territory now comprised within the frontiers of France.

---

[1] On the relations of royal and baronial Jews cf. Regné, *La Condition des Juifs de Narbonne*; REJ, LIX, pp. 62 ff.

[2] Matthew Paris, *Chron. Maj.*, ed. Rolls Series, V, p. 361.

[3] L. Brunschwicg, *Les Juifs de Nantes*; REJ, XIV, p. 85; and *idem, Les Juifs d'Angers, ibid.*, XXIX, p. 233.

[4] Teulet, III, No. 3783, p. 73.

[5] Mossé, *Hist. des Juifs d'Avignon*, p. 87.

[6] *Les Juifs d'Angers*; REJ, XXIX, p. 238.

[7] Laurière, I, p. 317.

[8] G. Saige, *Les Juifs de Languedoc*, p. 223.

For as the second cycle was ending the third was concurrently beginning. The Jews were readmitted to the royal demesne some time before 1268 and to other parts of the kingdom at various dates. Philip IV recognised their presence, but forbade them to receive usury. In fact, their situation seems to have reverted to what it was before the first expulsion in 1182. From the copious documents dealing with the sale of their properties after their next expulsion in 1306, it is evident that they were prosperous, but it is also evident that they followed many commercial and industrial occupations. That they also lent at usury we have documents to prove[1]. The expulsion by Philip IV in 1306 completed the third cycle, but had nothing to do with moneylending. It was rather a barefaced seizure of their property similar to that practised by John of England in 1210. But it proved difficult to recover that part of the property which was represented by loans, and Jews had to be called back to assist the king in tracing these sums[2].

In 1311 a partial liquidation of debts took place, but when in 1315 the fourth cycle began, there were still valid outstanding debts of which the Jews were allowed to collect a part[3]. As had happened previously, the Jews had only fled across the frontier; they returned from Burgundy, Dauphiné and Provence, where they had taken refuge[4]. The fourth cycle was a very short one. Yielding to the request of the royal administration, and also of the nobility, Louis X in 1315 persuaded rather than allowed them to resettle[5]. They were encouraged to work with their hands, but allowed to charge twopence per week if by any chance they did lend money. But again it was not usury which caused their downfall within six years of their return—they had been promised twelve years, and then reasonable notice of expulsion if they were to be expelled—but an accusation that with the help of the lepers they had planned to poison the

[1] E.g. No. x, *Catalogue des Documents*, etc., ed. S. Luce, in REJ, II, p. 28.

[2] Laurière, I, p. 488.

[3] *Ibid.*, pp. 553 and 604.

[4] Prudhomme, *Hist. des Juifs en Dauphiné*, p. 139, and S. Kahn *Les Juifs de Tarascon*, REJ, XXXIX, p. 97.

[5] *Shebet Yehuda*, trans. M. Wiener, p. 91; cf. Laurière, I, p. 595, which gives as reason the ' commune clameur du peuple '.

wells. This was in 1321, and closed the fourth cycle prematurely. The fifth and final cycle has already been fully described and, like the first, their last expulsion was primarily due to usury.

If we compare these five cycles and their termination, we find two expulsions primarily due to usury and its ruinous effects on the population (1182 and 1394), one due to greed for their wealth (1306), one due to superstition (1321), and one due to genuine piety (1254). This kind of proportion would obtain if we considered in detail similar cycles in other countries.

While such an exhaustive survey is unnecessary, it is well to remember one factor connected with these expulsions which is of considerable importance for the general situation of the Jews at the time. However great their commercial ability, and however unscrupulous may have been their financial activities, the only possible result of any group being subjected to this treatment is complete ruin. In none of the cases quoted did the Jews leave the country with all their possessions, and very few cases exist elsewhere where such occurred. If it was a usurious expulsion, their loans were either cancelled or confiscated, and at most they might recover a proportion of the capital. If superstition dictated it, then there was probably an enormous fine as a penalty for the incident which had aroused the feelings of the population. The alleged conspiracy with the lepers cost the Jews of Paris £150,000 according to the chronicler, William de Nangy[1].

Apart from the competition of Christian financiers, these events, and the thinning of their ranks by massacre and execution, explain how Jewish finance dwindled from loans to kings and princes in the twelfth century to petty pawnbroking in the fourteenth, and how the end of the Middle Ages found them so completely ruined that their share in the beginnings of the new commercial and industrial order was negligible.

[1] Ed. Géraud, II, pp. 31 ff.

EPILOGUE

In the preceding pages the story of Jewish Christian relations is carried a stage beyond the point at which it was left in *The Conflict of the Church and the Synagogue*. That volume, dealing with the Roman period and the coming of Christianity, traced antisemitism to its origin in the influence of the picture drawn by the theologians of a deicide and God-accursed people, and to the embodiment of this picture in the legislation of the Christian empire. The pagan emperors had found a place for a monotheistic nation amongst their polytheistic subjects: the Christians could not willingly accept a deicide people within the frontiers of their orthodox empire. They began to limit the scope of Jewish citizenship; they found it unseemly that Jews should hold high office; that they should receive the honours accorded to rank; that they should exercise authority over Christians; that those who killed the Saviour should hold in servitude or subjection those whom He had redeemed. But it is never possible to hold a people permanently in a position of modified inferiority; either they will revert to equality, or the inferiority will grow steadily more and more marked as it sinks into the minds of the common citizens that here are some who are to be treated as below themselves. Even less is it possible to arrest at a determined point the licence to oppress, to persecute, and to assault. The Church saw to it that the Jew should not climb back to equality; the medieval popes found that they could not protect from violence those whom they proclaimed the fitting objects of oppression and contempt.

In this sense the Church was directly responsible for the decline in the status of the Jew which marked the disappearance of the Roman conception of citizenship and the birth of the new Germanic societies; but the new position which he came to assume, and with which the first half of this volume deals, had its origin more in Germanic than in ecclesiastical concepts. The early history of the *servitudo camerae* is lost in the obscurities of the tenth and eleventh centuries, but there is no question but that everywhere in northern Europe kings, princes and barons came to consider the Jews as their own private property by the time that religious fanaticism, aroused by the Crusading movement, made it essential for them to know to whom they were supposed to turn for protection. The Roman citizen, when he lost the rights and duties embodied in the Roman codes, passed naturally into the new relationships of the new society by the simple fact of his being a Christian. It was the simple fact that he was not which prevented the Jew from following suit, and compelled him to accept a very inferior position.

The rightlessness which resulted is the keynote of the medieval period. In practice, of course, the ordinary daily life of the Jew passed in a fashion very similar to that of the Christian. The limitations of his existence once accepted, he had sufficient scope for his activities to be able to earn his living and accumulate possessions. His contacts with Christians were continuous, and must have been mostly friendly or, at least, carried on with mutual toleration. As the period developed, this daily mutual toleration certainly declined. The charters and other documents of the fourteenth and fifteenth centuries reveal this clearly. In the same way the Jew must ordinarily have been able to calculate sufficiently on the actions of his owner to conduct his relations with him on a satisfactory basis. The knowledge of how to humour an autocrat is a common possession of all subject peoples.

Yet, when every concession has been made for the ability of human beings to adapt themselves even to the most unfavourable circumstances, the conditions described reveal a basic and long-continuing insecurity which is bound to have affected profoundly the mentality of the people which endured it. The rightlessness was so complete—death, the confiscation of their entire property or banishment, decreed at any moment, and no appeal against the edict except by bribery. Against others it might suit their owner to give them even more than legitimate protection; but if their owner turned against them, they had no hope elsewhere. Moreover, this condition of rightlessness lasted not decades but centuries. Even if arbitrary violence grew less as society in western Europe grew more polished, for a large proportion of the Jewish people conditions remained essentially the same from the tenth century to the twentieth, and the present day has seen the old medieval insecurity affect the lives of millions of Jews who had believed that it had at last become a thing of the past.

To accentuate the tragedy, that which gave the medieval Jew the greatest security on the side of his owner was that very aspect of his life which made him most hated of his neighbours. His usury secured him official protection at the price of public detestation. It was only for the *absent* Jewish usurer that the poets waxed sentimental; it was only in contrast to the still greater scourge of the Christian practitioner that the Jewish appeared tolerable; in actual fact, his financial activities were also an intolerable scourge. It is the extortionate charges of the Jewish usurer, deeply imprinted upon the memory of Europe, enshrined in popular literature, canonised in Shakespeare's Shylock, which provides the foundation for economic antisemitism. Viewed apart from its causes and its setting, putting the responsibility on the usurer, not on the conditions out of which he was created, Jewish usury merits the execration which it has received. But, once the situation is analysed, it becomes transparently clear that the usurer himself merits sympathy and pity rather than blame, and that the responsibility lies elsewhere. It has been shown how usury amongst both Christians and Jews arose out of contemporary economic conditions. There is no sign of that inherited aptitude for exploitation, beloved of certain writers, which is supposed to have led the Jews themselves to initiate Europe into the gentle art of money-making. Usury arose because people wanted to borrow money, and the first lender was often the Church. With the growth of industry and commerce the merchant came to be the chief lender, and in this indirect way the Jews came to take their part in the whole business— their part, for an even more common myth is that which draws from the canonical prohibition the conclusion that all usurers were Jews. That the canonical doctrine was never successfully applied has been shown in the narrative of the long and unsuccessful chase of the Church after the ever-inventive Christian usurer. It was in the description of this battle that the real responsibilities emerged.

The main responsibility, not merely for Jewish usury, but for all medieval usury, must lie with the intellectual leaders of the age, who made no proper provision for a universal

CC

social want. The lending of money without security must always be a risky business, but nearly all medieval lending was on the security of land or objects of value. Had the lender been a recognised and respectable member of society, had political and religious condemnation not added to the risks of the profession, and to the hostility between the two parties to the transaction, interest might have been much lower, and society served much more competently.

If the main responsibility for usury as a whole lies with the Church, amongst whose servants the intellectual leaders were alone likely to be found, the special responsibility for the usury of the Jews lies with the medieval princes. It was because the Jews were part of the political and revenue system of the medieval state rather than a cog in the wheel of medieval commerce that Jewish usury assumed such proportions and earned such hatred. It was because the princes wished to secure revenue from their transactions, not because the Jews were experts in the art of exploitation, that they were so unjustly favoured in the law-courts, so vigorously protected until the moment came for their expulsion. Unquestionably, the Jew learnt from his experience, as would any other in his circumstances, and became himself an expert in evasive contracts, subtle scheming and dishonest practices, but he learnt this in his serfdom to the treasuries of Europe, not on the hills of Judaea. It is a product of his history, not of his blood.

This change in Jewish life has to be set against the lurid background of the massacres of the First Crusade to obtain its real values. The security shattered in those months of terror was never restored. Both the political and the economic developments of the centuries which followed were deeply affected by them. On prince, populace and Jew alike they left their mark.

In this volume only part of the medieval story has been told. Church and populace played their part also in shaping the history of those centuries. Yet from this partial survey essential contributions to the historical understanding of modern antisemitism emerge. It is in this period that the Jew begins to be involuntarily the part-author of his own misfortunes. For the first time it became possible to use the contemporary behaviour of the Jew as an argument against him, as a justification for the hatred of him. Hatred of the usurer came in the minds of the Christian public to justify the killing of the deicide. Nor was it much comfort to ruined Christian debtors that the Jewish usurer himself was but the victim of circumstances which he could not control. For if the birth of economic antisemitism is observable in the usury of the Middle Ages, it was accompanied by, and directly the consequence of, another aspect of the modern Jewish problem, the powerlessness of the Jew to direct his own destiny, with all the psychological consequences which that involves. The necessity of cringing before an owner with absolute power, and a populace moved by religious fanaticism, greed and hopeless indebtedness, inevitably produces unattractive characteristics. The Jew became what circumstances made him: his main, almost his only, responsibility in the creation of those circumstances was his desire to remain loyal to his Judaism. It was Christendom which decided that the price of that loyalty should be psychological and social degradation.

APPENDICES

APPENDIX ONE

SPECIMEN CHARTERS

I. Diploma of Louis the Pious to Domatus (*c.* 825) (Bouquet, VI, pp. 649 ff.).

Omnibus Episcopis, Abbatibus, Comitibus, Gastaldiis, Vicariis, Centenariis, Clusariis, seu etiam Missis nostris discurrentibus, necnon et omnibus fidelibus nostris, praesentibus scilicet et futuris, notum sit quia istos Hebraeos, Domatum Rabbi et Samuelem nepotem ejus, sub nostra defensione suscepimus ac retinemus. Quapropter per praesentem auctoritatem nostram decernimus atque jubemus ut neque vos, neque juniores, seu successores vestri memoratos Hebraeos de nullis quibuslibet illicitis occasionibus inquirere [l. inquietare], aut calumniam generare praesumatis, nec de rebus eorum propriis, unde praesenti tempore legaliter vestiti esse videntur, aliquid abstrahere, aut minuere ullo unquam tempore praesumatis; sed neque teloneum, aut paravereda, aut mansionaticum, aut pulveraticum, aut cespitaticum, aut ripaticum, aut portaticum, aut pontaticum, aut tranaticum, aut coenaticum a praedictis Hebraeis exigere praesumatis. Similiter concessimus eis de rebus eorum propriis commutationem facere, et proprium suum cuicumque voluerint vendere; liceatque eis secundum legem eorum vivere, et homines Christianos ad eorum opera facienda locare, exceptis festis, et diebus Dominicis. Habeant etiam licentiam mancipia peregrina emere, et infra Imperium nostrum vendere. Quod si Christianus causam vel litem contra eos habuerit, tres idoneos testes Christianos et tres Hebraeos similiter idoneos in testimonium suum adhibeat, et cum eis causam suam judicet. Et si illi causam vel litem contra Christianum habuerint, Christianos testes in testimonium sibi assumant, et cum eis eum convincant. Suggesserunt etiam iidem Judaei Celsitudini nostrae de quibusdam hominibus, qui contra Christianam Religionem suadent mancipia Hebraeorum sub autentu [l. obtentu] Christianae Religionis contemnere dominos suos, et baptisari; vel potius persuadent illis ut baptisentur ut a servitio dominorum suorum liberentur; quod nequaquam sacri Canones constituunt, immo talia perpetrantes districta anathematis sententia feriendos dijudicant. Et ideo volumus ut neque vos ipsi praedictis Hebraeis hoc ulterius facere praesumatis, neque juniores vestros usquam facere permittatis; certumque teneatis quia quicumque hoc perpetraverit, et ad nos delatum fuerit, quod absque sui periculo, et rerum suarum damno evadere non poterit. Et hoc vobis notum esse volumus, ut jam, quia supra scriptos Hebraeos sub mundeburdo et defensione nostra suscepimus, quicumque in morte eorum, quamdiu nobis fideles extiterint, consiliaverit, aut aliquem interfecerit, sciat se ad partem Palatii nostri decem libras auri persoluturum; et nullatenus volumus ut praedictos Judaeos ad nullum judicium examinetis, id est, neque ad ignem, neque ad aquam calidam, seu etiam ad flagellum, nisi liceat eis secundum illorum legem vivere vel ducere.

II. Charter of Henry IV to the Jews of Worms (1090) (R. Hoeniger, *Zur Geschichte der Juden in Deutschland im Mittelalter*, ZGJD, I, pp. 137 ff.).

In nomine sancte et individue trinitatis Fredericus divina favente clemencia Romanorum imperator semper augustus. Omnibus episcopis, abbatibus, ducibus, comitibus, necnon omnibus regni nostri legibus obnoxiis notum sit, qualiter Iudeis de Wormacia et ceteris sodalibus suis statuta proavi nostri imperatoris Henrici tempore Salmanni eorundem Iudeorum episcopi nostra quoque auctoritate lege semper valitura confirmamus.

(1) Quia erga volumus, ut de omni iusticia ad nos tantum habeant respicere, ex nostre regie dignitatis auctoritate precipimus, ut nec episcopus, nec camerarius, nec comes, nec scultetus nec quisquam penitus nisi quem ipsi de se elegerint, de aliqua re vel iusticie alicuius exaccione cum eis vel adversus eos tractare presumat, nisi tantum ille, quem ex eleccione ipsorum, ut prefati sumus, ipse imperator eis prefecerit, presertim cum ad cameram nostram attineant, [prout] nobis complacuerit.

(2) De rebus eciam quas iure hereditario possident, in areis, in ortis, in vineis, in agris, in mancipiis seu in ceteris rebus mobilibus vel immobilibus nullus eis quicquam aufferre presumat. In comoditate quam habent in edificiis in muro civitatis, infra vel extra, nullus eos impediat. Si quis vero contra hoc edictum nostrum eos in aliquo inquietare temptaverit, in graciam nostram reus sit, ipsis autem rem, si quam abstulerit, duplo restituat.

(3) Habeant eciam liberam potestatem per totam civitatem cum quibuslibet hominibus canbire argentum, excepto tantum ante domum monetaream vel sicubi alibi monetarii ad cambiendum consederint.

(4) Intra ambitum regni nostri libere ac pacifice discurrant negocium et mercimonium suum exercere, emere ac vendere; et nullus ab eis theolonium exigat, nullam exaccionem publicam vel privatam repetat.

(5) In domibus eorum sine consensu ipsorum hospites non recipiantur; nullus ab eis equum ad profectionem regis vel episcopi aut angariam regie expedicionis requirat.

(6) Si autem res furtiva apud eos inventa fuerit, si dixerit Iudeus se emisse, iuramento probet secundum legem suam quanti emerit, et tantundem recipiat et rem ei cuius erat restituat.

(7) Nullus filios aut filias eorum invitos baptizare presumat, aut, si captos vi vel furtim raptos vel coactos baptizaverit, duodecim libras auri ad erarium regis persolvat; si autem aliquis eorum sponte baptizari voluerit, triduo reservetur, ut integre cognoscatur, si vero christiane religionis causa, aut pro aliqua illata sibi iniuria legem suam deserat, et sicut legem patrum suorum reliquerunt, ita eciam relinquant hereditatem.

(8) Mancipia quoque eorum pagana nullus sub obtentu christiane religionis baptizans a servicio eorum avertat; quod si fecerit, bannum, id est tres libras argenti, persolvat et servum domino suo reddat, servus vero per omnia preceptis domini sui obediat, salva nichilominus christiane fidei observacione.

(9) Liceat eis ancillas et nutrices Christianas habere et Christianos ad opera facienda conducere, exceptis diebus festis et dominicis, nec hoc contradicat episcopus vel aliquis clericus.

(10) Non liceat eis christianum servum emere.

(11) Quod si Iudeus contra Christianum vel Christianus contra Iudeum contenderit, uterque, prout res est, secundum legem suam iusticiam faciat et rem suam probet; et sicut licet unicuique Christiano per suum

et unius testis utriusque legis publicum iuramentum probare, fideiussores Iudeo per eum positos absolvisse, sic eciam Iudeo liceat per suum et unius Iudei et unius Christiani publicum iuramentum probare, fideiussores Christiano per eum positos absolvisse, nec amplius ab actore vel iudice sit cogendus.

(12) Et nemo Iudeum ad ignitum ferrum vel ad calidam aquam vel frigidam cogat, nec flagellis cedat, nec in carcerem mittat, set iuret secundum legem suam post quadraginta dies; nullus testibus nisi simul Iudeis et Christianis convinci possit qualibet de causa; pro quacunque re regiam appellaverint presenciam, inducie eis concedantur. Quicunque eos contra hoc edictum nostrum fatigaverit, bannum, id est tres libras auri, persolvat imperatori.

(13) Si quis adversus aliquem eorum consilium fecerit aut eis insidiatus fuerit, ut occidatur, uterque et consiliator et occisor duodecim libras auri ad erarium regis persolvat; si vero eum vulneraverit, et non ad mortem, libram unam auri componat, et si sit servus qui illum occiderit vel vulneraverit, dominus eius aut supradictam composicionem inpleat, aut servum ad penas trahat; quod si pre paupertate predictum solvere nequiverit, eadem pena plectatur qua ille punitus est tempore Henrici imperatoris, proavi nostri, qui Iudeum nomine Vivum interfecit, scilicet oculi eius eruantur et dextra manus amputetur.

(14) Quod si ipsi Iudei litem inter se vel causam aliquam habuerint determinandam, a suis paribus et non ab aliis iudicentur, et si aliquando inter eos perfidus alicuius rei inter eos geste occultare voluerit veritatem, ab eo qui est episcopus eorum veritatem fateri cogatur. Si autem de magna causa inculpati fuerint, inducias ad imperatorem habeant, si voluerint.

(15) Habeant preterea vinum suum pigmenta et antidota vendere Christianis licenciam, et sicut prediximus, nullus ab eis exigat palefridos vel angariam vel aliquam exaccionem publicam vel privatam.

Et ut hec concessionis auctoritas omni evo inviolata permaneat hanc cartam inde conscribi et sigilli nostri inpressione iussimus insigniri. Huius rei testes sunt:

Follow Signatures.

III. CHARTER OF JOHN TO THE JEWS OF ENGLAND AND NORMANDY (1201)
(*Rot. Cart.*, i, 93. English translation in J. Jacobs, *The Jews of Angevin England*, pp. 212 ff.).

John, by the Grace of God, &c.

I. Know that we have granted to all the Jews of England and Normandy to have freely and honourably residence in our land, and to hold all that from us which they held from King Henry, our father's grandfather, and all that now they reasonably hold in land and fees and mortgages and goods, and that they have all their liberties and customs just as they had them in the time of the aforesaid King Henry, our father's grandfather, better and more quietly and more honourably.

II. And if any dispute arise between a Christian and a Jew he who summons the other to answer his complaint should have witnesses, viz.: a lawful Christian and a lawful Jew. And if a Jew has a writ about his complaint, the writ shall be a witness for him, and if a Christian have a complaint against a Jew, let it be judged by peers of the Jew.

III. And when a Jew dies his body shall not be detained above earth, but his heirs shall have his money and his debts, so that he shall not be disturbed therefore if he has an heir who may answer for him and do what is right about his debts and his forfeit. And let it be lawful for Jews to receive and buy without difficulty all things that may be brought to them except things of the church or blood-stained cloth.

IV. And if any Jew is summoned by anyone without testimony, he shall be quits of that summons on his sole oath on his Book. And on the summons of those things that belong to our crown he shall be quits on his sole oath on his roll. And if there is a dispute between Christian and Jew about accommodation of some money the Jew shall prove the capital and the Christian the interest.

V. And let it be lawful to the Jew to sell his pledge after it is certain that he has held it for a whole year and one day. And Jews shall not enter into pleadings except before us and before those who guard our castles in whose bailiwicks the Jews dwell.

VI. And wherever the Jews may be let it be lawful for them to go when they will with all their chattels just as our own property, and let none stop or prevent them in this.

VII. And we order that they be free through all England and Normandy of all the customs and tolls and modiation of wine just as our own chattels. And we order you to guard, to defend and to maintain them. And we prohibit anyone from summoning them against their charter on the above points on our forfeit such as the charter of King Henry our father reasonably declares. Witnesses Godfrey son of Peter Earl of Essex &c. &c. Given at Marlborough the tenth day of April in the second year of our reign.

II

John, by the Grace of God, &c.

Know that we have conceded and by this present charter of ours confirmed to our Jews in England that excesses which may arise among them except those which belong to our crown and justice, as homicide, mayhem, premeditated assault, burglary, rape, theft, arson, and treasure-trove, shall be brought before them according to their law and remedied, and they shall do justice thereon among themselves. And we also grant to them that if any of them summon another on a charge which pertains to us, we will compel none of them to witness against any other, but if the summoner has a reasonable and suitable witness let him bring him with him. But if some criminal and overt deed occur among them which pertains to our crown and justice, as in the aforesaid pleas of the crown, although none of them has become an accuser thereon, we will cause that charge to be investigated by our lawful Jews of England, as the charter of King Henry our father reasonably testifies. . . .

(Same witnesses, place and date as preceding.)

IV. CHARTER OF EDWARD I TO THE JEWS OF ENGLAND (1275) (*Statutes of the Realm* [*Rec. Com.*], I, pp. 221 ff.).

Forasmuch as the King hath seen that divers Evils, and the disheriting of the good Men of his Land have happened by the Usuries which the Jews have made in Time past, and that divers Sins have followed thereupon; albeit he and his Ancestors have received much benefit from the Jewish People in all Time past; nevertheless for the Honour of God and the common benefit of the People, the King hath ordained and established, That from henceforth no Jew shall lend any Thing at Usury, either upon Land, or upon Rent, or upon other Thing: And that no Usuries shall run in Time coming from the Feast of Saint Edward last past. Notwithstanding, the Covenants before made shall be observed, saving that the Usuries shall cease. But all those who owe Debts to Jews upon Pledges of Moveables, shall acquit them between this and Easter; if not they shall be forfeited. And if any Jew shall lend at Usury contrary to this Ordinance, the King will not lend his Aid, neither by himself nor his Officers, for the recovering of his Loan; but will punish him at his discretion for the Offence, and will do justice to the Christian that he may obtain his Pledge again.

And that the Distresses for Debts due unto the Jews from henceforth shall not be so grievous, but that the Moiety of the Lands and Chattels of the Christians shall remain for their Maintenance; and that no Distress shall be made for a Jewry Debt, upon the Heir of the Debtor named in the Jew's Deed, nor upon any other Person holding the Land that was the Debtor's, before that the Debt be put in Suit and allowed in Court.

And if the Sheriff or other Bailiff, by the King's Command hath to give Seisin to a Jew, be it one or more, for their Debt, of Chattels or Land to the Value of the Debt, the Chattels shall be valued by the Oaths of good Men, and be delivered to the Jew or Jews, or to their Proxy, to the Amount of the Debt; and if the Chattels be not sufficient, the Lands shall be extended by the same Oath before the Delivery of Seisin to the Jew or Jews, to each in his due Proportion; so that it may be certainly known that the Debt is quit, and the Christian may have his Land again; Saving always to the Christian the Moiety of his Land and Chattels for his maintenance as aforesaid, and the Chief Mansion.

And if any Moveables hereafter be found in Possession of a Jew, and any Man shall sue him, the Jew shall be allowed his Warranty, if he may have it; and if not, let him answer therefore: So that he be not herein otherwise privileged than a Christian.

And that all Jews shall dwell in the King's own Cities and Boroughs, where the Chests of Chirographs of Jewry are wont to be: And that each Jew after he shall be Seven Years old, shall wear a Badge on his outer Garment; that is to say, in the Form of Two Tables joined, of yellow Felt, of the Length of Six Inches, and of the Breadth of Three Inches. And that each one, after he shall be Twelve Years old, pay Three pence yearly at Easter of Tax to the King, whose Bond-man he is; and this shall hold place as well for a Woman as a Man.

And that no Jew shall have Power to infeoff another, whether Jew or Christian, of Houses, Rents or Tenements that he now hath, nor to alien in any other Manner, nor to make Acquittance to any Christian of his Debt, without the especial Licence of the King, until the King shall have otherwise ordained therein.

And, Forasmuch as it is the Will and Sufferance of Holy Church, that they may live and be preserved, the King taketh them under his Protection, and granteth them his Peace; and willeth that they be safely preserved and defended by his Sheriffs and other Bailiffs, and by his Liege Men; and commandeth that none shall do them harm, or damage, or wrong, in their Bodies or in their Goods, moveable or immoveable; and that they shall neither plead nor be impleaded in any Court, nor be challenged or troubled in any Court, except in the Court of the King, whose Bond-men they are. And that none shall owe Obedience, or Service, or Rent, except to the King, or his Bailiffs in his Name; unless it be for their Dwellings which they now hold by paying Rent; saving the Right of Holy Church.

And the King granteth unto them that they may gain their living by lawful Merchandise and their Labour; and that they may have Intercourse with Christians, in order to carry on lawful Trade by selling and buying.

But that no Christian, for this Cause or any other, shall dwell among them. And the King willeth that they shall not by reason of their Merchandise be put to Lot or Scot, nor in taxes with the Men of the Cities or Boroughs where they abide; for that they are taxable to the King as his Bondmen, and to none other but the King.

Moreover the King granteth unto them that they may buy Houses and Curtilages, in the Cities and Boroughs where they abide, so that they hold them in chief of the King; saving unto the Lords of the Fee their Services due and accustomed. And that they may take or buy Farms or Land for the Term of Ten Years or less, without taking Homages or Fealties, or such sort of Obedience from Christians, and without having Advowsons of Churches; and that they may be able to gain their living in the World, if they have not the Means of Trading, or cannot Labour; and this Licence to take Lands to farm shall endure to them only for Fifteen Years from this Time forward.

V. CHARTER ASCRIBED TO PHILIP AUGUSTUS TO THE JEWS OF FRANCE (c. 1190) (Laurière, XI, p. 315).

Universis Baillivis per Franciam & Normaniam constitutis. Mandantes vobis praecipimus quatenus de unaquaque villa eligatis duos legitimos homines, qui per juramentum suum fideliter custodiant sigillum Judaeorum, & in sigillo suo sigillabunt per assensum utriusque partis conventiones praestitorum quae fient inter Christianos & Judaeos à sexaginta solidis & supra, & illi Jurati rescripta illarum conventionum penes se ad opus nostrum retinebunt. Hic est autem modus conventionis; videlicet, quod si ad primum terminum qui ponetur in Charta, Christianus debitum suum Judaeo non rediderit, ex tunc post ipsum terminum elapsum, Christianus tenebitur reddere Judaeo per hebdomadam pro una quaque libra, duos denarios usque ad unum annum tantum. Si tamen Christianus tandiu voluerit debitum retinere & Judaeus noluerit ei dimittere, neque ultra illum annum Judaeus a Christiano usuras exigere poterit, occasione ipsius debiti, cum amplius quam per annum unum debitum ipsum non possit currere ad usuras.

Volumus autem & praecipimus ut ad probanda debita Judaeorum contra Christianos, vel Christianorum contra Judaeos, non admittantur in testimonium tam Christiani quam Judaei, nisi eo modo quo statutum est, et sicut solent circa haec testes admitti.

Vobis autem praecipimus quatenus ispsis Judaeis cum ab eis fueritis requisiti debita sua per ius, & absque omni dilatione, in nostris Bailliviis reddi faciatis, ita quod exinde verbum amplius non audiamus.

NOTE.—This is probably the earliest French charter. It is simpler than the other charters of the same King issued in the second half of his reign.

VI. CHARTER OF JOHN II TO THE JEWS OF FRANCE (1361) (Laurière, III, pp. 473 ff.).

Johannes Dei gratia Francorum Rex. Solet munificentia Regia illos quibus se liberalem exhibet, offerre [efferre] favoribus graciosis, Privilegiisque [et] Libertatibus insignire, sine quibus ea commode stare non possent, que dixit [duxit] primitus concedenda: Cum igitur carissimus Primogenitus noster dum Nobis absentibus, Regnum nostrum regebat, Universitati Judeorum ex certis & legitimis causis utilitatem Regni tangentibus, introitum & moram in Regno nostro per suas Literas prius

concesserit usque ad viginti annos, Nosque post modum per nostras
Literas, dictam gratiam per nostrum Primogenitum factam, approbando
& confirmando, habitis super hoc cum nonnullis Prelatis & aliis de nostro
Genere, Gentibus Cleri, Ducibus, Comitibus, Proceribus, Militibus &
aliis habitantibus, prudentibusque Regni nostri, concesserimus prefatis
Judeis, eorum Uxoribus & familiis ipsorum, introitum & moram in
Regno nostro usque ad vigenti annos a data presentium continue
numerandos, sub certis conditionibus mediantibus, quod certis tributis
vel subventionibus Nobis propter hoc solvendis & prestandis, ipsosque
in nostris speciali et Salva gardia ac nostro salvo condictu [conductu]
suscipiendo, prout in ipsius Primogeniti nostri(s) literis prius, & per
nostras Literas postea super hoc concessas, lacius continetur, dictique
Judei, prout nobis suppliciter insinuare curavit [curaverunt] in dicto
Regno nostro morari pacifice nequirent, nisi certa Privilegia & Libertates
concederemus iisdem, quibus perversorum vel emulorum astuciis,
necnon opprobriis & conviciis occuratur, dignum sancimus ut ipsi
Judei nostra liberalitate gaudeant & utantur, eisdem Libertates &
Privilegia concedere, quibus a noxiis, molestiis & gravaminibus defen-
dantur: nam eo magis quiete in Regno nostro poterunt habitare, & Nobis
promissa & debita subsidia persolvere, quanto per Nos adjuti fuerint &
uberiori liberalitate fulsiti [fulciti]. Notum itaque facimus Universis
tam presentibus quam futuris, Nos hiis attentis, Privilegia, Libertates,
immunitates & alia que secuntur, eisdem concessisse de nostris autoritate
& plenitudine Regie potestatis, ex certa scientia & de gratia speciali.
 (1) In primis etenim volumus & eisdem Judeis & eorum cuilibet in
Regno nostro moranti, concedimus ut ipsi possint habere domos et
habitationes pro eorum mansionibus, & plateas pro ipsorum corporibus
inhumandis, ac etiam pro aliis ipsorum neces.itatibus faciendis, prout
inter Judeos tempore quo in Regno nostro alias habitabant, fuit hactenus
consuetum, absque eo quod super hoc, per quemcumque vel quomodolibet valeant impediri.
 (2) Item. Ipsos Judeos & Judeas & eorum quemlibet in Regno nostro
morantes, ab omnibus Justiciariis, Judicibus nostris & aliis quibuscumque aut quibuscumque Commissariis quavis auctoritate, prorogativa,
potestate, commissione vel Privilegiis, tam in casibus civilibus quam
criminalibus †vel quasi, aut aliis quibuscumque, nisi ab eisdem & preter-
quam† a Nobis vel a Nobis deputandis dumtaxat, eximimus ac exemptos
teneri volumus & jubemus, Nobis vel Gardiano ipsorum vel aliis eisdem
per nos deputandis, de & super causis suis quibuscumque & casibus ipsos
tangentibus, cognicionem & decisionem, ipsorumque punitionem in
casibus de quibus punitio ad nos spectare debebit, tenore presencium
penitus reservantes; nisi ab eisdem Judeis nostri Judices requirerentur:
inhibendo omnibus & singulis Justiciariis [et] Commissariis dicti Regni,
cujuscumque dignitatis vel preeminentie existant, vel quacumque
auctoritate fungantur, ne de ipsorum vel causarum eorumdem cognitione
vel ipsorum punitione se quomodolibet intromittere presumant, quicquid
in contrarium fecerint, nullius decernentes esse efficacie vel momenti,
quicquid in contrarium factum repererint, revocando, anullando, & ad
statum pristinum & debitum reducendo indilate [et] faciendo reduci.
 (3) Item. Quod si sit aliquis vel aliqua Judeus vel Judea, qui vel
que non sit ydoneus, sufficiens aut dignus, suis demeritis publicis vel
occultis exigentibus, morari vel remanere in Regno, ipsi ad relationem
duorum Magistrorum Legis dictorum Judeorum, & quatuor aliorum
Judeorum quos eligerent, quorum Dicto vel arbitrio stabitur et credetur,

† . . . † text corrupt.

punietur vel bannietur a Regno absque revocatione, vel prout ipsi juxta facti qualitatem per eos considerandam † prout fuerint faciendum; † solvendo tamen Nobis per dictos Magistros, centum Florenos de Florencia boni ponderis, una cum bonorum dicti puniti vel banniti confiscatione Nobis acquirenda, absque eo quod Nos, Justiciarii nostri aut quilibet alius possit petere, vel quod ipsi causam propter quam hoc factum fuerit, dicere teneantur.

(4) Item. Si ipsi Judei vel Judee in & sub aliorum Justiciariorum vel Dominorum Jurisdictione velint habitare vel morari, hoc facere poterunt, absque eo quod servitutes & redebentias alicui preterquam Nobis, solvere vel reddere teneantur; exceptis dumtaxat census vel redditus suarum domorum & habitationum, quos Dominis quorum intererit, solvere debebunt, prout alii Regnicole eadem annuatim persolvunt.

(5) Item. Volumus & eisdem concedimus quod in Regno nostro intrare, venire & in eodem morari, absque eo quod virtute cujusdem marque vel gagiamenti marque, Privilegii vel aliis quibuscumque, valeant arrestari, impediri vel vexari.

(6) Item. Nec propter quamcumque causam capi vel arrestari valeant, quam propter casum criminalem: Sed si capi [capti] fuerint, ipsos deliberari volumus indilate, prestando bonam & ydoneam cautionem Christianorum vel Judeorum.

(7) Item. Et quia ipsi Judei vel Judee vel eorum aliqui, pridem forsam [forsan] ante ipsorum ultimo recessum a Regno, aliqua crimina potuerunt commisisse, propter que possent nunc vel alias molestari vel puniri, eadem omnia & quolibet [quaelibet] eorumdem, que ipsi Judei vel Judee seu aliqui ipsorum vel ipsarum, nunc usque in Regno vel alibi commiserint, sive sint crimen Lese Majestatis, false Monete, homicidii, raptus, furti, mutilacionis vel aliud crimen capitale, aut aliud quoscumque [quodcumque] & quovis nomine censeatur, omnemque penam corporalem, criminalem & civilem quas ob eadem incurrere potuerunt, remittimus, quittamus & penitus indulgemus, Procuratore nostro ceterisque quibuscumque Judicibus nostris, silentium perpetuum super hoc imponendo; nolentes ipsos vel eorum aliquem propter hoc inquietari, molestari vel vexari quomodolibet in corpore sive bonis, sed quicquid secus fuerit attemptatum, ad statum pristinum & debitum reduci celeriter volumus & jubemus.

(8) Item. Eisdem occasione [l. concedimus] domus quod in Regno nostro quamdiu in ipso morabuntur, possint mercari [et] contrahere tam suis denariatis & mercaturis quam suis denariis, & ipsos prestare possint; ita tamen quod ipsi non possint ultra quatuor denarios pro libra, recipere seu exigere qualibet septimana.

(9) Item. Quod possint sua Ministeria vel opera, currecterias, artes speculativas, praticas atque mechanicas, exercere & facere prout alibi sunt consueti.

(10) Item. Quod ipsi alias in Regno, & nunc etiam soliti sunt Christianis, duntaxat, ut asserunt, pecunias prestare, volumus & eisdem concedimus ut in Regno nostro quamdiu trahant ibidem [moram] suas pecunias valeant prestare seu mutuo tradere, sub omnibus pignoribus vel ypothecis aut aliter; exceptis dumtaxat Reliquiis sacris, Calicibus, Libris, ornamentis & aliis rebus Deo dicatis, vomeribus, cultris & ferramentis carrucarum & molendinorum: Solvendo videlicet per recipientes pecuniam, ut predicitur, pro qualibet libra sive viginti solidos, nisi quatuor denarios in qualibet Septimana, sub omnibus pignoribus; predictis exceptis.

† . . . † text corrupt.

(11) Item. Credetur eisdem per ipsorum Legem, Juramentum vel fidem, de omni eo quod asserent se super pignora mutuo tradidisse & eisdem deberi, ac de & supra conventionibus super hoc factis, & terminis super pignorum custodia & super hec statutis per eos vel prefixis.

(12) Item. Si super hujusmodi pignorum custodia nil fuerit conventum inter Partes, ipsi non ultra annum & diem tenebuntur pignora custodire, nec illis quorum fuerint, restituere tenebuntur, donec eisdem fuerit solutum id quod super hoc asserent, ut prefertur, se mutuo tradidisse, nec nominare tenebuntur personas que eisdem dicta pignora tradiderunt.

(13) Item. Nec restituere tenebuntur aliquid quod eis sponte datum, traditumve fuerit insolutum.

(14) Item. Si ipsi Judei vel Judee quicquid ultra quatuor denarios pro libra, de pecunia per eos tradita receperint, ipsi pura sorte contentabuntur, sed [l. et] restituere tenebuntur id quod ultra sortem receperint, & Parti expensas ab hoc factas.

(15) Item. Volumus & hoc promittent Judei memorati, quod si aliquis vel aliqua ipsorum Judeorum, de Villa in Villam vel de patria in patriam se duxerint transferendum, aliquaque pignora teneant vel habeant, super que mutuo tradiderint pecuniam, ipsi priusquam dictam Villam vel patriam in quibus morabuntur, exeant, tenebuntur facere preconisari dicta pignora que tenebunt per tres subastationes vel preconisaciones solempnes, in locis publicis & consuetis, Literam inde a dicti loci Justitia capiendo: et si predicta pignora ultra fuerint vendita quam super hoc debeatur, residuum reddatur illis quorum erunt dicta pignora, vel ponetur in manus Justitie sub qua erunt dicta pignora, vel sub qua vendita fuerint, ut prefertur.

(16) Item. Ipsos ab omnibus Imposicionibus, subsidiis, maletoltis, gabellis & subventionibus, exercitu, equitaturis, Villarum vel Fortaliciorum custodiis, & ab omnibus servitutibus vel redibenciis quovis nomine censeantur, persolvendis quibuscumque, ob quamcumque causam & cuicumque persone concessis vel concedendis, ubicumque per Regnum nostrum se transferant, quittos remanere volumus & immunes; exceptis duntaxat tributis superius nominatis, & subsidiis pro nostra liberatione ordinatis vel etiam ordinandis.

(17) Item. Non tenebuntur solvere alicui subditorum nostrorum, pedegia, transversa vel calceyas, nisi antiqua & consueta.

(18) Item. Nolumus quod Procuratores nostri alicubi in Regno contra ipsos Judeos vel aliquem ex eisdem, se partem facere presumant vel audeant, nisi prius fuerint super factis eisdem impositis, sufficienter & debite informati.

(19) Item. Quod nullus contra ipsos per viam denunciacionis admittatur, nisi se Partem faciat contra ipsos: et si subcumbat, quod ipsi solvat expensas.

(20) Item. Et quia forte possint per nonnullos Christianos ipsorum emulos vel ipsos oprimere [volentes], res alique in suis domibus supponi, quamobrem possint de furto, latrocinio vel alio scelere reprehendi, & propter hoc vexari vel puniri, Nolumus quod propter quamcumque rem vel bona mobilia in ipsorum domibus vel habitacionibus reperta, ipsi Judei vel Judee vel eorum aliqui, ultra rei ipsius restitucionem possint super hoc prosequi per quemcumque, nec de furto, latrocinio vel aliter propter hoc reprehendi, molestari vel puniri; nisi reperta fuerit dicta res in scrinio vel archa firmatis, de quibus clavem deferat Dominus vel Domina domus, Judeus videlicet, vel Judea.

(21) Item. Concedimus eisdem quod nulli Magistri Hospiciorum nostrorum, municionum nostrarum, Equitatores, Captores, Forerii, aut alii Officiarii nostri Liberorumque nostrorum, ac aliorum de nostro

Genere, vel quorumcumque aliorum Ducum, Prelatorum vel Baronum, equos, pecudes, Jumenta, quadrigas, blada, vina, fenum, avenam, superletilem, utensilia, aut bona aliqua mobilia dictorum Judeorum vel Judearum, ubicumque existentia, capiant vel capere faciant quomodolibet pro quacumque necessitate, vel virtute cujuscumque commissionis vel potestatis sibi date: Et si aliquis dictorum Officiariorum contrarium facere conetur vel attemptet, eisdem per dictos Judeos vel Judeas ipsorum vel Gentes impune volumus non pareri: quinymo eisdem concedimus ut ad [a] dictis bona sua capere presumentibus, possint dicta bona restituere ab eisdem sine emenda.

(22) Item. Nolumus quod ob quodcumque crimen, delictum vel maleficium eisdem Judeis vel alicui eorum impositum, vel super quod quisquam ipsum prosequi accusare vel deferre voluerit, provocari valeat ad Duellum.

(23) Item. Nolumus quod aliquis Judeus ad quamcumque predicacionem vel quemcumque Sermonem Christianorum accedere, ire vel stare possit compelli, nisi de ipsius mentis voluntate et assensu.

(24) Item. Volumus et eisdem concedimus quod ipsi Judei & Judee possint unum vel duos in qualibet Villa, ex ipsis eligere, ad taillias faciendas super ipsos, et colligendas pro suis negociis faciendis, & ipsos propter hoc & non aliter, congregare: quodque dicti Electi vel commissi possint levare dictas taillias vel collectas, & quod ipsi Judei vel Judee contradicentes vel rebelles, per loci Justiciam sub qua morabuntur, ad hoc possint compelli.

(25) Item. Quod omnes Tabelliones & Notarii dicti Regni possint recipere & in scriptis redigere omnes Literas, omnesque contractus dictorum Judeorum vel Judearum, inter se ac cum quibuscumque alii[s] faciendo[s].

(26) Item. Quod nulle Litere impetrate vel impetrande contra Privilegia dictorum Judeorum, a Nobis vel nostris Predecessoribus Regibus Francie concessa eisdem, ullius sint efficacie vel momenti, nisi ad hoc accesserit sui Conservatori[s] assensus.

(27) Item. Eisdem concedimus quod volumini [volumina], rotuli vel Libri dictorum Judeorum, per quemcumque Officiarium seu alium Christianum nullatenus capiantur.

(28) Item. Volumus insuper & eisdem concedimus quod omnia bona, Privilegia, Libertates, Franchisiae, Immunitates eisdem concessa & indulta per inclite memorie Dominos & Predecessores nostros Reges Francie, presentibus Literis non contraria, de quibus poterunt ostendere per cartas, Registra, Vidimus vel transcripta sub sigillis Regiis confecta, eisdem confirmabuntur per Nos quocienscumque eis placebit & ipsa ostendere poterunt, Nosque super hoc fuerimus requisiti.

Mandamus autem atque districtius injungimus omnibus & singulis Senescallis, Baillivis, Rectoribus, Vicariis, Prepositis, Majoribus, Juratis, Scabinis, Commissariis, Justiciariisque nostris vel dicti Regni, quatinus omnes & singulos Judeos & Judeas universaliter & singulariter, conjunctim & divisim, omnibus & singulis Privilegiis & Libertatibus supradictis ac ipsorum quemlibet uti pacifice faciant & gaudere, ipsos in contrarium nullatenus molestando vel molestari in corporibus sive bonis, per quoscumque vel quomodolibet permittendo: Sed quicquid in contrarium factum vel attemptatum repererint, ad statum pristinum & debitum reducant reducive celeriter [faciant], ac Nobis propter hoc emendari condigne, si casus exigerit, faciant & procurent. Et quia dicti Judei vel Judee generaliter vel particulariter, Literis presentibus vel aliquibus articulis contentis & expressis in eisdem, forsitan poterunt indigere, & habere presentes Literas, cum opus fuerit eisdem, nequirent,

Volumus & eisdem concedimus de gratia speciali, quatenus Vidimus vel transumpto Literarum presencium, vel Clausule qua ipsi ꝗvel eorum aliqui indigebunt, vel habere seu extrahi voluerint de premissis, sub sigillo Castelleti Parisiensis vel alio Regio confectis, adhibeatur plena fides ac si presentes Litere exhiberentur. Quod ut roboris obtineat firmitatem, Literas presentes nostri sigilli fecimus appensione muniri: salvo in aliis Jure nostro, & in omnibus quolibet alieno. Actum Parisius, Anno Domini MCCCLX, Mense Marcii.

VII. CHARTER OF DUKE FREDERICK TO THE JEWS OF AUSTRIA (1244) (Scherer, pp. 179 ff.).

Fridericus dei gratia dux Austrie et Styrie et dominus Carniole omnibus hanc literam inspecturis salutem in perpetuum. Quoniam uniuscuiusque conditionis in nostro dominio commorantes [homines] volumus gratie ac benevolentie nostre participes inveniri iudeis universis et in districtu Austrie constitutis haec iura statuimus ipsis inviolabiliter observanda:

(1) Statuimus itaque primo ut pro pecunia mobili aut re immobili aut in causa querimoniali que tangit personam aut res iudei, nullus christianus contra iudeum nisi cum christiano et iudeo in testimonium admittatur.

(2) Item si christianus iudeum impetit asserens, quod ei sua pignora obligavit et iudeus hoc diffitetur, si christianus iudeo simplici verbo fidem adhibere noluerit, Iudeus iurando super equivalente sibi oblato suam intentionem probabit et transiet absolutus.

(3) Item si christianus obligaverit pignus iudeo affirmans, quod iudeo pro minori pecunia obligavit, quam iudeus confiteatur, iurabit iudeus super pignore sibi obligato et quod iurando probaverit, christianus ei solvere non recuset.

(4) Item si iudeus christiano non assumptis testibus dicat, se pignus mutuasse, et ille negaverit, super hoc christianus suisolius iuramento se expurget.

(5) Item iudeus recipere poterit nomine pignoris omnia que sibi fuerint obligata quocumque nomine vocentur nulla de hiis requisitione facta exceptis [vestibus] sanguinolentis et malefactis [recte madefactis] quas nullatenus acceptabit.

(6) Item si christianus impetiverit iudeum, quod pignus, quod iudeus habet, ei furtim aut per violentiam sit ablatum, iudeus iuret super illo pignore, quod, tamen recepit, furtim esse ablatum aut raptum ignorarit, hoc in suo iuramento implicito, quanto sit ei pignus huiusmodi obligatum, et sic probatione facta christianus sortem et usuras ei persolvet medio tempore accrescentes.

(7) Item si per casum incendii aut per furtum aut per vim res suas cum obligatis sibi pignoribus amiserit et hoc constiterit et christianus quod obligavit nichilominus eum impetit, iudeus iuramento proprio absolvatur.

(8) Item si iudei de facto inter se discordiam moverint aut guerram, iudex civitatis nostre nullam sibi iurisdictionem vendicet in eos, sed ipse dux aut summus terre sue Camerarius iudicium exercebit. Si autem vergebit in personam, soli duci hic casus observabitur iudicandus.

(9) Item si christianus iudeo vulnus qualecumque inflixerit, reus duci solvat duodecim marcas auri, sue camere deferendas, vulnerato XII marcas argenti et expensas, quas pro suimet curatione impenderit medicine.

(10) Item si christianus iudeum interemerit, morte digno iudicio puniatur et omnia rei mobilia et immobilia in ducis transeant proprietatem.

DD

(11) Item si christianus iudeum ceciderit, ita tamen, quod sanguinem eius non effuderit, solvet duci IV marcas auri, percusso IV marcas argenti. Si pecuniam habere non potuerit, per truncacionem manus satisfaciat pro commisso.

(12) Item, ubicumque iudeus dominium nostrum transierit, nullus ei aliquod impedimentum preparabit nec molestiam inferat nec gravamen, set si aliquas merces aut alias res duxerit, de quibus muta debeat pervenire, per omnia mutarum loca non nisi debitam solvat mutam, quam solveret unus civium illius civitatis, in qua iudeus eo tempore demoratur.

(13) Item si iudei iuxta suam consuetudinem ex mortuis suis aut de civitate ad civitatem aut de provincia ad provinciam aut de una terra in alteram terram deduxerint, nichil ab eis a mutariis nostris volumus extorqueri; si autem mutarius aliquid extorserit, ut predatio mortui qui volgariter reraub dicitur, puniatur.

(14) Item si christianus cimiterium iudeorum quacumque temeritate dissipaverit aut invaserit, in forma iudicii moriatur et omnia sua perveniant camere duci quocumque nomine nuncupentur.

(15) Item si aliquis temerarie iactaverit super scolas iudeorum, iudici iudeorum duo talenta volumus ut persolvat.

(16) Item si iudeus iudici suo in pena pecuniali, que dicitur wandel, reus inventus fuerit, non nisi XII denarios solvat ei.

(17) Item si iudeus per edictum sui iudicis primo et secundo non venerit, pro utraque vice solvet iudici IV denarios. Si ad tertium edictum non pervenerit, solvat XXXVI denarios iudici memorato.

(18) Item si iudeus iudeum vulneraverit, suo iudici duo talenta in penam, que wandel dicitur, solvere non recuset.

(19) Item statuimus ut nullus iudeus iuret super rodali preter quam ad nostram presenciam evocatus.

(20) Item si iudeus dampno fuerit interemptus, ut per testimonium constari non posset amicis suis, quis eum interemerit, si post inquisitionem factam aliquem suspectum habere ceperint, nos iudeis contra suspectum pugilem volumus exhibere.

(21) Item si christianus alicui iudee manum iniecerit violentam, manum illius volumus detruncari.

(22) Item iudex iudeorum nullam causam ortam inter iudeos in iudicium deducat, nisi per querimoniam fuerit invitatus.

(23) Item si christianus a iudeo pignus absolverit, ita quod usuras non persolverit, si easdem usuras infra mensem non dederit, illis usuris accrescant usure.

(24) Item in domo iudei nullum volumus hospitari.

(25) Item si iudeus super possessiones aut litteras magnatum terre pecuniam mutuaverit et hoc per suas litteras et sigillum probaverit, nos iudeo possessiones assignabimus obligatas et ei eas contra violentiam defendemus.

(26) Item si aliquis vel aliqua puerum iudei abduxerit, ut fur volumus condempnari.

(27) Item si iudeus receptum a christiano pignus per spacium unius anni tenuerit, si pignoris valor mutuatam pecuniam et usuram non excesserit, iudeus iudici suo pignus demonstrabit et postea vendendi habet libertatem. Si quod pignus per annum et diem apud iudeum remanserit, nulli super hoc postea respondebit.

(28) Item quicumque christianus iudeo per vim abstulerit pignus suum aut violentiam in domo eius exercuerit ut dissipator camere nostre graviter puniatur.

(29) Item contra iudeum nisi coram suis scolis nusquam in iudicio procedatur nobis exceptis, qui eos possimus ad nostram presenciam evocare.

(30) Item statuimus ut et iudei de talento per singulas ebdomadas non nisi octo denarios participant [recte : percipiant] in usuris.

Follow Signatures.

VIII. CHARTER OF JAMES I OF ARAGON TO THE JEWS OF LERIDA (1268)
(F. Darwin Swift, *The Life and Times of James the First*, pp. 296 ff.).

Noverint universi quod nos Jacobus Dei gracia rex Aragonum Majoricarum et Valencie comes Barchinone et Urgelli et dominus Montispesulani, per nos et nostros damus et concedimus vobis aliame Judeorum Ilerde et aliorum locorum ad comune vestrum spectancium et vestris in perpetuum quod non teneamini respondere alicui vel aliquibus personis in aliquibus petitionibus quas vobis moveant super aliquibus que asserant in libris vestris ebraicis contra fidem nostram contineri, nisi ea fuerint desonrries nostri domini Jhesu-Christi vel beate Virginis Matris ejus vel sanctorum eorundem, et quod de hoc simus nos vel nostri et non alii cognitores, auditis prius partium racionibus: que cognicio determinetur per nos vel nostros ubicumque fuerimus et non alibi. Preterea damus et concedimus vobis et vestris imperpetuum quod possitis emere a Christianis et eis vendere omnia quecumque victualia et alia prout actenus facere consuevistis libere et sine alicujus impedimento, et quod carnes que judayce in juderiis vestris interficiuntur vendantur in locis hucusque consuetis et non alibi. Damus etiam et concedimus vobis et vestris perpetuo quod illi vestrum qui oficio de coiraterie uti voluerint possint hoc facere libere et absque aliquo impedimento. Preterea damus et concedimus vobis et vestris imperpetuum quod habeatis et possideatis sinagogas vestras quas hodie habetis et possidetis prout melius et plenius ipsas actenus habuistis et possedistis, et quod ipsas etiam sinagogas decenter aptare possitis cum hoc fuerit ipsis necessarium. Item damus et concedimus vobis et vestris perpetuo quod ciminteria vestra sint in locis quibus modo sunt et non mutentur aliqua ratione nisi de vestra fuerit voluntate. Item damus et concedimus vobis et vestris perpetuo quod pro usuris vestrorum debitorum seu lucro possitis accipere et accipiatis quatuor denarios pro libra in mense et expleta vendere et emere cum Christianis, prout jam vobis concessimus cum cartis nostris ut in eisdem continetur confirmantes vobis omnia debita que vobis debentur, dummodo ad rationem predictam sive lucrum fuerint mutata. Item per nos et nostros damus et concedimus vobis et vestris in perpetuum quod non teneamini ire ad abscultandam predicacionem alicujus patris ordinis predicatorum minorum vel alicujus alterius extra vestras juderias nec ad hoc per aliquem compelli valeatis : et hoc vobis concedimus quia in predicationibus que vobis fiebant extra juderias vestras fiebant vobis pluries per Christianos vituperium et dedecus. Et si predicti fratres vel alii intus sinagogas vestras voluerint predicare, non veniant ad ipsas sinagogas ad ipsam predicationem faciendam cum multitudine populi set tantum cum decem probis hominibus Christianis et non cum pluribus. Concedimus etiam vobis et vestris perpetuo quod super aliquibus non possit vobis fieri aliqua innovatio, nisi prius per nos vel nostros judicati fueritis super ipsis rationibus primitus auditis. Predicta autem omnia et singula vobis et vestris concedimus perpetuo ut dictum est, non obstantibus aliquibus cartis per nos in contrarium concessis: mandantes bajulis justiciis curiis paciariis et aliis officialibus et subditis nostris presentibus et futuris quod predicta omnia et singula firma habeant et observent et faciant observari et non contraveniant nec aliquam contravenire permitant aliqua ratione. Datum Ilerde V idus novembris anno Domini M. CC. LX.octavo.

Follow Signatures

APPENDIX TWO

SPECIMENS OF RECORDS OF INDEBTEDNESS

I. I.O.U. TO A JEW IN WHICH THE AMOUNT LENT AND THE USURY ARE CONCEALED UNDER THE FACT THAT REPAYMENT IS IN KIND (from J. Jacobs, *The Jews of Angevin England*, p. 66).

Know all men present and future that I, Robert, parson of Bisebrok [co. Rutland], owe Aaron, Jew of Lincoln, 25 soams of hay, Stamford measure, and I have agreed that every two loads shall make one great bundle, Lincoln measure, and all this corn I will render to him within fifteen days of his summons and I make an affidavit to keep this, and I, Richard of Bisebrok, am surety for all the aforesaid corn and owe the said Aaron of my own part 40 soams of hay of the same measure to be tendered similarly within fifteen days of his summons and this I have made an affidavit to render.
[A.D. 1179.]

II. I.O.U. IN WHICH THE SUM BORROWED IS NOT MENTIONED, SO THAT THE AMOUNT OF USURY CANNOT BE DISCOVERED, AND IN WHICH COMPOUND INTEREST, CHARGEABLE IF REPAYMENT IS DELAYED, IS INSCRIBED AS THOUGH IT WAS THE ONLY INTEREST CHARGED (from J. Jacobs, *The Jews of Angevin England*, p. 67).

Know, &c., I, Herbert, parson of Wissinden, owe Aaron Jew of Lincoln 120 marks to be returned at the second feast of St. Michael after the death of Richard de Luci [*ob.* 1179] in six years, viz.: each year 20 marks at two terms of the year, at Rogations 10 marks and at the chains of St. Peter 10 marks, and so on, from year to year, till the whole debt is paid. The first term for receipt is at the second Rogations after the death of Richard de Luci. And if by chance any one of those terms shall pass, I will give him every week twopence interest for every pound, so long as I shall hold the debt by his grace, and I make my affidavit, and have confirmed it with my seal.
[A.D. 1179.]

III. OPEN RECORD OF A SUM BORROWED AND REGULAR INTEREST CHARGED (from J. Jacobs, *The Jews of Angevin England*, p. 66).

Know, &c., I, Richard of Bisebrok, owe Aaron the Jew of Lincoln ten pounds sterling which I received from him at the octave of St. Michael next after the death of Richard de Luci [*ob.* 1179] and for each pound I will give him every week two pence for interest as long as I keep the debt by his favour, and for the whole debt aforesaid, viz. capital and interest, I have pledged to him all my land of Bisebrok till he has the debt aforesaid, viz. capital and interest, and if I cannot warrant this land to him I will give him equivalent of its value at his pleasure and this I make affidavit to keep and I, Robert, parson of Bisebrok, am surety for the whole debt aforesaid, viz. capital and interest, for satisfying the said Aaron within 15 days of his summons unless the aforesaid Richard has done it and this is my affidavit.
[A.D. 1179.]

APPENDIX THREE

CORRECTIONS TO VOLUME ONE, 'THE CONFLICT OF THE CHURCH AND THE SYNAGOGUE'

p. 7. For ' Sybil ' read ' Sibyl '.

p. 10. The Patriarchate dates from the century following the destruction of the Temple. The 'didrachm' was paid to the Temple until the war of A.D. 68.

pp. 58 and 59. The Epistle to the Hebrews used to be considered to be an exhortation to Palestinian Jewish Christians, and was related to the temptations which beset them at the time of the siege of Jerusalem by Titus. It was considered as an appeal to them not to be tempted by false patriotism to throw in their lot with the Jews. Such a view is now rejected, because the author deals, not with the daily ritual of the Temple, but with the theoretical ritual of the Tabernacle. He is concerned with a type, not with an existing activity. Its origin, authorship, and date are therefore quite uncertain. Its purpose, however, is clear. It is concerned with ' worship ', and with ' the Law ' only as it contains prescriptions for sacrificial worship. As such it made nothing perfect. The rest of the argument on p. 59 remains valid.

p. 60. On the new view detailed above, the Epistle to the Hebrews is not necessarily addressed to Jewish Christians. It is written to convince any Christian that all the sacrifices of the Old Testament were but anticipations of the supreme Sacrifice of Christ.

p. 86. For ' prescription ' read ' proscription '.

p. 90. For ' Mellito ' read ' Melito '.

p. 93. For ' Trajan ' read ' Hadrian '.

p. 112, note 3, should be part of note 2. The reference for note 3 is: *Sermon on the Resurrection* of Eusebius of Emesa in *Analecta Bollandiana*, XXX.

p. 118. The Dialogue in question is more probably related to that of Timothy and Aquila. See Lukyn Williams, *Adversus Judaeos*, pp. 117-123.

p. 133. For ' Ubricius ' read ' Urbicus '.

p. 205. Valentinian III also excluded the Jews from the Bar; Const. Sirm., *loc. cit.*

p. 214, line 6 from bottom. The word is probably a personal, not a geographical name; perhaps Tamnus or Nostamnus.

p. 248. Justinian was not the first to exclude the Jews from the Bar. Valentinian III did it in the West, and Leo the Thracian did the same in the East (C.J., 1.4.15 and 2.6.8) in 468.

p. 280, l. 3. This should read: The references to the Jews in this poem consist merely in a violent diatribe against them as, etc. The poem deals with other questions also. Note 1. The title should be *Trostschreiben Jacobs v. Sarug an die himaritischen Christen.*

p. 296. For ' efficacity ' read ' efficacy '.

p. 304. On the ritual of conversion, see S. Krauss in *Festskript* . . . *David Simonsen*, Kopenhagen, 1923.

p. 313. Work was done on the Syrians earlier by Scheffer-Boichorst, in *Mitteilungen für oesterreich. Geschichtsforschung*, VI, 1885. See also H. Laurent, in *Byzantion*, VII, 1932.

p. 316. There is a reference to a Jewish moneylender in *Vita S. Pauli*, 3-5; *Analecta Bollandiana*, XI, pp. 377-79.

p. 325. On *advena* see Du Cange, s. *proselyti*.

p. 390. Under ' legal profession ' add Const. Sirm., vi; and the C.J. reference should read 1.5.12.

p. 395. In the third Profession of Faith, l. 5, for ' home ' read ' throne '.

p. 403. The name ' Manean ' should be ' Manaen '.

p. 424. Under Jerusalem should be included: Council of, 50. To ' capture of ' add 205—Under ' Occupations of Jews ', ' Doctors ', add 268.

p. 427. Add ' Noachian commandments ', 50.

p. 428. Under ' Promises ' add ' cannot be fulfilled twice ', 279.

INDEX

INDEX

Names in italics are those of authors whose works are discussed in the text or chapter bibliographies

A

Aaron of Lincoln, 106, 343, 346, 349
Aaron of York, 346
Abbeville, Lombards at, 319, 374
Abbeys, indebtedness of, 348 n. 2
Abduction of Jewish children, 69, 164, 180
Abrabanel, Isaac, 347
Abraham of Saragossa, 159
Abrahams, B. L., 147 n. 3, 220 n. 1, 222 n. 1, 223 n. 3
Abrahams, I., 220 n. 1
Ackermann, A., 337 n. 4
Acts of the Apostles, The, xii, 3 ff., 54 n. 2; xv, 29, 6 n. 1
Adalbert, St., Bishop of Prague, 46
Adam, Hammaburg. Eccl. Pontif. Gesta, 57 n. 1
Adhemar, Bishop of Puy, and the First Crusade, 62-4
Adhemar, Historia, 33 n. 1, 34 n. 4, 38 n. 2, 44 n. 1, 56 n. 5
Adler, S., 118 n. 2, 203 n. 1, 369 n. 6
Adolf of Nassau, 113
Advocates of the Jews, 244
Aenham, Council of, 28 n. 7
Agde, Council of, 27
Agnellus Abbas, Lib. Pont., Vita Damiani, 57 n. 2
Agobard, Archbishop of Lyons, 159, 211; on baptism of slaves, 46-7; on conflict with Louis the Pious, 46; correspondence of, 19, 27; Jews: at Lyons, 50; Christian relations with, 29; conflict with, 20; 'Master of the Jews', 243; social and religious conduct of, 49; under a curse, 30; undue familiarity with, 26; sale of meat and wine to Christians, 48; on Slave-trade, 46
Agobard:
Consultatio et Supplicatio . . . ad Proceres Palatii de baptismo Judaicorum mancipiorum, 41 n. 4, 47 n. 2
Epistola ad Proceres Palatii contra Praeceptum impium de bap-

tismo Judaicorum mancipiorum, 41 n. 4
De insolentia Judaeorum, 27 n., 28 n. 6, 29 n. 3, 41 n. 4, 48 n. 1, 51, 55 n. 1, 2
Epistola Agobardi, Bernardi, et Eaof de Judaicis superstitionibus, 26 n. 3, 27 n. 6, 28 n. 1, 30 n. 2, 53 n. 3
Epistola . . . ad Nibridium Episcopum Narbonensem de cavendo convictu et societate Judaica, 30 n. 3, 40 n. 4, 54 n. 6, 8
Alaman, Cardinal Legate of Aragon, 139
Alazrach, Jew of Saragossa, 235
Albert of Habsburg, 113
Albi, Council of, 214 n. 2, 283, 366 n. 3
Alcolea, charter to Jews of, 1320, 189
Alcuin, 56
Alexander II, Pope, 58, 85, 213 n. 2
Alexander III, Pope, 130-1, 211, 279, 282, 283 n. 7, 309
Alexander IV, Pope, 137, 368 n. 2
Alexandria, Jews of, 3, 4
Almoravides, persecutions by, 186-7
Alpertus, De diversitate temporum, 35 n. 3
Alphonse of Poitiers, 120, 137, 209, 368, 380; *Correspondence of*, 120 n. 1, 137 n. 4, 369 n. 3
Alphonso I, of Aragon and Navarre, 186
Alphonso II, of Aragon, 150 n. 2
Alphonso V, of Aragon, 139
Alphonso VI, of Castile and Leon, 185
Alphonso XI, of Castile, 230, 232
Alphonso, Infante, of Aragon, 115, 189
Alsace, Jews in, 208-9, 226, 333, 351
Alsatian Chronicle, 228 n. 1
Altenahr, massacres of Jews at, 76
Altercations (see Disputations)
Amatus, 49